THE ARCHAEOLOGY OF SKYE AND THE WESTERN ISLES

THE ARCHAEOLOGY OF SKYE AND THE WESTERN ISLES

Ian Armit

EDINBURGH UNIVERSITY PRESS
in association with Historic Scotland

For William Armit
1920–1992

© Ian Armit, 1996

Edinburgh University Press Ltd
22 George Square, Edinburgh

Typeset in Monotype Plantin Light
by Nene Phototypesetters, Northampton,
and printed and bound in Great Britain by
Redwood Books, Trowbridge, Wiltshire

A CIP record for this book is available
from the British Library

ISBN 0 7486 0858 3 Hardback
ISBN 0 7486 0640 8 Paperback

Contents

	Acknowledgements	vi
1	Introduction	1
2	The Environment	18
3	Hunters and Gatherers	33
4	The First Farmers	42
5	Tombs and Standing Stones	67
6	Beakers and Bronze	86
7	The Atlantic Roundhouses	109
8	Wheelhouses	136
9	Picts and Scots	159
10	The Vikings	186
11	Lords of the Isles	205
12	Tracing Change	227
	Appendix: Radiocarbon Dates from Skye and the Western Isles	236
	Bibliography	247
	Index	258

Acknowledgements

I would like to thank the following individuals and institutions for their help and encouragement through the protracted process of putting this book together.

Several colleagues made available details of their work in progress: Patrick Ashmore provided information relating to his excavations at Callanish and provided calibrations for radiocarbon dates prior to 8000bp; data on his excavations and surveys in Skye was made available by Roget Miket; information on Viking Age hoards was provided by Olwyn Owen; and Trevor Cowie provided much valuable information on his work in Lewis. Equally valuable technical advice was forthcoming from Dr Bruce Walker regarding the reconstruction of Cnip wheelhouse, and Dr Euan Campbell on Hebridean pottery sequences.

Sponsorship for the illustrations was provided by Historic Scotland, and original illustrations were drawn by Alan Braby. Permission to reproduce illustrative material was granted by a number of individuals and institutions: Historic Scotland (Crown Copyright: Figures 7.8, 11.2, 11.4 and 11.7); RCAHMS (Crown Copyright: Royal Commission on the Ancient and Historical Monuments of Scotland: Figures 1.4, 7.2, 11.6, 11.9 and 11.10); the Centre for Field Archaeology (Figures 6.4, 10.4 and 10.5); Glasgow Archaeological Society (Figure 10.3); Museum nan Eilean (Figures 7.10 and 8.3); the Prehistoric Society (Figure 4.9); the Society of Antiquaries of Scotland (Figures 6.6, 8.6, 9.7 and 10.6); Nick Bridgland (Figure 1.3); Dr Euan Campbell (Figure 8.6); Professor John Coles (Figure 6.6), Dr Anne Crone (Figure 4.9), Professor Dennis Harding (Figures 5.5, 7.4, 7.5 and 7.9); Richard Welander (Figure 10.6); and Caroline Wickham-Jones (Figures 3.2 and 3.3). Roger Miket supplied information for Figure 7.12.

The text has benefited greatly from comments by a number of friends and colleagues; Patrick Ashmore, Gordon Barclay, Trevor Cowie, Andrew Dunwell, Dr Bill Finlayson, Dr Noel Fojut, Dr Sally Foster, Professor Dennis Harding, Dr Alan Lane, Dr Coralie Mills, Olwyn Owen, Richard Langhorne and Dr Ian Ralston. None of them, however, should be held responsible for any views or interpretations expressed which remain stubbornly those of the author.

On the organisational front, thanks are due to Dr David Breeze and Dr David Caldwell. Finally, I would like to thank all at EUP for their infinite patience.

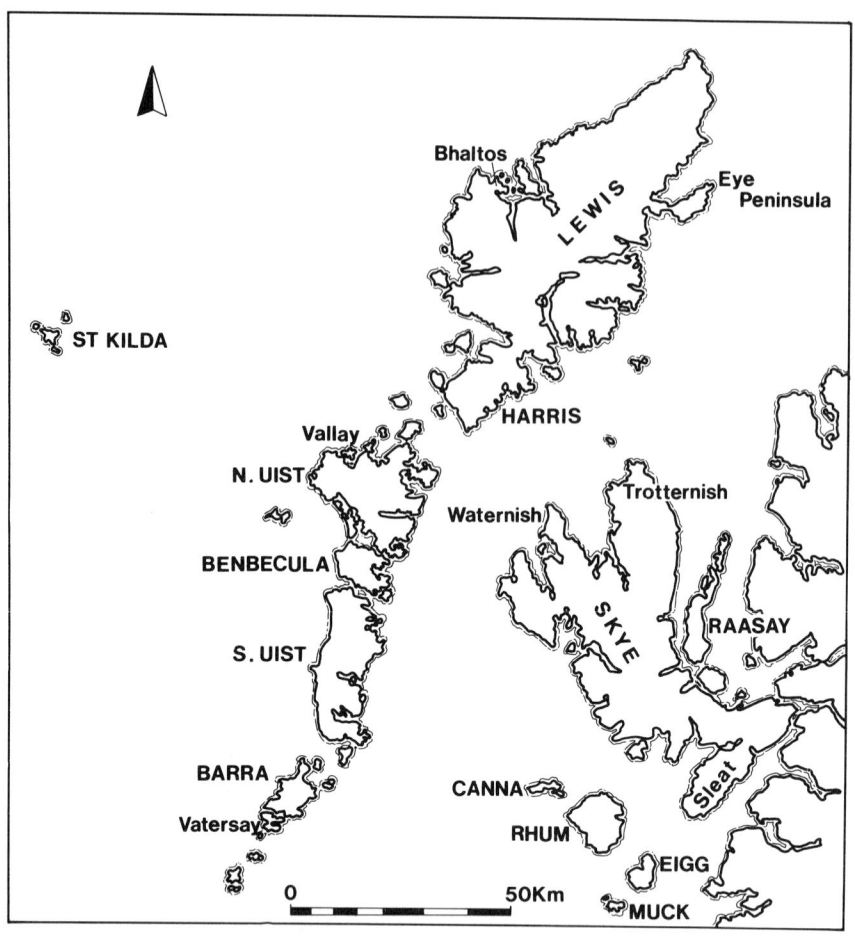

FIGURE 1.1. Map of Skye and the Western Isles showing the main islands and areas.

1 Introduction

This book attempts to tell the story of Skye and the Western Isles from the earliest human occupation through to the recent past. Although very little of this story was ever written down in contemporary records, there is still a vast range of material to draw upon: relict buildings and landscapes dating back over 5000 years; the tools, pottery, jewellery and other artefacts found in excavations; place names, inscriptions and gravestones; pollen and other environmental data; all combining to create the rich archaeological record of the islands.

The island of Skye lies only half a mile from the mainland of Scotland and measures some fifty by twenty-five miles at its widest points. The actual land mass is much less than these figures suggest, though, as the island is formed of a series of jagged peninsulas divided by long sea lochs (Figure 1.2). These peninsulas, such as Waternish, Duirinish, Trotternish and Sleat, break the island up into naturally defined territories which probably had considerable local importance at various times in the past. They also suggest one of the possible derivations of the name 'Skye', from the Norse word '*sgiath*' meaning 'wing', which may refer to the island as the 'winged isle'. Or perhaps another Norse word '*ski*', for 'mist', gave us the more obviously descriptive 'misty isle'. For the landscape of Skye is dominated by mountains, and the Cuillin Hills in the southern part especially are often clad in a grey misty shroud (Figure 1.3).

Skye has never been densely settled and the only town of any size is Portree which, like the main settlements of the Outer Isles, is a relatively recent creation. Today the island population numbers slightly less than 9000, although this is seasonally swelled by a substantial tourist inflow, particularly during the summer months. Skye is surrounded by smaller islands, including Raasay and Scalpay to its east and Rhum, Canna, Muck and Eigg to the

2 THE ARCHAEOLOGY OF SKYE AND THE WESTERN ISLES

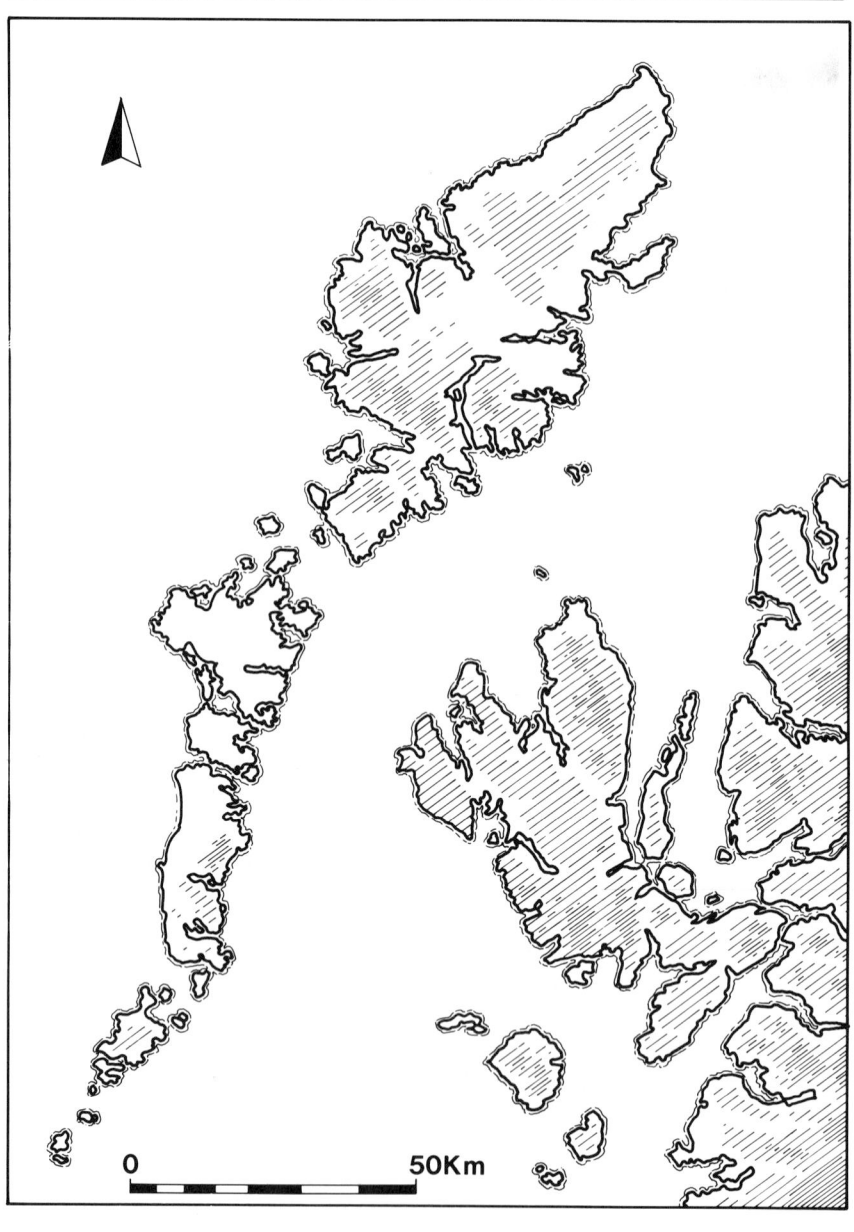

FIGURE 1.2. Topography of Skye and the Western Isles.

FIGURE 1.3. A view of the Cuillins, Skye.

south. Each of these small islands has, like Skye itself, formed a focus for human settlement since prehistoric times.

Some sixteen miles distant from Skye at their nearest point and beyond the reach, so far, of mainstream tourism, lie the Western Isles, or Outer Hebrides. This island chain stretches for some 150 miles from the Butt of Lewis in the north to the small islands south of Barra. To sail for the first time into Stornoway or Lochmaddy is to know that you are entering a place which is culturally as well as geographically far removed from the population centres of modern Scotland. The islands have been known by various names, initially by Roman scholars as Ebudaes, mistranscribed subsequently as the more familiar Hebrides. Later names convey something of the cultural affiliations of the islands. To the Norse, they were the Sudreyar or southern isles, as opposed to the Nordreyar of Orkney and Shetland, while at the same time to the mainland Gaelic Scots they were Innsegall or the 'isles of the strangers'. Like Skye, the Western Isles have their outlying islands, the most important for our present purposes being the St Kilda group some forty miles west of North Uist.

At something under 30,000, the population of the Western Isles is more than three times that of Skye, but apart from the major population centre of Stornoway in Lewis, people are spread equally thinly in both areas. Like those of Skye, the present townships are sited along the coasts, although the interiors of the islands are made inhospitable not by mountains but by thick blanket peats and low rocky hills (Figure 1.4). The Western Isles landscape can be characterised in general terms by a contrast between the machair – miles of white shell sands which fringe the west coasts of the chain and are at their most spectacular in the Uists and Benbecula (Figure 1.5) – and

FIGURE 1.4. Loch Obisary, North Uist.

the peatlands. The gentle slope of the west coasts, where the machair meets the sea, stand in stark contrast to the rocky cliffs and inlets of the east coast. The only mountains of any note are the Harris Hills, which serve to separate the habitable areas of Lewis and Harris and give them in the public mind the status of separate islands.

Atlantic Scotland and Hebridean Archaeology

Skye and the Western Isles have had a long and respectable history as a unit of archaeological study. The area is the same as that covered by the Royal Commission on the Ancient and Historical Monuments of Scotland (RCAHMS) in their original survey of 'the Outer Hebrides, Skye and the Small Isles', published in 1928, which formed the basis for much subsequent work. Skye and the Western Isles share a similar range of monuments, for example the Iron Age broch towers and Neolithic chambered tombs: they also tend to display similar types of site within these broad categories – markedly different from nearby Argyll, particularly in the Iron Age and Early Historic periods.

By the mid-1st millennium AD the region was peripheral to the emerging Dalriadic kingdom centred in Argyll, also falling outwith the core of the historical Pictish kingdom. At many periods the islands were markedly different from the Northern Isles in their range of monuments and areas of outside contact, for example in the Later Neolithic and Early Bronze Age when radically different types of pottery predominate in each area. Although there is some justification for identifying an 'Atlantic Province' during much of prehistory which encompassed all of the Highlands and Islands, there is per-

FIGURE 1.5. Traigh na Berie: a machair landscape in Lewis.

haps also justification for seeing within that province a Hebridean zone which varied in cohesion and cultural affiliation through time. The archaeology of Skye and the Western Isles is ultimately a definable unit of study, recognisably related to but different from, say, an archaeology of Orkney (Renfrew 1985), of Argyll (Ritchie 1995), or of Caithness and Sutherland.

An Island-centred Geography

It can be tempting to regard Skye and the Western Isles as peripheral or marginal areas for human settlement, and many archaeologists in the past have done just that whether explicitly or implicitly. Such perceptions are important and deeply colour the way the past is viewed. When the islands were seen as inherently peripheral it was natural to view them as cultural backwaters; receivers of ideas rather than places where innovations occurred. In old-style diffusionist archaeology, when cultural change was seen as the product of invasion, colonisation and migration, the north and west of Scotland was seen as more or less the last place where anything innovative was likely to happen. The major breakthroughs in technology or developments in social organisation apparently broke like waves from the Near East and Mediterranean, crashing across the mainland of Europe before ending up as rather sad ripples in the outer reaches of the Scottish islands.

Marginality of course does depend on your perspective. For the study of, for example, the growth of capitalist economies and urbanisation, the islands are indeed marginal. But the assumption that the islands were always and inherently peripheral simply projects modern social and economic neglect into the past (Armit 1996). Indeed it is possible to make a case for the view that it has been the role of Scottish and later British mainland authorities to render the islands peripheral, due in part to their cultural and economic distance from the relatively recent centres of power.

The islands have not existed in the past as a peripheral outpost of a Scottish or British state. Prior to the urbanisation of Scotland the balance of population between the highlands and the central and eastern mainland was far more even. The potential to intensify agricultural production and support major industries and towns was not a relevant factor until relatively recently. In the earliest periods of human colonisation in Scotland the range of coastal and other natural resources in the Hebrides would have made them desirable settlement areas. Prehistoric societies in the islands were comfortably able not just to survive but to engage in the construction of great monuments. Much later they occupied a pivotal place in the Norse and Medieval Kingdom of the Isles.

To understand the archaeology of the area we should not picture the weather map view of Scotland as we commonly see it, with the islands off in one corner. Instead we must try to think in terms of an island-centred geography where travel by sea was of prime importance and where modern political perceptions were simply irrelevant (Figure 1.6). Archaeology shows up paths of prehistoric communication which emphasise the Atlantic connection. Cultural traits, for example megalithic tombs, spread along the Atlantic coasts of Europe. Links varied through time and in various periods we must consider communications and possible cultural connections with Ireland, with France and England, the Isle of Man, with the Northern Isles and Scandinavia; links such as these perhaps outweighed the communications routes with which we are most familiar today, which tie the islands to the population centres of modern Scotland.

From Antiquarians to Archaeologists

Any attempt to tell the story of an area through its archaeology relies heavily on the actions and ideas of previous generations of archaeologists and antiquarians. To understand the way in which the archaeological record is built up we have to spend some time considering the activities and motivations of the people through whose efforts our present knowledge accumulated. The developing archaeology of Skye and the Western Isles was, until recent years, highly dependent on the work of a small number of researchers and often only lightly tempered by the varying fashions of mainstream archaeological thought. Research agendas, concentrations on particular periods, known distributions of many types of monument, and numerous other aspects of the archaeological record which dominated the archaeology of the islands prior to the 1980s, were often established very many years ago.

Early Days

Tourist interest in island archaeology is no new thing. In 1773 the broch of Dun Beag, near Struan in Skye, was visited by Dr Johnson on his celebrated Hebridean tour, where he speculated at some length on the function of the

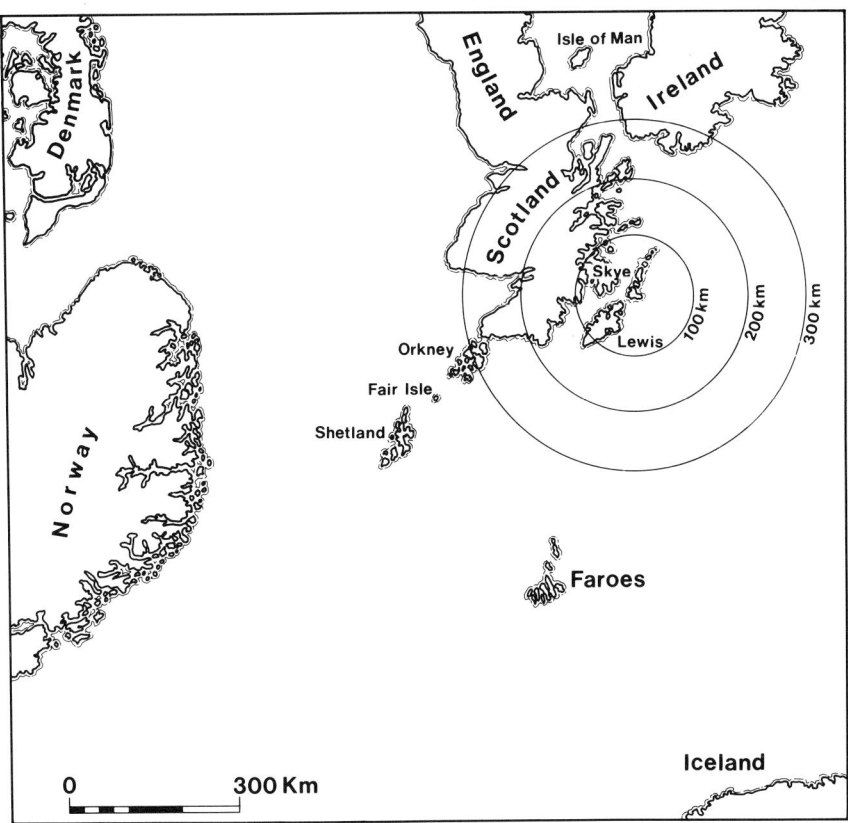

FIGURE 1.6. An island-centred geography.

strange stone tower, with its narrow entrance, massively thick walls and small mural cells (Johnson 1774, 64–5). Even earlier, in c.1695, the traveller Martin Martin had recorded the Callanish stones and prepared a plan of the monument for inclusion in his book on the islands (Martin 1716, 9). Numerous other writers with an antiquarian interest recorded the existence and characteristics of the most prominent monuments of the islands, providing fascinating insights into the emerging awareness of the broad outlines of Scotland's distant past.

It was during the nineteenth century though that the study of archaeology really began to evolve and it is mostly through the work of a few individuals since the latter part of that century that ideas on the nature of Hebridean archaeology have emerged. Neither Skye nor the Western Isles witnessed the degree of nineteenth century antiquarian zeal that was directed at some other rich archaeological areas. In Orkney, for example, large numbers of Iron Age brochs were dug into while in many parts of Scotland the same treatment was applied to Neolithic and Bronze Age burial monuments. Although the damage done to important sites and the quantity of information lost is regrettable, the material recovered in this period provided the essential building blocks from which Scottish archaeology was constructed. The concentration on the most imposing monuments, principally the funerary mounds and cairns of the Neolithic and the forts and broch towers of the Iron Age, was to set the research agendas for much of the early research on Scottish archaeology.

Perhaps the birth of archaeology of the Western Isles can be traced to 1857 when, under the instruction of the landowner Sir James Matheson, the thick blanket of peat was removed fully to expose the magnificent Callanish stones. This was perhaps more an exercise in presentation than a search for knowledge of the past. The first real excavations in Skye were instigated by the Countess de Latour and carried out by her workmen on two brochs; Dun Iardhart at Dunvegan and Dun Beag, Struan. The absence of stratigraphic understanding on these excavations was typical of the period. Nonetheless, the excavations were recorded well enough at least to enable subsequent publications of both sites (MacLeod 1915; Callander 1920). Much store was set by the recovery of artefactual material and J. Graham Callander, publishing Dun Beag, noted that Countess de Latour had all two hundred tons of material from the broch 'sifted through the fingers' to recover artefacts (ibid., 110). Nonetheless, much of the information that would have been of most use to us today was simply unachievable at the time when the work was carried out.

The Western Isles were rather better served by antiquarian enthusiasm than were Skye or the Inner Isles. The first substantive archaeological work there was carried out by Captain F. W. L. Thomas, a naval officer, who surveyed a number of sites, particularly Iron Age monuments including the brochs and wheelhouses, in the late nineteenth century (Thomas 1870, 1890). Thomas excavated relatively little and recorded a great deal, and his records are of considerable value to the modern archaeologist, particularly where they describe sites which have since suffered through stone-robbing or erosion. A little after Thomas, another visitor to the islands, the Rev. Odo Blundell came to extend his work on the crannogs or lake-dwellings of Scotland. Blundell's work was limited in scope but some new sites were recorded and published (Blundell 1913) and the concept of the Hebridean crannog entered the archaeological record.

The first real Hebridean excavator was Erskine Beveridge, an incomer to the islands who built a home on the tidal islet of Vallay off North Uist in the early part of this century. This impressive building now stands in ruins, surrounded by a cluster of lesser structures: it is itself now a prime archaeological monument of North Uist, resonant of late Victorian optimism (Figure 1.8). Beveridge's enthusiasm and energy were immense and by 1917 he had excavated a vast range of sites in the Vallay Strand area, centred around his home. Most of these sites dated from the first millennium BC and first millennium AD, although a few were undoubtedly earlier. Even now the Vallay Strand ranks as perhaps the most thoroughly excavated area of its size

FIGURE 1.7. A visit to Dun Torcuill, North Uist (from *Beveridge 1911*).

FIGURE 1.8. Erskine Beveridge's house on Vallay.

in Scotland and, despite very basic levels of recording, our knowledge of the area is arguably superior to any comparable part of the Western Isles.

Beveridge's book *North Uist* was published in 1911 and is a beautifully compiled volume including many photographs of the island's monuments. Beveridge had done a certain amount of archaeological work on the islands of Coll and Tiree in the Inner Hebrides prior to his Western Isles work. Nonetheless he was not a key figure in the mainstream of Scottish archaeology and he does not seem to have been too concerned with the wider implications of his work. Beveridge made little effort to classify his sites or analyse his results and seemed content to accept classifications and ideas from other areas. For the Iron Age sites, including the broch towers and other Atlantic roundhouses, this meant deferring to the ideas generated by the more theoretically-aware workers in Orkney a few decades earlier.

This tendency towards an avoidance of ideas and a concentration on data was to set a pattern in the Western Isles. Theories have tended to be derived from work elsewhere and have been extended to the islands without too much thought as to their suitability. The outstandingly rich data from the Western Isles has thus never been fully assimilated into archaeological thinking.

Consolidation and Progress

In 1914 the RCAHMS began fieldwork which was to lead to the publication of an inventory of Hebridean monuments in 1928. The volume covered the 'Outer Hebrides, Skye and the Small Isles' and represented a major benchmark in Hebridean archaeology, collating and classifying monuments of all periods up to 1707.

Obviously 1914 was not an ideal time to begin a major archaeological survey and, not surprisingly, the fieldwork was beset by difficulties over a protracted period. The RCAHMS surveyors had an often unenviable task, particularly in the Western Isles where so many monuments are sited on islets in lochs. Seldom with access to a boat, the surveyors had to make many descriptions of the numerous islet sites from the shores of the lochs or attempt to negotiate the rickety and semi-submerged causeways often 'at the cost of a wetting' (RCAHMS 1928, v). The survey work suffered numerous interruptions and involved a great deal of patience and perseverance. In the end though, all of the islands were covered, including even St Kilda, where information was provided by a Captain Grant 'late of the Indian Army, who happened to be visiting the island' (ibid., vi).

The resulting volume is an invaluable document summarising knowledge up to the time of its publication, even though it did not include extensive field-walking which might have revealed many more sites. This admirable inventory, thus, tended to fossilise the somewhat skewed pattern of fieldwork which had previously taken place. The distribution of crannogs, for example, was more or less a reflection of the travels of Odo Blundell, while there was a tremendous concentration of wheelhouses centred around Erskine Beveridge's house on Vallay. The distributions of monuments of all classes which were available in the mid-1980s still preserved the activities of the early field-workers giving a biased picture of Hebridean settlement patterns. So little survey has been carried out in so many areas, even today, that it is often only the distributions of the most obvious monuments, such as the Atlantic roundhouses and chambered cairns which even broadly represent the original spread of sites.

In terms of excavation there was something of a lull in archaeological activity in the islands after the death of Erskine Beveridge, until the work of Sir Lindsay Scott began in the 1930s. Scott is one of the major figures in Hebridean archaeology and should have carried a similar stature in the archaeology of Scotland as a whole had his ideas not met with a rather bemused indifference from the archaeological establishment of the time. Although Scott carried out notable excavations on the Neolithic chambered tombs of Rudh an Dunain in Skye and Unival and Clettraval in North Uist (Scott 1934, 1947a, 1948), it was his work on the Atlantic roundhouses of the Iron Age which was of most lasting importance. Scott saw the brochs not as a unique class of site set apart for special study, but as part of a drystone-building tradition which encompassed wheelhouses, duns and a range of other forms (Scott 1947, 1948). His landscape study of these structures in Barra and North Uist was rudimentary but, at least in retrospect, exciting and insightful for its time. While his analysis was still framed within the ideas of diffusionism (where migrations and invasions explained most changes in the archaeological record), Scott was clearly striving to break free from the contemporary consensus on the brochs. Scott's work presaged many of the results of excavation and interpretation in the 1980s, much of which was subsequently summarised in the book *Beyond the Brochs* (Armit 1990).

It was unfortunate for the development of Atlantic Scottish archaeology that Scott's immediate successor in the islands, Alison Young, abandoned his more radical and important ideas and retreated to a rather traditional position in which brochs, duns and wheelhouses were seen as chronologically separate responses to various implied historical invasions and migrations (Young 1961). This was not surprising given the archaeological climate of the times but, after Scott, it has to be seen as disappointing. It was Young, rather than Scott, who was to establish the framework for the Iron Age archaeology of the Hebrides which has lasted into recent times.

The 1960s and '70s

The archaeology of the Hebrides during the 1960s and '70s was dominated again by the study of brochs. Arguments raged over the origin and spread of these monumental towers with various authorities favouring either Skye or the Northern Isles. Debate tended to focus on the architectural *minutiae* of the best preserved monuments, but underlying the divergence of opinion over broch origins was a shared set of assumptions about the date and function of brochs and their introduction via colonisation from the south.

Skye was an important focus of broch studies at this time and excavations were carried out at Dun Ardtreck by Euan MacKie, one of the major figures in broch studies, in which he set out to test some of his theories on broch origins. By contrast the Western Isles sites, sadly as a result of prevailing perceptions of Scott's work, were seen as atypical and peculiar - definitely not suitable for determining the origins and spread of the brochs. While debate continued as to whether the first broch was built in Orkney or Skye, the rich Iron Age archaeology of the Western Isles was all but eclipsed.

A good deal of other important work was done at this time on other periods. Audrey Henshall's mammoth work on the chambered tombs of Scotland was one of the most significant, and drew together the data on these Neolithic burial cairns from all parts of Scotland (Henshall 1963; 1972). The all-encompassing approach of this study ensured that the material from Skye and the Western Isles was considered as a valuable part of the wider whole. In a similar fashion, Steer and Bannerman's collation and classification of Late Medieval monumental sculpture in the West Highlands drew the Hebridean monuments into a wider sphere of analysis (Steer and Bannerman 1977).

Between the 1950s and the mid-1980s, though, there was little interpretative work specifically on the archaeology of Skye and the Western Isles, despite a steady flow of excavations on sites of several periods. Notable campaigns of excavation were pursued, for example by Professor Derek Simpson at Northton in Harris (1976), by Ian Shepherd at Rosinish in Benbecula (1976) and by the then Central Excavation Unit, headed by John Barber, in the Uists (forthcoming), as well as extensive coastal surveys by Shepherd and Cowie. Excavations at the Udal in North Uist have also continued over an extended period since the early 1960s (Crawford n.d.). The results of these and other excavations of the time will be discussed in the chapters which follow. The great problem has been that the results of work in the Western Isles have tended not fundamentally to affect wider interpretations in Scottish archaeology. The archaeology of the region has been seen in terms of models devised elsewhere, or in terms of Alison Young's classification of the Iron Age sites. The idea of marginality has reigned.

Recent Years

Work in recent years, while still often focused on the first millennia BC and AD, has tended to attempt a broader reconstruction of the Hebridean past. More attention has been paid to the development of landscapes rather than individual sites and to the interaction of human populations with their environment. The information available for different historical periods is still very uneven and there are spans of time, such as the Later Bronze Age and Medieval periods, for which whole classes of archaeological information are all but absent. Nonetheless we are beginning now to approach a much broader understanding of the development of human settlement in the islands than was available in the past. Of course, individual site excavations have continued and their value is increased by the ability to see them now in the context of this more wide-ranging work. One of the most important of these has been Caroline Wickham-Jones's work at the Mesolithic site of Kinloch in Rhum, which has opened up a whole new period of study in the region.

In 1985 Edinburgh University's Callanish Archaeological Research Project was set up in Lewis by Professor Dennis Harding. Although the original aims of the project included a programme of work on prehistoric farming practices, it was the associated excavation programme which has had most impact on the archaeology of the islands. A series of excavations and surveys were carried out in Bhaltos, a peninsula on the west coast of Lewis, set out to examine the later prehistoric settlement of one relatively small, self-contained area. The results were to be of central importance in establishing the development of buildings, settlements and material culture for the area and formed a basis for the re-evaluation of a great deal of earlier work. At last it was possible, for one period at least, to establish a distinctively Hebridean archaeology which did not rely on importing models from outside. The chapters in this book which deal with the period from the first millennium BC until the Norse incursions, *c.* AD 800 owe much to the results of work in Bhaltos (Harding and Armit 1990).

Since the late 1980s a further landscape-based project has been underway in the southern part of the Western Isles, focusing on Barra and South Uist. The SEARCH Project run by Sheffield University has directed its efforts particularly at the environmental background to settlement in the islands and has included extensive surveys in a range of environments.

In North Uist the Loch Olabhat Research Project has carried out intensive survey and selective excavation in part of the Vallay area which formed the focus of Erskine Beveridge's work in the early part of this century. As well as the results of the major excavations, at sites like Eilean Domhnuill for the Neolithic and Eilean Olabhat for the Iron Age and later, the survey work there complements that in Bhaltos and the work of the SEARCH project. The forthcoming publication of a series of excavations and palaeoenvironmental studies on eroding machair sites in the Uists carried out by John Barber in the early 1980s will also add significantly to our understanding of past human exploitation of these coastal areas.

Skye has not witnessed the upsurge in work seen in the Western Isles but there have been significant recent developments. Perhaps the most important has been the appointment of a Museums Officer, Roger Miket, who has carried out extensive surveys and a series of excavations in the island. These have been particularly concerned with sites of relatively recent periods with a poor record of previous archaeological excavation, for example shielings, but have also encompassed work on prehistoric hut circles and souterrains (e.g. Wildgoose, Burney and Miket 1993). The RCAHMS has carried out important survey work in advance of forestry on Skye, particularly in the Waternish peninsula, again treating the landscape rather than the individual site as the unit of study. More recently the RCAHMS has carried out surveys on Canna, as has John Hunter of Bradford University (Hunter 1994).

Many of the projects discussed here are still in progress or awaiting publication. But taken as a group they have already added considerably to our knowledge of Hebridean archaeology. The interpretations given in the following chapters are, in many ways, provisional, as all archaeological accounts must be. Nonetheless the various projects of recent years, as well as the re-evaluation of older ideas and data, has led us to a point where we can begin, at last, to present a coherent picture of the development of human settlement and societies in the islands from the earliest times to the recent past.

A Brief Outline

The chapters which follow are arranged more or less chronologically and a brief initial overview might be helpful in setting out the overall picture and highlighting some of the main themes which recur in different periods. After a discussion of the evidence for the changing environment of the islands, the story begins with the first colonisation of the islands following the retreat of the last ice sheets. Evidence for this period is scanty in the extreme: the loss of the contemporary coastlines in the Western Isles has probably robbed us of most early settlements, at least in the Uists. Only in Rhum, at the site of Kinloch, has a settlement of that period been found and excavated, and that site, along with a solitary cave midden site at An Corran in Skye and evidence drawn from Argyll, provides most of our information.

Some time after 4000 BC society was changing with the introduction of farming augmenting and perhaps sometimes replacing traditional food gathering. The introduction of farming has tended to be recognised by rather indirect means – by items of material culture such as stone axes and pottery, etc. rather than by the presence of crops or domesticated animals. There will be some discussion in Chapter 3 about just how valid our assumptions are regarding major economic changes at this time, while Chapter 4 traces the development of farming communities in the Hebrides principally through recently excavated sites such as Eilean Domhnuill and Bharpa Carinish, both in North Uist.

The Neolithic is better known for its monuments than its settlements, and the stone circles and chambered tombs form the basis of Chapter 5. The peculiar concentrations of these monuments – the chambered tombs in North Uist and the stone circles at Callanish in Lewis – raise questions about the distribution of populations in these periods and the possibility of ritual or sacred areas. Interesting patterns of similarity and difference emerge between the Western and Northern Isles at this period, as well as with other parts of Scotland, which might shed some light on the nature of Neolithic society.

Chapter 6 examines the evidence for Bronze Age societies in the Hebrides. The evidence here remains rather disparate from a large number of generally small, and mostly unpublished excavations dominated by small domestic buildings and burial monuments. After the wealth of Neolithic and Early Bronze Age material the Later Bronze Age is difficult to trace, particularly in settlement terms. Artefactual material shows the continuity of settlement and it may be that many settlement sites of the period lurk unnoticed under the later Atlantic roundhouses, particularly on islet sites in the numerous lochs of the Western Isles.

The Atlantic roundhouses, a general term encompassing the various types of massive drystone circular buildings of the Iron Age, form one of the best surviving groups of monuments in the region. These sites survive in such numbers and with such a degree of visibility that we can begin to explore in much more detail questions of population, economy and site function. Chapter 7 addresses these questions principally through the study of several important recent excavations, particularly in the Western Isles.

By contrast with the visibility of the Atlantic roundhouses, manifested most clearly in the broch tower sites such as Dun Carloway in Lewis, the wheelhouses which succeed them represent a wholly different type of structure. These houses, sunk into the earth, do however show their own kind of monumentality. They have also provided a mass of data on ritual and religious practice in the Iron Age which is hard to parallel elsewhere in Scotland. Chapter 8 examines the meaning of this material and the question of why the massive roundhouses gave way to such radically different structures.

In Chapter 9 we are entering a period when documentary records start to play a part. The role of Skye and the Western Isles in the period of the historical Picts and Scots in the first millennium AD is hard to ascertain but there is a body of evidence nonetheless which may provide some clues. The arrival of the Norse in the ninth century AD is discussed in Chapter 10, and here again documentary evidence and archaeology have complementary roles. Place names and burials with clear Scandinavian affiliations show the impact of the Norse incursions, but in the absence of a good body of settlement data the nature of the interaction between Norse and native remains difficult to gauge.

As the present millennium progressed the quantity of contemporary documentation grew enormously. During the period of the Norse and Medieval Kingdom of the Isles we know the names of the key historical players and have a fair knowledge of political and military manoeuvring. This wealth of historical knowledge of specific people and events, however, tends to disguise the absence of information relating to the culture and lives of the mass of the population. Some such information is now becoming available through recent surveys and excavations. In Chapter 11 we will examine the evidence for this period, prior to the disaster of the '45 rising, during which the varying relations between the Gaelic world and the Scottish throne (and latterly the British state) came increasingly to affect life in the islands. In the late and Post-Medieval period too, archaeology has a part to play in enhancing the information provided by the documentary sources. Despite the wealth of written records, many aspects of daily life remain unclear and a vast amount of archaeological data lies buried in the former *baile* settlements and other sites of the period. The combination of written and archaeological data here also provides some interesting perspectives on the relationship of archaeological evidence to historical processes and events and these insights may increasingly be of use in understanding the archaeology of prehistoric periods.

A number of themes arise repeatedly in writing the archaeology of the region. These include the relationship of social and economic development to the changing natural environment, the role of population change, the related phenomena of monuments and elaborate artefacts, and the shifting relationship of the Western Isles communities to the wider world. Continuity of settlement locations and economy over time and across archaeological period divisions is another of the most striking features of Hebridean archaeology. In some cases individual sites or areas were occupied almost continuously over thousands of years. At the Udal in North Uist for example there was occupation of a small area of the machair coast from the time of the earliest farming communities of the Neolithic through to the Post-Medieval period, with remarkably few breaks in the sequence of deposits (c.f. Crawford and Switsur 1977).

In the final chapter I will make some attempt to tie together these various themes and the other ideas put forward throughout the book, sketching a tentative picture of Western Isles archaeology as it stands today.

Note on Chronology

Throughout the book the dating of archaeological sites and periods will be based substantially on radiocarbon dating. The dates quoted will be calibrated into 'calendar' years BC and AD using the methods available as of 1994, and generally without qualification on the basis of sample material or statistical standard deviations. Full details of the available dates for the area are given in the appendix, and these should be referred to for fuller information on any specific dates.

2 The Environment

Even in the few thousand years that have passed since the islands first came to be settled, the Hebridean environment has been transformed in numerous ways. A series of dynamic processes – principally sea level change, climatic fluctuation and soil and vegetation development – have combined over that period to produce an ever-changing environmental backdrop to the development of island communities, their economies and their social development. The environment forms, however, more than a simple background against which human lives were played out. It established the possibilities and constraints within which people operated and had an enormous effect on people's perceptions and attitudes to the world. Climate and soils, for example, establish the potential for economic development; topography compresses settlement into certain areas and establishes patterns of communication.

Human beings, however, are not simply pawns of their environment, and whilst environmental constraints might limit the options for human economies and societies, they do not dictate the solutions. Very often communities flout environmental constraints, at least for a time, with manifestly ill-adaptive practices, whether it be with self-destructive farming practices or through the devotion of valuable resources to the construction of economically pointless monuments. Nonetheless, the changing environment is something with which all communities ultimately have to come to terms and it is impossible to understand any human society, especially as it changes through time, without an understanding of the environment. So, although from time to time people might behave in ways which suggest a disregard for economic necessity, in the long term their survival depends upon existing within environmental constraints.

Today's unfavourable climate is part of a much longer-term development which has been in train since the last glaciers disappeared from Scotland around ten thousand years ago. There have long been a variety of hints that earlier Hebrideans enjoyed a more lenient environment – for example, the timber structures of crannogs exposed in loch drainage, and the presence of tree stumps under the peat suggest that woodland was once more widespread. Modern plantations have shown that given the right conditions a variety of woodland species can thrive even today in what have long been open treeless wastes.

Attempts to reconstruct the environment of the islands in prehistory, and indeed relatively recent historic periods, are beset with difficulties and can only be approached through a series of indirect means. These involve making inferences from the study of vegetation and fauna of former periods which are preserved in various ways in the archaeological and palaeo-environmental record.

Climate

The summer visitor to the Hebrides must often reflect with some dread upon the nature of these islands in winter. The maritime climate of the Hebrides today, as is the case for much of western Scotland, is notorious for its unpredictability and occasional ferocity, even though their northern location is tempered by the presence of the Gulf Stream. This provides a warming influence that gives the islands a fairly mild climate compared to other areas at a similar latitude. There is only a small annual variation in temperature and precipitation, which, whilst making the summers cool and wet, at least saves the islands from unduly severe winters.

The wind is probably the dominant climatic characteristic of the Hebrides. High winds are common all year round and their effects are accentuated by the lack of trees and general openness of the landscape. This is particularly so in the Western Isles, whilst Skye is somewhat more sheltered.

Rain, too, is common throughout the year, although it is the changeability of the weather from hour to hour, rather than the actual amount of rain which is so striking. Rainfall, associated with depressions moving eastwards from the Atlantic, is greatly influenced by relief and altitude and is therefore very variable even within such a relatively small region. The low altitude of much of Lewis, coupled with the modicum of shelter provided by the Harris Hills, means that this area gets least rainfall, perhaps 1000–1200 mm per annum (Figure 2.1). The rather more completely exposed but low-lying Uists and Barra average 1200 mm, whilst in the Harris Hills and particularly in parts of Skye it can be around 1600 mm in the most heavily settled areas, reaching 3200 mm in the Cuillins. Snow and frost, by contrast, are rare away from the mountainous areas of Skye and Harris.

Although winters in the Hebrides, particularly the Western Isles, are relatively mild in terms of temperature and precipitation, the combined effects of wind and northern latitude ensure that the seasons remain well-

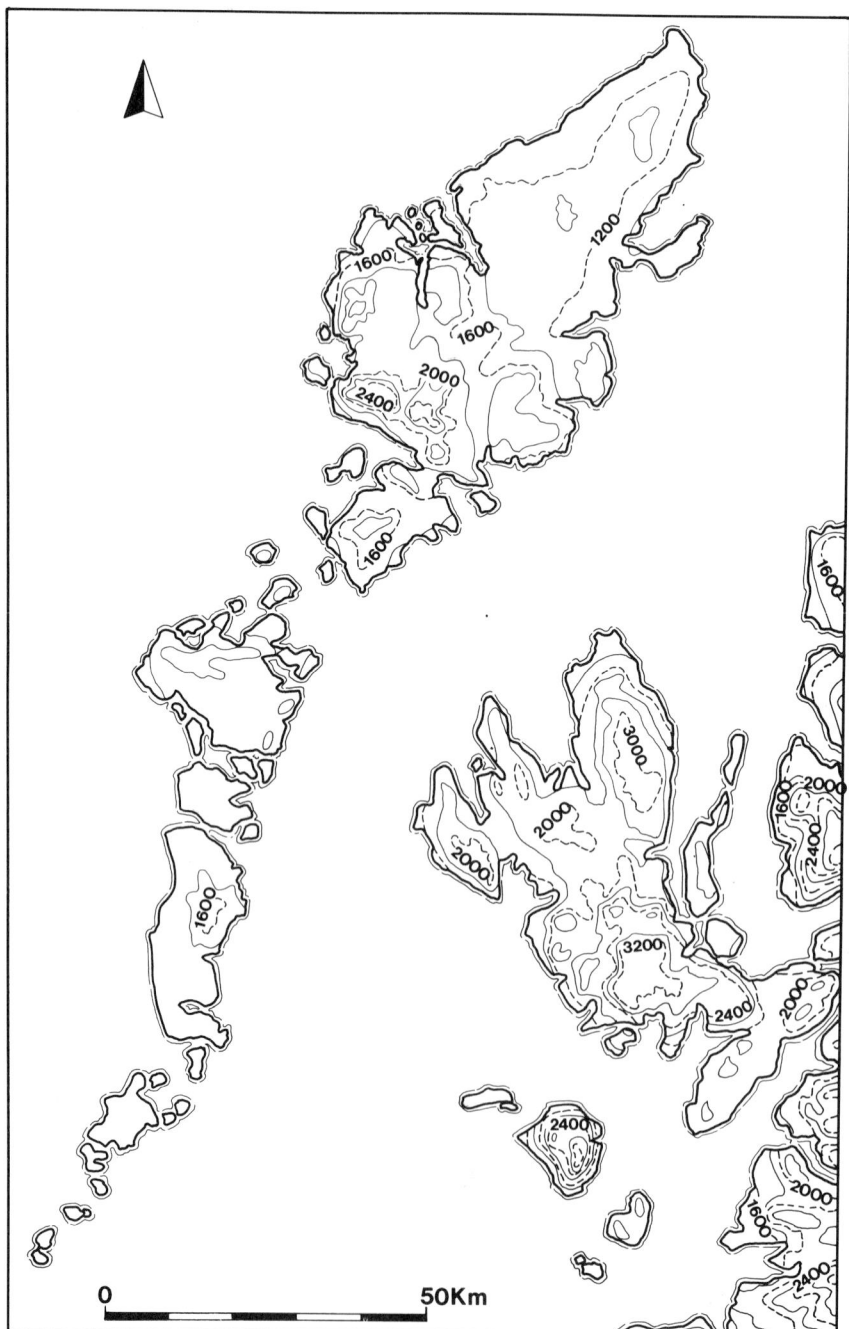

FIGURE 2.1. Rainfall in Skye and the Western Isles – measured in mm.

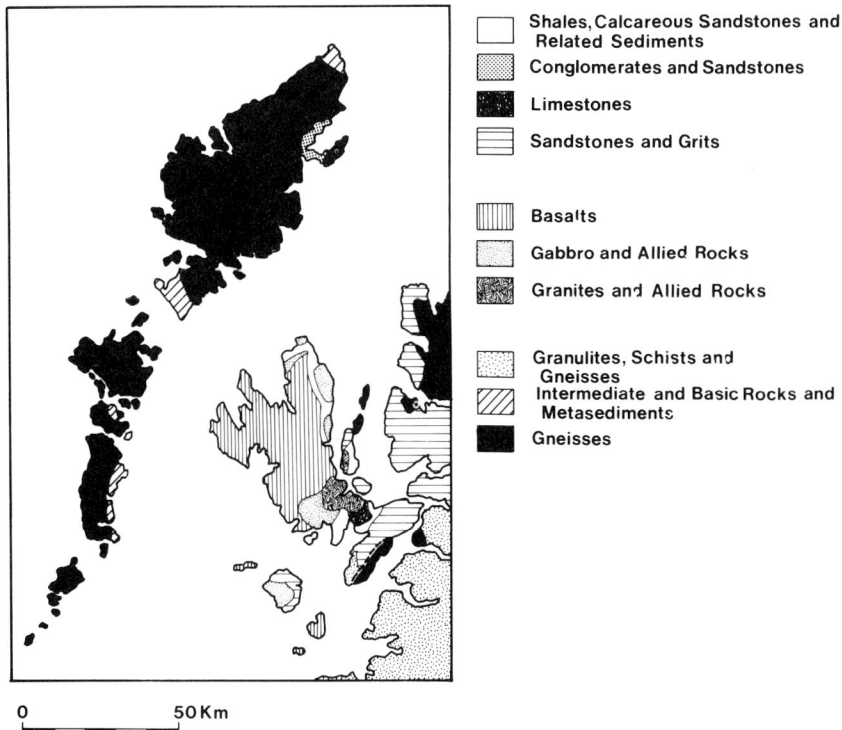

FIGURE 2.2. Geology of Skye and the Western Isles.

defined. In remote prehistory, as today, the latitude of the islands dictates that the hours of daylight shrink to a brief midday window in the pit of winter, whilst midsummer daylight can last until almost midnight. Seasonal rhythms such as these would have formed the framework for much of the economic and social life of the islanders from the earliest times.

Geology and Topography

The Hebrides, despite the shared cultural background of much of their prehistory and history, encompass a wide range of geological and topographical variation (Figure 1.2). In particular, there is a contrast between the Western Isles, and Skye and the other Small Isles (Rhum, Mull, Eigg and Canna), these latter sharing much more in common with the west mainland of Scotland.

Western Isles

The Western Isles are formed almost entirely of Lewisian gneiss, an extremely ancient rock formed around 3000 million years ago (Figure 2.2). This long chain of islands represents the weathered surface remnants of a long ridge of gneiss stretching to the north as far as the west of Shetland. Over a vast span of time the mountains of this gneiss formation have been eroded to a series of low, fragmented islands with few of the remaining hills attaining any great height. Clisham in Harris is the highest peak in the chain at around 800 m. The only exception to this geological homogeneity lies around Stornoway in Lewis where there is an area of much younger sandstones (Figure 2.2).

The ice sheets of the Quaternary period compounded earlier erosion by scouring the valleys and low-lying ground. This geologically recent process is responsible for the characteristic pock-marked landscape of low rounded hills and small lochs, as water filled the hollows gouged out by the ice. This is seen most clearly in North Uist where the eastern part of the island is a maze of small freshwater lochs and low hills and there is almost as much water as land. Indeed, although the land area of the Western Isles is only 1.3 per cent of Great Britain, they contain an impressive 15.8 per cent of its standing waters (Angus 1993a).

The ancient geology of the islands did not leave a particularly rich inheritance for their human inhabitants. Lewisian gneiss is not a good building stone and there are few mineral resources of any value. Most importantly though, the rock produces thin, acid soils of limited agricultural value. It is probably no coincidence that the area around Stornoway, underlain by sandstone rather than gneiss, was one of the first areas settled in the Neolithic period – presumably because of its richer soils. Elsewhere agriculture has traditionally been concentrated on the machair (the extensive coastal shell sand plains created by processes of sea-level change after the end of the last Ice Age).

Skye and the Small Isles

The geology of Skye is more varied than that of the Western Isles, and although Lewisian gneiss is present, particularly in the southern part of the island, it does not dominate as it does in the Western Isles (Figure 2.2). The predominant rock formations in Skye and the Small Isles were created by volcanic activity in the Tertiary period around 60 million years ago. It was at this time that the Cuillins were thrown up, as well as the mountains of Rhum to the south. The basalt plateaux, characteristic of the north and west of Skye, were also formed in this period.

Subsequently, like the Western Isles, the rock formations of Skye and the Small Isles were sculpted and scoured by the great movements of ice that characterised the Quaternary period. In Skye these processes resulted in the formation of the numerous characteristic U-shaped glacial valleys. The movement of the ice carved out great gorges subsequently filled by the sea, like that which separates Raasay from Skye and Skye itself from the mainland.

In terms of their potential for human settlement, the soils of Skye and the Small Isles are no better than those of the Western Isles. The volcanic soils provide moderate grazing but lack the fertility often associated with volcanic soils elsewhere. Cultivation in these areas has tended to focus on the more sheltered valleys where boulder clays and gravels were laid down by the retreating ice sheets. Arable cultivation is not practised above 150 m above sea level, these lands being used instead for grazing. Elsewhere localised geological factors influence land quality and agricultural potential. At Ord, west of Sleat, for example, the underlying limestones have produced unusually fertile conditions and support limited woodland (Figure 2.2).

The Past Environment

Woodland and Peat Growth

Since the end of the last glaciation the climate has broadly followed the cyclical pattern of previous warm intervals. As temperatures gradually increased and the ice sheets retreated northwards, soil formation began and plant communities started to develop. Forest cover became established, the initial hazel and birch scrub was replaced by dense woodland, and soils gradually became enriched. As plant communities developed conditions became more conducive for larger land mammals and, as these species spread, human populations too moved north. These people lived in small, mobile bands, surviving by gathering and hunting a wide range of plant and animal resources.

By around 3500 BC the climate was in its interglacial prime, significantly warmer than it is now. As in all previous interglacials, however, the climate eventually began to get cooler and wetter. Almost as soon as the first settlers had reached the islands their natural environment was in decline.

The Hebrides today are virtually treeless: natural woodland is restricted to isolated pockets of scrub on islets in the numerous lochs, out of the reach of sheep, or else in small sheltered clefts in the more mountainous areas. Vast blankets of peat shroud the inland areas. These peats have formed over the millennia as a result of a combination of factors; principally the coolness and wetness of the climate and poor drainage, which have conspired to inhibit the decomposition of organic matter. The resulting soils are infertile, wet and acidic and have been of little economic use to the human inhabitants of the islands other than as a fuel. They support a restricted range of vegetation and have inhibited any regeneration of woodland. Agriculture has generally been confined to the coastal machair or areas of locally fertile soils, although much effort was spent at times laboriously reclaiming peatlands.

It was not simply climatic decline that caused the disappearance of woodland from the islands. Human interference played a significant part. As yet this has to be largely inferred from indirect archaeological evidence, e.g. episodes of early forest burning, the timber requirements of broch towers and related structures. As elsewhere in Britain, grazing would have prevented the natural regeneration of areas once cleared. But with or without human help, peat expansion would have signalled the end of extensive Hebridean forests many centuries ago. In recent years evidence from a variety of sources, most significantly pollen analysis and the study of preserved sub-peat tree stumps, has begun to build up an ever-improving picture of how woodland developed, declined and eventually disappeared.

The Western Isles

During the 1970s Birks and Madsen carried out an analysis of the pollen which had accumulated over thousands of years in the valley mire at Little Loch Roag on the west coast of Lewis (Birks and Madsen 1979). The site was chosen for its relative proximity to prehistoric activity at Callanish, 11 km to the east, and because of the lack of destructive peat cutting in the area. Birks and Madsen found remarkably low levels of tree pollen for the whole of the post-glacial period; sufficiently low in fact to suggest that the area had never supported extensive woodland (ibid., 836).

More recent studies have radically altered this perception. Pollen analysis on the site of Tob nan Leobag in Lewis, just outside the township of Callanish, produced a very different picture of former woodland to that suggested at Little Loch Roag (Bohncke 1988). During the Mesolithic period the area around Callanish appears to have been covered by substantial stands of birch along with some elm and oak (Edwards *et al.*, 1994). Early human incursions are hinted at by the increased incidence of forest fires represented by charcoal fragments in the peat from around 5000 BC. These fires were probably deliberately caused by hunter-gatherers trying to create clearings to attract their prey. Cereal pollen appeared later, indicating the beginnings of farming in the area from around 3300–2500 BC (ibid.). By around 2000 BC tree cover seems to have been much reduced, possibly because the sea had encroached, flooding the valleys that now form Loch Roag. At Dun Bharabhat in the Bhaltos peninsula barley appears in the pollen record at around 1500 BC perhaps suggesting an intensification of agriculture in the locality. By the Iron Age the Callanish area was much more open and there are indications of more extensive agriculture. Significantly though, in the last centuries BC birch was able to regenerate even in this most exposed area of west Lewis. During the first millennium AD heather increased markedly and the area became wetter, although cereal cultivation continued for several centuries.

Recent work around Loch Lang on the east side of South Uist has further revised the environmental picture for the islands (Bennett *et al.*, 1990). In this study it was found that woodland had formerly covered around half of the land area in the early post-glacial period with the expected birch and hazel supplemented by oak, elm and possibly pine. From around 2000 BC this woodland began to decline, probably as a result of intensification of grazing on the hills. Blanket peat which had begun to appear some time before this became increasingly dominant. A similar picture derives from work at Loch Hellisdale, also on South Uist, where forest clearance intensified slightly later, at around 1000 BC and soil erosion possibly associated with cultivation was apparent by around 600 BC (Kent *et al.*, 1994).

This less pessimistic view of the extent of former woodland gains additional support from John Evans' work on the mollusc species present at the machair site of Northton in Harris (Evans 1971a). Shade-dwelling species indicate woodland in the Neolithic with a more open environment beginning to develop in the Later Neolithic and Bronze Age. Woodland appears even have regenerated to some extent prior to renewed clearance, almost certainly by human populations in the Iron Age (Evans 1971b; 1975, 122).

Much of this work represents essentially local snapshots of former environmental conditions in specific parts of the island chain. Work during the early 1980s on preserved timbers exposed by peat cutting has provided insights into the more general development of the Hebridean forests (Wilkins 1984). These sites, all located in Lewis and Harris, represent the waterlogged remnants of the final generations of woodlands which were engulfed by peat. Numerous samples of pine, birch and willow were analysed and dated, providing an indication of the dates for the disappearance of woodland at various localities.

The dates obtained from these preserved tree stumps provided some interesting patterns. Willow gave consistently the earliest dates, from *c.*7190–6600 BC, whilst birch was slightly later at *c.*6030–3080 BC. The pine samples dated to 2920–1960 BC and came from sites more remote from human settlement. The patterns of dates and locations suggest that while pine forest developed from earlier birch-dominated woodland in some areas of the Harris Hills, peat was already encroaching on the woodland of surrounding areas and had already engulfed some areas where woodland had never fully developed. From the point of view of human occupation two important points emerge from this study: firstly it is clear that from the earliest human settlement of the Outer Isles, woodland was under threat from peat expansion; the other is that despite this, pine forest remained established in the more remote parts of Lewis and Harris well into the Bronze Age and in the more secluded and better-drained valleys it may have survived longer still. It may be significant that among the bones recovered from Iron Age sites in Lewis are included those of wildcat and blackbird, both suggestive of some degree of woodland survival (Barber 1985, 17). Timber might not have been plentiful but it did exist locally and must have been a prized resource. Bennett (1990) has pointed out that the latitudinal range of the Outer Hebrides covers a diverse range of mainland vegetation zones and that therefore we should not expect to see any particular uniformity in former woodland composition from island to island.

The proportions of tree species represented in the pollen record of Wilkins' sub-peat sites actually correspond well with the earlier work of Birks and Madsen. It was the small absolute values of tree pollen – possibly resulting from the displacement of windblown pollen by the Hebridean gales –

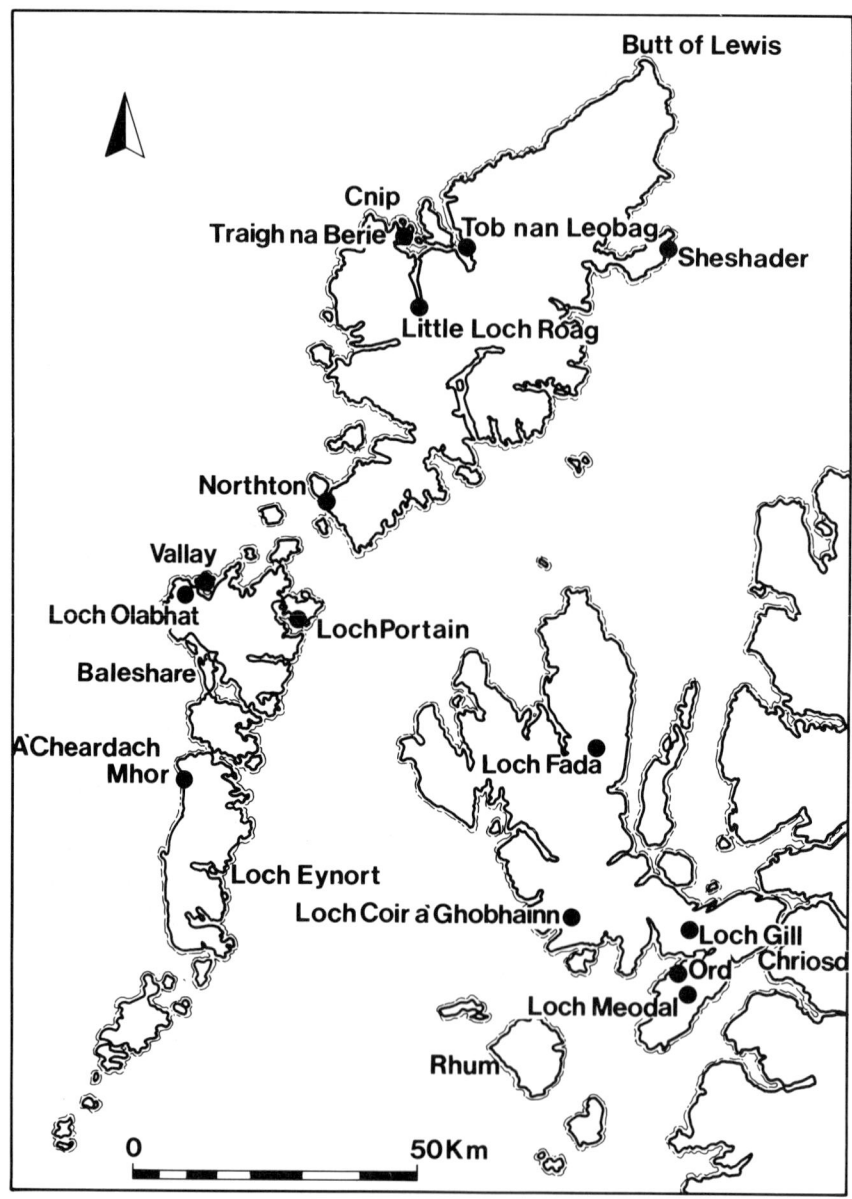

FIGURE 2.3. Location of palaeo-environmental sites.

which had led to their dismissal as 'background' readings in the earlier work. Even the original Little Loch Roag sample site, therefore, may not have been as devoid of woodland in prehistory as had first been thought.

Skye and the Small Isles

More woodland survives today in Skye than in the Western Isles. Areas of birch scrub can be found particularly in parts of the south and east of the island. The topography of Skye, and the relatively small areas of intensive prehistoric settlement, may have given woodland a better chance of survival than in smaller, more exposed and more intensively occupied areas like the Uists. Pine forest with birch flourished in eastern parts of Skye and the island may also have witnessed a limited presence of oak although it is adjudged to have been close to the north-western margins of both pine and oak (Hirons 1990). This information is supplemented by a handful of clues from near-contemporary historical records, suggesting that woodland of sorts lasted rather longer here than it did in the Western Isles. Adomnan's *Life of St Columba* written in the late seventh century AD, relates a story in which the saint encountered a wild boar on the island, suggesting the presence of a decent spread of woodland. Even as late as the sixteenth century Dean Monro wrote of the 'maney woods' of Skye, although by then it is hard to envisage the survival of much closed woodland. The Statistical Account of 1792, however, records that remnants of old woodland survived even then at Portree and Sleat.

The recent excavations of the Mesolithic settlement site of Kinloch in Rhum generated a certain amount of palaeo-environmental work relating to the Small Isles (Hirons 1990). It appears that Rhum was late in receiving woodland relative to the mainland and the larger island of Skye. By around 6000 BC though, birch, hazel and oak were present and are represented in the pollen record. Stumps of pine have also been identified indicating some incidence of that species too on the island. By around 2000 BC, however, during the Neolithic, there are signs that here, as throughout the Hebrides, a more open vegetation was developing, along with the expansion of peat (ibid., 137). This change was brought about primarily by climatic factors but human interference with the natural vegetation certainly played its part at least locally. In Rhum, for example, agriculture seems to have led to soil erosion as early as 2700 BC (ibid., 143).

Sea and Sand

The Western Isles

The relationship between land and sea in the Western Isles has been central to the development of human settlement in the islands from the earliest times. Unlike Skye and the Inner Isles which had for long been buried under the weight of the immense mainland ice sheets, the Western Isles saw little appreciable land level rise after the melting of the glaciers to counteract the rising seas. The process of sea level rise is in this sense simpler in the Western Isles and there are no raised beaches in these islands. Instead the rising seas since the end of the last Ice Age have steadily engulfed former areas of dry land, reducing the size of the land mass and fragmenting it into an ever increasing number of separate islands.

Whilst the steep and rocky east coasts have probably lost fairly little land, the shallow west coasts, running out under the sea at a slope of around 1 in 250, have been extremely vulnerable to shifts in sea level. John Barber has calculated that at a likely figure of 1 m rise in sea level each 1000 years, the islands have lost on average 1.25 km from their western margins since the Neolithic. This means that the coastline and coastal plains of that period and before have long since been submerged. Even the shape of the land mass encountered by the first settlers, and the number and configuration of the islands would have been unrecognisable to us. Coastal resources were of even greater importance to the earliest inhabitants than to subsequent generations, who had farming to supplement their subsistence, so we have probably lost the main areas in which they lived and in which their economies focused.

The near-continuous plains of machair which fringe the Uists and Harris, and the substantial but fragmented bays of Lewis, have been the most intensively cultivated parts of the islands in historic times (Figure 2.4). They also contain exceptionally rich and detailed archaeological evidence for past human societies who lived in and around them. Their agricultural wealth is only relative to other soils in the islands though, since the machair is highly alkaline, unstable and prone to winter flooding. Understanding its complex formation processes and development is one of the most pressing palaeoenvironmental issues in Hebridean archaeology. The study of machair formation and development as well as wider questions of sea level change have been most extensively studied by Ritchie (e.g. 1966; 1967; 1976; 1979; 1985) and in a series of volumes published by the Institute of Terrestrial Ecology (e.g. Ranwell 1974; 1980).

The machair consists of shell sands thrown up by the rising sea and then reworked by the wind into a complex formation of coastal sand dunes fronting a more stable sandy plain. These sands cover a buried landscape continuous with that further inland, and thin out gradually away from the coast except where the local topography blocks their way, leading to deep accumulations of sand against the low inland hills. The machair remains in continuous flux, constantly changing configuration as sea levels rise and push the whole formation landward. Numerous sites of the Iron Age have been found in recent years eroding from the modern beach front. These appear to have been sites originally set well back behind the coastal dunes and in many areas the prehistoric machair has probably all but disappeared. Steady erosion of the beach front has been supplemented by occasional submergence of large level areas of former coastal plain when the frontal dunes

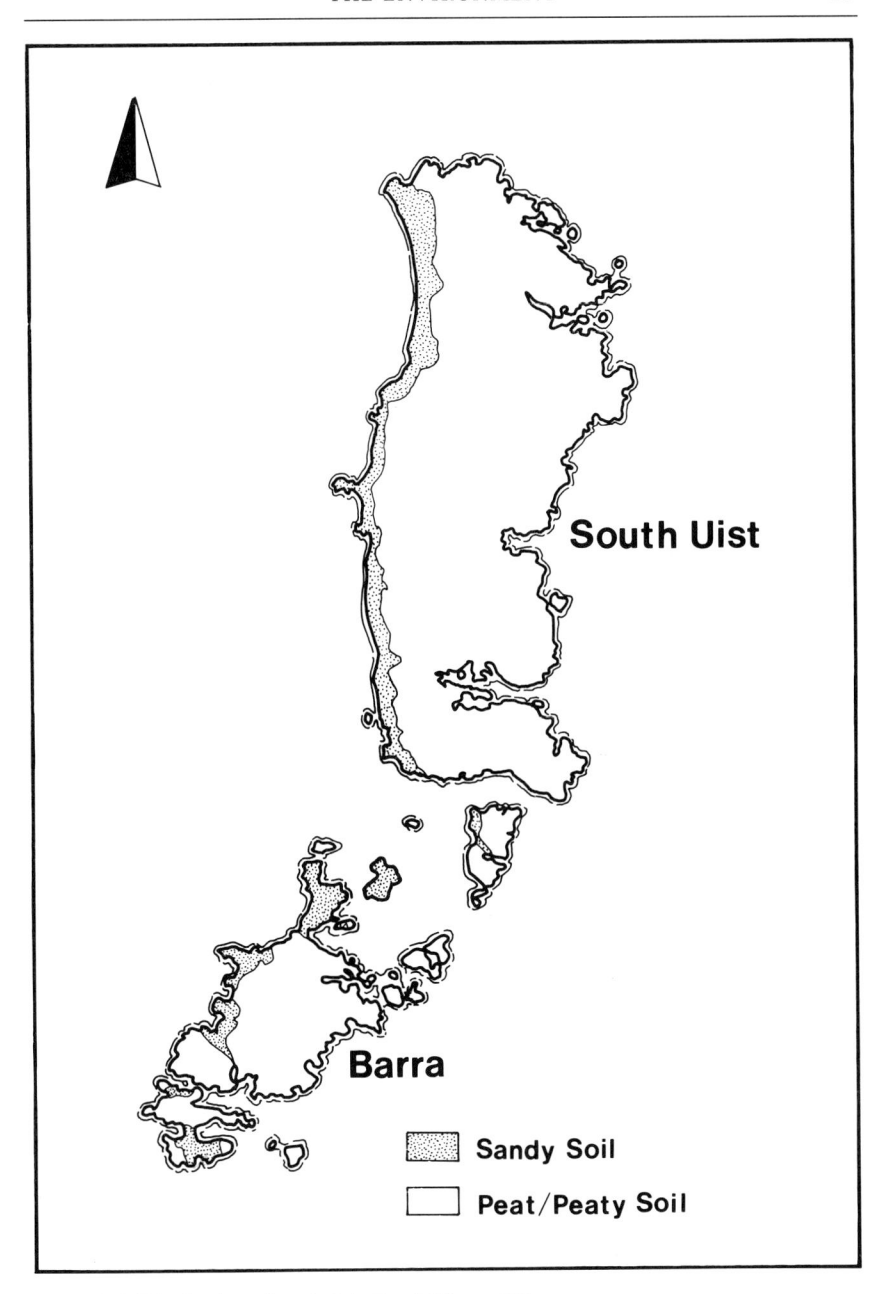

FIGURE 2.4. Distribution of machair in South Uist and Barra.

are breached. This appears to have happened, for example, on the Vallay Strand in North Uist, and would have had disastrous consequences for the prehistoric inhabitants of the area.

In relatively recent centuries machair change has continued apace. There are numerous historical accounts of the catastrophic loss of agricultural lands on the machair or even the loss of whole settlements (Angus and Elliot 1992). The settlement on the west coast of Baleshare off North Uist was lost to the sea as recently as the eighteenth century. Baleshare itself only became an island cut off from North Uist in fairly recent times.

It is not simply the rising sea which has kept the machair on the move. The light sandy soils are highly vulnerable to any surface disturbance: once openings are made the wind can quickly set about the wholesale removal of even major sand-hills. Agriculture too, by removing the vegetation cover and exposing the soil to the elements, has contributed greatly to machair instability and change. The introduction of rabbits has further destabilised the machair: many archaeological sites have been riddled with burrows and subsequently ripped apart by the wind, leaving little but a mixed and useless mess of stone, sand and earth.

Skye and the Small Isles

The retreat of the last ice sheets caused immense environmental changes throughout northern Europe. In the islands one of the major processes set in train was the fluctuation of sea level relative to the land. The meltwaters of the retreating glaciers caused the level of the sea to rise, over-running large tracts of land and filling many of the gorges and bowls gouged out by the ice. The fragmented coastline of western Scotland and the chains of separate islands began to take on something approaching their present shape, with their numerous peninsulas and sea lochs.

The process was not simply one of sea level rise. The weight of the ice which had borne down on the land mass of Scotland had now been lifted and the land itself thus begun to rise at the same time as the sea. The inter-play between these two processes meant that, although in absolute terms the sea was rising, the relative sea-level fluctuated enormously. At several stages the coastlines of much of Scotland were raised above the level of the sea to be preserved as inland raised beaches. Many of these can be recognised today in Skye, particularly at Uig and Broadford where their relatively fertile soils have made them a focus for subsequent human settlement. In Rhum too there is extensive evidence for the presence of former coastlines, now raised above the sea.

Fauna

One of the natural resources of most relevance to the first settlers in the islands was the fauna. The hunter gatherers of the Mesolithic lived entirely on wild animals and plants and the range of the former is almost as difficult to reconstruct as we have seen to be the case for the latter. The post-glacial fauna of the islands can for our purposes broadly be divided into three categories: land mammals, birds and sea-life.

The range of Hebridean land mammals prior to human introductions would have been very limited. It has been argued recently that the red deer could not have colonised the Western Isles without human intervention (Serjeantson 1990, 11), though Skye would have been in easy reach of mainland deer populations. It is perhaps most likely that red deer were introduced as early as the Mesolithic and this species remained an important resource long after the adoption of farming. There are certainly parallels for the deliberate introduction of wild deer to islands in the Mediterranean, such as Cyprus and Sardinia, at an equally early date (ibid.). Even in the early centuries AD red deer were the main food animal at the wheelhouse site of Cnip in Lewis, although this was almost certainly a fairly localised phenomenon. Roe deer are still found in Skye today but are absent from the Western Isles. Wolves were present in Skye until the eighteenth century when they were hunted to extinction. Foxes and otters too, maintain a precarious existence in the islands.

The majority of the present terrestrial fauna of the islands are species introduced by humans. The range of domesticated animals which made their appearance from the Neolithic onwards was derived exclusively from external sources. Cattle, sheep and goats had no wild ancestors in the Hebrides and, although wild boar may have been present in the past (although the single tooth known from the islands may have been part of an imported ornament), domestic pigs were derived from outside the islands. Dogs may have been domesticated a little earlier than meat-bearing species. Later introductions included the horse which becomes apparent in the Iron Age, for example at the wheelhouse of A' Cheardach Mhor in South Uist (Finlay 1985). Rats and rabbits made a less welcome appearance in Medieval or later times, while ferrets were subsequently introduced to control the latter. A number of introductions date to much more recent times; these include the hedgehog, deliberately introduced in an attempt to reduce the slug population, and the mink, whose feral population originated in island fur farms.

Fowling was an important part of the economy of many parts of the Hebrides and several species of seabird were valuable for their meat, oil and feathers. Martin records the organised slaughter of cormorants in parts of Skye (1716) whilst in St Kilda the gannets, fulmars and puffins that inhabited the rocky cliffs were a staple food on which survival often depended. At the Butt of Lewis the annual cull of gannets persisted into recent centuries. The bones of species such as the (now-extinct) great auk and gannet are common on archaeological sites in the Western Isles while other species such as swan also occur.

From the earliest times the sea played a central part in the lives of the Hebrideans. Fishing was always vital to island communities, as was the collection of shellfish. The remains of both are prominent in archaeological sites of all periods, although fish bones have been adequately recorded only in relatively recent years. Numerous species were available in the seas around the Hebrides, including cod, ling, saithe, pollack, whiting, haddock, conger eel, wrasse, herring and mackerel. Flatfish and sharks of various species have also been recorded from archaeological sites in the Western Isles. Shellfish species include cockles, periwinkles, scallops, whelks, mussels, razorshells and oysters.

Another coastal resource which has long provided a welcome, though unpredictable, supplement to the subsistence economies of Hebridean communities was the stranding of whales and other cetaceans. Whalebone is common on archaeological sites, often fashioned into a variety of tools, and a wide range of other resources could be obtained from these occasional windfalls: flesh, blubber, oil and skins. The frequency of strandings is difficult to gauge and inevitably modern comparisons may have only a limited bearing on the situation in the past. Nonetheless detailed modern records suggest that in Lewis and Harris alone there were seven such strandings during 1990, including pilot whales, sperm whales and white-beaked dolphins (Angus 1993b). Seals, mostly the common and grey varieties, were also plentiful and provided both meat and skins.

People and the Environment

It would be false to separate out the natural environment from human activity. The activities of human populations since their first arrival, through farming, tree-clearance and burning, peat-cutting, etc., have had immensely important effects on the development of the Hebridean landscape. In the following chapters this relationship will surface repeatedly to complicate the story of both the development of the environment and of human societies.

3 Hunters and Gatherers

The First Colonisation

It is impossible now to tell when people first colonised the Hebrides. The destructive forces of climatic and environmental change over thousands of years have obliterated most of the slight remains of the earliest settlers. Although there is evidence for the presence of humans in England as early as 500,000 years ago, there are few indications of people in Scotland until the end of the last glaciation. This is probably due to a combination of the scouring away of former sites during the last Ice Age, and also partly to the paucity of investigations of those areas, such as caves, where remains might fortuitously have survived. It is likely that some Palaeolithic groups would have visited Scotland hunting herds of wild animals in milder periods of previous interglacials, but it is not until the Mesolithic – or Middle Stone Age – that the permanent occupation of extensive areas of Scotland becomes archaeologically visible.

Mesolithic communities in temperate regions of Europe lived by exploiting a diverse range of resources. The herds of reindeer and other large mammals prevalent during the Ice Ages had disappeared from these regions as woodland gradually became established and spread northwards carrying more diverse fauna and flora. Mesolithic economies relied heavily on the exploitation of plant resources such as fruits, nuts, seeds and roots, etc.; the hunting of species like red deer, boar and small mammals probably took second place in terms of nutritional importance. Coastal, lacustrine and riverine resources were vital, and probably dominated the diet in many areas. Areas, like the Hebrides, which could give access to a variety of environmental zones and a wide range of resources would have been prized.

Since wild foods in a temperate region are fairly thinly spread and often only seasonally available, Mesolithic communities are thought to have lived in small bands, moving around a great deal, perhaps on an annual cycle. By around 10,000 years ago communities like this were firmly established in Scotland. Most areas of the country were probably inhabited by that time although, since these people were living off wild foods, populations could never be particularly large.

Some of the best evidence for Mesolithic settlement in Britain comes from the west coast and southern Hebrides where the early inhabitants left large middens of food debris which can be analysed to provide a wealth of detail on their lifestyles and economy. The small island of Oronsay, off Colonsay in the southern Hebrides (Figure 3.1), contains a series of extensive shell middens which have been partially excavated (Mellars 1987). A wide range of stone and bone tools were recovered from these sites but perhaps more important were the environmental remains relating to the foodstuffs of the Mesolithic inhabitants. Evidence from otoliths (small ear bones) of the saithe demonstrated that the occupants of Oronsay were engaged in the harvest of this fish throughout the year. A range of shellfish was exploited, probably on a seasonal basis, and it is their remains that form the physical bulk of the shell middens. In terms of dietary significance however, shellfish were less important than fish, birds and both marine and terrestrial mammals.

There is evidence from various excavations in the southern Hebrides and west coast area that Mesolithic communities were highly mobile and travelled frequently by sea. Some groups may have routinely incorporated several islands or mainland areas into their seasonal round. It is easy to envisage in this 'island-hopping' context the gradual spread of people to new areas and the progressive colonisation of the west coast. Such economically-driven movement would undoubtedly have brought people to Skye and the Western Isles, all of which are easily intervisible and accessible to early sea-craft.

In terms of the area covered by this book, excavated evidence for human settlement in the Mesolithic is extremely sparse. Only at Kinloch, on the island of Rhum south of Skye, has a Mesolithic settlement been excavated. Few indications of Mesolithic settlement have been found in Skye itself, though this is probably due mainly to a lack of appropriate fieldwork. In the Western Isles the problems are much greater due to a series of environmental factors. Mesolithic settlement in the Hebrides would have been primarily coastal. In the Western Isles sea levels have risen greatly since the Mesolithic and most of the contemporary coastlines have long since sunk beneath the Atlantic (see Chapter 2). Assuming that there were inland Mesolithic sites in the islands these are most likely covered by thick peat or shell sand and their discovery is more likely to be a matter of chance than careful research.

One of the most exciting recent archaeological discoveries in the Hebrides was made in 1993 at the coastal cave site of An Corran in Skye (Miket, pers. comm.). This cave contains middens rich in both bone and stone tools and associated debris. The worked stone assemblage contains a range of forms including microliths characteristic of the Mesolithic and bone tools of

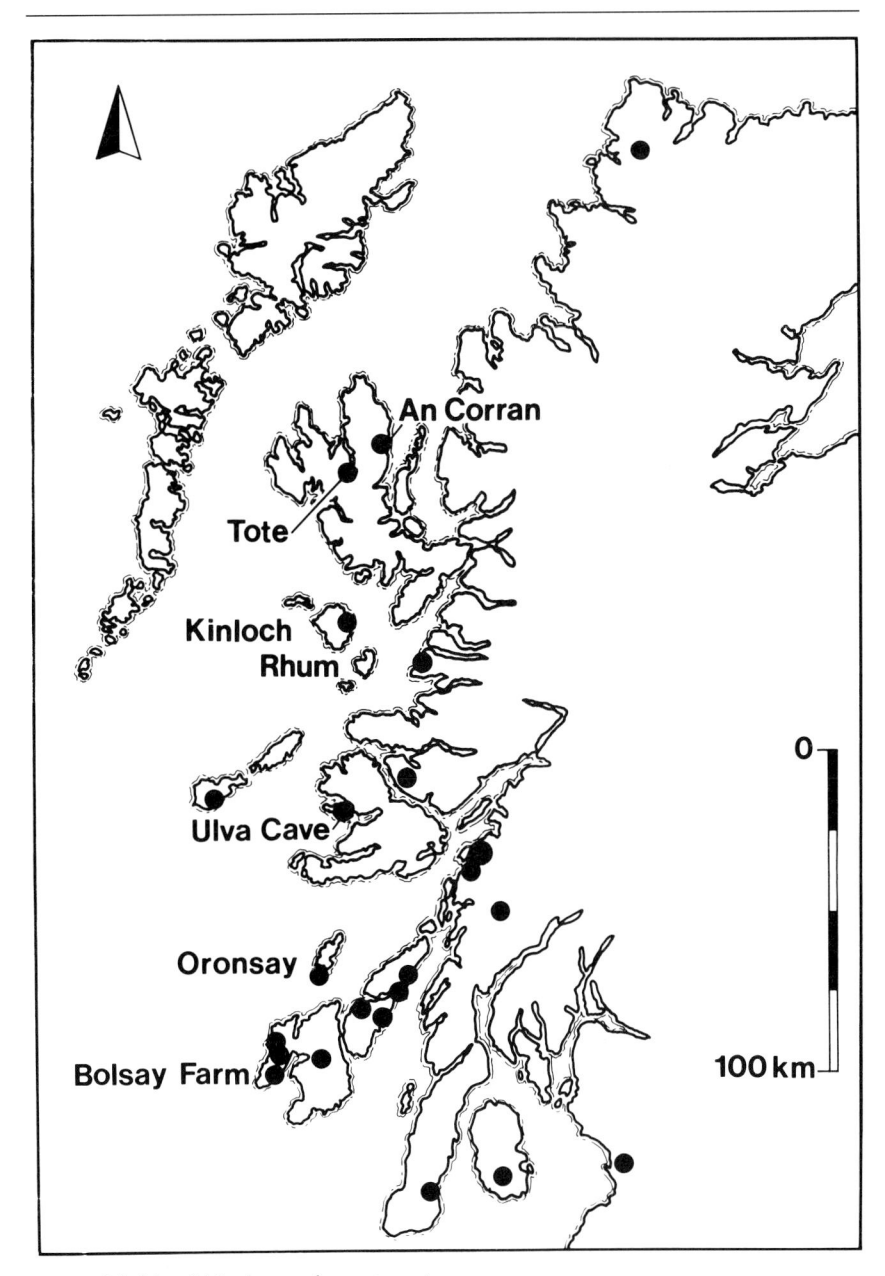

FIGURE 3.1. Mesolithic sites on the west coast.

Obanian type. Indeed this is the first occurrence of these two technologies in direct association and appears finally to refute the idea that they represented different Mesolithic populations. Among the midden material are the bones of small mammals, birds and fish with the potential to greatly augment our understanding of Mesolithic subsistence strategies in the Hebrides. Although it has yet to be subject to full excavation, An Corran highlights the tremendous potential which still exists to add to our understanding of these earliest parts of Scotland's history.

At present, with the exception of the excavations on Rhum and the cave at An Corran, only tantalising glimpses of mesolithic settlement in the area are available from the environmental record. At Leobag in Lewis the burning of vegetation around 5000 BC is suggested by a drop in tree pollen and the presence of charcoal in the peat. Similar indications appear even earlier at around 7000 BC at Loch Lang in South Uist (Bennett 1990). Such episodes have often been interpreted as deliberate human interference designed to create woodland clearings which will attract wild animals to graze. So far, such slender threads are as close as we can get to the Mesolithic people of the Western Isles.

Kinloch and the West Coast Mesolithic

The recent excavations at Kinloch, on the east coast of Rhum at the head of the sea loch, Loch Scresort (Wickham-Jones 1990), have revealed traces of the earliest settlement so far found in Scotland, dating back to around 6700 BC (ibid., 163). Although only some 10 per cent of the site was exposed, the excavations greatly increased our knowledge of settlement in Scotland at this period and highlighted the potential for the recovery of mesolithic sites.

The settlement at Kinloch was preserved in a very fragmentary state. The remains of former structures were represented by scatters of stake holes, pits and hollows, while the occupied area was strewn with flint and other stone tools and debris from tool manufacture. Many varieties of stone tools were present, suggesting that Kinloch was a site for domestic occupation rather than a temporary camp where some specific activity was carried out. It seems to have been occupied over several thousands of years, although possibly sporadically. The area of settlement probably shifted periodically so that the whole site may never have been occupied at any single time. The later occupants used pottery and were thus, in conventional terminology, Neolithic, although there is little sign of any change in the way the site was used and there is no indication of farming or of substantial domestic buildings.

The excavator was able to offer some suggestions for the reconstruction of the dwellings based on the fragmentary structural elements, parallels drawn from other Mesolithic sites, and anthropological observation (Figure 3.2). The main structural fragments were a series of arcs of stake holes which can be interpreted in various ways. A minimalist interpretation might be that

FIGURE 3.2. Artist's reconstruction of the mesolithic houses at Kinloch.

they represent windbreaks, supporting light shelters. A view somewhat more attuned to the exigencies of the Hebridean climate (even the kinder mesolithic variety) might be more inclined to see them as parts of circular buildings, supporting walls of skin or brush. Nonetheless, this suggestion does not account for the missing halves of the arcs. Another suggestion is that the arcs represent the rear ends of ridge-pole structures of a kind similar to those found amongst the Inuit, where only one earthfast stake supported the front end (Figure 3.2). Although no hearths were found in these 'buildings', heat-fractured hearth-slabs were found dumped in pits, and quantities of stone dumped in an infilled watercourse might well be fragments of dismantled Mesolithic wall-footings.

Aside from the dwellings themselves, other pairs of stake holes around the site have been interpreted as emplacements of racks or frames. A range of other, even more ephemeral constructions may have left no trace at all in the plough-ravaged subsoils.

Although there are few comparable excavated structures of this period elsewhere in Scotland, there is no *a priori* reason to expect that even mobile Mesolithic communities did not occupy moderately substantial houses. At Mount Sandel in Ireland a series of Mesolithic houses has been excavated. These were circular timber-framed huts up to 6 m in diameter with central hearths, and provide some idea of the types of dwelling that might be expected of Mesolithic communities in the unreliable climates of northern and western Europe (Woodman 1985).

The problems of interpreting a site like Kinloch are typical of the Scottish Mesolithic and are due to the limited preservation. Artefacts that survive are almost exclusively those made of stone, bone or antler, and the latter two materials survive only in rare soil conditions. Rich expressions of Mesolithic culture must surely have existed in more perishable materials, such as wood, basketry and leather but these simply do not survive in normal conditions. One result of this has been the understandable concentration of work on extracting as much information as possible from worked stone.

Stone tools were clearly vital to Mesolithic communities and some work has been done recently on the ways in which the raw materials were obtained. Flint-bearing gravels occur in various parts of western Scotland but it is likely that most flint was obtained from beach pebbles, transported from undersea deposits (Wickham-Jones 1978). Such material could find its way far from its original location, in the roots of drifting seaweed for example, and sufficient quantities were available on most Hebridean islands to provide for a range of tools. Flint could be chipped or knapped to produce a range of tools for various purposes. The Later Mesolithic is characterised by the production of small flint tools known as microliths (Figure 3.3), which formed elements of composite tools such as arrowheads. For many utilitarian purposes more abundant local alternatives to flint were called into service. Chert shares many of the properties of flint and was more easily obtained whilst often, as at Kinloch, even such obstinate materials as agate and quartz were used.

Occasionally stone sources can be pin-pointed with some confidence and these demonstrate the mobility of some Mesolithic communities at least in terms of their stone procurement. Bloodstone from the eponymous Blood-stone Hill on Rhum was found, unsurprisingly, as a major component of the chipped stone assemblage at Kinloch. But the same material has also been found at a range of Mesolithic and later sites in other parts of western Scotland.

Mesolithic Society and the Spread of Farming

Understandably, given the nature of the surviving material, archaeologists have been reluctant to speculate on the nature of Mesolithic societies. There has been a tendency to assume that social organisation was fairly loose and egalitarian, with people moving around in bands of perhaps ten to twenty people with little in the way of social differentiation or territorial awareness.

The coherence of regional traditions and styles of flint-working in the Mesolithic period suggests that individual bands must have had considerable contact with each other and maintained active and widespread cultural links. It would have been a biological necessity for people to move between groups and, although actual archaeological evidence for such contact is presently negligible, we must envisage a web of social mechanisms which regularly brought people together in the routine course of their seasonal movement.

Evidence for Mesolithic religion and ritual practice is similarly scarce, although sporadic finds from Europe attest the elaborate burial of the dead and the provision of offerings as if for an afterlife. In the British Mesolithic the best examples of ritual activity are the deer 'frontlets' at the site of Star Carr in North Yorkshire. These comprised parts of the skull and the antlers

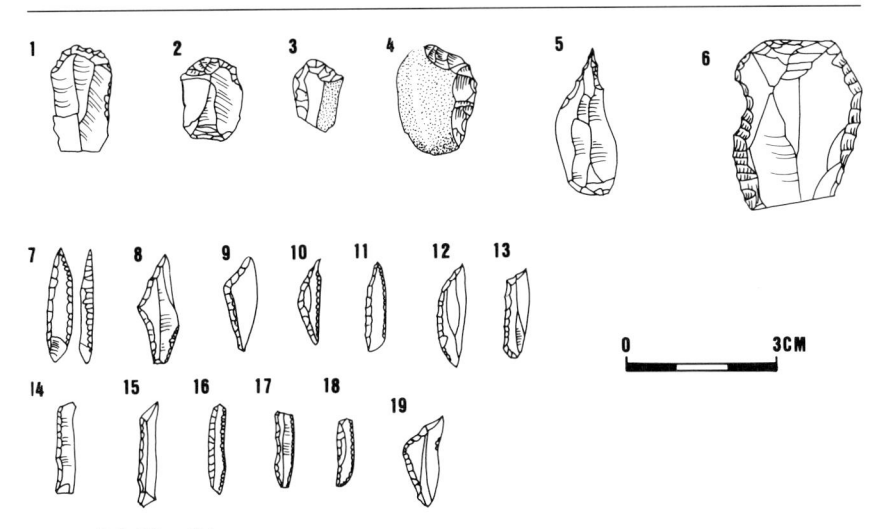

FIGURE 3.3. Microliths.

skull of stags and may have been worn in some form of shamanistic ritual, perhaps associated with hunting. That similar items have been found at Bedburg in Germany illustrates the shared cultural background of much of the European Mesolithic.

In parts of Europe there are clear signs of complex Mesolithic societies. In southern Scandinavia in the fourth millennium BC, communities known as the Ertebolle appear to have developed a semi-sedentary way of life, with more or less permanent coastal base camps from which task groups periodically set out to exploit specific seasonal resources. The Ertebolle are remarkable in that they appear to have co-existed with early farming communities to the south, from whom they adopted the principles of pottery manufacture, although they developed their own distinctive ceramic styles. They also had formal cemeteries and a degree of social stratification but, despite these apparently advanced traits, they did not practise agriculture. This distinctive way of life lasted until around 3100 BC when farming came to be widely practised. Some have suggested that climatic factors led to the dwindling of coastal resources which finally destabilised the Ertebolle and led to their eventual adoption of the new farming lifestyle (Rowley-Conwy 1983; 1985); others that an increasing population meant that the natural resources had to be augmented by food production (Jensen 1982). Alternatively the adoption first of pottery, tailored to their own needs, and subsequently food production, may have related more to the internal development of the Mesolithic Ertebolle communities themselves than to any external environmental forces.

In other parts of Europe similar piecemeal adoption of cultural and economic traits from farming communities have been observed in local Mesolithic communities. For south-west France William Barnett has suggested that pottery and domesticated animals were adopted by Mesolithic communities because of their prestige value (Barnett 1995). Such communities, as we have suggested, were engaged in constant social contacts and these may often have involved feasting and the display and provision of exotic objects and foods. Far from filling a basic subsistence need the adoption or 'accumulation' of certain domestic animals and crops, and very probably pottery, may have been intended to enhance the prestige and social status of certain groups of people.

In Scotland the evidence for Mesolithic social complexity is still slight but there is little reason to suppose that Mesolithic communities here were any less complex than those in the rest of northern and western Europe. The environmental conditions of the west coast were at least as favourable as those that supported the Ertebolle in Scandinavia. Recent analyses by Bill Finlayson have suggested that some Mesolithic bone tools were used in the labour-intensive processing and softening of skins for the manufacture of elaborate hide clothing (Finlayson 1993). Furthermore this activity may have taken place at specialist production sites. This hypothesis implies that substantial resources were devoted to activities unrelated to basic subsistence and argues for specialisation both of labour and of processing sites (ibid.).

There are also signs of economic intensification in the Later Mesolithic with the development of a range of specialised bone and antler tools of the so-called Obanian culture and the appearance of substantial shell middens (Finlayson 1993). Mesolithic cemeteries are lacking in Scotland although human remains in potentially ritual contexts have been found at both MacKay Cave and MacArthur Cave on the west coast (though their attribution as Mesolithic is far from secure, c.f. Pollard 1990; Saville and Hallen 1994). Pottery in the Scottish Mesolithic is presently a conceptual impossibility since the very presence of pottery on a Mesolithic site is taken to indicate a Neolithic presence.

The First Hebridean Farmers

Around 4000 BC we begin to see for the first time traces of communities in the British Isles that practised farming, at least to a degree, used pottery and buried their dead in formal and elaborate tombs. The adoption of a farming economy was eventually to transform human societies all across Europe. It dictated a basically sedentary lifestyle and strengthened the link between the community and its territory. It opened up tremendous potential for population expansion since food production could generally be increased by the application of more human labour. The combination of population expansion and territorial awareness created a scenario in which inter-community conflict was more likely. In addition to its massive impact on human society, farming was to lead to the clearance of woodland for agriculture and the spread of grasslands for grazing, destroying forever the natural, postglacial environment of Scotland.

Traditionally archaeologists tended to assume that the advent of farming in Britain meant the immigration of new peoples, bringing domestic crops and animals from their homelands in the south. After all, the wild progenitors of the domestic crops and animals derived mainly from the Near East, whence farming was thought to have spread over Europe and ultimately to the British Isles. The spread of pottery and burial ritual across Europe too, seemed to signal a colonial 'wave of advance', presumably fuelled by the spread of farming.

It seems that the initial spread of farming in Europe did happen in this way. The Central European *Linearbandkeramik*, or LBK, culture seems to have expanded northwards and westwards along the major river valleys carrying with it farming and other cultural traits such as ceramics, polished stone axes, elaborate houses and enclosures. But contrary to the notion of 'progress' which underlay early attempts to trace the development of human societies, farming has no inherent advantage over hunting and gathering as a mode of subsistence. It can involve great risk and large investments of labour. This, along with the wealth of the natural environment, may explain why the advance stalled long before it reached the northern and western fringes of the continent.

Although communities tend to be interpreted as Neolithic if they have any of a range of traits, e.g. pottery, chambered tombs or signs of domesticated plants or animals, recent research has indicated that there is no necessary connection between these various traits and that they need not all have been adopted as a 'Neolithic package' (Armit and Finlayson 1992). In other parts of Europe and Africa for example, pottery seems to have spread wholly independently of agriculture (Armit and Finlayson 1995). It appears that stable and successful communities, such as the Ertebolle, co-existed with farming groups for centuries, adopting and tailoring to their own requirements only those cultural and economic traits which fitted with their existing social strategies, for example the accumulation of exotic goods for gift exchange or feasting.

Kinloch is not the only west coast site with evidence for Neolithic occupation on an earlier site. On the small island of Ulva, off Mull, Clive Bonsall has found both Neolithic pottery and the bones of domestic animals in the upper levels of middens which originated in the Mesolithic. The precise nature of the change-over from Mesolithic to Neolithic on these sites is far from clear, but evidence is at least now emerging of the adoption of Neolithic cultural traits by the native, Mesolithic Hebridean communities.

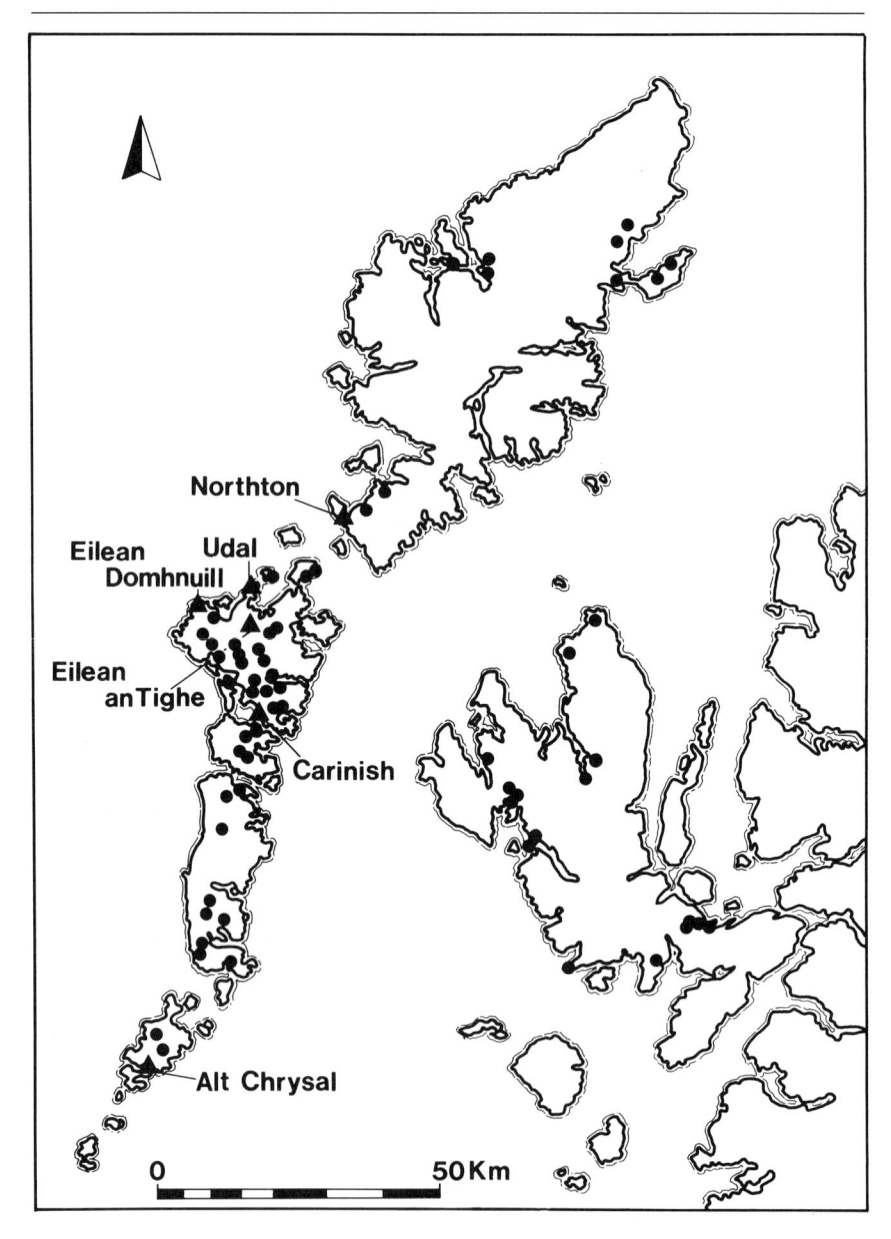

FIGURE 4.1. The Hebridean Neolithic: settlements and chambered tombs.

4 The First Farmers

The settlements of the early Hebridean farming communities remain elusive. None have yet been identified in Skye despite the presence there of several chambered tombs dating to the same broad period (Figure 4.1). In the Western Isles the few known settlements tend to comprise slight and ephemeral structures which have left little in the way of surface remains. The impermanence of these Hebridean Neolithic houses contrasts sharply with the monumental 'houses of the dead', the chambered tombs which dominated the contemporary landscape.

Most of our present information comes from a series of recent excavations, notably at Eilean Domhnuill and Bharpa Carinish in North Uist, and from excavations carried out in the 1960s at Northton in Harris. From these sites and from a reassessment of older excavations it is becoming possible to piece together a tentative picture of Hebridean Neolithic settlement and to attempt to identify where we might find and how we might recognise further sites.

Settlement

Eilean Domhnuill, Loch Olabhat

Loch Olabhat (pronounced Olavat) is a small, shallow loch in the far north-west corner of North Uist (Figure 4.2). The islet of Eilean Domhnuill (pronounced Ellen Donall) lies off the southern shore of the loch to which it is connected by a causeway of large slabs and boulders. The first excavations on Eilean Domhnuill were carried out by Erskine Beveridge sometime in the first decade of the twentieth century and recounted in his book, *North Uist*:

FIGURE 4.2. Eilean Domhnuill, Loch Olabhat (*from* Beveridge 1911).

In Loch Olavat [sic] ... is the site of another island-fort with a causeway which still remains in good preservation. This islet is locally known as *Eilean Domhnuill a' spionnaidh* (or 'island of Donald of strength') and has evidently been walled around; its central portion rising to a height of 5 or 6 feet above the present water-level, although there are distinct indications that the loch was formerly three feet deeper. Partial excavation of the summit yielded little result beyond confirming the statement that this island was at one time occupied by a fort, apparently measuring about 43 feet in diameter over its main wall, but now obscured by the foundations of two secondary buildings placed side by side. The existence of an earlier structure is further proved by the fact of these secondary walls standing upon a thick deposit of kitchen midden ashes; while similar remains, intermixed with small fragments of ancient pottery, were also found near the centre of the island at a depth of from 12 to 17 inches beneath the later floor. Here were unearthed specimens of patterned pottery, together with a saddle quern and a stone pounder.

So the site passed into the archaeological literature of the Western Isles as a rather unexceptional island dun of likely Iron Age date with some later, perhaps medieval, buildings set into its ruins. In the summer of 1985, a survey by the author aimed at identifying possible antecedents of the numerous island duns of the Western Isles located a second enclosed site on a promontory jutting into the loch close to Eilean Domhnuill. The position of the enclosing bank showed that when this promontory was occupied Eilean Domhnuill would have been submerged, thus the two sites related to different periods. Such a demonstrable relationship is relatively rare and trial excavations were subsequently carried out to establish the chronology of these two sites. It was during the course of these small-scale operations that the real significance of Eilean Domhnuill became apparent. The two sites did indeed relate to different chronological periods. The promontory, Eilean Olabhat, was an Iron Age and later settlement and metal-working site (see Chapter 9), but Eilean Domhnuill was shown to be a partially waterlogged settlement with a complex sequence of occupation dating to the period of the first Hebridean farmers (Armit 1988a; 1990a; 1992).

While Beveridge's observations had been basically sound, his interpretation of the site was misleading. What he had considered to be a wall around the islet was in fact the jumbled stone displaced from former buildings and deposited around an old shoreline. Excavations revealed no trace of any later prehistoric activity, far less an island dun. What had appeared to be intrusive later structures were simply the last phase of Neolithic settlement, capping the deeply stratified layers of former houses and middens which Beveridge had noted in the lower parts of his trench. The initial trial excavations carried out in 1986 quickly established that there was no apparent evidence for any post-Neolithic occupation on the site and, judging from its relationship with the adjacent Iron Age site, the islet appears to have lain submerged below the loch surface for perhaps thousands of years.

Excavations from 1987 until 1989 subsequently began to unravel the complex history of the islet and to uncover the remains of successive buildings and deposits. It became apparent that the story of the islet's development was closely bound up with the history of loch level fluctuations. Initial occupation of the site lies well below modern loch levels but as the islet grew higher with the accumulation of generations of occupation debris so the loch level also rose, although here the mechanisms are much less clear. These twin processes of loch level rise and settlement accretion have presented an extremely complicated picture of the settlement sequence.

That part of the islet now visible above the water is wholly man-made (Figure 4.2). No natural rock foundation has been found during the excavations and, although it may originally have been founded on a small outcrop or a raised area of the loch-bed, the present islet is entirely composed of the debris of human settlement – the remains of structures and domestic middens. In an attempt to establish the depth of this occupation debris and to try to gain some understanding of the islet's structure, a trench was excavated underwater. This work established that occupation floors are preserved well below the modern loch level. Furthermore these deposits extend several metres from the present shore of the islet, showing that, in its earlier phases, the islet was far larger than it is now. The general trend appears to have been that the islet grew gradually smaller as the loch waters engulfed its periphery, although numerous fluctuations of the loch complicate this simple picture.

The waterlogged conditions have aided the preservation of organic materials which have generally long since decayed on contemporary dryland sites. Although the uppermost deposits have dried out, the excavations on the islet itself penetrated into layers close to the modern loch level where structural timbers were well preserved. The divers found even better preservation of fragile organic materials under the modern water level. This material provides enormous potential for the future study of the Neolithic environment, economy and the construction of domestic buildings.

The Sequence of Occupation

Absolute dating of the excavated phases at Eilean Domhnuill awaits the processing of radiocarbon dates but the relative sequence of structures and deposits is fairly well-understood. In the earliest excavated phases the settlement on Eilean Domhnuill may already have been in decline. Occupation at this time was characterised by a sequence of single domestic buildings fronted by a series of entrance works which were periodically re-built as loch levels rose. These phases of occupation have been numbered 1–11 from the top down (i.e. Phase 1 was the phase of most recent occupation), since it is impossible to tell how many phases underlie those so far excavated. Indeed from the depth of material exposed in the underwater trenches it seems that the excavations have done little more than scratch the surface of the site.

An artist's impression shows how the islet might have looked at the time when these earliest excavated occupation levels were being formed (Figure 4.3). Approaching the islet across the timber walk-way one would have encountered a facade of stone slabs, surmounted by a timber palisade. This façade may have extended around the perimeter of the islet as it seems to have done in earlier phases, known only from the underwater work, but the evidence remains ambiguous. Stepping from the walkway onto the stone paving of the entrance one would have walked towards the interior through a narrow corridor flanked by timber uprights. Once inside a single principal house could have been seen set to the side, probably built of turf on stone footings. Around it would have been various activity areas and possibly slight, stake-built outbuildings and structures. There would have been traces of the mounds of old, demolished structures and heaps of domestic waste. These mounds of largely organic debris decayed and became compressed over time forming many of the thin dark soil layers that make up most of the visible islet. The great density of pottery in these layers exaggerates the original quantities deposited since the decomposition of the surrounding organic waste has removed most of its original bulk.

The reconstruction drawing naturally encompasses a great many unknowns. It is impossible to tell how high the perimeter fence and façade were: perhaps there was a timber gate and perhaps the entrance corridor was covered. Evidence for the activities carried out in much of the interior is also lacking. Nonetheless, it gives the general impression of a fairly imposing settlement, shielded from view and with tightly controlled access, dominated by a single domestic building.

The entrance façade seems to have been one of a long series of such works;

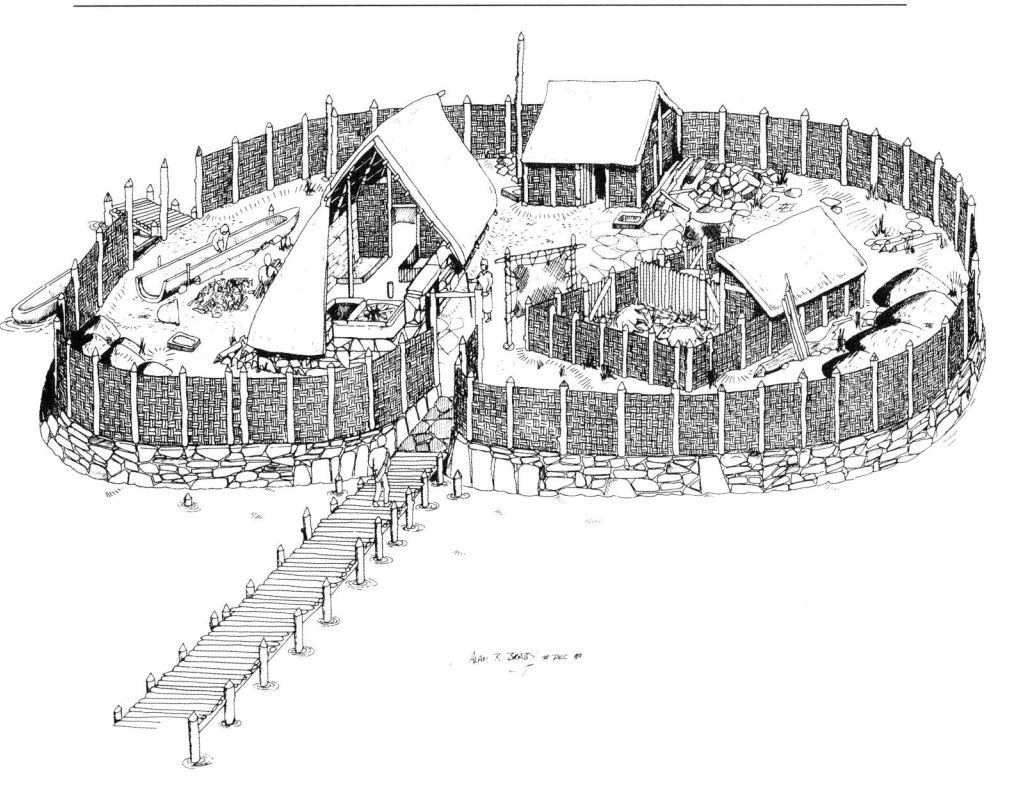

FIGURE 4.3. Artist's impression of the settlement at Eilean Domhnuill.

earlier timber structures had been levelled for its construction whilst the remains of still older stone footings can be seen under the loch waters further out from the islet. This phase of occupation (Phase 9 in the sequence) came to an end at a time of rising loch levels which apparently necessitated the dismantling of the entrance façade. A new timber and slab façade was built a few metres back from the earlier one, using parts of the wall of an abandoned house. The remains of the timber superstructure of this later construction were found crushed flat against the slab revetment. By Phase 5, after the construction and abandonment of a series of further houses, the now-ruinous façade was again replaced on two occasions each marginally further back from the water's edge.

At the end of Phase 5, though, the waters closed in completely and the site was drowned. For a time the islet was under water and occupation must have shifted elsewhere. After an abandonment of unknown duration, marked by the deposit of a thin, uniform layer of lake silt across the site, the stone causeway was built and occupation resumed on the somewhat reduced interior without the elaborate entrance works which accompanied the earlier occupation. The occupation of these last buildings (Phases 1–4) seems to have been terminated by a further and final episode of flooding, after which it seems that the site lay submerged for several thousands of years.

The structures

The recovery of so many structures on Eilean Domhnuill, despite their poor preservation, is an important addition to our knowledge of Neolithic settlement in northern and western Europe. Outside the heartlands of early agriculture in Central Europe evidence for houses from the earlier part of the Neolithic remains scarce, and only a handful of buildings of this period are known from Britain and Ireland.

Combining the evidence from the various excavated structures on Eilean Domhnuill it is possible to gain some idea of the nature of the buildings. As they survive, the houses are defined by rough stone alignments which are mostly fragmentary and heavily displaced by demolition and later disturbance. Hearths dominated the central floor space (Figure 4.4), but few other internal features survived. The hearths of most of the buildings had been flattened and replaced on numerous occasions; hearths made up of small cobbles were found in two buildings whilst structure 8.1 contained a large rectangular hearth which had been carefully paved and kerbed. It is difficult to envisage functional reasons for these different constructions but they clearly had some specific meaning to the Neolithic inhabitants of the islet. The two cobbled hearths, for example, relate to entirely different phases of occupation, and thus are unlikely to be the products of individual whim.

The interiors of the houses were clogged with layers of occupation debris formed by spillage from the hearths and the decay of organic floor coverings, bedding materials and food waste. They contained few substantial postholes, suggesting that the roofs rested on the walls rather than on internal supports. Numerous stake holes, however, represent former internal wooden fittings and partitions. In the lower, partially waterlogged, levels charred stakes and fragments of wattlework hurdles survive suggesting that these unexcavated levels will contain an enormous amount of information on the internal arrangements of these buildings.

With one exception, all of the buildings were of elongated oval or rectilinear form with rounded corners and all had long axes aligned between N/S and NE/SW. The internal dimensions were fairly constant with the largest measuring approximately 6.8 by 4.4 m (structure 7.1) and smallest 5.2 by 3.2 m (structure 1.2). The best preserved structures (1.1 and 1.2) had stone-faced walls packed with earth and rubble, surviving to a height of up to 0.5 m and originally 0.6–0.8 m thick. It seems that these walls would have originally been somewhat higher and surmounted by a turf or thatched roof. The rubble around the edge of the islet (mistaken by Beveridge for a collapsed defensive wall) presumably derived largely from these structures.

The earlier structures had all been dismantled to their foundations and

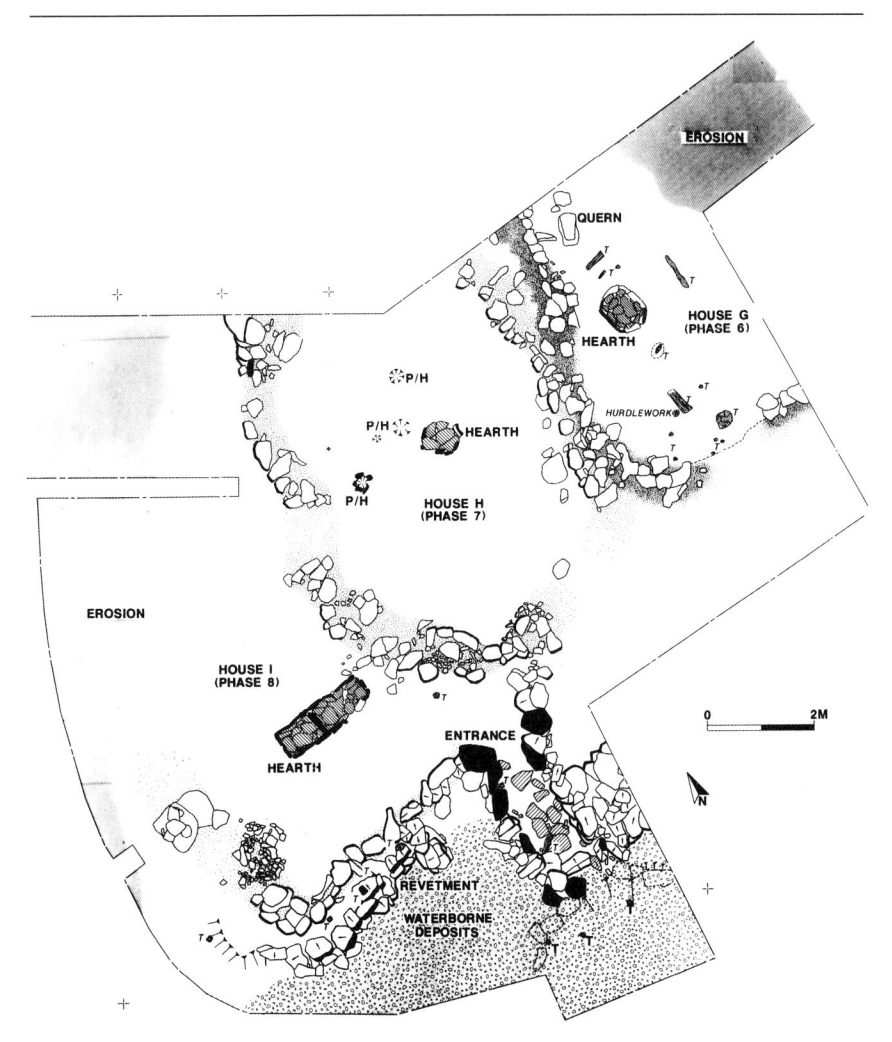

FIGURE 4.4. Structures on Eilean Domhnuill; combined evidence from Phases 6–8.

may not have been of the same construction. Only rarely did any indication of coursed walling survive and there was no rubble in these layers to suggest the former presence of substantial stone walls. One possibility is that the walls were of turf, founded on stone footings. This might explain the absence of both rubble and signs of timber walling; turf walls once dismantled make a valuable fertiliser and would probably have been spread on the fields around the settlement as was the case in medieval times.

Structure 3.1 was of markedly different character to the others, being oval with wall-footings formed of rounded boulders. This structure also incorporated small post holes along the course of the wall-footings and may have had a frame of light timber stakes. It may be significant then that this structure belongs to the period of initial reoccupation immediately after the re-emergence of the site from beneath the loch waters.

The closest Scottish parallel for the rectilinear houses on Eilean Domhnuill are those at Knap of Howar in Orkney excavated by Anna Ritchie (Ritchie 1983). This settlement, dating from around 3700–2800 BC, comprised two adjoining rectilinear houses strikingly similar in plan to the Eilean Domhnuill examples though somewhat larger (Figure 4.5). Irish settlements in the earlier part of the Neolithic, for example those at Tankardstown and Ballyglass (O'Nuaillain 1972, Gowen 1988), also seem to have involved small rectilinear houses, although these were generally built of timber rather than stone or turf. A general pattern of fairly small, isolated farmsteads comprising no more than one or two houses may have characterised much of northern and western Europe in the earlier part of the Neolithic.

Eilean an Tighe

Long before the excavations at Eilean Domhnuill, another North Uist islet settlement had been partially excavated by Sir Lindsay Scott in Loch nan Geireann a few miles to the east of Loch Olabhat (Scott 1950). Eilean an Tighe (literally 'island of the house') is a small, natural islet, measuring some 60 by 15 m with no visible causeway. The water level of the loch has been completely altered by the construction of a dam in the nineteenth century and it is difficult to tell what size the islet would originally have been or how far it would have been from the shore.

The site was originally identified, as was so often the case in North Uist, by Erskine Beveridge, who noted the presence of stone structures and found Neolithic pottery fragments eroding from the shore (Beveridge 1911, 221–2). Scott's subsequent excavations produced a wealth of stratified Neolithic structures and artefacts.

In contrast to those on Eilean Domhnuill, the visible structures on Eilean Tighe seem to date to a period substantially later than the Neolithic although the evidence is not as conclusive as might be hoped. Underneath these structures, however, were the fragmentary remains of earlier buildings and deposits very similar to those on Eilean Domhnuill. The stratigraphy of the deposits demonstrated that the features were not all contemporary and a sequence of hearths could be identified. Scott interpreted these insubstantial structures as the remains of a pottery workshop and this view underpins his published description of the remains. Although, like Eilean Domhnuill, the islet was strewn with fragments of Neolithic pottery, Scott's interpretation has since been largely discounted on the basis of the lack of evidence for actual manufacture in the form of wasters (c.f. Simpson 1976).

The location of the site, the fragmentary nature of the structures, and the similarities in the pottery assemblage, all demonstrate the close relationship between Eilean an Tighe and Eilean Domhnuill. The lack of a stone causeway at Eilean an Tighe probably indicates that it was reached by a timber

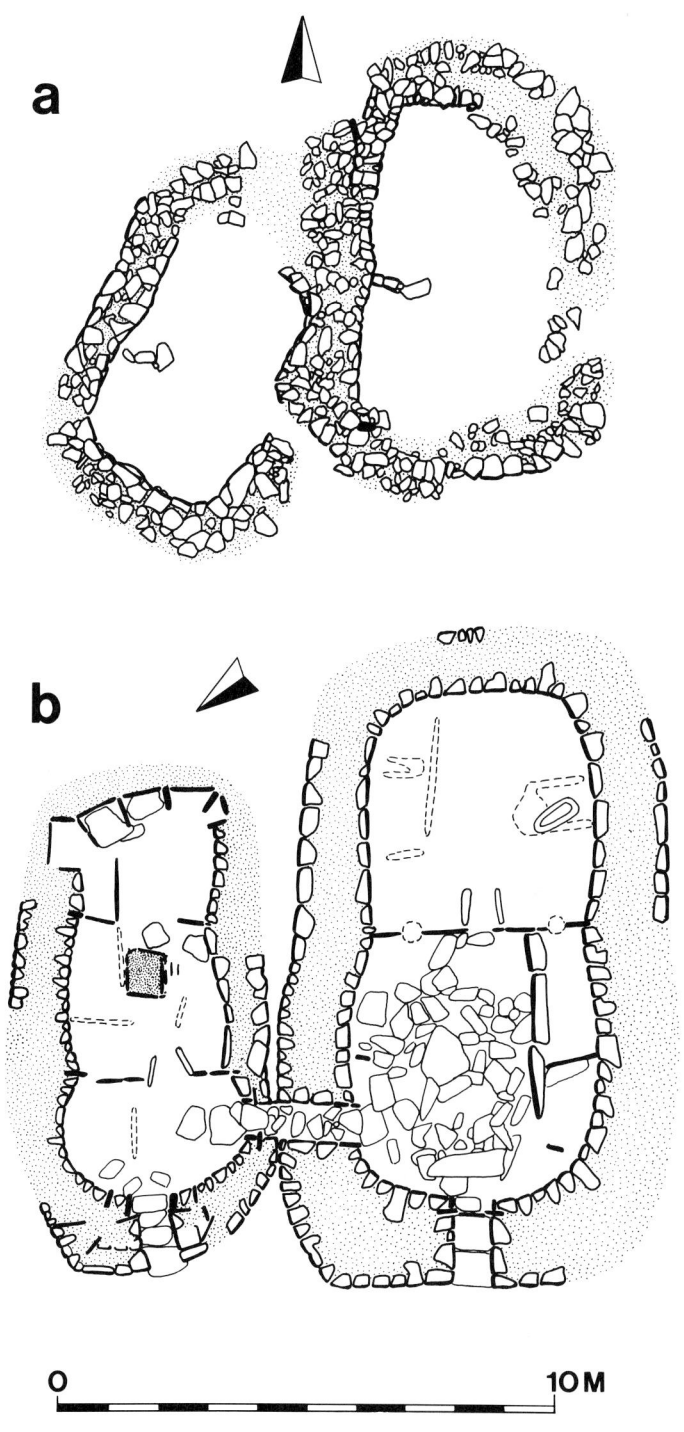

FIGURE 4.5. Comparative structures: (a) Eilean Domhnuill, Phase 1; (b) Knap of Howar.

walkway which was never translated into stone as was the case in the latter stages of the Eilean Domhnuill occupation. Almost certainly then, Eilean an Tighe, like Eilean Domhnuill, represents a Neolithic islet settlement.

Islet Settlements

Before the excavations at Eilean Domhnuill a great many other causewayed islets had been identified as poorly preserved Iron Age brochs or duns although they contained little or no evidence to suggest the former presence of such massive stone structures. In the light of the Eilean Domhnuill excavations it seems quite possible that many such islets are the sites of similar Neolithic settlements. North Uist contains a number of such causewayed islets (Figure 4.6), mostly to be found in the interior or eastern parts of the island. These peat-drenched and ill-drained areas have long been the least favoured for human settlement in the island and were probably abandoned long before the Iron Age (Armit 1992). Many islet sites in these areas may well represent early settlements which failed prior to the Iron Age whilst their more favoured contemporaries around the coast have been masked by the massive stone constructions of their successors (Armit 1992a). Even where later structures have not hidden their remains, such settlements may have been submerged under inland lochs or, as at Eilean an Tighe, the absence of a stone causeway may hamper their recognition.

A few specific sites are known where there is some indication of an early date. A scattering of Neolithic pottery fragments found on the remote Pygmies Isle, off the Butt of Lewis, suggests that this islet might be the site of another settlement like those at Eilean Domhnuill or Eilean an Tighe (MacKenzie 1905), although its location off the cliff-bound coast is clearly quite different. Loch drainage operations in the late nineteenth century exposed a timber crannog (or artificial islet) at North Tolsta in Lewis, which seems likely to have dated to the Neolithic or Bronze Age when sufficient timber may have been available for its construction (Blundell 1913).

Crannogs are common in Scotland and Ireland and were inhabited, if not constructed, even in relatively recent centuries (Morrison 1985). The majority of Scottish crannogs seem to date to the Iron Age or Early Historic periods, although lake dwellings of various kinds are known from the Bronze Age in other parts of Britain (Barber and Crone 1993). In the Hebrides at least, the concept of living on small islets clearly originated in the Neolithic, and is perhaps most obvious in the Iron Age (see Chapter 7) although it persisted well into the medieval period. The islet of Finlaggan in Islay, for example, was a major centre for the Lordship of the Isles in historic times. The numerous small natural islets in the loch-pocked Hebridean landscapes meant that often it was unnecessary to create crannogs from scratch as was often done for example in Loch Tay or Loch Awe (Morrison 1985).

But why live on an islet? Such locations were obviously impractical for construction, use and maintenance. The initial effort required to raise such

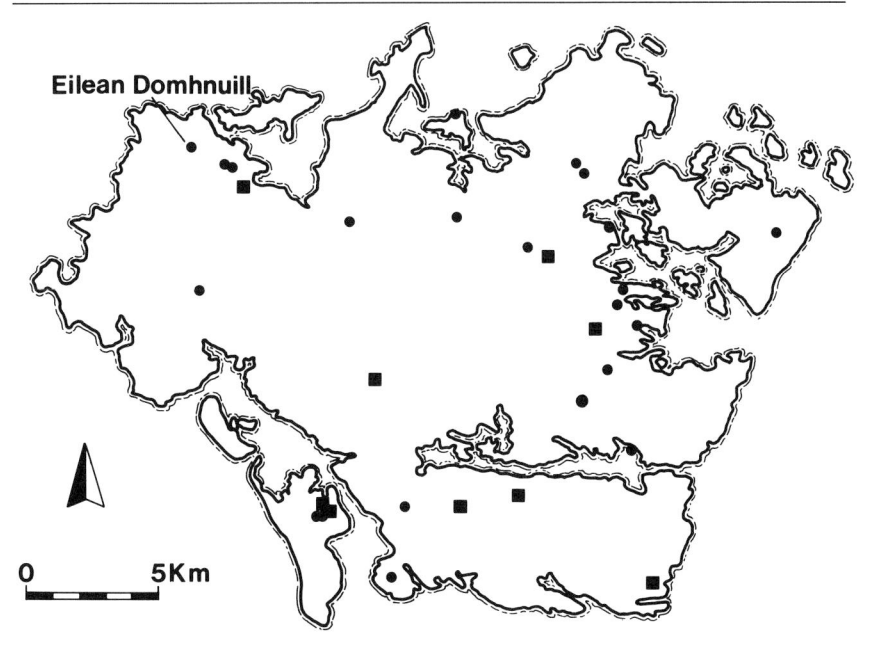

- **Causewayed Islets**
- **Walled Islets**

FIGURE 4.6. Distribution of islet settlements on North Uist without substantial stone structures.

a structure sufficiently high above the loch waters would have been immense. Houses would have been at risk of periodic flooding and subsidence; the former was certainly the case at Eilean Domhnuill. Timbers, whether in the walkway or revetments, would have been exposed to accelerated decay in the standing water. The sites were inevitably exposed to the elements and highly inconvenient of access.

There must, therefore, have been important reasons for the construction of such structures and for their persistence in the archaeological record over thousands of years. Archaeologists have tended to assume that the need for defence was the prime motivation for crannog construction. Certainly, access would easily have been controlled by means of the narrow walkway or causeway. Evidence for warfare or physical conflict in the Scottish Neolithic, however, is fairly sparse; a flint arrowhead lodged in the back of an elderly man in the chambered tomb of Tulloch of Assery B in Caithness is a rare sign of violence at this time (Ashmore, forth.). No recognisable weapons have been found in Hebridean Neolithic sites and there are no indications of the deliberate destruction of any settlements. Even in the chambered tombs, where we might perhaps expect some recognition of warriors or warfare, no weapons were deposited. In any case there are numerous other ways in which defence could have been achieved with less effort and risk than the building of an islet; for example, by the construction of a simple rampart and ditch. Crannogs, it has been suggested, may have been designed for protection from animal rather than human predators but it is unlikely that any natural predators survived long into the Neolithic in North Uist (if they were ever present at all) and again, rather less labour-intensive measures could have been taken to exclude them.

Recent archaeological research has stressed the symbolic aspects of many aspects of past societies, their homes as well as their tombs and temples. Communities in many parts of Europe who had newly adopted a farming way of life often seem to have established elaborate homes and settlements (c.f. Hodder 1990). The control over nature implicit in farming – the domestication of formerly wild animals and plants – would have had radical implications for the way in which early farming communities saw the world. New concepts of society would have emerged which increasingly set humans apart from nature. It is in this context that deliberate attempts to separate culture and nature – human society and the untamed natural world – may have originated. Elaborate houses and enclosed settlements formed boundaries between the realm of human culture and the realm of the wild. Similar concerns affect our perceptions of architecture in the western world today where the threats of an untamed natural world have been replaced by the dangers of a chaotic urban environment (Tuan 1979). Homes continue to represent havens from the external forces which threaten to undermine our way of life and considerable effort goes into their decoration and maintenance.

Crannogs, at least in the Neolithic, seem to fit well into this view of early farming societies. The crannog presented the community as isolated and apart from the world. Its construction and maintenance forged a sense of group identity and created a feeling of ownership and a sense of place. Along with the chambered tombs in the hills beyond the fields around the loch, the elaborate settlement helped to structure the landscape and stamp a human imprint upon it. Whatever the explanations for the continued use of crannogs in the Iron Age and later, their initial adoption may be explicable as part of a wider move towards the creation of a cultural landscape involving both the homes of the living and the tombs of the dead.

Settlement Below the Peat: Bharpa Carinish

Neolithic settlement was not exclusively focused on islet sites. Anne Crone's recent excavations on the site of Bharpa Carinish sprang initially from a programme of archaeological prospecting in peat-cuttings close to a chambered tomb, Caravat Barp, in the southern part of North Uist (Crone 1993). A combination of sub-surface probing and small-scale excavation identified an area of settlement, occupied prior to the onset of peat growth, as well as a series of later enclosures.

The Carinish site represents the remains of a settlement of insubstantial buildings in a fragmentary state of preservation. Isolated arcs and alignments of boulders, occasional stake holes and a series of hearths stubbornly refused, as at other Hebridean Neolithic sites, to add up to a coherent series of buildings, although the excavator was able to identify three 'hearth complexes' which may represent distinct structures (Crone 1993). None of the post holes exceeded 0.15 m in depth and it seems improbable that they held substantial structural timbers. Indeed the character of the deposits at Carinish is strikingly similar to those excavated at Kinloch in Rhum (see Chapter 3).

As at Eilean Domhnuill, deposits of ash and charcoal were spread around the site, containing significant quantities of fragmentary pottery of Unstan and Hebridean Ware forms. A series of accompanying radiocarbon dates suggest that the hearth complexes were at least broadly contemporary in the period between 3300–2900 BC.

It is not clear how far settlement remains might extend in the area around Bharpa Carinish: the site lacks the boundedness and formality of the islet settlements. As at Eilean Domhnuill, settlement might have shifted slightly down the generations and, without the constraints of the islet site, might have spilled over a much wider area, somewhat reminiscent of the Mesolithic occupation site at Kinloch in Rhum. It is also not clear how the Carinish settlement related to the adjacent chambered tomb. Was it an opportunistic 'squatter camp', pillaging stone and shelter from the earlier monument? Did it represent a temporary home for the cairn builders? Or was it earlier than the tomb and did the tomb in some way commemorate an abandoned settlement and its ghostly occupants? Observations on the relationships between houses and tombs in the Neolithic right across Europe gives more credence to the latter interpretation than we might have expected a few years ago. Tombs very often seem to take the form of houses (Hodder 1994) and may in some cases be built over them. In the case of Carinish though, much more excavation would be necessary even to begin to address this question.

Coastal Settlement

The machair coasts of the Western Isles contain a wealth of settlement remains of various periods including two excavated Neolithic settlements at Northton and the Udal. The site of Northton on Toe Head peninsula in the south-west corner of Harris contains a sequence of Neolithic, Bronze and Iron Age occupation and a rich artefactual assemblage (see Chapter 6 for the later development of the site). The two successive occupation phases relating to the Neolithic lay at the base of the sand deposits, separated by windblown sand from the layers above. The remains of the first occupation lay directly on the boulder clay which underlies the machair showing that, in this location at least, the machair had not yet formed (Simpson 1976). It is possible that the contemporary machair lay further out, adjacent to an earlier, now-submerged coast. There may even at this time have been a land bridge between southern Harris and the small islands off its coast, if not to North Uist (Evans 1971).

In terms of artefacts the earliest phase of occupation at Northton yielded only scraps of plain pottery and bone fragments. Studies carried out on the land molluscs preserved in the sands, however, gave an indication of the types of habitat available close to the site during this period and testified to considerable forest clearance in the vicinity at this time (Evans 1971b; Simpson 1976, 221). The second phase of Neolithic occupation contained quantities of Hebridean and Unstan Ware, with some pieces of plain bowls, echoing the material from Eilean Domhnuill and Bharpa Carinish. This phase at Northton has been radiocarbon dated to around 3200–2900 BC, a date comparable with those from Bharpa Carinish. Aside from areas of burning, the sole structural remains comprised 'one short length of drystone walling' and a number of other boulders which had clearly been deliberately brought to the site (Simpson 1976, 221). Such fragmentary and insubstantial structures would not be out of place on any of the sites already discussed. More formal structures have been claimed at the Udal but these have yet to be substantiated by publication (Crawford 1985, 7).

Excavations by a team from Sheffield University at Alt Chrysal on the rocky and inhospitable south-west coast of Barra have recently produced yet another site with evidence for Neolithic occupation. As elsewhere there appear to have been no substantial structures, but rather numerous ashy spreads, hearths, stone alignments and post holes suggestive of frequently replaced, fairly slight dwellings (SEARCH 1992, 1993). The whole complex seems to have centred on a stone platform levelled into the irregular rocky hillside. Although the excavators have suggested that the site may have been an activity area for the manufacture of pottery and stone tools, and for grain processing (SEARCH 1993), there seems little at present to distinguish it from other excavated settlements.

Settlement Interpretation

It is interesting that Scott interpreted Eilean an Tighe as a pottery workshop, and Crone initially interpreted Bharpa Carinish as possibly a ritual area, essentially because of the unconvincing nature of the structures on both sites (Scott 1950, Crone 1989). Even in the 1990s the lack of clear structures at Alt Chrysal prompted the excavators to believe that it must be a specialist activity area whilst the 'proper' settlement must be somewhere else (SEARCH 1992). Only with the depth of material on Eilean Domhnuill and the evidence built up from the numerous buildings did it become clear that this was indeed the form of Neolithic Hebridean settlement. There was perhaps an unspoken feeling that a 'Hebridean Skara Brae' would eventually be found. This now seems unlikely. Eilean Domhnuill shows us that many, if not all, of the domestic buildings which accompanied the massive and monumental chambered tombs were relatively slight and transient.

A distinction seems to be emerging between the islet settlements which were, at least in the case of Eilean Domhnuill, extremely impressive structures, although individual buildings on them were slight, and sites such as Northton and Bharpa Carinish where there seems to have been no formal demarcation of the settlement. In this respect these latter sites appear to have more in common with Mesolithic settlements even though they were clearly occupied by communities with at least some commitment to farming. It is possible that islet settlements like Eilean Domhnuill were permanent bases, occupied all year round, whilst the machair and peatland sites were more transient or seasonal activity areas. Alternatively, the difference may be based on the relative social status or human resources of the various sites. The nature of the relationship between these various forms of Neolithic settlement in the Hebrides remains to be established by future research.

ARTEFACTS

Pottery

Well over 20,000 sherds of round-based pottery have been found on Eilean Domhnuill, including several complete or near-complete vessels. Most of this pottery is profusely decorated and a range of recurrent forms and motifs have been identified which can be compared with pottery from settlements and tombs in the Hebrides and elsewhere. The Carinish assemblage contained around 500 sherds and fell into the same general range as the Eilean Domhnuill material, although predictably (given its smaller size) lacking the variety observed in the larger assemblage. Pottery from the early phases at Northton and from Eilean an Tighe again echoed the same range of forms and profusion of decoration. In terms of the conventional typologies the pottery falls into three main groups – Unstan Ware, Hebridean Ware and Plain Bowls – although the definition of these categories remains unsatisfactory and their relevance far from proven (Figure 4.7).

Plain bowls occur throughout the sequence at Eilean Domhnuill although their numbers are always few. They are ubiquitous in the Scottish Neolithic though their absence of distinctive traits means that this is less than surprising and need imply no connection between the various occurrences. Unstan Ware is characterised by shallow, open, carinated bowls with incised decoration above the carination and simple rims. It has been found at sites outwith the Hebrides, principally in Orkney although a recent find has extended the distribution as far as Stonehaven on the north-east coast of Scotland (Alexander pers. comm.). Interestingly Unstan Ware was the predominant pottery type in use at Knap of Howar in Orkney, further strengthening the parallels between this site and Eilean Domhnuill. In the Hebrides it remained in use for a considerable period, and is found in all phases at Eilean Domhnuill in close association with other pottery forms (Figure 4.7).

Hebridean Ware is a more localised style, so far known only from the

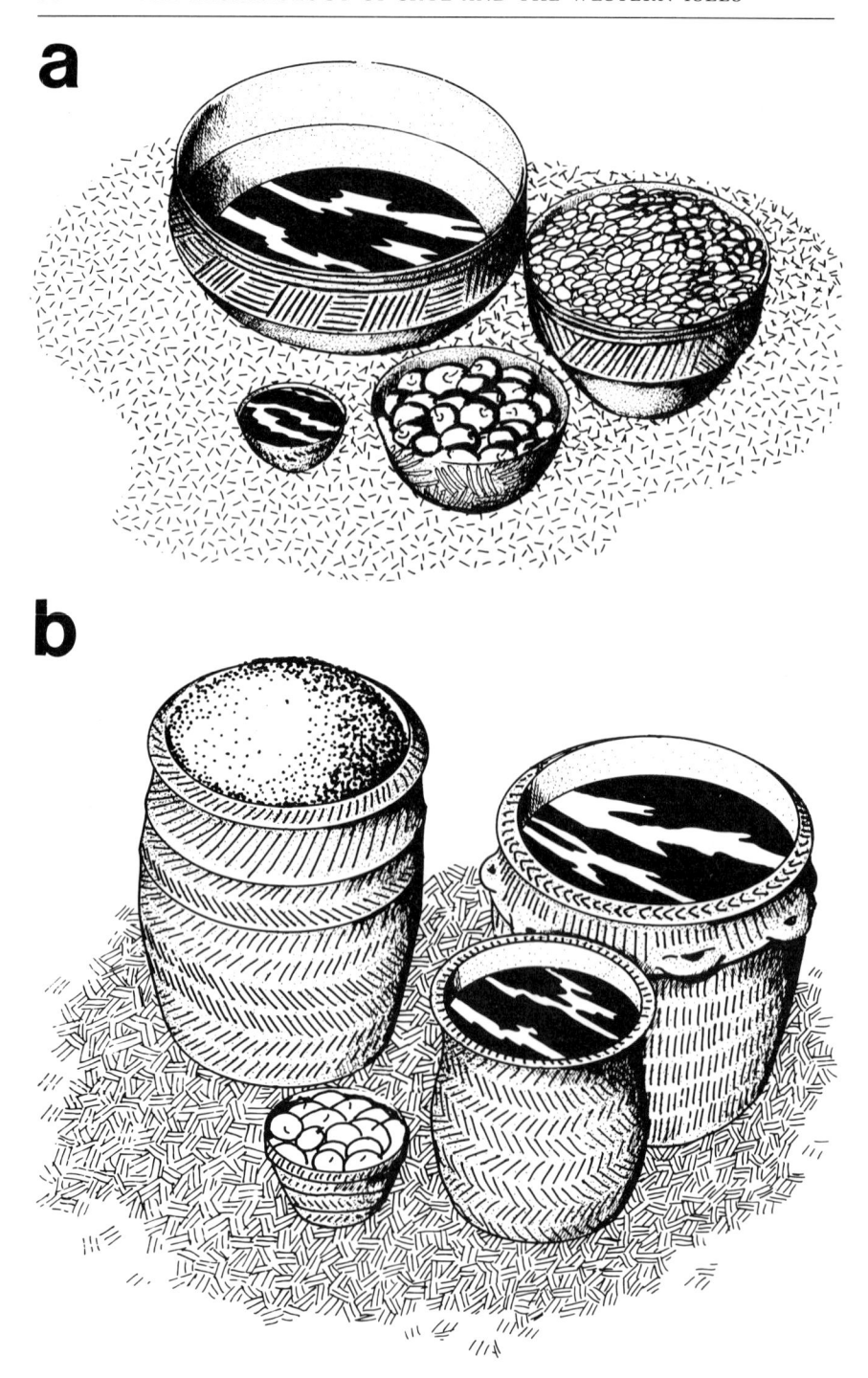

FIGURE 4.7. Neolithic pottery styles in the Hebrides: (a) Unstan Ware; (b) Hebridean Ware.

Western Isles (Kinnes 1985, 49). Hebridean vessels are characteristically deep jars with multiple carinations; their upper parts are profusely decorated, generally with incised herringbone patterns. The term hides a tremendous amount of variation which the detailed examination of the Eilean Domhnuill material may help eventually to address. Many vessels refuse to fit neatly into existing typologies; a near-complete pot found in a North Uist peat bog, for example, seems to meld Hebridean and later traits (Atkinson 1953).

Two further ceramic objects from Eilean Domhnuill so far defy explanation: it is possible that they may be clay phalluses (Figure 4.8). The two very similar objects are decorated in a style similar to Hebridean Ware vessels with herringbone decoration and both appear to have endured the same processes of breakage and abrasion. They appear not to have formed part of ceramic vessels and were found in different parts of the site, both spatially and chronologically. Their close similarity implies a uniformity of purpose and their shared condition suggests that both went through the same, presumably ritual, process. If these pieces do represent ceramic phalluses, their shared decoration with Hebridean Ware could be important.

Like islet settlements themselves, elaborately decorated pottery was to be a recurrent trait of Hebridean prehistory until almost the end of the Iron Age. The quantities of ceramics and the effort put into their decoration shows that pottery played an important role for the communities of the Hebridean Neolithic. In functional terms it provided containers for cooking and food storage. It also held offerings which were placed in the chambered tombs. It may also have played a role in feasting and ritual activities about which we know as yet very little. There is an apparent separation of formal ceramic styles that, with their recurrent combinations of form and motif, must have held meanings for their makers and users, perhaps relating to the social status, age or gender of its owners or users, or the ethnicity of its makers (Armit and Finlayson 1995).

The wealth of material and the abundance of decorative motifs have so far defeated any attempts to reconstruct the social role of Neolithic ceramics in Scotland but the field remains in its infancy. Eilean Domhnuill for the first time presents a substantial and well-stratified domestic rather than funerary assemblage within which some of these ideas might begin to be explored.

Stone

Compared to the wealth of pottery from Hebridean Neolithic settlements, chipped stone assemblages are generally fairly impoverished. Flint tends to be rare with chert being used as a substitute and quartz seems to have been used extensively for basic tasks. As in the Mesolithic, there is some evidence for the movement of materials. Pitchstone, a volcanic glass somewhat like obsidian from Arran in the Firth of Clyde, has been found not only in Hebridean Neolithic sites, but up to 300 km away in north-east Scotland.

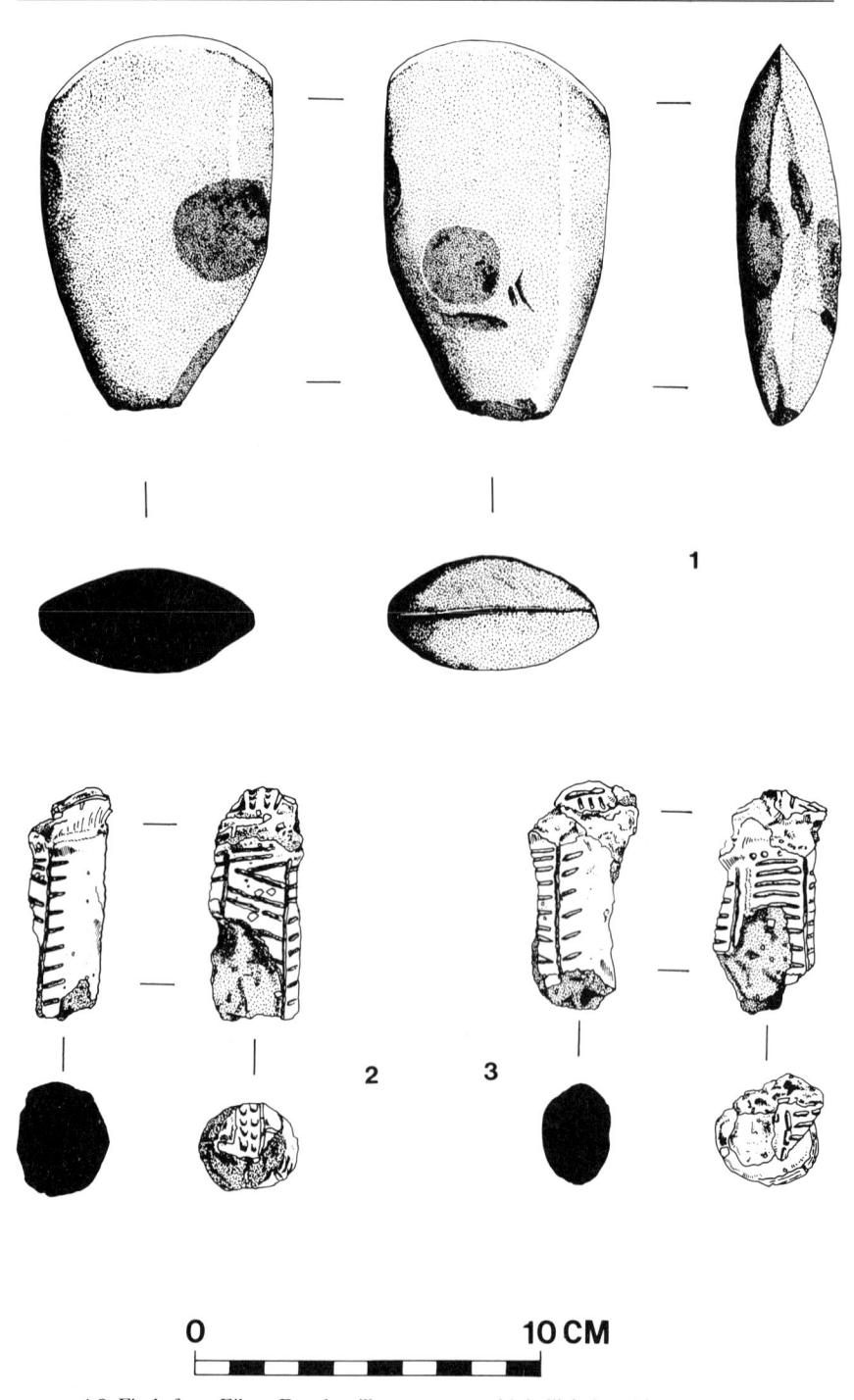

FIGURE 4.8. Finds from Eilean Domhnuill: stone axe and 'phallic' clay objects.

Rhum bloodstone continued to be used, as it had been in the Mesolithic, and has been identified in the cave deposits at Rudh an Dunain in Skye. Banded mudstones from north-west Skye have also been found outwith their source area, for example at Northton in Harris (Wickham-Jones 1986, 7).

Another material found commonly on Eilean Domhnuill is pumice. It appears to have been used in tool manufacture, and to shape and polish organic materials such as bone and wood. One piece does, however, appear to have been made into a pendant (Andrea Smith, pers. comm.). Pumice was also found at Eilean an Tighe where, again, many pieces displayed the characteristic concave surfaces and grooves caused by the working and finishing of tools (Scott 1950, 37).

Perhaps the artefact that most distinguishes Neolithic from earlier and later communities is the stone axe, a tool that, amongst its many functional uses, symbolises the clearance of woodland for cultivation. These items could be very elaborate in manufacture and were often exchanged far from their source areas. Axes quarried at Great Langdale in the Lake District, for example, were found throughout Scotland, as were the products of 'axe factories' at Killin in Perthshire (Sheridan 1992). Numerous stray finds of stone axes have been made in areas without identified Neolithic settlement; in Skye for example and in the area around Stornoway in Lewis. Few, however, have been found in secure contexts in the Hebrides. One example from Eilean Domhnuill (Figure 4.8) was of an imported igneous material and another from Eilean an Tighe was made of porcellanite from Rathlin Island in Co. Antrim (Megaw and Simpson 1961, 69). A total of thirteen axes of this Irish material have been recovered from the islands, to which they were brought either as finished products or as raw materials. These appear to have been deposited deliberately, as votive offerings, never having been used. Seemingly these imported axes had a special status as exotic items and were reserved for ritual rather than practical use. Generally the stone axeheads have been found in isolation; the only Hebridean axe with its wooden haft substantially intact (Figure 4.9) was found in 1982 during peat cutting at Shulishader on the Eye Peninsula in the east of Lewis (Sheridan 1992, 198–201). The hawthorn haft was carefully worked to hold the axehead without the requirement of any resin or binding material (ibid., 200). The haft has now been radiocarbon dated to around 3150 BC.

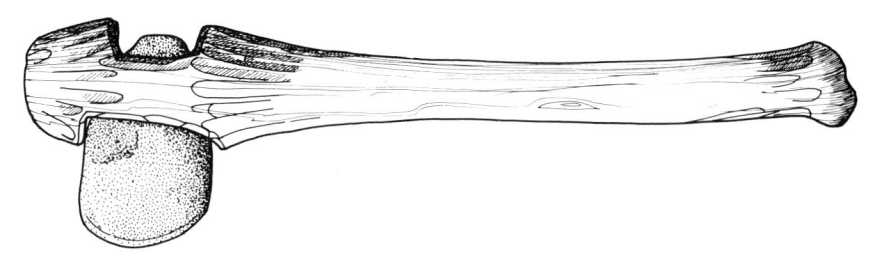

FIGURE 4.9. Hafted axe from Shulishader, Lewis.

Several of the stone objects from Eilean Domhnuill have no obvious utilitarian explanation. Perhaps the most notable of these was a carved stone ball, incised with patterns similar to those found on the pottery (Figure 4.10). Around 400 carved stone balls are known from the Scottish Neolithic (the majority from north-east Scotland), although a few have been found on excavated sites and many are much more elaborate than the Eilean Domhnuill example.

Bone

Very little Neolithic bonework is known from the Hebrides primarily because most of the excavated sites lie in acid soils unconducive to its survival. The machair sites are, however, an exception to this and Northton has produced evidence of a range of simple bone points and rubbers as well as an antler mace-head similar to items found in the Later Neolithic of Orkney (Simpson 1976). Burnt bone and antler survived to some extent on Eilean Domhnuill and unburnt material was obtained from the limited underwater excavations. The few worked pieces included a gouge-like tool and various simple points.

Waterlogged Material

It is hard to exaggerate the importance of the lower, waterlogged levels of Eilean Domhnuill as a resource for the future study of the Neolithic. The structures and material preserved in these deposits will have relevance far beyond the Scottish or even British Neolithic. Only the uppermost parts of these deposits have been excavated but even this limited work has provided evidence of preserved structural timbers and wattlework. Artefactual material has included a small piece of rope and fragments of worked bone. Many pieces of worked and shaped wood have been identified although the apparent absence of wood-chips, at least from preliminary inspection, suggests that most of the woodworking may have been carried out off the islet. The earlier structures may be expected to retain a great deal of evidence for the timber and other organic elements of their construction. Exploration of this material must wait, though, for a future campaign of excavation.

ENVIRONMENT AND ECONOMY

The Economic Base

As elsewhere, the first Hebridean farmers had no reason to abandon traditional wild resources and were probably still dependent on them for much of their subsistence. Fishing and fowling, in particular, probably retained a central role. Neolithic communities in Scotland seem generally to have incorporated elements of a mixed farming economy within traditional

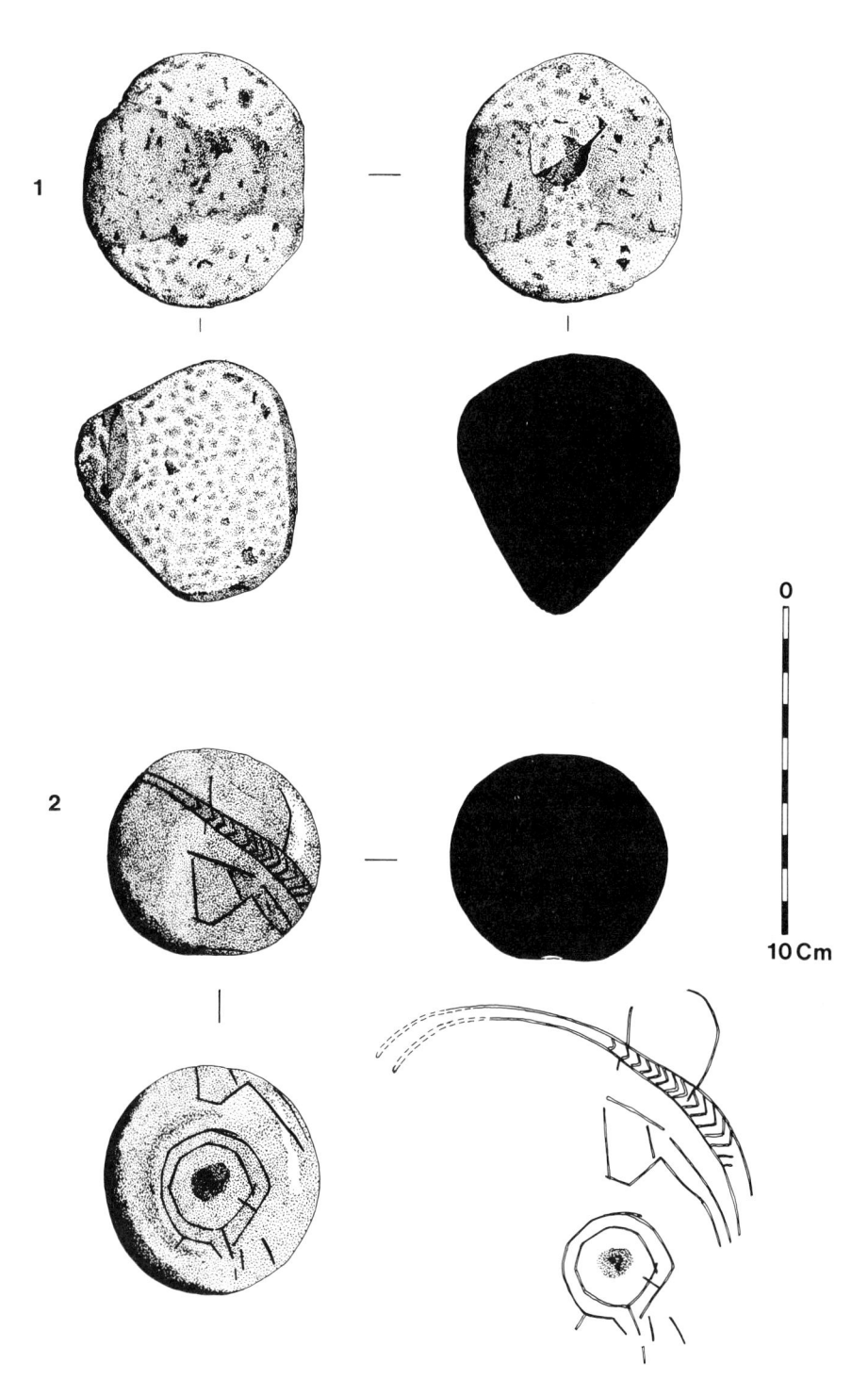

FIGURE 4.10. Finds from Eilean Domhnuill: carved stone balls.

subsistence strategies based on the intensive exploitation of wild resources. The balance and relative importance of these various resources no doubt varied greatly from place to place. It is unlikely for example that the economic base of communities on the intensively occupied island of North Uist would have exactly paralleled that of their neighbours on the less crowded islands of Lewis and Skye.

One of the main archaeological indicators of arable production is the presence of saddle querns used for grinding grain. Numerous examples have been found at Eilean Domhnuill and a saddle quern embedded in the floor deposits of structure 6.1 suggests that some grain processing took place inside the houses themselves. Charred grain recovered from Bharpa Carinish suggests that the principal cereal crop was probably naked six row barley, although emmer wheat was also present (Boardman 1993). The dominance of this type of barley seems to reflect a general pattern across Neolithic Scotland (Boyd 1988). At Carinish, as at Eilean Domhnuill, hazelnut shells were plentiful, and crab apple pips too were present suggesting that wild plant resources were still important (ibid.).

Our knowledge of the domesticated animals kept on Hebridean Neolithic sites is still very limited. The small bone assemblage recovered from Eilean Domhnuill may not be representative, even of the stock-rearing regimes practised by the islet's inhabitants, but it does at least gives some indication of the species which were present. Sheep and cattle were fairly common with a primitive domesticated sheep, similar to the mouflon, apparently being the dominant species (Hallen 1992). The bone assemblage from Northton indicates that both sheep and cattle were kept there too, with the remains surviving in more or less equal numbers (Simpson 1976). There is some suggestion from the range of bones represented, that animals were slaughtered on Eilean Domhnuill (Hallen 1992), although the unmixed nature of the excavated deposits seems to indicate that livestock were not routinely kept on the islet. The single pig bone recovered from Eilean Domhnuill reflects a rarity of this animal also noted at both Northton and the Udal (Finlay 1985, 35 and 47). It has been suggested that this animal was not introduced in the west in any numbers before the Bronze Age, although pigs were kept much earlier at Knap of Howar in Orkney (Ritchie 1983). The presence of domesticated dogs was attested both by the actual bones and by evidence for the gnawing of the bones of other species.

Evidence for the exploitation of wild animals is rather patchy. The almost complete absence of deer at Eilean Domhnuill (only a single tooth was recovered) suggests that these animals were not locally available in the somewhat crowded Neolithic environment of North Uist. Whalebone from the site probably represents a share of the spoils of the occasional beaching – a windfall that would have produced a wide range of useful products. Wild birds were also represented at Eilean Domhnuill by the bones of both seaduck and redshank (Hallen 1992). With the exception of Northton there is little evidence so far for the exploitation of fish or shellfish but this probably reflects the limited range of excavated sites and the problems of survival. In Orkney in the same broad period there is evidence at Knap of Howar for the exploitation of numerous wild species including deer, seal, whale, otter, sea birds, fish and shellfish (Ritchie 1983).

Environmental Effects

The distribution of chambered tombs (Figure 4.1) suggests that Neolithic North Uist was, as has been mentioned, quite densely populated. This picture would be strengthened still further if the distribution of causewayed islets, in the now inhospitable peatlands, is indicative of Neolithic settlement (Figure 4.6). Although the density of settlement on North Uist may not have been representative of the Hebrides as a whole – there are far fewer chambered tombs in Skye, for example – it still has implications for the environmental effects of human settlement in large tracts of the Hebridean landscape.

Eilean Domhnuill seems to exemplify the effects of the environmental stresses that Neolithic settlement might have caused. The principal visible effects are the apparent scarcity of timber and the instability of the loch level. Only four tree species were identified at Eilean Domhnuill – birch, hazel, willow and larch – suggesting an impoverished local woodland at least in the latter stages of the site's occupation. Larch in particular could only have been obtained as driftwood from across the Atlantic, and its use as a structural timber strongly suggests that wood was in short supply. The Eilean Domhnuill wood remains seem fairly typical of the material from other sites of the period. Charcoal fragments show that hazel, birch, willow and rowan were used as fuel at Bharpa Carinish (Crone 1993), for example; and hazel, birch, pine, willow and poplar charcoal was recovered from Eilean an Tighe (Scott 1950, 24). Tree cover would have been subject to clearance for farmland, building materials and fuel in the intensively occupied Uists and grazing animals would have hampered regeneration. From the combination of the evidence of site distribution and the evidence for wood availability on individual sites it appears that timber had become a scarce resource in the Uists some time before the end of the Neolithic.

The removal of tree cover from the Uists would have necessitated new arrangements for the provision of timber, perhaps involving inter-community exchange. Woodland certainly survived considerably longer in areas such as the Harris Hills and parts of Skye for example. Deforestation was, however, just one aspect of the environmental decline initiated by farming and a worsening climate. Perhaps the most likely explanation for the rising loch levels and periodic floods at Eilean Domhnuill is that deforestation and cultivation of the surrounding area contributed to an increased flow of both water and, more importantly, sediment into the loch. This could have had quite rapid consequences for the absolute level of the loch and for the degree of fluctuation which prolonged bad weather might cause. The testing of this idea is one of the main aims of post-excavation work shortly to be carried out on sediments cored from the bed of Loch Olabhat.

By the end of the Neolithic period much of the Hebridean landscape would have been transformed from its Mesolithic state. A great deal of the woodland cover would have gone, particularly in the coastal areas and on the better soils. Locally, soils may have become seriously impoverished through intensive cultivation and soil erosion may have been a problem in many areas. These problems would have added to the natural effects of a worsening climate and the local onset of peat growth. In short, even by the end of the first phase of farming settlement the environmental conditions for human settlement were in steep decline.

5 Tombs and Standing Stones

The Neolithic period in the Hebrides is characterised not by the homes of the living but rather by the tombs of the dead and the megalithic monuments where communal rituals were acted out. The discrepancy of scale and permanence between houses and tombs is reflected elsewhere in Europe, where tomb architecture may often echo that of the domestic house, transformed from transient timber to permanent stone. Monument building seems to have originated at around the same time as the inception of farming in many parts of Europe, although there is no reason to suppose that the two were part of some indivisible cultural package (Armit and Finlayson 1995). The Hebridean monuments comprise numerous chambered tombs, a smaller number of stone circles and a sprinkling of single standing stones and small settings (Figure 5.1). These ritual monuments have been used, much more than the settlements of the period, by archaeologists in their attempts to reconstruct the nature and development of Neolithic societies in Scotland. The relatively massive amounts of labour devoted to these monumental, but economically unproductive, projects dispels any notion that the Neolithic communities of the Hebrides were simple peasant farmers little different from rural communities of recent times. Their entire world view and ideology were fundamentally alien to our own. It is only by studying the ways that they moulded and transformed the landscape – through the construction and use of monuments, fields and settlements – that we can begin to understand how they lived and how they saw their world.

Neolithic Chambered Tombs

The chambered tombs of the Hebridean Neolithic form part of an extensive north and west European series of funerary monuments built mostly

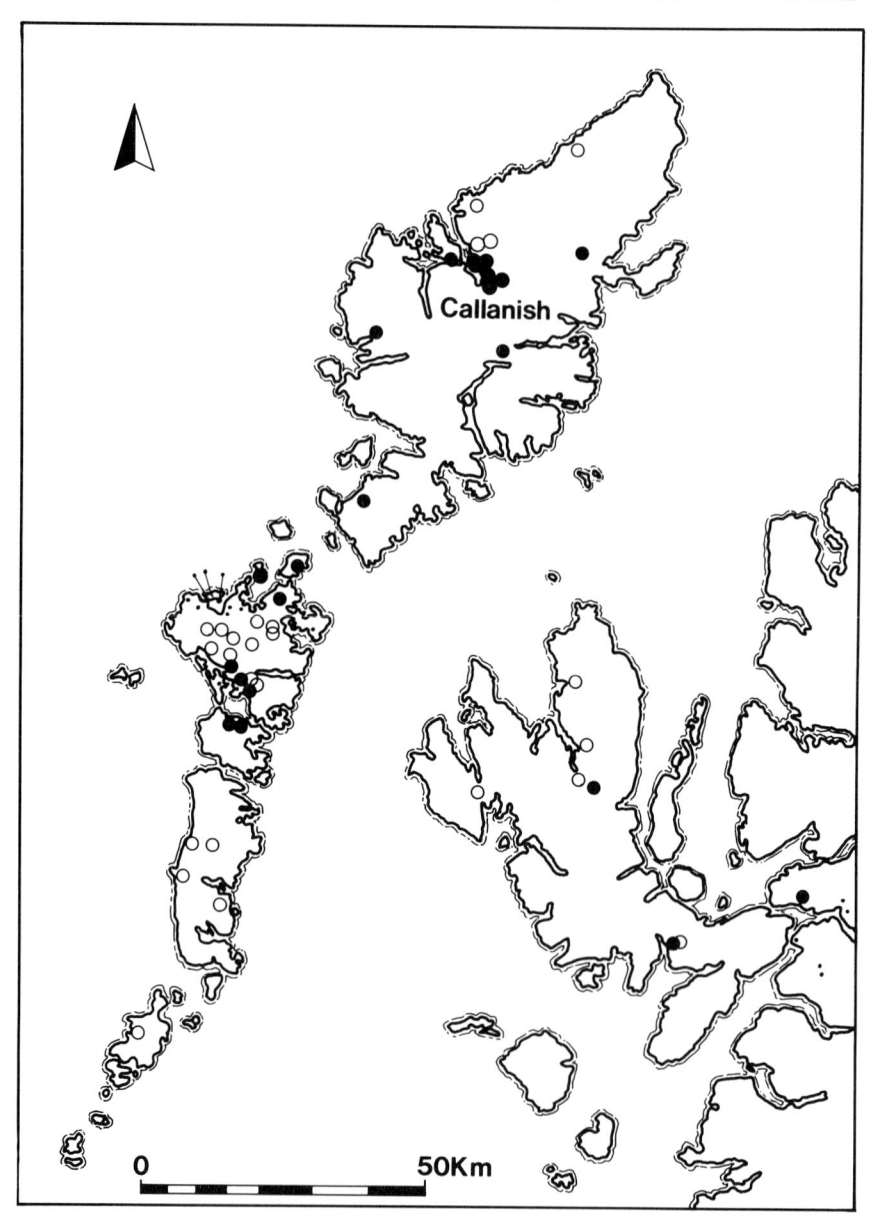

FIGURE 5.1. Stone circles, standing stones and cup-marked stones in Skye and the Western Isles.

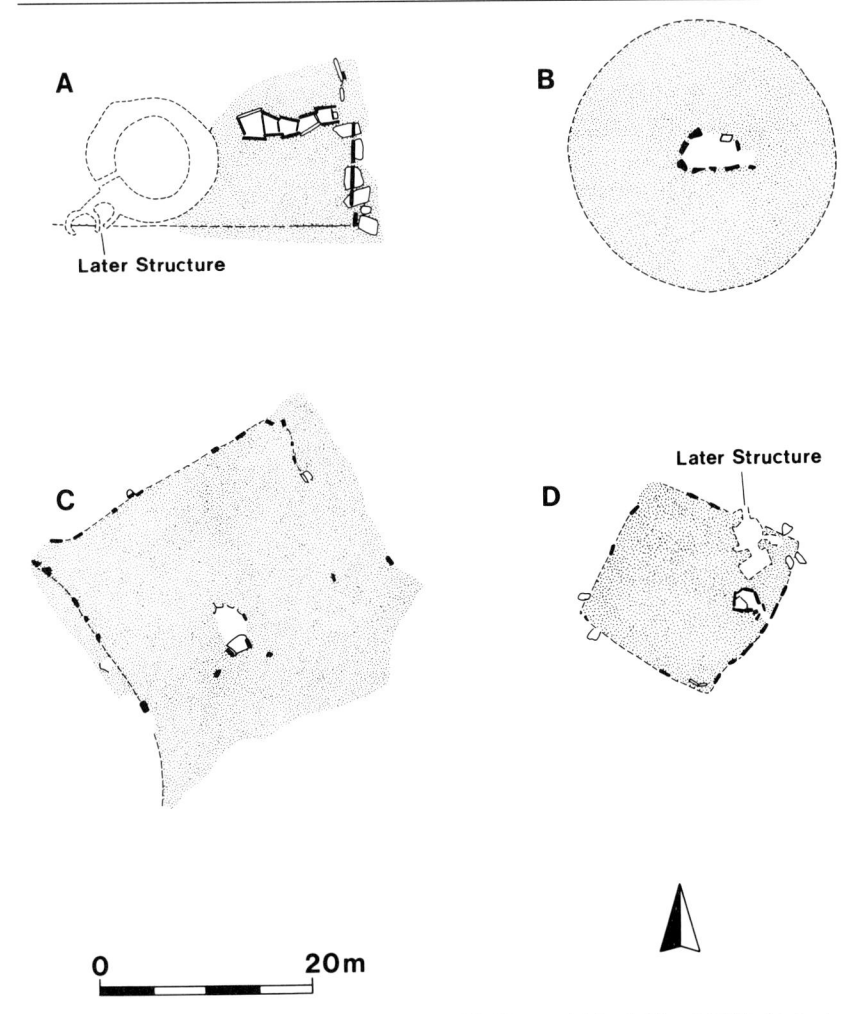

FIGURE 5.2. Comparative chambered tomb plans: (a) Clettraval, North Uist; (b) Ullinish Lodge, Skye; (c) Carn Liath, Balgown, Skye; (d) Unival, North Uist (after Henshall 1972).

between around 4000 and 2000 BC. These megalithic monuments each comprise a stone-built chamber generally housing human remains, set within a large cairn of stones (Figure 5.2). Their construction involved the gathering or quarrying, movement and emplacement of the massive stone slabs – the eponymous megaliths – used to construct their chambers and sometimes their façades. Such enterprises must have diverted significant amounts of labour from the routine subsistence activities of farming, fishing and the gathering of food.

Chambered tombs vary widely in form and many local and regional types have been identified. Audrey Henshall, whose comprehensive study of the Scottish tombs forms the basis for all subsequent research, identified two types of chambered tomb in the Hebrides: passage graves and Clyde cairns. These two types are distinguished principally by the form of the chamber (Henshall 1972): in the passage graves a narrow passage leads from the outer edge of the cairn to an inner chamber; in the Clyde cairns (so-called because of their geographical concentration) the simple rectangular chamber is entered directly from outside. The Hebridean passage graves belong to Henshall's Orkney/Cromarty/Hebridean series signifying the general geographical spread of closely related types (ibid.). They are generally set within round cairns surrounded by a stone kerb and often with a slightly indented forecourt. Some of the Orcadian examples are greatly elaborated versions of this basic design, with elongated or multiple chambers, but in general the Hebridean examples are fairly simple. By contrast, the Clyde group tend to be set in long cairns as at Bharpa Carinish and Clettraval, both in North Uist, and in some cases their chambers are elongated and subdivided by sill-stones and portal slabs (Figure 5.2).

These typological distinctions tend to become rather blurred when the Hebridean tombs are examined individually. The shapes of the cairns, for example, have often been modified during their periods of use so that round cairns may lie under and within long cairns.

Typology aside, all chambered tombs share some basic traits. They tend to be associated with the disposal of human remains, often partial or disturbed bodies, suggesting periodic reuse of the tomb and occasional removal of skeletal fragments. This implies that the physical remains of the ancestors retained an importance in the rituals and religious activities of the living long after their death.

The remains from single tombs often represent many individuals, sometimes deliberately mixed up and probably deposited in the chamber over several generations. Thus the people using the tombs did not see the dead as individuals but rather as a community of ancestors. In some areas such as Orkney the over-representation of larger bones suggests that bodies arrived at the tomb with the flesh already gone, probably after exposure of the corpse as a ritual purification. The tombs tend to contain offerings such as pottery and food (represented by animal bones) and could be used for many centuries before being finally sealed. These, however, are generalisations drawn from different tombs and different areas and it remains to be seen whether they are relevant to the use of the Hebridean tombs. To examine this question we must look at the evidence from the best studied and excavated examples.

Barpa Langass, North Uist

Barpa Langass is a well preserved Hebridean passage grave set high on a bleak moorland hillside looking out over what are now the barren peaty wastes of the interior of North Uist (Figure 5.3). At 5 m high and about 25 m in diameter, the great stone cairn still dominates the landscape as it was

FIGURE 5.3. Barpa Langass, North Uist.

intended to do when it was first built around 5000 years ago. The tomb would originally have had a more regular and deliberate appearance than it does now. The kerb of large slabs would have served to retain a cairn that now has the appearance of a jumble of loose boulders.

The tomb was entered through a forecourt facing slightly south of east. This orientation is significant since tombs in different parts of Britain tend to maintain similar alignments, possibly set to accord with basic astronomical events such as midsummer or midwinter sunrise or sunset. The narrowing of the forecourt serves to direct attention inwards towards the entrance to the passage. It is probably significant that a larger group could assemble outside the tomb looking in towards this entrance than could have passed through the passage at one time. The very structure of the monument seems to establish a hierarchy of access among the different people using the tomb.

The entrance passage is low and narrow, about 4 m long and less than 1 m wide, walled with massive stone slabs and topped by drystone walling. This passage was clearly built for single-file access. The roof lintels are still more or less intact but loose rubble and earth on the floor prevents any estimate of their exact original height. At its end the passage opens out into an irregular chamber some 4 m long by around 2 m wide, formed by enormous orthostatic slabs filled with careful drystone walling, and capped by lintels. The roof of the chamber, as in most passage graves, is higher than that of the passage, increasing the sense of space on entering.

Little is known about the deposits inside Barpa Langass since these were substantially pillaged even before the antiquary, Erskine Beveridge, was able to examine the monument sometime before 1911. Evidently pottery, charcoal and cremated human bones were found littered on the floor. Its good state of preservation probably left the tomb open to the inspection and scraping around of the curious long before more formal antiquarian interest in such monuments began. The few recorded pottery fragments include sherds of beaker pottery (see Chapter 6) demonstrating that some use of the tomb, presumably still as a funerary monument, continued into the Early Bronze Age.

Rudh an Dunain, Skye

Although Barpa Langass is by far the best preserved Hebridean chambered tomb, perhaps better evidence for the use of these monuments comes from several less imposing examples where there has been more controlled archaeological excavation. As for many other aspects of Hebridean prehistory, the work of Sir Lindsay Scott is central to our understanding of these monuments. Scott excavated three Hebridean chambered tombs – Rudh an Dunain in Skye, Unival and Clettraval in North Uist – during the 1930s and 40s and published detailed accounts of his findings.

Rudh an Dunain lies in the western part of Skye on a peninsula overlooked by the Cuillin Hills (Scott 1932). Although it lies at only 10 m OD, the monument is locally prominent and would have been an imposing landscape feature in its time. Like Barpa Langass, Rudh an Dunain is a passage grave and there are clear similarities between the ground plans of the two monuments, each having a round cairn, kerb and funnel-shaped forecourt facing slightly south of east (Figures 5.2 and 5.4). The cairn at Rudh an Dunain is, however, considerably denuded, standing only around 3.5 m high. The kerb was exposed during Scott's excavations and was shown to have been built of large orthostats approximately 1 m apart, the gaps being filled with drystone walling of rectangular slabs. By contrast the cairn itself was built with rounded, beach boulders. Entry to the chamber demanded movement first through the forecourt, then the short passage and an ante-chamber, both marked off by portal and sill-stones, finally into the chamber itself (Figure 5.4).

The excavations revealed that the forecourt, as might be expected, had been the focus of some activity although the nature of that activity remains obscure. A large hollow in front of the cairn was filled by two distinct layers of soil and stones, and the 'floor' showed some indications of burning and the deposition of quartz pebbles. Artefacts in the excavated area of the forecourt were restricted to a very few sherds of Neolithic pottery and a number of pieces of pumice and quartz. Other than supporting what might be assumed on the basis of the tomb's design, i.e. that the forecourt was a focus for communal gathering, this evidence does not get us very far.

The excavated deposits within the chamber appear to have been thoroughly mixed and disturbed through repeated use, making their interpretation difficult. Scott divided the material into three levels providing a broad depositional sequence but one which is of limited use in our endeavours to understand the history of the use of the tomb. The lowest 0.3 m

TOMBS AND STANDING STONES 73

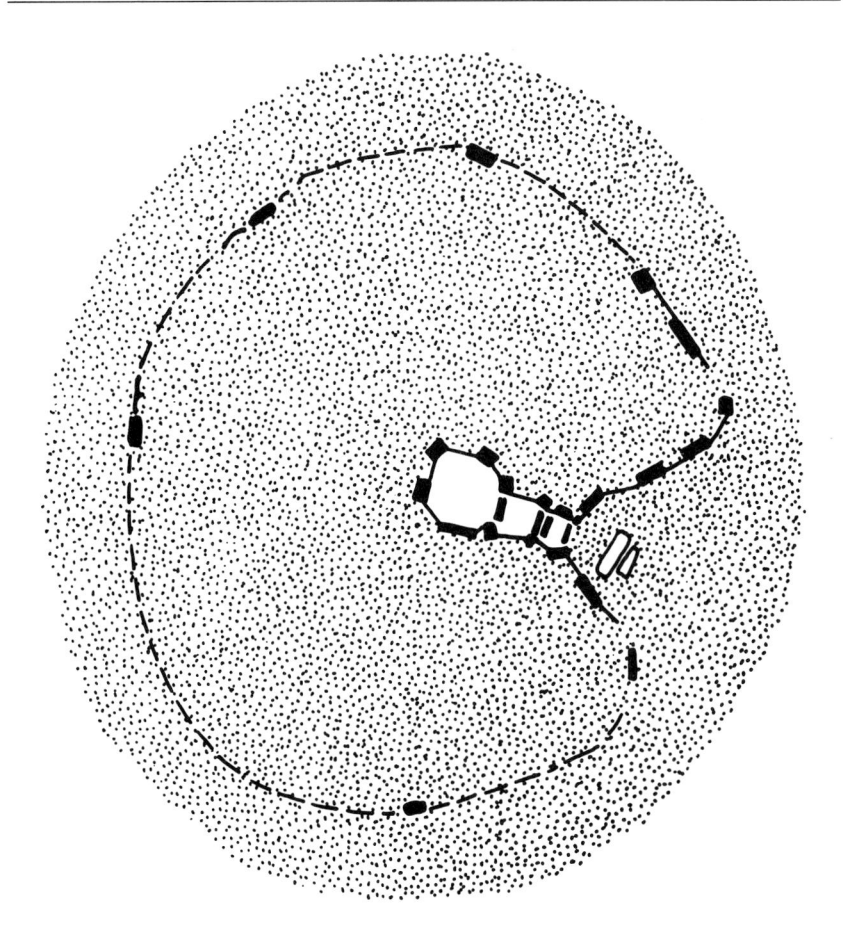

FIGURE 5.4. Plan of Rudh an Dunain.

or so was a thick black earth and above this lay brown earth and stones still containing debris from the ritual use of the tomb; the upper fill was composed of sterile earth and stones. The numerous finds included human remains belonging to at least six people. Jaw-bones of two individuals, one probably a middle-aged male, were found in the primary deposits while parts of skulls and teeth of four further individuals were found in the slightly higher levels. Animal bone was restricted to a single sheep or goat bone from the lower levels of the chamber and a small collection of bird, cattle and possibly human bone from under one of the chamber orthostats.

The deposits of human bones had been accompanied by pottery and the fragments from the chamber show that two distinct types can be linked with the lower and middle levels respectively. In the lower levels were sherds from two round-based bowls of Neolithic form (Henshall 1972, 310), whilst from the middle levels came a near-complete beaker of somewhat later date. A number of pieces of flint and quartz including two flint scrapers were found in the lower deposits in the chamber and ante-chamber. Pieces of quartz, pumice and chert were also found in the slightly higher levels from which the beaker was recovered. All of these are likely to have been deliberate deposits subsequently displaced by reuse of the chamber. Indeed it is probable that the finds assemblages from most tombs represent a fairly small proportion of material originally deposited, with other material being periodically cleared out (Henshall 1972, 165).

The soil which filled the tomb prior to Scott's excavations is of considerable interest in itself. Henshall noted that the passage, although still partially lintelled, was filled to the roof with stones and earth while the ante-chamber was similarly filled almost to the roof. It is impossible to tell when the roof of the chamber was removed but it seems unlikely that all of this material could have accumulated naturally. It is possible, as has been suggested for both Neolithic settlements and tombs elsewhere in Scotland, that this filling was carried out deliberately to mark the formal and final closure of the monument. In the next chapter we will see how the adoption of beaker pottery seems to have been associated with major changes in the nature of burial and ritual. It remains possible that the closure of the tomb followed immediately upon the deposition of the final burial, associated with the beaker pot.

Unival, North Uist

A further passage grave excavated by Scott was the tomb of Unival lying on the slopes of the hill of the same name in the southern part of North Uist at around 80 m OD, surmounted by a cluster of Iron Age domestic buildings (Scott 1947a). This cairn is roughly square with sides some 16 m long; a short passage leads into a chamber some 1.8 by 2 m, set off centre and entered from the south-east facing side (Figure 5.2). Compared to Barpa Langass it was a small, low and roughly built structure with a tiny chamber and lacked the forecourt which characterises many Hebridean passage graves.

Much of the space in the chamber was occupied by a slab-built cist which stood around 0.5 m high. This cist contained part of the articulated skeleton of a woman probably over twenty five years of age, and a few ribs of a younger person, possibly the remains of an earlier burial displaced from the cist. It appears that burning charcoal had been tipped onto the skeleton long after the burial when the flesh had already decayed. So, at this late stage in its use, the tomb was still visited for the purpose of carrying out rituals not involving actual burial. Other charred bones found throughout the chamber might have been displaced from the cist at an earlier date.

Amongst a rich assemblage of Neolithic pottery comprising numerous bag-shaped and highly decorated Hebridean vessels were a near-complete Grooved Ware bowl and fragments of a beaker. Grooved Ware is rare in the Hebrides although found widely across Britain in the Later Neolithic. Fragments of a cinerary urn seem to suggest that the tomb continued to receive burials well into the Bronze Age although the beaker appears to have been the latest deposit in the chamber itself. Other finds included a piece of pumice pierced as a pendant, possibly intended to replicate a bronze flat axe similar to Breton examples (Megaw and Simpson 1961, 69).

Clettraval, North Uist

Lying close to the summit of one of the low hills of the interior of North Uist at around 120 m OD, the tomb of Clettraval looks out over extensive barren tracts of Uist peatland down to the coastal machair. As at Unival, subsequent Iron Age building has disturbed the cairn but Scott's excavations provided a considerable degree of information about its structure and the deposits within it (Scott 1935).

Unlike Barpa Langass, Rudh an Dunain and Unival which are all passage graves, Clettraval is a Clyde tomb with a trapezoidal cairn around 30 m in original length (Figure 5.2). The east-facing entrance occupied the wider end which, if symmetrical, would have been around 25 m wide. This façade was lined with orthostats which would have given the tomb an imposing appearance. Although lacking the funnel-shaped forecourt of the passage graves, Clettraval appears to have had a paved area approaching the tomb from the west and further paving along the base of the façade. The subsequent collapse of the latter and the disturbance caused by later occupation has obliterated most of the evidence which might have existed for the use of this area.

A chamber, some 12 m long, led in directly from the entrance and was partitioned into five compartments by a series of high sill-stones which also served to support the side slabs, stopping them from slipping inwards. Each compartment was formed by a pair of orthostats, each slightly overlapping the next (Figure 5.2). The compartments both widened and rose in height closer to the centre of the mound creating a hierarchy of spatial zones similar to that seen in the architecture of the passage graves. The surviving floor, partially natural gneiss and boulder clay and partially paved, indicated the original height of the walls which graded from around 1.5 m at the entrance to over 2 m in the inner compartment.

The primary fill of the chamber was a black earth around 0.6 m deep with stones in its upper levels. Subsequent filling may have occurred with the dismantling and reuse of the tomb during the Iron Age or perhaps even earlier. Various stone features seem to relate to the original ritual use of the site including a cist-like structure in the inner compartment and a stone pillar standing 1.5 m high in the penultimate compartment.

Considerable quantities of pottery and other finds were recovered from Clettraval but the deposits appear to have been so thoroughly mixed that there is little hope of understanding the processes by which they were deposited: fragments of one vessel, for example, were found in the lower, middle and upper layers of the chamber (Henshall 1972, 511, pot 24). The upper layers contained mainly Iron Age material from the subsequent domestic occupation of the monument. Human remains were restricted to a few small pieces of burnt bone from the lower layers.

Many of the pottery vessels from the tomb were of forms similar to the material from contemporary settlement sites like Eilean Domhnuill and Eilean an Tighe. Notably absent, however, were Hebridean vessels with multiple carinations and Unstan bowls, and there was a predominance overall of somewhat plainer and simpler vessels than were common, for example, at Eilean Domhnuill. As well as the Neolithic pottery remains of at least eight beaker vessels were recovered showing that Clettraval, like Rudh an Dunain in Skye, was used for burial into the Bronze Age.

The nature of the relationship between passage graves and Clyde cairns in the Hebrides is hard to understand. In North Uist, the association of Clyde-style chambers with long cairns at Clettraval and Gerisclett contrasts sharply with the round and square cairns of the passage graves among which they lie. Other long cairns are found in the islands but the form of their chambers is unknown. The architecture of the two groups seems to be attuned to the same basic forms of ritual organisation: there is elaboration of the forecourt in both types, and in both there appears to be a hierarchy of space with the most important area being the innermost compartment or chamber which is higher and larger than the passage or compartments leading to it. There are no obvious differences in the alignments of entrances. Perhaps an ethnic or tribal distinction existed between communities using the two types, rather than any significant difference in the nature of the rituals carried out. Or perhaps the difference was chronological, with the Clyde tombs coming first and rapidly being replaced by passage graves. The Beacharra style of pottery associated with Clyde tombs elsewhere may even have been an influence on the early development of Hebridean ceramic styles (c.f. Henshall 1972, 112). A passage grave lies only a few hundred metres from the tomb at Clettraval and may have replaced it, although the deposition of beaker pottery in the latter shows that it remained in use for many centuries after the construction of its near neighbour.

Tomb Siting and Function

Just as the form of the tombs varied from area to area so in all likelihood did their function. We must be wary, therefore, of attempts to establish one overall interpretation for chambered tombs. Virtually all seem to have involved the disposal of the dead, but the nature and disposition of human remains varies widely. The problem is exacerbated in the Hebrides by the poor state of bone preservation. Clearly, however, chambered tombs were not built simply to provide a convenient container for the deceased; nor were they even the Neolithic equivalent of family burial vaults, for although they were used repeatedly their use was never restricted to burial.

The most concentrated distribution of chambered tombs in the region lies in North Uist. Most of these tombs occupy prominent locations on the slopes of the hills which form the island's core. Today they command extensive views and they were probably designed to do the same when they were first built, given that the light forest cover of the island was probably removed early on in the Neolithic. It is noticeable, though, that they tend not to be sited on hilltops and they may relate to specific tracts of land rather then being simply sited for maximum visual impact. The locations of the tombs avoid modern-day areas of good land and are instead associated with areas of the island peripheral to settlement in recent centuries. As we have seen in Chapter 4, however, these areas may have been occupied fairly densely in the Neolithic period before becoming unworkable with the onset of peat growth and climatic deterioration from around the second millennium BC.

It has been suggested that chambered tombs acted as territorial markers. Renfrew used the dense distribution of tombs on the Orcadian island of Rousay to suggest that they symbolised the rights of small communities to hold individual parcels of land (Renfrew 1979, 216). Renfrew saw the early farming communities in Orkney as representing a segmentary society, each largely autonomous with its own settlement, fields and tomb. The huge investment of labour needed to live off the land during the Neolithic must have made land rights a central preoccupation of early farming communities. Links between land and community took on a new level of importance replacing the more mobile and fluid situation which probably pertained in the Mesolithic. The association of chambered tombs with the bones of the ancestors makes this an attractive hypothesis, symbolising the timeless link between land and community through generations of clearance and tillage.

Chambered tombs cannot, however, have been simply territorial markers. In most regions there are distinct concentrations of tombs in certain areas – Rousay is one, North Uist in the Western Isles is another – which do not appear to be simple products of fieldwork biases (Armit 1990b). So the areas which seem to support the idea of segmented societies each with their own tomb are the exception rather than the rule. Such peculiarities of distribution suggest that we cannot assume a one-to-one link between early farming communities and chambered tombs.

Neolithic People

The acid Hebridean soils generally prevent the survival of good human bone assemblages. This makes it unlikely that we will ever be able to gain a clear idea of how many people were buried in the tombs or what proportion of the community they represented. However, work on the well-preserved bones from hundreds of individuals in tombs such as Isbister and Quanterness in Orkney has produced important information on the composition and condition of the population of Neolithic Orkney (Hedges 1984). The bodies from Isbister seem to contain a cross-section of age and sex groups suggesting to the excavator that the whole population of the local community, with the exception of new-borns, ended up in the monument (ibid.).

There are obvious problems in transposing interpretations based on the bodies in an Orcadian tomb into the Hebridean Neolithic. Although Isbister seems to have contained a cross-section of a farming community without any obvious status differentiation or selection this does not necessarily mean that this situation applied elsewhere. The burial rites practised at Unival, for example, have no clear parallel in Orkney. Nonetheless the information from the Isbister bones gives a rare insight into some aspects of Neolithic society which are far from obvious amid the more standard components of the archaeologist's armoury.

The most striking feature of the Isbister population is their low life expectancy (Hedges 1984). Even after high levels of child mortality, most of those surviving to puberty could not be optimistic about surviving past the age of thirty. Very few individuals reached fifty and most of those seem to have been male, the rigours of childbirth evidently adding to the stresses on the female population. Such a population structure is not uncommon among pre-industrial societies in present and recent centuries and it would have had significant effects on the ways in which communities were organised. Much of the burden of economic production would have fallen on the very young who made up a significant proportion of the population. Old age would have been sufficiently rare to give these individuals a special, and perhaps venerated, status. Household or family composition would have been highly variable due to the unpredictable culling of individuals of all ages by a variety of ills. Extended, rather than nuclear, family groupings would have been more or less dictated by the population structure. Hedges has also calculated that to remain stable the Isbister population must have practised forms of population control similar to those observed widely in pre-industrial societies, for example abortion and infanticide. Such mechanisms might partially explain the attitudes behind the exclusion of new-born children from the tomb.

The Isbister bones also enabled Hedges to discuss more detailed aspects of the population. For example, average heights could be calculated at 5'7 for men and 5'4 for women: these are close to modern averages and the small differences might be explained by relatively poor diet. All of the Isbister dead had been highly muscular and there was no indication of a 'leisure class'. Many of the women had cranial deformation caused by carrying loads by means of a 'brow-band' and at least half of the adults had degenerative diseases of the spine resulting from heavy labour. It is intriguing to speculate that the additional labour devoted to economically unproductive tasks like the very construction of the Isbister tomb may have contributed in no small way to the physical condition of those subsequently buried inside it.

The Isbister population model is probably not far removed from the situation which would have pertained in Skye and the Western Isles. Many of its characteristics are, after all, the inescapable result of pre-industrial, farming lifestyles. It would be unwise to picture these people as uniquely unfortunate in their conditions of existence since such conditions were prevalent in European rural communities far more recently than we might imagine. Similar studies of the bones of medieval and later populations from the eroding remains of a cemetery on the small island of Ensay in the Sound of Harris produced a picture of a broadly similar peasant community with massive levels of child mortality around twelve times the levels of modern populations in the islands (Miles 1989).

The implications from the bones that all of the Isbister people were involved in heavy labour lends some support to the view that chambered tombs were essentially communal monuments of an egalitarian society, organised by co-operative action rather than by authoritarian decree. This Orcadian picture may not necessarily apply to the Hebridean tombs. The Callanish tomb for example (see below) is very small and seems unlikely to have served the size of population which would have been required to construct the standing stones in which it is set. Sadly, there is as yet no bone assemblage from any Hebridean tomb which might let us compare the west coast population with that of the Northern Isles.

Despite many indications that the earlier part of the Neolithic was a period of broadly egalitarian societies with relatively little status differentiation, the architecture of the Hebridean tombs suggests unequal access to the ancestors and strict division of roles in ritual life. Given the relative profusion of the tombs and the implication from Isbister that nobody was exempt from the day-to-day labours of economic production it seems likely that status differentiation may have been based on age or gender groups within relatively small social units.

Cup-marked Stones

One group of prehistoric sites that sit rather uneasily in chronological terms are the cup-marks; groups of hollows pecked into natural rock outcrops or megaliths. These appear to date to the Later Neolithic and Bronze Age and, on mainland Scotland, are often associated with chambered tombs and stone circles. They appear to mark out sacred places, whether these are defined by artificial constructions such as tombs or natural places unaltered by humans.

The Hebridean examples have not been studied in great detail and the known distribution is undoubtedly a mere fraction of these yet to be found, judging by the recent discoveries of Margaret and Ron Curtis in Lewis and Harris. Many of these examples are at, or near, present-day high water marks suggesting that further study might well reveal significant patterning in the relationship of cup-marked stones to the wider landscape.

Ritual Monuments of the Later Neolithic

In the later part of the Neolithic period the appearance of large ritual centres signalled the emergence of elite groups able to marshal labour on a scale not previously witnessed. In Orkney, for example, the tradition of chambered tomb building continued to develop with the construction of increasingly elaborate and complex structures. Elsewhere in Scotland enormous earthwork structures built for communal ritual were constructed, including a henge complex at Balfarg in Fife (Barclay 1993), timber circles and avenues at Dunragit in the south-west, and a large ceremonial enclosure at Blackshouse Burn in Clydesdale. Such centres seem to have had more than simply local significance and may have acted as focal points for communication between elite groups and for the exchange of goods. This apparent process of increasingly concentrated and centralised power shown by communal ritual and elaborate building projects extended throughout Britain and Ireland and suggests widespread social change at this time. New artefact types such as Grooved Ware pottery were adopted in widely separate areas such as Orkney and Wessex (the earlier alternate name 'Rinyo-Clacton' Ware exemplified the widespread distribution of the style) and seem to be recurrently associated with the new monuments. Megaw and Simpson even noted that the Grooved Ware pot from the tomb at Unival had 'a very "Wessex" look about it' (1961, 69).

The Hebrides lack any of the henge monuments which are so characteristic of much of the Later Neolithic in Britain, but their numerous stone circles and standing stones belong to the same broad tradition of communal ritual monuments (Figure 5.1). The larger stone circles, like henges elsewhere, represent a scale of construction and a manipulation of communal labour significantly more developed than would have been required to build the Hebridean chambered tombs. Although stone circles and henges are sometimes associated with burials these seem to have been peripheral to the primary purpose of the monuments. The ancestors seem to have gradually lost their central role in defining group identity.

FIGURE 5.5. Callanish, Lewis.

Callanish, Lewis

By far the most impressive concentration of megalithic monuments in the Hebrides lies in the area around Loch Roag near the modern township of Callanish on the west coast of Lewis (Figure 5.5). The Callanish standing stones occupy a rocky ridge commanding extensive views over tracts of formerly cultivated boggy peatland and the waters of Loch Roag. Before the sea drowned the low-lying ground this would have been, by Hebridean standards, a fairly rich area for early farming communities, as pollen analysis on the nearby peats has shown (Bohncke 1988). Indeed much of the now-submerged Loch Roag basin would have been dry land and available for farming in the earlier part of the prehistoric period. Subsequent deterioration of the landscape was such that many of the stones themselves were engulfed by peat to a depth of 0.5 m before being dug out under the orders of Sir James Mathieson in 1857.

One early visitor to the Callanish stones was the writer and traveller Martin Martin who was greatly impressed by their 'number, bigness and order' (Martin 1716, 9). On enquiring of the local people for what purpose these stones had been set up Martin was told that 'it was a place appointed for worship in the time of heathenism, and that the chief druid or priest stood near the big stone in the centre, from whence he addressed himself to the people that surrounded him' (ibid.). Druids aside it is still hard to progress substantially from this analysis.

The main setting at Callanish is well known, adorning the covers of numerous books on Scottish and British archaeology (e.g. Evans 1975; Ritchie and Ritchie 1981). Less well known are the numerous associated monuments in the vicinity, including at least three other circles, several arcs, alignments and single stones, many intervisible with the main site. The profusion and scale of the monuments in this locality show that the area was of enormous importance in the ritual life of the neolithic people of the Hebrides.

The visible remnants of the main setting at Callanish are the products of a lengthy sequence of development over many centuries. On the basis of limited excavations in 1980–1, Patrick Ashmore has been able to delineate a broad history of the monument (Ashmore 1984 and n.d.). The first traces of human activity are no longer visible above ground. A broad, shallow ditch is all that remains of some early structure or enclosure which was virtually obliterated by cultivation in the centuries around 3000 BC. These ephemeral traces may represent a precocious monument signifying an already sacred area or, perhaps less likely given the scale of the ditch, may relate to some more mundane domestic building. Whatever its original purpose the site, after being cultivated for a time, was subsequently allowed to grass over before the central monolith, almost 5 m high, and near-circular ring of thirteen standing stones, about 12 m in diameter, were set in place around 3000 BC.

An avenue formed of two more or less parallel rows of standing stones runs out from the circle approximately, but by no means exactly, to the north for around 80 m creating a formal approach to the monument. This design echoes the processional qualities of other linear constructions of the Later Neolithic including the great cursus monuments associated with Stonehenge in Wessex and elsewhere in Britain. Further alignments run approximately east, west and south to complete a cruciform plan. The stones which form the avenues and circle could have been quarried fairly locally and Burl has estimated that it would have taken 'thirty or forty men' to shift them (1993, 61). The effort of quarrying, transportation and finally emplacement should not be underestimated. Burl has highlighted the complexity of the stone arrangements; the stones forming the avenue, for example, are graded in height with the highest at either end and lowest in the centre; the stones on the western side are consistently smaller than those on the east, a trait shared with megalithic monuments in the north of Ireland (ibid., 61).

Circles formed of tall standing stones are also widespread in western

Britain and similar examples to Callanish include the Stones of Stenness and Ring of Brodgar in Orkney. A parallel for the grouping of monuments around Callanish can be found in the stone circles of Machrie Moor in Arran. Although the cruciform plan of Callanish singles it out from these other sites it seems to be a characteristic of the great ritual centres of Neolithic Britain that no two are exact replicas of each other and each appears to represent an individual re-working of elements from a shared repertoire of architectural ideas and symbolic forms.

Some time after the emplacement of the standing stones a small chambered tomb was inserted between the eastern part of the circle and central monolith (Ashmore n.d.). Although in general the chambered tomb tradition flourished before that of stone circles, there was considerable overlap and it may be significant that the Callanish tomb was of a most unusual type for the Hebrides, with a subdivided, drystone walled chamber much more like the tombs found in Orkney and Caithness in the same period.

The Callanish tomb was used for several centuries judging from the many fragments of pots which appear to have been cast out of the chamber when it was despoiled in the course of subsequent cultivation. Preliminary analysis of the pottery by Audrey Henshall shows not only the expected Hebridean jars and bowls but also numerous sherds of beaker vessels probably dating to around 2000–1700 BC. Some of the beaker sherds were from fine and fairly early all-over-corded vessels of a higher quality than those usually found in chambered tombs. Also present were sherds of Grooved Ware (from contexts dating between the construction of the stone circle and the construction of the chambered tomb) and sherds impressed with cord, a technique common throughout eastern Scotland and northern England. Grooved Ware, whilst widespread in Later Neolithic Britain generally and common in Orkney, is markedly rare in the Western Isles. Along with the unusual nature of the tomb this ceramic evidence points to the potential importance of Callanish as point of contact between people from different areas and as a ritual centre where cultural influences were absorbed and exotic possessions flaunted.

At some time between around 1500–1000 BC the monument fell out of use and was, perhaps deliberately, despoiled by Bronze Age farmers cultivating close around the stones. Subsequent modification of the tomb may signal a brief period of domestic occupation but there is no apparent evidence for any further veneration of the monument (Ashmore 1984). Judging by the nature of the pottery deposited with them, the last burials on the site seem to date to around the same period as those in the tombs of Rudh an Dunain, Unival and Clettraval.

It is impossible presently to determine why the Callanish area should have assumed such ritual significance in the Later Neolithic. On the basis of the somewhat earlier concentration of chambered tombs, North Uist might have seemed the most likely place for such a centre to arise. Aside from Callanish there are numerous less spectacular stone circles and many more isolated standing stones throughout the Hebrides. Possibly the Callanish area developed as a key ritual centre from an origin as one of a number of smaller ritual foci throughout the Hebrides. The development of the main monument may, for example, have been the culmination of a growing regional importance perhaps initially centred around one of the slighter stone circles in the vicinity of Callanish.

The Purpose of the Callanish Stones

As might be expected, much antiquarian and academic ink has been spilt over the years in an effort to penetrate the minds of the builders of the Callanish stones and the innumerable other megalithic monuments of all shapes and sizes throughout Europe. Early antiquarian theories of celestial alignments encoded in the stones evolved into the work of more recent astro-archaeologists (e.g. Hawkins 1965) and the detailed researches of Thom (1967). Hawkins and Thom believed that the stones were set up to provide a prehistoric lunar observatory just as other megalithic monuments seemed to relate to the movement of the sun. Such ideas have been challenged by recent research using more accurate survey data (c.f. Roy 1980), although Margaret and Ron Curtis have made a detailed case more recently for the possible use of the stones to observe the interplay of the moon and the Clisham range (Curtis and Curtis 1994). Critics of the astronomy theories have also pointed out that the irregularity of the stones, weathering and displacement since their erection, and their great bulk means that numerous alignments will inevitably be preserved in a monument of any size by chance alone. Detailed examination of the topography appears to show that Hawkins' lunar observations would be impossible to make from the monument (Roy 1980, 6).

Although Callanish was probably not a precocious temple of astronomy, observation of the heavens was undoubtedly important to its builders and, in a less precise way, the setting probably did indeed tie human rituals into the celestial realm and link human with divine authorities. In this sense such monuments as Callanish played a political role. Their construction formalised the social structures already existing in society and provided a stage on which rituals reinforcing that authority were played out. Many such monuments were embellished over the centuries as the scale and formality of ritual centres helped to make earthly power seem natural and inevitable. Even in the very act of construction those providing labour demonstrated, albeit perhaps unconsciously, their subservience to those directing and organising the work.

Status differentiation in the later part of the Neolithic was apparent not only within the local social and economic unit. Certain groups of people had emerged as an elite able to draw upon labour from widespread communities and to develop links with other élites in other regions. Their power was manifested through the construction of great monuments of communal ritual, perhaps related to a religion based on celestial powers rather than on the ancestors. This power was, seemingly, not established through war or conquest. The Scottish Neolithic has no evidence of forts or defensive enclosures, for example. Of the hundreds of people buried at Isbister only around 2 per cent had suffered broken bones during their lifetimes (Hedges 1984) and there was no sign of deliberately-inflicted injury. The internal development of Neolithic societies simply seems to have led inexorably to the progressive centralisation of power.

6   Beakers and Bronze

From around 2000 BC the great ceremonial monuments of Later Neolithic Britain, the henges and stone circle complexes, seem to have become less significant whilst monuments celebrating the individual became increasingly important. For the first time elaborate single burials, whether in stone cists or under small cairns or barrows, came to prominence. At more or less the same time a new type of pottery appeared across Europe. Beaker pottery, as it is known, typically comprised a range of fine, fairly small drinking cups profusely decorated with a series of recurring motifs (e.g. Figure 6.1). These vessels were often placed with the dead, in single graves, along with a variety of other grave goods drawn from a new repertoire of personal jewellery (including occasionally objects of gold or jet), weapons and items associated with archery.

The end of the Neolithic and beginning of the Bronze Age appears to have seen the emergence of societies involved in the exchange of prestige or exotic goods, sometimes over large distances. Such movement of exotica was presaged by the exchange of polished stone axes in earlier periods but appears to have assumed greater importance at this time. The making of bronze itself demanded a degree of trade or exchange since the necessary copper and tin ores are seldom found in close proximity. Access to exotic items, particularly non-utilitarian ones such as personal jewellery, seems to have become an important means of demonstrating the power and prestige of the individual. Indeed the earliest use of metal was almost exclusively focused on non-utilitarian items and it appears that the prestige goods economy, as it has been termed, was a key factor in creating a demand for metalwork.

Perhaps the earliest known occurrence of metal in the islands is the small splash of arsenical bronze from the beaker period occupation at Northton

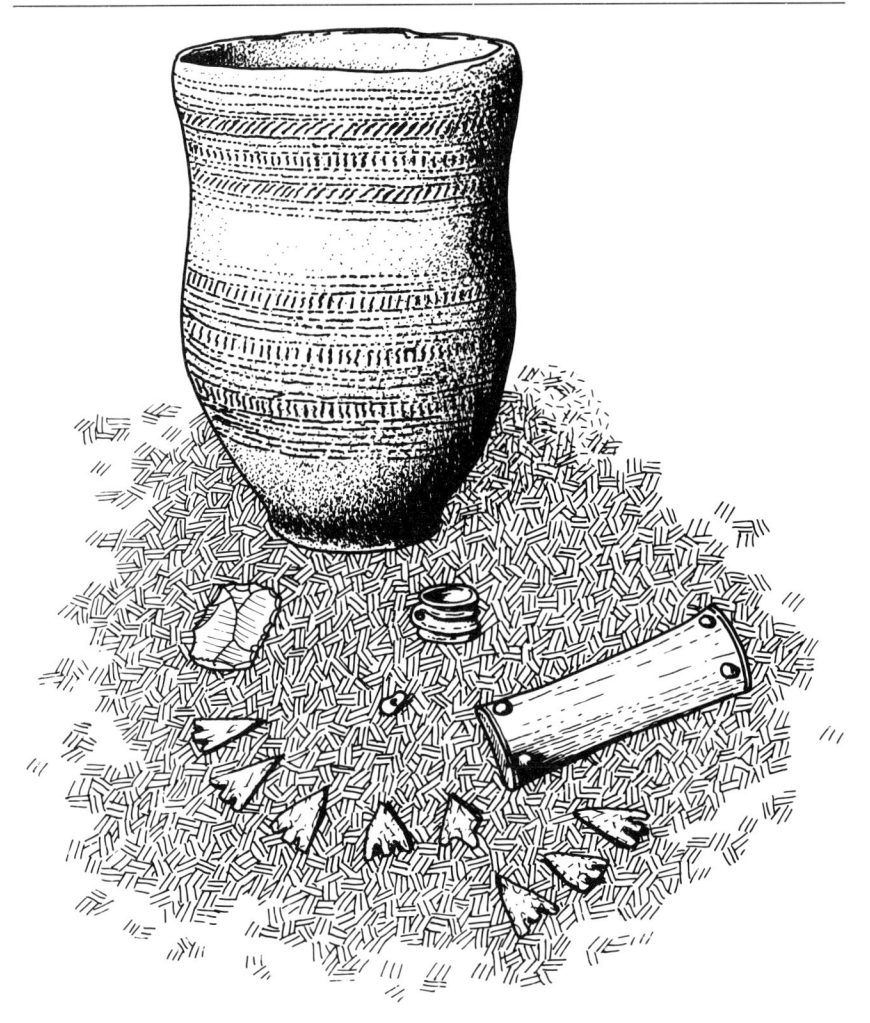

FIGURE 6.1. Beaker vessel and associated artefact types.

(Simpson 1976, 224). Another fragment of copper alloy was found among the debris from the eroding middens of the same broad period at Dalmore in Lewis (Ponting and Ponting 1984, 235). Nonetheless, there is little sign that bronze made any significant impact on the day-to-day lives of Hebridean communities. The necessary ores were not easily available in the Hebrides although a few copper and gold sources have been identified on the west mainland (Coles 1969, 32). It was not until close to the end of the Bronze Age that bronze appeared in any quantity, and even then its principal use seems to have been for the manufacture of high status weaponry.

The evidence from the Hebrides for this period fits uneasily into the wider chronological frameworks of British prehistory. For the purposes of this chapter a rather arbitrary division can be made between the Earlier Bronze Age, to which several settlements and burials relate and within the earlier part of which beaker pottery was in use, and the Later Bronze Age when artefactual material dominates.

Beakers

For many years the spread of beaker pottery, together with associated artefacts and burial practices, across large parts of Europe was seen as signifying the movement of a new people – a 'Beaker Folk' – as conquerors and colonisers. There is, however, little evidence of any large scale population movement in this period. There is instead considerable continuity in many aspects of material culture in most areas where beakers are found. Alternative theories, of course, abound. One current view holds that beakers formed part of a 'cult package' associated with alcoholic drinks. Analysis of residues adhering to excavated beakers seems to suggest that they may have formerly contained mead or beer (c.f. Ashgrove; Fife in Ritchie and Ritchie 1981, 66). Such intoxicants may have spread as part of a quasi-religious practice involving a specific set of material culture. A parallel from more recent times is the spread of the peyote cult among native American communities from Mexico to Canada after about 1850 (Burgess 1980). The associated paraphernalia of rattles, carved staffs, drums and fans represents a recurring material assemblage that may parallel the prehistoric beaker 'package'.

Alternatively, the common association of beakers with archer's wristguards and with barbed and tanged arrowheads has prompted suggestions that an ideology based around the hunter or warrior may have emerged at this time. The appearance of single graves commemorating particular individuals may lend some weight to this argument, although of course these two views are far from mutually exclusive.

Earlier Bronze Age Settlement in the Hebrides

The concentration of known settlements with beaker pottery in the Hebrides, specifically the Western Isles, is virtually unparalleled elsewhere in Europe (Figure 6.2). None of the recently identified islet settlements typical of the Neolithic period have yet produced evidence of second millennium occupation but there are numerous other sites, particularly on the machair, where material of this period survives in abundance. This pattern probably reflects little more than the instability of the machair and perennial outpourings of pottery from beneath wind-torn and sea-battered dunes. Certainly occupation of islet settlements occurred widely in the first millennium BC and given the paucity of excavation on these sites there is every chance that Bronze Age islet dwellings still await discovery.

BEAKERS AND BRONZE 89

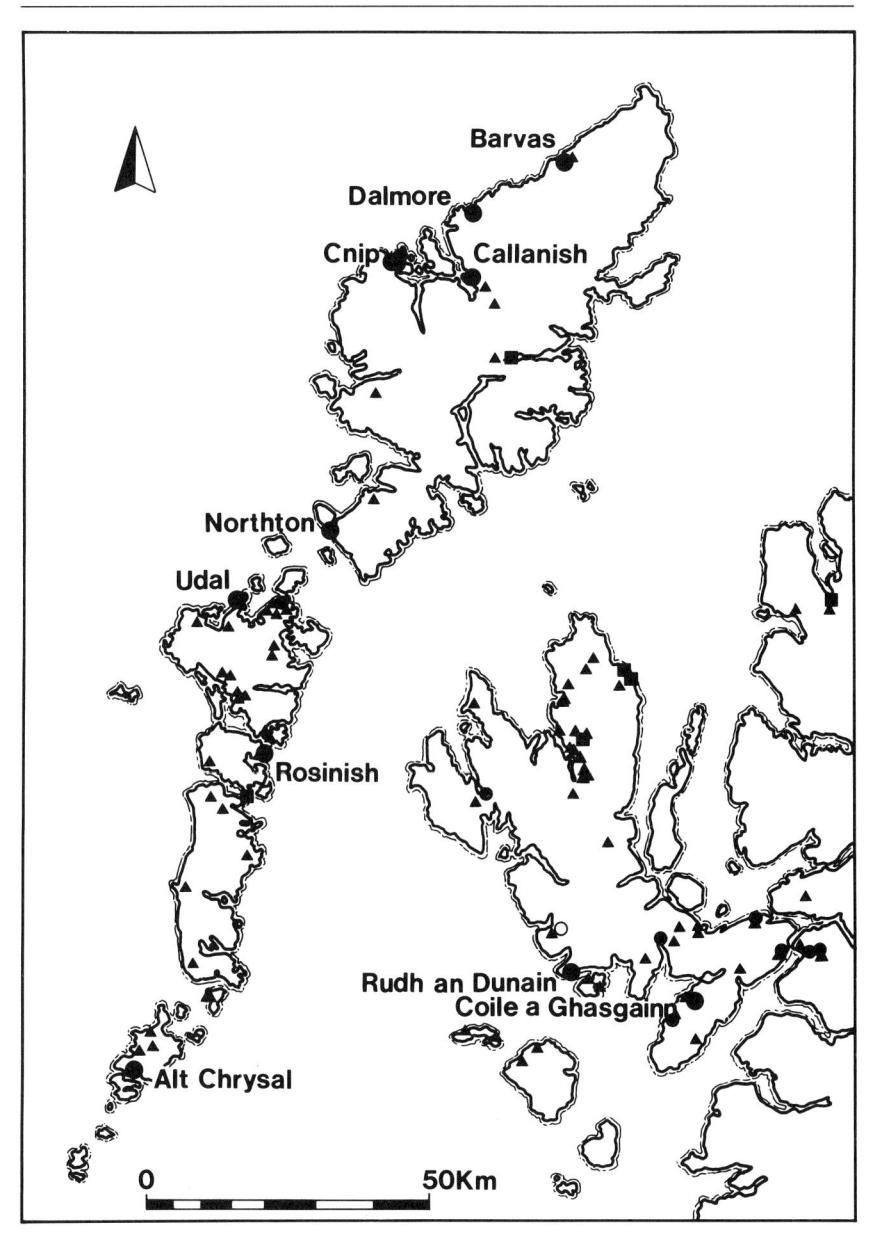

- ■ Beaker Burials   ● Settlements
- ● Urn Burials
- ▲ Unaccompanied Burials

FIGURE 6.2. Bronze Age sites in Skye and the Western Isles.

Northton, Harris

The Neolithic occupation at Northton, buried under the machair at the south-western corner of Harris, has already been discussed in Chapter 4. Professor Simpson's excavations at this site have, however, also produced the most complete picture yet of a Hebridean beaker period settlement, stratified above the earlier occupation (Simpson 1971, 1976).

In the lower of two levels of beaker period occupation dating from around 2090–1890 BC were two houses, aligned north-east to south-west, one of which was complete enough to provide a detailed ground plan (Figure 6.3). This building was around 7 m long by 4.5 m wide and had few internal features other than a scatter of stake holes, a hearth and adjacent pit. Its entrance faced south-west, towards the sea. Both structures were dug into the sand dunes and revetted with drystone walling, a technique which was to remain common on machair locations at least until the Norse period. Although the excavator suggested that the internal stakes may have supported a light skin roof (Simpson 1971, 138) there seems no reason to suppose that a more substantial timber-framed roof did not rest on the sand dune at the wall head as was the case with later prehistoric sand-revetted buildings. The wall probably stood around 2 m high and this kind of roofing would have enabled free movement around the building.

The site yielded sherds of numerous beakers (typologically part of Clarke's Northern British series) from house floors and middens (Simpson 1971, 140). Perhaps surprisingly, much of this material was of a very high quality more usually associated with burial (Burgess 1980, 219). Bone and antler tools including points and combs complemented an impoverished chipped stone tool-kit reminiscent of those from the earlier, Neolithic settlements.

The absence of any signs of agricultural processing at Northton along with the lack of grain impressions on the abundant pottery has led to suggestions that the inhabitants were involved in a predominantly pastoral economy (Evans 1971a). The environmental evidence, predominantly in the form of land molluscs, indicated the clearance of substantial tracts of woodland, perhaps specifically to promote grazing (ibid.). The substantial faunal assemblage included sheep and cattle but also had fairly high proportions of red deer and abundant wild resources including cetaceans, shellfish and birds (Simpson 1976, 224).

The Udal, North Uist

Another site which seems to have evidence of beaker settlement continuing on a site occupied in the third millenium is the machair site of the Udal in North Uist (Crawford and Switsur 1977). Reports of substantial ritual structures as well as middens and buildings have emanated from this site (Crawford n.d.) but the dearth of published information makes these hard

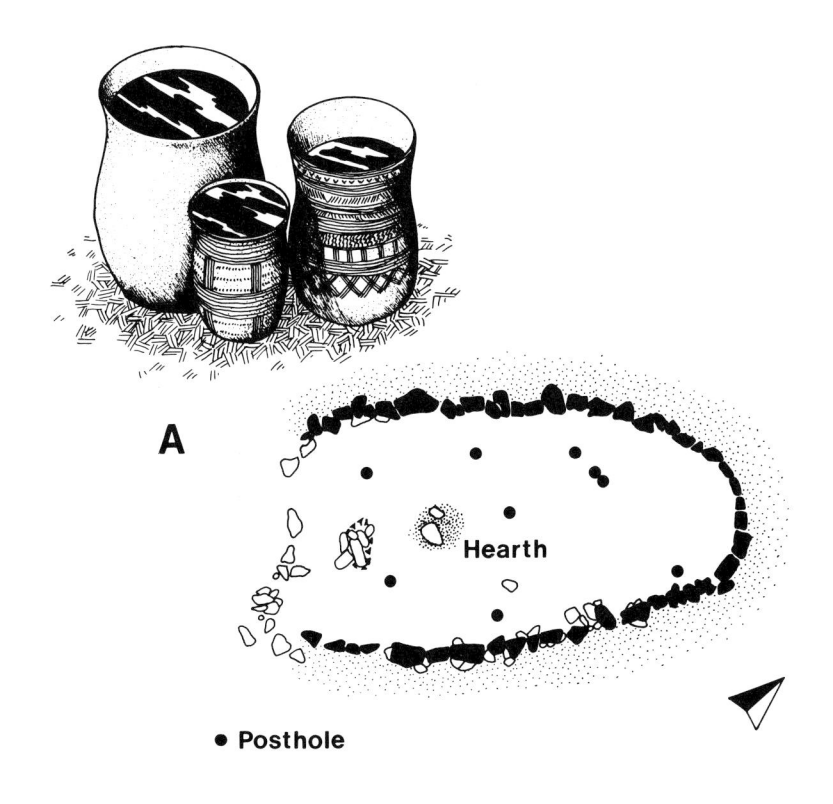

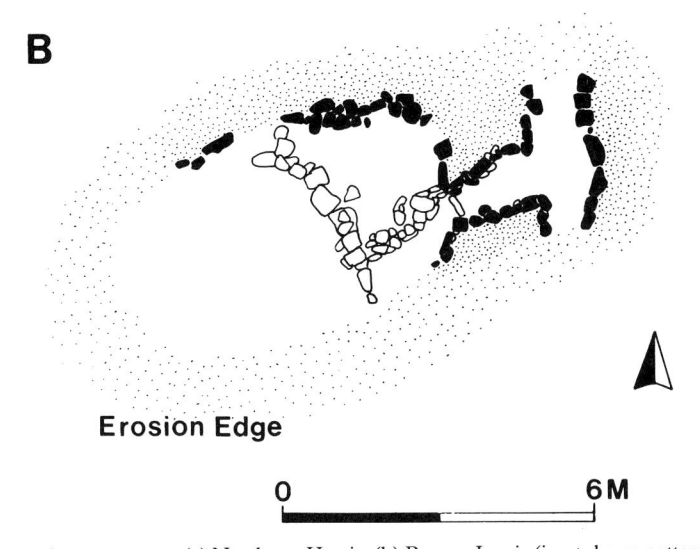

FIGURE 6.3. Bronze Age structures: (a) Northton, Harris; (b) Barvas, Lewis (inset shows pottery based on vessels from Northton).

to evaluate. Nonetheless it seems that here, as at Northton, in the first half of the second millennium BC, people making and using beaker pottery styles carried on living in the same locations as their ancestors of earlier centuries.

Dalmore, Lewis

Further middens and structures were exposed by coastal erosion of the machair at Dalmore on the west coast of Lewis in the late 1970s (Ponting and Ponting 1984). As the sea tore at the beach-front quantities of bone and antler tools and pottery were recovered, the latter including numerous beaker sherds and other fragments with perhaps earlier, Neolithic affiliations.

Subsequent, limited excavations revealed a sand-revetted building with several phases of construction; what began as an oval structure was subsequently remodelled as a small circular house and yard, and finally reduced still further to a small rectangular hut (Sharples 1984, 235). These structures contained few internal features but the concentration of hearth debris in the circular building lay close to a well-constructed pit (ibid.), a relationship which also occurred in the house at Northton. The pottery associated with the buildings at Dalmore suggested that occupation may have continued throughout the second millenium BC (Sharples, pers. comm.). In a late phase of use the structure seems to have served as a workshop for the manufacture of barbed and tanged arrowheads from a local quartz washing up on the Dalmore beach.

Sharples has suggested that the location of the site (in deep shadow from the neighbouring hills throughout the winter months) together with the paucity of fish bones, shellfish and animal bone, implies that Dalmore was a highly specialised site. It may have been only seasonally occupied although the extent of the midden deposits suggests that there was considerable, if not continuous, activity at the site. This pattern of use is consistent with the idea that logistic economies, where task-groups operate seasonally from a permanent or semi-permanent base, persisted into the second millennium BC in the Hebrides (indeed considering shielings, fishing, fowling and peat-cutting it could be argued that logistic economies remained prevalent until very recent times).

Rosinish, Benbecula

Further south in the Western Isles the machair hill of Rosinish projects above the low northern coastline of Benbecula (Figure 6.2). Excavations here, as at Northton, have revealed that, under the medieval and Iron Age midden deposits, lies an extensive and complex beaker period site including settlement, agricultural and funerary components (Shepherd 1977).

Two principal layers of beaker period midden were investigated and, despite the limited scale of the excavations, at least one building was found: a U-shaped stone structure some 10 by 3 m (Shepherd 1977). Its poor state of preservation prevents detailed comparison but its size, construction and shape are, at least, not alien to the building tradition represented at Northton and earlier sites. The radiocarbon dates appear to place this site in the second half of the second millennium BC although it should be borne in mind that they derive from notoriously unreliable marine shell.

Numerous sherds of beaker pottery were found, including both coarse and fine examples, but with notably small quantities of the finer vessels common in beaker burials. Other sherds showed clear affiliations to local Neolithic ceramic traditions with which they shared forms and motifs (Shepherd 1976). The stone assemblage from Rosinish was predictably poor, with the few flints including a number of scrapers but the bulk of the assemblage formed by quartz.

Underneath the beaker period and later middens a fragile record of early Hebridean agriculture was preserved. Marks made in the sand by an early stone-tipped wooden plough or ard, possibly employing human traction, as well as spade impressions and a possible field boundary ditch, were sealed beneath the later deposits showing that here, perhaps in contrast to the situation at Northton, agriculture was indeed practised. Analysis of the ard marks showed multiple 'layers' of ploughing, cross-cutting on various alignments. The marks may have been made using a crook ard similar to forms dated to the second millennium BC in Scandinavia, for example at Hvorslev (c.f. Fowler 1971, 158). Carbonised grains from the excavated deposits give a good indication of the sorts of crop grown in these fields: naked barley was overwhelmingly the dominant crop, with hulled barley and emmer wheat making up the meagre remaining portion (Shepherd and Tuckwell 1977).

Alt Chrysal (or Alt Easdal), Barra

As at Northton, beaker period remains appear to overlie Neolithic settlement at Alt Chrysal (discussed in Chapter 4); although here, perhaps, there is more evidence for direct continuity (SEARCH 1993). From preliminary indications this site appears to represent the painless introduction of the beaker ceramic style into existing cultural traditions. A further small site close to the main excavations at Alt Chrysal produced a substantially intact beaker associated with a small stone structure of uncertain purpose (ibid., site T19). The occurrence of these sites in contexts which could not have been identified as of Bronze Age date from surface traces, suggests that many more sites of similar date await discovery.

Rudh an Dunain Cave, Skye

Close to the chambered tomb of the same name, Sir Lindsay Scott excavated an area of beaker period occupation within a small cave at Rudh an Dunain, an isolated promontory in the shadow of the Cuillins in the west of Skye (Scott 1934b). Whether this cramped enclave, cut into a vertical rock-face well above the shoreline, was ever a permanent settlement is hard to tell; Scott thought not (ibid., 201). If it was, it must have been shielded in some way from the elements since its tiny interior, only 5 m wide and 3 m deep, would have been regularly flushed out by driving rain from the west. Daub fragments, one grooved as if from a wattle and daub structure, may relate to such a construction (ibid., 215). A group of hut circles on lower ground nearby may, however, as Scott suggested, have been the permanent settlement to which the cave was an occasional adjunct (ibid., 201).

The earliest deposits above a floor of sand contained sherds of beakers and sufficient quantities of stone-working debris to prompt Scott's suggestion that the cave was a knapper's workshop. The ubiquitous impoverished stone industry of sparse flints, chert and quartz was found along with bloodstone fragments from Rhum, some ten miles to the south (Scott 1934b, 205).

Discussion

In the Beaker period and Bronze Age, as in the Neolithic, settlements in the Hebrides seem to have been restricted to small units of one or two houses. The settlement at Northton, in particular, seems closely related to the much earlier settlement at Eilean Domhnuill, down to the details of house form and size, despite the differences of location and the intervening centuries. Similar forms of settlement seem to have been in use further south, as at Ardnave on Islay where a small oval stone-built house again occupied a fertile machair environment (Ritchie and Welfare 1983). Extensive machair middens of the same broad period occur for example at Kilellan on Islay (Burgess 1976) and Sorisdale on Coll (Ritchie and Crawford, 1978). The type of settlement nucleation seen in Orkney, for example at Skara Brae or Rinyo, seems, however, not to have occurred in the Hebrides, or at least it has certainly not yet been observed.

It seems likely that the present concentration of beaker period settlement on the machair relates to the vagaries of discovery. As has been mentioned before, too few islet settlements have been investigated to establish whether their use extended into the second millennium BC. Sites like Rudh an Dunain and Alt Chrysal are particularly encouraging because they show that occupation does survive away from the machair and off the islets, suggesting that we may at least aspire to a more comprehensive understanding of Bronze Age settlement in the islands.

Burials

Beaker Burials in Chambered Tombs

Mention was made in Chapter 5 of the fairly numerous beaker associations with chambered tombs. Fragments of at least eight such vessels were counted among the pottery assemblage from Clettraval in North Uist for example.

More were found among the debris cast out of the despoiled tomb in the centre of the Callanish circle although this tomb itself has been described as 'aberrant' and late in the tomb-building tradition of the Hebrides (Henshall 1972, 283).

It remains possible that the deposition of human remains with beakers in the Hebridean tombs were the final acts of burial and were associated with the sealing of the tomb. In effect what had been a communal and periodically re-used tomb was transformed finally into a closed monument to an individual. Such a process is implicit in the associations of beaker pottery with late or last burials at Clettraval. It is even more emphatically stated at Rudh an Dunain, where the tomb appears to have been deliberately blocked with earth which contained beaker sherds. A similar situation applies at Unival where the associated pumice pendant helps date this blocking to around the middle of the second millennium BC based on similar material associated with jet beads at Taversoe Tuick chambered tomb in Orkney (Henshall 1972, 196). The inclusion of sherds from two cinerary urns also found in this blocking may suggest that it occurred quite some time after the first adoption of beakers in the Hebrides.

Beaker sherds and associated material have also been found in tombs which have not been subject to formal excavation, notably beaker sherds from the Clyde cairn of Gerisclett on North Uist (Henshall 1972, 515–6) and from a probable tomb at Garrafad on Skye (Close-Brooks and Ritchie 1978, 101). Further sherds were recovered by Erskine Beveridge from Barpa Langass (1911) while two archer's wristguards, made of stone, from the tomb at Liveras in Skye suggested to Henshall that a secondary beaker burial had occupied the closed tomb (Henshall 1972, 190–1). A further secondary cist was also built into the side of the chambered tomb at Kensaleyre in Skye, this time without any obvious beaker trappings (Henshall 1972, 143).

In sum there is little to suggest that beaker pottery was used in the communal funerary rites of which chambered tombs originally formed a part. The formal blocking of many tombs, even where there may have been no accompanying burial seems to testify to a desire to suppress the former active role of the ancestors in everyday life. By the time beakers were in use these tombs, while retaining their symbolic importance, were being usurped as the burial places of particular individuals. Their function as living, communal monuments, repeatedly entered and re-used, was replaced by a static role as closed tombs commemorating the power of specific people and by extension their descendants and heirs.

The number of beakers found in the Hebridean chambered tombs probably somewhat exaggerates their abundance relative to Neolithic pottery forms. Since beakers were late in the sequence of deposition and possibly related often to the closure of tombs, they will have been less exposed to disturbance and removal during subsequent rites. Therefore any tomb in which beakers were deposited is likely to contain some evidence for the practice. The same is clearly not true of pots deposited in previous centuries.

Cairns and Cists

Cnip (formerly 'Kneep') Headland is a rocky promontory separating the broad sandy beaches of Traigh Bhaltos and Traigh na Berie on the Bhaltos peninsula on the west coast of Lewis. Deep sands which formerly shrouded the east-facing slopes of the headland are gradually being peeled back by the wind, revealing year by year the remains of two old ground surfaces (Armit 1994a). The lower of these is occupied by Bronze Age cairns (Figure 6.4) and the upper by a Viking Age cemetery (see Chapter 10).

In the 1970s the first Bronze Age cairn to appear was excavated by Dr Joanna Close-Brooks (in press). The excavations demonstrated that the, superficially simple, stony cairn had a complex history of use and modification. First the area had been cultivated, as witnessed by numerous ardmarks similar to those at Rosinish, although the settlement of these farmers has yet to be identified (two nearby hut circles represent possible candidates but remain unexcavated). Subsequently a low stone cairn with a slab kerb, measuring 6.8 by 5.8 m north to south, was built around a central rectangular short cist in which was placed the corpse of an adult around 35–45 years old (ibid.); elderly by the standards of the day.

The D-shaped ground plan of the cairn is unusual, most others of the period being round, but Close-Brooks has identified a smattering of parallels around Scotland, for instance in the borders, the highlands and the southwest, most of which were under later round cairns (Close-Brooks in press). The rather incoherent distribution of these parallels suggests that there is no particular connection between them, and the excavator's suggestion that the D-shape derives from the straight facades of earlier chambered tombs is an appealing explanation.

Around fifty short cists analogous to the one within the Cnip Headland cairn have been reported in the Western Isles although the poverty of dating evidence and the lack of detailed analysis on the structure of the burials, for example the possible presence of covering mounds, makes this material difficult to use (Megaw and Simpson 1961). Most have been found in the machair of the Uists and Barra, though this probably relates to their relative ease of discovery in the sands. A cist containing a flexed inhumation at the Udal apparently dates to around 1900–1600 BC (raw data published in Crawford and Switsur 1977, 129). Pottery from these cists, where present, tends to comprise local variants of the collared urn tradition, commonly associated with Bronze Age cremation burial elsewhere. None are associated with beakers. Collared urns are one of a succession of Bronze Age pottery styles associated with burial and ritual use and their *floruit* occurs some time after that of beakers. A further local tradition appears to be the inclusion of quartzite pebbles in the grave fill (Megaw and Simpson 1961, 66).

Oddly there appears to be a fairly even mix of inhumations and cremations from Hebridean short cists and the two rites are seemingly represented together under one mound at Sithean an Altair in the Vallay area of North Uist

BEAKERS AND BRONZE 97

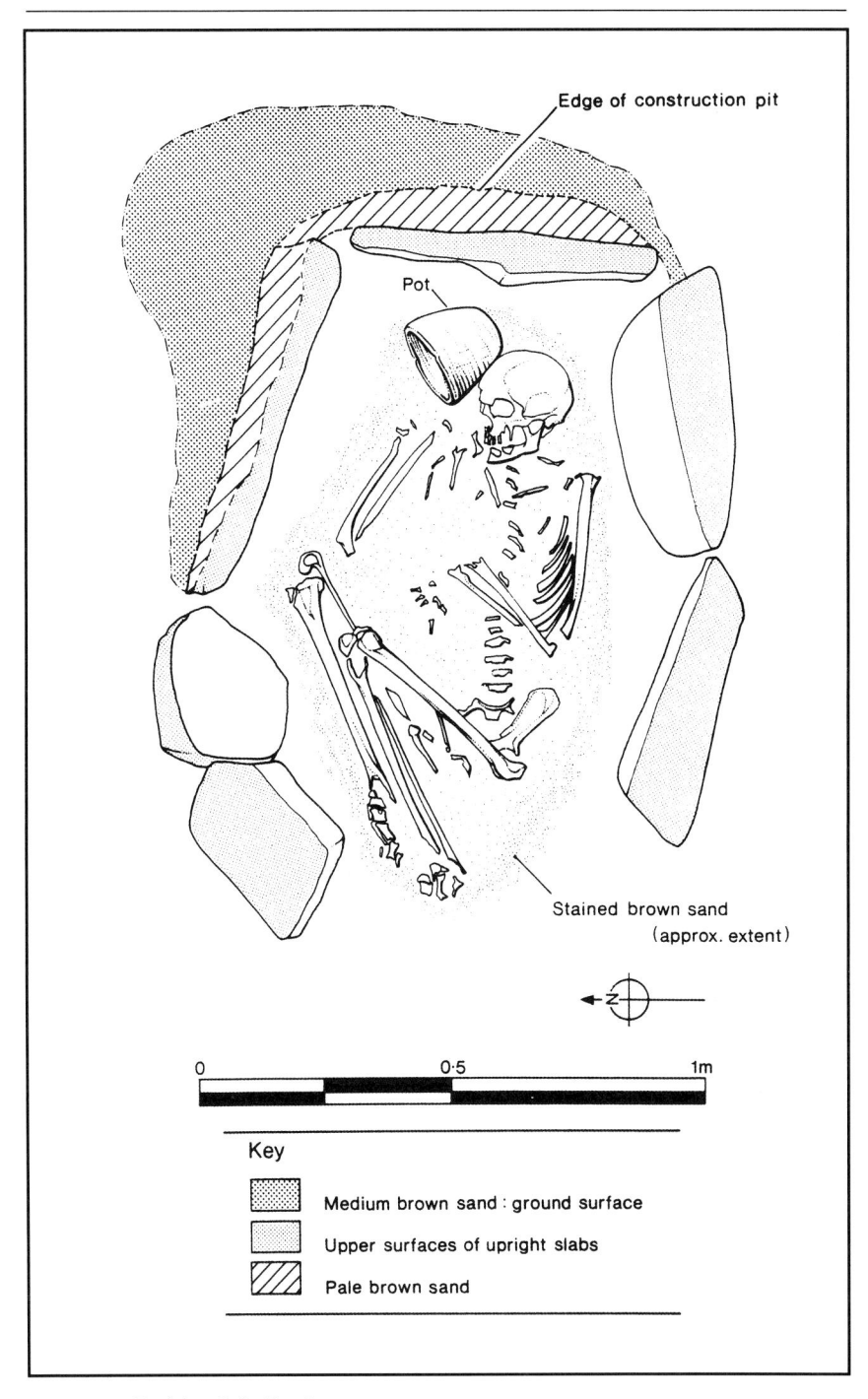

FIGURE 6.4. Burial at Cnip, Lewis.

(ibid.). This is perhaps surprising because of the considerable differences in funeral rite implied by the two forms of deposition; cremation requires a complex succession of processes including the construction of a funeral pyre. Whatever irretrievable complexities were involved in either rite we can be fairly sure that quite different attitudes to the dead were involved in the acts of cremation and inhumation, and that both were used throughout the Hebridean Bronze Age.

Some time after its construction the Cnip headland cairn was radically modified for the insertion of a new burial; this time cremated and deposited in an upturned urn (Close-Brooks in press). This deposit was placed in a carefully constructed corbelled cist dug into the cairn and through the older burial, parts of which were rudely scattered amid the building debris. The cist was formed of vertical slabs for its lower courses, capped by corbelling and presumably held in place by a capping of turf or sand. A C-14 sample from burnt organic material (probably the remains of food) inside the urn was dated to between around 1780–1670 BC. Similar construction was observed in the corbelled cist dug into the middens at Rosinish (Crawford 1977) although this held inhumations (of a male around forty years old and two women of around twenty) rather than cremations. Two small satellite cists were found outside the small setting of stones which eccentrically ringed the corbelled cist (ibid.). Interestingly, the pots from both Cnip headland and Rosinish are hard to parallel outwith the Western Isles and testify to the persistence and distinctiveness of Hebridean ceramic traditions during this period. A further corbelled cist was the only clear structure in the upper levels of the former beaker settlement at Northton (Simpson 1976, 224). This time the occupant was a middle-aged woman buried with a polished bone pin which presumably was all that remained of her clothing or burial shroud (ibid.). Other, less formal burials were also recorded at Northton (ibid., 224): away from the stratified deposits of excavated sites such burials would be hard to date without recourse to C-14 determinations which are seldom judged appropriate for stray finds of human remains.

But the corbelled cist did not mark the end of the Cnip Headland sequence. Some time later, possibly several centuries after the construction of the corbelled cist, a kerb cairn was constructed over the earlier features (Figure 6.4). Kerb cairns, essentially low stony mounds demarcated by a kerb of larger boulders, appear to belong to the later second millennium or earlier first millennium BC although too few have yet been securely dated to be sure (Ritchie et al., 1975). At Cnip an inner, boulder-defined kerb some 3 m in diameter was encircled by an irregular kerb some 6 m in diameter. The inner space was packed with smaller stones. Amid the stones was mingled burnt material containing cremated human bone (of a young adult) and animal bone, perhaps the remnants of feasting or food offerings made at the funeral pyre (Close-Brooks in press).

In 1992 further excavations by the Centre for Field Archaeology (initially focused on the eroding Viking graves from the upper levels on the site) located the remains of a further cist burial which had just emerged from under deep sand close to the kerb cairn. This burial comprised a small cist, 1.2 by 0.9 m, cut into the old ground surface in which lay the crouched skeleton of a man over forty years of age laid out east to west (Dunwell et al. forth.). The bones showed the tell-tale signs of hard, physical work suggesting that this was not a member of any leisured class. A simple, bucket-shaped vessel lay beside his head and some staining of the sand might mark the position of long since decayed organic offerings, perhaps of food. Interestingly this unfortunate individual had suffered severe facial trauma during his life which although it had healed had probably caused prolonged discomfort. The nature of the damage suggested that the cause had been a 'baseball bat' injury, i.e. a fierce blow to the face with a blunt object. Whether this injury was the result of violence or accident is, of course, unknowable. A radiocarbon date from the skeleton suggests that the man died between around 1730–1580 BC, remarkably close to the date of the corbelled cist in the adjacent cairn and suggesting that the two burials, despite one being an inhumation and one a cremation, relate to the same period of use of the site. An outer irregular kerb of boulders around this cist may echo the outer kerb of the larger cairn and there were indications (though it was too damaged to be sure) that the cist had originally been corbelled under a turf or sand mound. Further cairns have been reported in the locality, as has a sherd of beaker pottery, but these structures can no longer be traced and may have eroded since their discovery (Cormack 1973, 48).

Considerable periods of time may have elapsed between each of the documented re-uses of the Cnip headland cairn, with each successive burial being a conscious decision to reclaim a long-established and symbolically-charged feature of the landscape. It is interesting that burials seem often to have been inserted into abandoned settlement as well as into older graves; in addition to the corbelled cist capping the Rosinish middens, scattered inhumations lie over eroded structures at Barvas in Lewis (Cowie 1986, 1987), while in the later beaker period at Northton there were apparently no houses and the site was instead used for burial.

THE LATER BRONZE AGE

By the end of the second millennium BC in the Hebrides archaeological evidence becomes increasingly sparse. Dated settlements are simply absent between around 1700 BC and the middle of the first millennium BC, although cultivation and midden deposits presumably associated with nearby settlement have been dated to the second half of the second millennium BC at Baleshare in North Uist (Barber forthcoming). Funerary evidence too is highly fugitive for this period although kerb cairns may extend into the Later Bronze Age.

One of the main archaeological manifestations of the Later Bronze Age in Britain as a whole is the deposition of hoards of metalwork (Figure 6.5).

●Socketed Axes ■Spearheads ▲Caledonian Sword

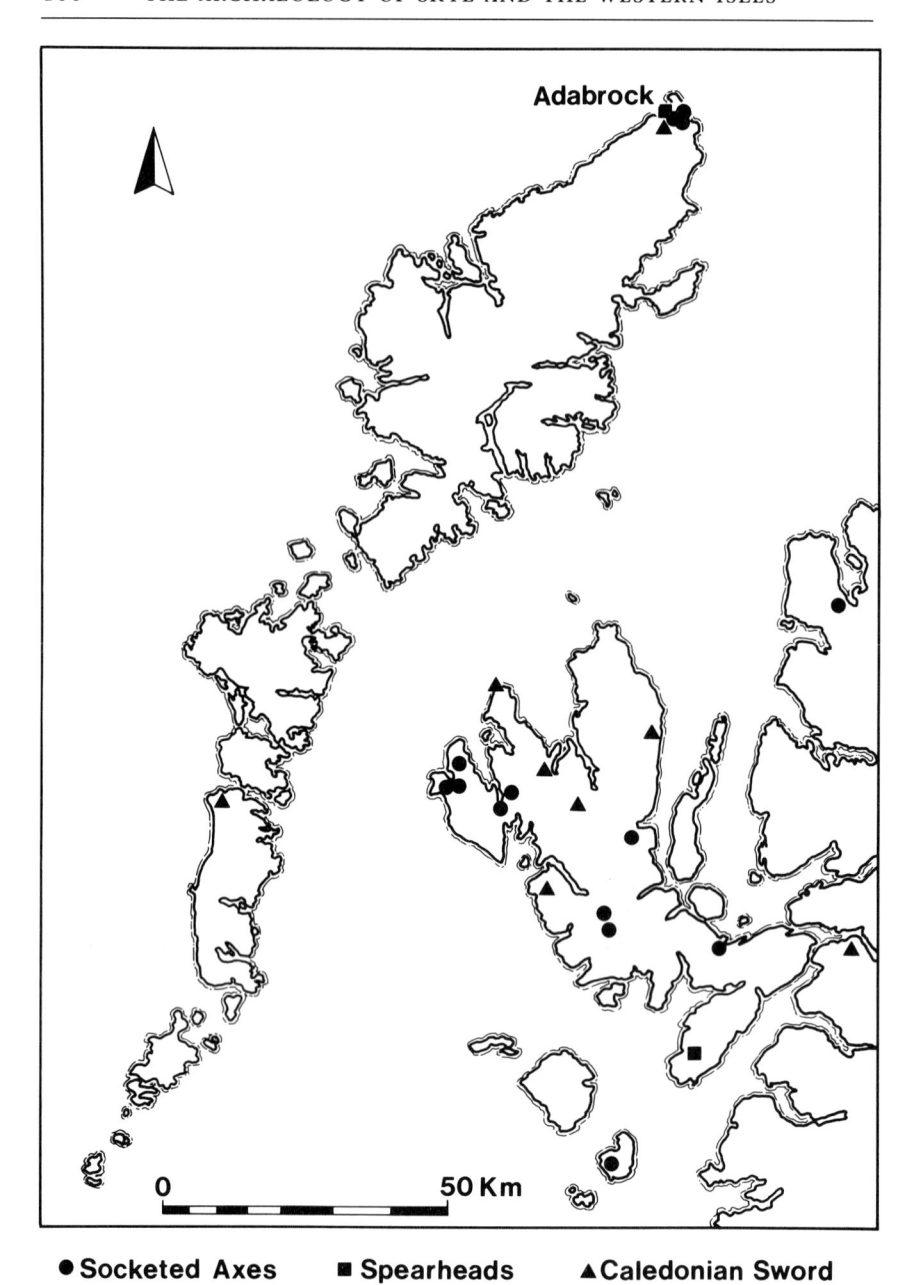

FIGURE 6.5. Bronze Age metalwork in Skye and the Hebrides.

Until quite recently archaeologists have tended to be fairly pragmatic in their explanations of these strange and often very rich deposits. They have thought that some were deposited for security in times of stress by people not fortunate enough to reclaim them later; others perhaps belonged to smiths and were deposited for later trading or re-working. Such explanations may account for some hoards but it is now generally accepted that a great many were deposited as religious offerings. Such hoards crop up in watery places, such as rivers, pools or peat bogs, natural places of significance for pre-Christian religious belief. Many could never have been easily recovered. Aside from acting as a display of piety, such conspicuous disposal of wealth might also have had a social and political impact, reinforcing the status and wealth of the owner. It is perhaps in this light that we should see the metalwork hoards and stray finds of the Hebridean Later Bronze Age.

Hebridean Hoards and Stray Finds

Metalwork that can be dated to the Early or Middle Bronze Age in the Hebrides is restricted to a couple of stray finds of flat axes from Skye and a gold torc dredged up from the Minch off the Shiant Islands (Coles 1964; 1969; Cowie 1994). This relative paucity of material suggests either that metal itself was scarce or alternatively that it was simply not being deposited in the sorts of locations where archaeologists are likely to recover it. This pattern changes markedly however in the early part of the first millennium BC. The most celebrated of these Later Bronze Age finds is the Adabrock hoard, found near Ness at the northern tip of Lewis (Figure 6.6). This collection of bronzes included a range of tools such as gouges, a hammer, socketed axe, chisel and whetstones, and weaponry including a spearhead, along with beads of amber, gold and glass (Coles 1960, 50). Also present were fragments of a beaten bronze vessel; the decoration under the rim, composed of horizontal grooving, maybe even echoes motifs from Hebridean pottery of earlier periods. The vessel is a particularly rare find for the Hebrides, although sheet bronze waste and rivets similar to those found with bronze vessels have been found quite recently on a metal-working site at Cnip in Lewis (Armit and Dunwell 1992). As yet these hoards are all dated, where they are dated at all, on the basis of artefact typology thus obscuring still further their potential chronological relationships with the various settlement forms.

Many other deposits of metalwork, whether as hoards or single objects, have been found in the Hebrides, generally in the midst of inland peat bogs (Figure 6.5). Enough bronze swords have been found to enable the definition of a distinct regional tradition. These 'Minch' or Caledonian swords, larger than their 'Ewart Park' cousins that typify the rest of Scotland at this time, are most common in Skye although they have been found in the Western Isles, for example in peat bogs at Iochdar in South Uist and Aird in Lewis (Megaw and Simpson 1961; c.f. Colquhon and Burgess 1988).

FIGURE 6.6. Selection of items from the Adabrock hoard, Lewis.

One from Talisker in Skye retained a bronze pommel (Coles 1960).

Some other peat bog finds can also be dated to the Bronze Age. A mysterious object known as the Sheshader 'Thing', was found recently in a Lewis peat bog. It consists of a pad of compressed cattle hairs attached to several cords, some of twisted wool and some of horse hair, dating to 1200–950 BC (Hedges et al., 1993). The survival of this curious article demonstrates the potential for very fragile objects to survive in wet conditions and shows how unrepresentative of the materials of daily life the conventional archaeological record is likely to be.

The Settlement Gap

Despite the presence of metalwork in some quantity we have as yet no settlements that can be assigned to the later second and first half of the first millennium BC, although tantalising sub-peat walls and enclosures in areas such as Callanish and Dell, both in Lewis, hint at substantial survivals in certain areas (Cowie, pers. comm.). The characteristic settlement of the Bronze Age in the southern Hebrides and west coast is the hut circle, represented for example at sites like Kilpatrick and Tormore on Arran (Barber 1982) and Cul a' Bhaile on Jura (Stevenson 1984). The Arran examples are associated with extensive field walls and clearance cairns while Cul a' Bhaile appears to have been at the centre of an enclosed settlement. Elsewhere in Scotland whole landscapes of Bronze Age settlement have been preserved with enclosures, field boundaries and clearance cairns intact, as for example in parts of Perthshire and Sutherland.

Hut circles and associated field systems have been identified widely in Skye but until recently there have been no excavations to provide dating evidence. Recent survey and excavation by Roger Miket and others in Skye have begun to rectify this imbalance and exciting results are emerging from their preliminary work.

The recent excavation of a hut circle at Coile a Ghasgain near Ord in Sleat has produced the first indications of early hut circle settlements in Skye. This structure, in a fairly marginal inland valley setting, is superficially representative of a widespread type of Hebridean monument (Wildgoose et al., 1993). A circular drystone wall, originally at least 1.2 m high surrounded an interior 5.2 m in diameter (comparable to the size of some later complex roundhouses e.g. Dun Bharabhat, Cnip, see Chapter 7). The surrounding wall expanded to 2.4 m wide at the entrance creating an entrance passage of exaggerated length reminiscent of earlier chambered tomb entrances and foreshadowing those of the later brochs (Figure 6.7). A kerbed central area inside the walls contained a well-built hearth (ibid.) and a circle of post-holes hint at the former presence of radial partitions. Taken together these various traits mark the appearance of an architectural form in which radially organised space becomes important for the first time. This form of spatial division was to persist in the islands throughout the Iron Age.

A solitary radiocarbon date from Coile a Ghasgain centres around 470 BC (Miket, pers. comm.), although the deviation of the date is wide and more determinations will be required to confirm the existence of a parallel tradition to those seen elsewhere in Scotland. Whilst the present date is lodged firmly in the Iron Age, it does suggest that at least some Hebridean hut circles may relate to the wider, west coast tradition which is known to

● Postholes

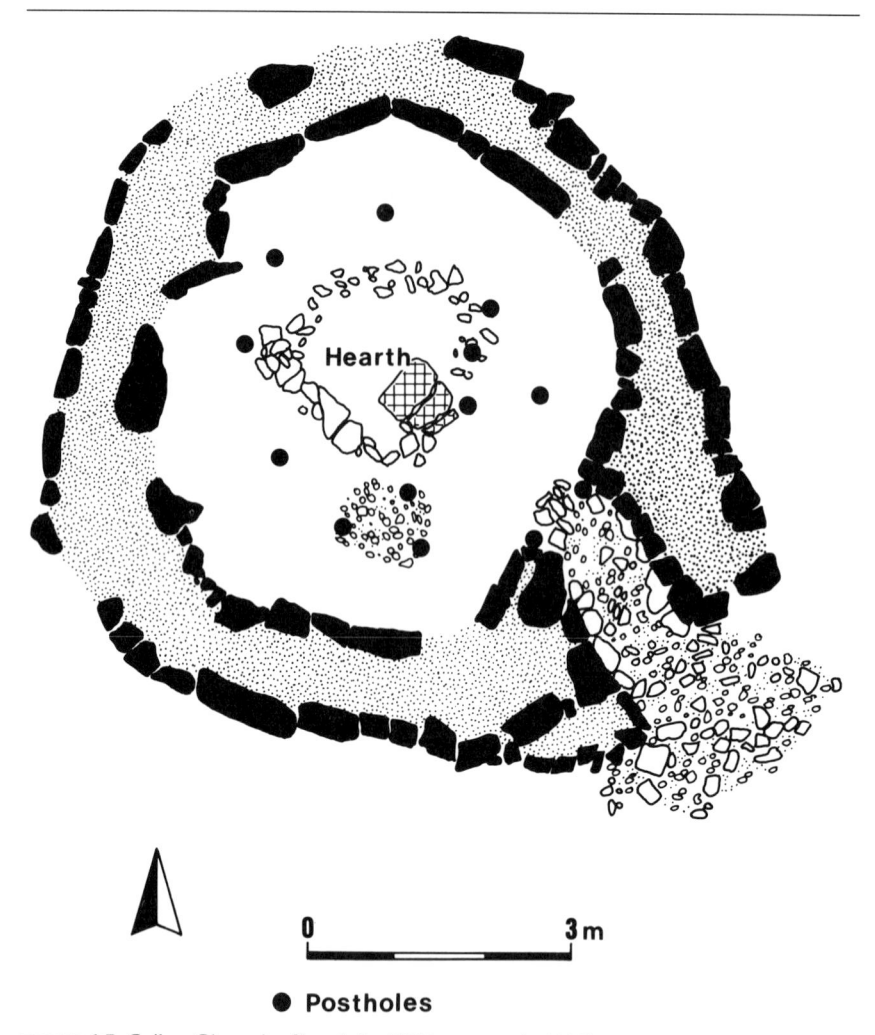

FIGURE 6.7. Coile a Ghasgain, Skye (after Wildgoose et al., 1993).

stretch back into the second millennium BC. The Skye examples occur widely across the island. Unlike those of the Scottish mainland they tend to occur singly although there are a few clusters, as at the site of Altnacloiche where recent excavations have revealed further structures with internal post rings similar to Coile a Ghasgain.

Miket has identified similar examples of hut circles with expanded entrances in the Western Isles (pers. comm.) although hut circles have not previously been a monument type associated with the chain of islands from Lewis to Barra. Instead, as mentioned earlier, there is circumstantial evidence that some of the numerous islet sites may have been inhabited in the

Bronze Age; certainly they were used in the preceding Neolithic and succeeding Iron Age. Some examples such as the North Tolsta 'crannog' in Lewis incorporated quantities of timber in their construction and may therefore be of fairly early date (Blundell 1913; Armit 1992; Chapter 10). Many complex roundhouse sites of Iron Age date have evidence of substantial underlying deposits (c.f. Armit 1985) and underwater excavations at Dun Bharabhat, Cnip in Lewis have suggested a lengthy pre-roundhouse period of occupation in the first millennium BC (Harding and Armit 1990). Radiocarbon samples from below Dun Bharabhat suggest occupation in the first half of the first millennium BC. The complex roundhouse of Dun Cromore in Lewis appears to overlie and earlier stone building of unknown date whilst at Dun Loch an Duin, Shader a 'ghost' islet or crannog with a causeway lies submerged only some 50 m from the surviving complex roundhouse site (Harding and Armit 1990).

Discussion

The study of the Hebridean Bronze Age is undoubtedly in its infancy and few of the sites discussed in this chapter have seen more than interim publication. The final publications of sites like Northton, Rosinish, Dalmore, the Udal, Barvas, Cnip Headland, recent excavations like Alt Chrysal and Coile a Ghasgain, and related west coast sites like Kilellan on Islay, will transform our understanding of the period. Nonetheless there are at least some provisional conclusions which can be drawn from the available information.

Beyond the 'Beaker Folk'

Archaeologists have often expressed surprise at the wealth of beaker material in the Hebrides, particularly the occurrence in domestic contexts of material associated elsewhere with burial (Burgess 1980, 219). This striking concentration is made more puzzling by the lack of beaker graves. The answer probably lies in the way we see beaker pottery and the mechanisms by which it was adopted across Europe.

The dominance of settlement over funerary associations for Hebridean beakers suggests that the pottery style was perceived, adopted and used in a wholly different way in the islands than in certain other regions, for example Wessex or Ireland. This does not mean that the Hebridean Bronze Age was in some way peculiar or retarded – the balance of beaker burials and settlement is highly variable throughout the British Isles (c.f. Case 1993) – but simply that the cultural meaning of artefacts such as beakers is highly malleable and will inevitably be adapted to fit indigenous social strategies (c.f. Armit and Finlayson 1992; 1995).

Looking at the earliest Hebridean settlements it is clear that profusely decorated domestic pottery was of central importance to the Neolithic islanders: such was the elaboration of these vessels and their quantity that we can be fairly sure that they were of considerable symbolic importance in addition to their utilitarian role as simple food containers and cooking aids. It should be no great surprise then that the Bronze Age descendants of these islanders carried this tradition forward by adopting exotic forms of pottery current among other groups with whom they were in contact. Beaker pottery was adopted in the context of pre-existing traditions of decorated domestic pottery and appears to have had no specific funerary associations; its occasional deposition with the dead simply carried on existing practices.

Even to refer to sites like Northton and Rosinish as beaker settlements is potentially misleading given the continuities of many aspects of Hebridean culture. The very presence of beaker sherds in an assemblage tends to bring the whole weight of beaker-theorising crashing down upon a site. In fact a 'veritable hotchpotch of ceramic styles' was in use in the Hebridean Bronze Age (Gibson 1984, 85) and Neolithic decorative traits freely adorn Hebridean beakers (e.g. the heavy use of horizontal grooving under the rim echoes local Unstan Ware motifs).

In Britain, beaker pottery was succeeded by styles known as Food Vessels and Urns, although the development of these styles was not strictly chronological. Bradley has suggested that pottery styles tended to slip down to the social scale over time so that beakers for example started as exotic and prestigious items but eventually became so widely adopted that new styles had to be developed (Bradley 1984). This process of competitive emulation of exotic goods may have helped create the succession of ceramic styles seen through the earlier part of the Bronze Age. In the Western Isles though there is little sign that specific pottery styles were associated with the social elite and we must be wary of imposing models that, whilst perhaps valid at the 'national' scale, have little bearing on the particular Hebridean situation.

Environment and Economy

The economy of beaker period settlements in the islands showed little change from that of the preceding Neolithic economy. Simpson has suggested that the inhabitants of Northton depended on pastoralism and wild resources, on the basis of the lack of querns and grain impressions on pots (1976, 226). Perhaps this reflected a local abundance of natural resources or perhaps Northton was one of a range of inter-dependent settlements forming parts of a logistic economy where sub-groups moved around from the home base to exploit seasonally available resources. There is marked variation in the bone assemblages from Scottish sites of this period again suggesting the specialised nature of individual sites and wide regional variation. For example, whilst cattle dominate in the bone assemblage from Kilellan on Islay, and wild species play an insignificant part, at Northton cattle and sheep are equally common and wild resources are a major component. Nonetheless, the small size of most of these assemblages suggests that we should exercise considerable caution in their wider interpretation.

It may be significant that two of the other second millennium sites, Dalmore and Rudh an Dunain, seem to have been occasional or seasonal activity areas rather than permanent settlements. The ard marks preserved in the sand demonstrate without a doubt that agriculture was practised at Rosinish and on Cnip Headland and these may signify the presence in the vicinity of more permanent settlements.

There were undoubtedly some innovations which had at least the potential to affect the subsistence economy; the horse hairs that form part of the Sheshader 'Thing', for example, might indicate the presence of horses in the Hebrides in the second millennium BC (unless of course it was acquired as an exotic item from outside the Hebrides), and the few finds mentioned above show the rather stuttering arrival of bronze (although a material so suitable for recycling may be expected to be rather fugitive archaeologically). It remains open to doubt, however, whether such innovations had any fundamental economic impact rather than simply a prestige value.

Social Change

Despite continuities in settlement forms and economy there were marked social changes from the Neolithic to the Bronze Age. The adoption of beakers seems to have coincided more or less with the final eclipse of communal burial traditions and the beginnings of elaborate single burial and it would be perverse to dissociate this from wider developments across Europe. The ritual closure of chambered tombs suggests that death had now assumed a finality not recognised in earlier religious beliefs. The physical presence of the ancestors was perhaps now less of a force in daily life and a less potent symbol of the power of the community and its timeless links to the land.

Alternatively the reminder of the communal tenure of land and resources that the tombs expressed may have been deliberately suppressed by those trying to establish themselves in positions of authority. The usurping of formerly communal tombs as personal graves may embody this change. The individual dead rather than the faceless mass of the ancestors were given the guardianship of the land through the monumental grave; their heirs could thus lay claim to rights formerly held in common.

The locations selected for new burial monuments were also significant. As we have seen, former settlements like Rosinish, Barvas and Northton, were often used, and older burial monuments were commandeered repeatedly, as on Cnip Headland. Burial rites varied quite dramatically, from cremation to inhumation, in the forms of monument, types of grave goods, and the dispositions of the dead. We need a large scale excavation of a Bronze Age cemetery (if such things existed in the Hebrides) before we can begin to come to terms with this variation and identify patterns within it.

There are relatively few indications in the Western Isles of the centralisation of power seen in Orkney in the Later Neolithic and Early Bronze Age; there are no especially elaborate chambered tombs like that at Maes Howe in

Orkney, and no clustered settlements like Skara Brae or Rinyo. Only the Callanish stones seems to suggest any degree of centralised authority and, even there, the profusion of subsidiary circles and settings scattered around the vicinity of Little Loch Roag suggests a rather slacker level of planning and control than the largest Orcadian monuments. The Hebridean monuments seem to suggest a loose affiliation of communities periodically coming together at places of shared sanctity rather than a tightly marshalled and hierarchical society. There is little to suggest that any individual or lineage held sway over particularly extensive areas or large populations although power relations within each community were probably more formally expressed than in the Neolithic. Interestingly, by the middle of the Bronze Age the apparently highly structured society of Orkney appears to have been replaced by more mobile and self-sufficient communities more akin to those of the Hebrides (Ovrevik 1985, 131). Some of the later funerary constructions there show affiliations with the Hebrides, for example the kerb cairns, although the Orcadian tradition of barrow building is seemingly not paralleled in the west.

If the earlier part of the Hebridean Bronze Age seems to emerge seamlessly from the Neolithic in the importance of burial and the continuance of settlement forms and traditions, the Later Bronze Age, from what little evidence presently exists, seems more to foreshadow developments in the Iron Age. The emergence of more substantial house forms, the radial organisation of domestic space and the disappearance of elaborate burial traditions all mark major transformations in the way Hebridean communities understood their world.

The adoption of beakers, single graves and subsequently elaborate bronze weaponry, strongly suggests that Hebridean communities were in touch with wider networks of contacts which extended ultimately across large areas of Europe. Coles has stressed the cosmopolitan nature of the Adabrock hoard, among which are items showing Irish and continental affiliations, whilst the use of amber suggests north European contacts (1960, 50). Certainly the upper echelons of Hebridean society, at least, were in contact with the wider world of early Celtic Europe in the early part of the first millennium BC. It was perhaps these contacts that maintained the power of the Hebridean elite; legitimised by their worldly power, material wealth and access to exotic goods, rather than by any appeal to the ancestors or the heavens.

7 The Atlantic Roundhouses

Ever since the time of the first farmers, the Hebridean landscapes had been dominated by tombs and religious monuments. Although settlements were undoubtedly numerous they were physically dwarfed by the chambered tombs and stone circles. This emphasis changed dramatically during the first millennium BC with the construction of the massive Atlantic roundhouses, among them the broch towers. Dun Carloway is the archetypal broch tower of popular perception: a massive, ragged ruin, isolated in the bleak, rocky peatlands of west Lewis. Even today it commands the landscape, towering over the later blackhouses and modern township (Figure 7.2). The Hebrides are, however, littered with the much less imposing, robbed-out remains of related and contemporary buildings that met with much harsher treatment both from the elements and at the hands of subsequent generations.

The convenient collapse of one side of Dun Carloway exposes the inner structure and architectural complexity of the building and demonstrates some of the key attributes of this architectural tradition (Figures 7.2 and 7.3). The two concentric walls are drystone-built, the space between them being bridged at intervals by circuits of large flat stones. These bridging slabs tied the walls together forming intra-mural galleries and stairs which enabled access between the floors and up towards the wallhead, the whole construction combining to create a tall and remarkably stable structure. Despite considerable variation in the ways in which these techniques were deployed, the principle remained simple. The hollow-walled construction minimised the weight of stone required whilst the tapering shape and bonding effect of the galleries helped to channel the weight stresses effectively to the base. From the outside this architectural complexity was cloaked in a forbidding drystone tower punctured only by one small and narrow entrance.

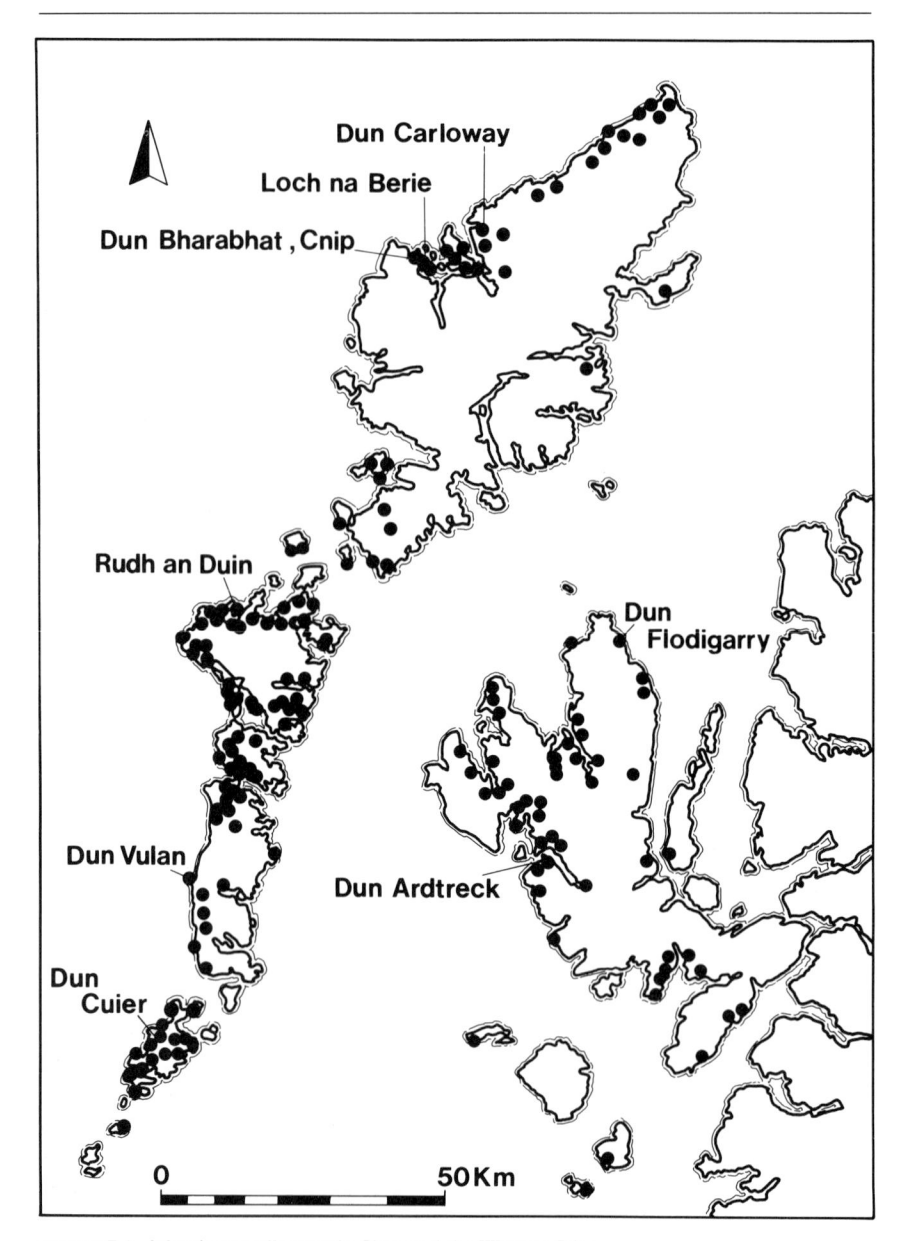

FIGURE 7.1. Atlantic roundhouses in Skye and the Western Isles.

FIGURE 7.2. An early print of Dun Carloway.

FIGURE 7.3. Dun Carloway.

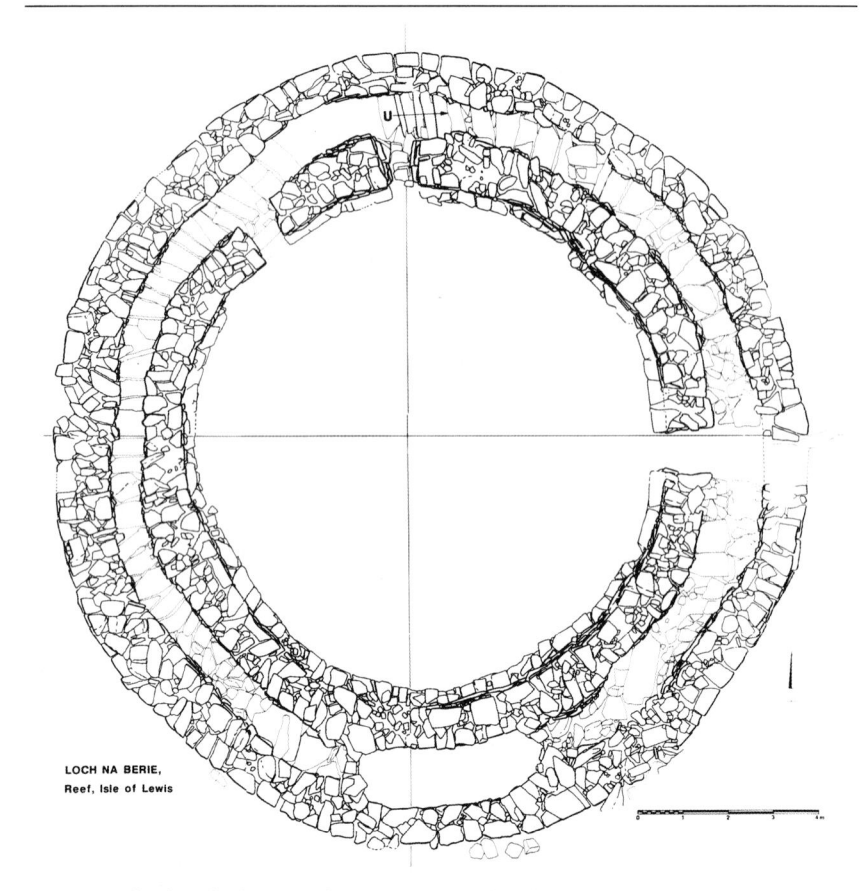

FIGURE 7.4. Loch na Berie, plan of the broch tower, first floor.

A range of other features of broch architecture are recurrent across the Atlantic regions of Scotland although they are not necessarily common to all sites. Ground level cells built into the walls and entered from the central area provide additional space in many broch towers; examples of these can be seen in the ground floor plans of Dun Carloway and the Loch na Berie broch tower (Figure 7.4). Scarcement ledges (protruding stone courses on the inner wall-face), at variable heights above floor level, played a part in supporting upper floors and roofs. Superimposed voids for ventilation of the intra-mural galleries are also to be found in some of the inner wall-faces of the broch towers, as at Dun Carloway (Figure 7.3).

Monumental Houses

It was once fashionable to view broch towers and related buildings as a peculiar architectural flourish in the remote northern outposts of the British

Isles; an odd phenomenon unrelated to events elsewhere. More recently though they have been linked with a more widespread tradition of monumental domestic building which can be seen in much of Britain in the middle of the first millennium BC when substantial timber roundhouses characterised many parts of the country. In the arable lowlands of southern and eastern Scotland, for example, numerous ring ditches recorded by aerial photography represent the ploughed-down remains of former timber roundhouses of similar dimensions to the surviving stone examples in the north. Large timber roundhouses of fairly elaborate construction were also found during the Iron Age in parts of England including Wessex. Generally, this phenomenon of monumental roundhouse-building was on the wane long before the end of the millennium. Along the Atlantic coasts of Scotland, however, monumental roundhouses achieved their finest expression after those elsewhere had largely disappeared.

Atlantic roundhouses are widespread throughout the Hebrides occupying most of the tolerably habitable areas, including many small islands long since abandoned for human settlement. The variable density of sites between different areas, for example the dense spreads over North Uist and Barra as opposed to rather less concentrated groups in Lewis and Harris and parts of Skye, may reflect, at least in part, the intensity of past surveys. Some areas, however, apparently have relatively few Atlantic roundhouses. This appears to be the case in South Uist and in the southern part of Skye. In the latter case the relative poverty of the land compared with the northern part of the island, coupled with a lack of intensive survey, may explain the paucity of sites.

The nature of the local landscape tends to dictate the locations favoured by roundhouse builders. In North Uist and Lewis, for example, islet locations are predictably common. In many cases these structures were simply built over older islet settlements. In Barra and Skye, by contrast, with fewer suitable lochs, rocky knolls and promontories were the favoured locations.

The Search for 'True' Brochs

Much effort has been spent over many decades in the analysis of the architectural minutiae of brochs in order to isolate a group of 'true' brochs. Once defined, the architecture, distribution and associated material culture of this select few could form the basis for the construction of theories on their invention and spread.

Extraordinary structures seemed to imply extraordinary events and in the climate of archaeological thought in the first half of the twentieth century this meant migration or invasion by new peoples. Prior to the 1970s there was a consensus that the brochs were built by incomers to Scotland, probably dispossessed elites chased out of southern England at the time of the Roman invasion. Despite the lack of comparable stone architecture in the supposed source areas, these ideas seemed more attractive than the notion that such ill-favoured island outposts could give rise to architecture of such mastery and solidity. Before the development of scientific dating methods, brochs could only be dated by reference to the few finds which could be matched and dated elsewhere. Inevitably the Roman period provided the only reliable benchmark and, since Roman material occurred on a scatter of broch sites, the brochs were generally placed in that period.

Excavations in Orkney in the late 1970s and early 1980s revolutionised the study of broch towers and related structures. Sites like Bu in Orkney showed that massive stone roundhouses, similar to the broch towers although lacking the architectural complexity, were being built in the Northern Isles from around 700 BC (Hedges 1985). This was far earlier than previously suspected and, equally importantly, it provided a viable ancestry for the broch towers which had previously seemed to have appeared fully-formed in the last centuries BC.

A combination of survey and excavation in the Western Isles during the 1980s demonstrated that broch towers were part of a structural continuum and could not be abstracted from the wider context of the Atlantic roundhouse group (Armit 1988, 1990, Harding and Armit 1990). The classification of individual sites as brochs had previously depended on their state of preservation since only positive evidence of the presence of upper floors would validate a structure as a 'true' broch. Since such survival of stone structures is extremely rare, the inevitable result was that very few structures were accepted as brochs, thus bolstering the argument that brochs were somehow different and special.

Their apparently sudden appearance along with the supposed architectural uniformity and purity of the brochs have been key props in the invasion hypothesis and without these there was no reason to question the indigenous development of broch architecture and the Atlantic roundhouse form. The broch towers were indeed extraordinary structures, but explanations for their origins and developments must be sought in the history of human settlement in northern and western Scotland, not in the adventures of down-at-heel expatriates from sunnier southern climes.

ATLANTIC ROUNDHOUSES

The term Atlantic roundhouse was introduced a few years ago to clarify the rather confusing typological morass which included brochs towers, galleried duns, semibrochs, island duns and an assortment of other variants (Armit 1990a, 1990b, 1991). It reflects the basic unity of the range of stone-built roundhouses in northern and western Scotland, many of which were previously condemned to the typological dustbin whilst the search proceeded for the origin of the brochs. Not all Atlantic roundhouses incorporate the traits of broch architecture. Indeed it is useful conceptually to separate the roundhouse form which relates to much wider traditions of house-building throughout prehistoric Britain, from broch architecture which was applied principally to roundhouses in Atlantic Scotland in the second half of the first millennium BC. Thus traits associated with broch architecture, such as intramural stairs, cells and scarcements, can also be identified in structures which were clearly not domestic buildings such as some Hebridean promontory forts and enclosures. The promontory fort on Barra Head, for example, contains two super-imposed galleries and a low entrance passage with bar-holes within an arc of walling cutting off the approach to a promontory (Armit 1992a, 94).

Within the overall class of Atlantic roundhouses we can identify a sub-group of complex roundhouses where elements of architectural complexity can be seen. Within this complex roundhouse class we can identify a further sub-group, the broch towers, where the elements of broch architecture were used to construct a tall tower-like building. Due to the vagaries of preservation, however, it is seldom possible to determine the height which most of the complex roundhouses attained and it is probably impossible ever to determine the proportion of complex roundhouses that originally stood as broch towers.

Simple Atlantic Roundhouses

The Atlantic roundhouse classification has been evolved to describe the field evidence in a way that recognises the limitations of the data. It need not imply any evolutionary scheme from simple to complex. Nonetheless, a review of the chronology of the Atlantic roundhouses shows that recent work is beginning to point to a gradual development of complexity from early simple versions to the elaborate broch towers (Armit 1990e, 1991), although this does not necessarily mean that simple roundhouses ceased to be constructed.

These simple Atlantic roundhouses seem generally to have stood alone, devoid of associated domestic buildings or substantial enclosures. They were essentially farmhouses, housing perhaps a single extended family, and gave no signs of serious defensive provision. The early roundhouses did, however, mark a significant break from older traditions of settlement. The characteristic Later Bronze Age settlement of the Northern Isles seems to have been the cellular complex, seen for example at Jarlshof in Shetland (Hamilton 1956). Still earlier Neolithic settlements such as Skara Brae and Rinyo in Orkney shared this cellular design. Atlantic roundhouses were the first domestic buildings in the area to mark out the settlement as a dominant landscape feature. Whilst earlier settlements, such as Skara Brae, were elaborate and highly structured internally, they would have been unprepossessing from the outside and certainly less prominent than contemporary chambered tombs. In the Iron Age though, the settlement itself, the centre of the domestic arena, became dominant.

There is no evidence so far of any simple Atlantic roundhouses in Skye or the Western Isles. In the fourteen structures which have been excavated to a sufficient degree for structural complexity to be recognised, all have been found to have incorporated intra-mural cells or galleries (Armit 1992). Although it is too early to be sure, it is possible that by the time that the first Atlantic roundhouses were being built in the Western Isles some of the elements of broch architecture had already been developed. This might sugest that the initial development of the Atlantic roundhouses occurred in the Northern Isles, although there is really no reason to believe that simple Atlantic roundhouses needed to exist before the concept of complex Atlantic roundhouses could arise.

In Orkney Atlantic roundhouses appear to have preserved the cellular form of earlier settlements within the confines of their massive circular walls as, for example, at Bu. The roundhouse form seems to have been necessary to create a massive and monumental structure, but the organisation of domestic life inside seems to have continued to follow the cellular patterns set in earlier, Bronze Age dwellings. This might suggest that the concept of monumental domestic construction was adopted from elsewhere and grafted on to existing settlement organisation. By contrast, the Hebrides may have had a tradition of circular domestic building prior to the initial appearance of the Atlantic roundhouses. The hut circles of Skye and the southern Hebrides, and possibly even of the Western Isles, probably originated prior to the mid-first millennium BC. The Hebridean Atlantic roundhouses do not appear to have had cellular interiors but rather a central open space (although the paucity of excavation means that we may yet find evidence for internal timber partitioning). Nonetheless, present evidence, sparse as it is, suggests that Atlantic roundhouses may have begun to be built rather later in the west than in the north.

Ultimately though, the search for broch origins is futile. Such was the heterogeneity of the Atlantic roundhouse group and the extensive area across which they developed over more than five centuries that there is unlikely to have been any one moment or place of invention. What is more relevant to the study of the Atlantic roundhouse tradition is the question of why the diverse communities of northern and western Scotland should turn their attention for the first time to the elaboration in stone of what had previously been simple and often transient houses.

Complex Roundhouses

Some time around the fourth century BC the northern Scottish Atlantic roundhouses appear to have acquired more complex architectural characteristics (Armit 1990e). Simple roundhouses, like Bu, generally built as isolated structures gave way to more complex structures, some with outer enclosures and ancillary buildings (Armit 1990a; 1990b). Crosskirk in Caithness exemplifies this transformation (Fairhurst 1984). Whilst apparently never attaining any great height, this structure incorporated intramural cells and stairs and was set in an enclosure with auxiliary buildings.

Its internal space was broken down into a cellular pattern demonstrating its continuity with earlier domestic buildings in the north. Early phases of construction at the multi-period site of the Howe in Orkney hint at the emergence of a similar complex roundhouse there at broadly the same period (Carter et al., 1984). The analysis of the chronology of these complex roundhouses remains in its infancy but a pattern does seem to be emerging of a development of both architectural complexity and enclosure from around the fourth century BC in the north. It is perhaps these complex roundhouses of the far north, with their variable levels of architectural elaboration, that the majority of the Hebridean structures resemble most closely (Armit 1992a).

Dun Bharabhat, Cnip

Dun Bharabhat is one of a number of sites of various periods to have been excavated in the Bhaltos peninsula on the west coast of Lewis (Harding and Armit 1990). It lies within a landscape rich in archaeological remains of all periods from the Early Bronze Age onwards including the Cnip Headland cairns described in Chapter 6.

Prior to excavation, Dun Bharabhat appeared as a rather dismal pile of rubble protruding above the surface of a small loch in the hills above Bhaltos (Figure 7.5). The stony islet was linked to the shore of the loch by a treacherous and often submerged causeway. Its modest appearance was shared with numerous other Atlantic roundhouse sites throughout the Western Isles and in many ways Dun Bharabhat seemed as close as could be expected to a typical 'island dun' with no indications of any architectural complexity

Excavation quickly revealed a very different story (Harding and Armit 1990). The structure was found to have been built using the principles of broch architecture, with intra-mural galleries, stairs and cells (Figure 7.5). The presence of intra-mural stairs suggests that Dun Bharabhat would originally have had an upper storey but its small size (only some 11 m in diameter) and wide gallery entrances suggested that it could never have achieved tower-like proportions.

Dun Bharabhat appears to have collapsed soon after completion and was subsequently reoccupied in a distinctly less monumental form during the first and second centuries BC (Harding and Armit 1990). Material from immediately below the primary floor of the roundhouse dates to around the eighth century BC demonstrating the presence of pre-roundhouse settlement on this islet site in the earlier part of the millennium. Excavations by divers working around the islet have confirmed that the excavated structure overlies an accumulation of earlier settlement and it seems that its premature collapse was in part due to its being founded on the unstable debris of this previous occupation. The nature of earlier settlement of the site cannot be ascertained without the removal of the surviving complex roundhouse but it is clear nonetheless that Dun Bharabhat represents a continuity of settlement

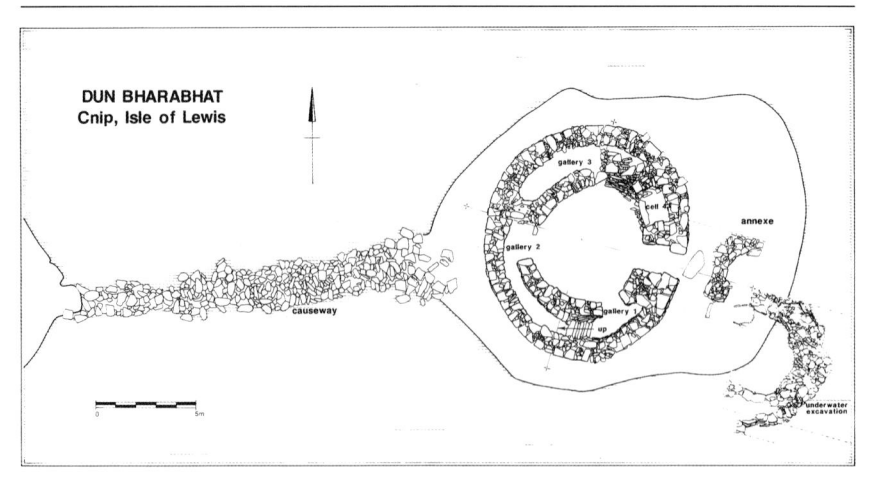

FIGURE 7.5. Dun Bharabhat, Cnip.

from the earlier part of the first millennium BC or perhaps much earlier. Many islet settlements, spanning the millennia that separate the Neolithic islets like Eilean Domhnuill and Eilean an Tighe from the Atlantic roundhouses, may lie in just such a situation, under the monumental ruins of their Iron Age successors.

The use of broch architectural techniques in a small, islet site of this kind has serious implications for the many other Atlantic roundhouse sites in the Hebrides. Many complex roundhouses were so irregular in plan that there can never have been any intention of building a tower-like form. The exigencies of the islet and promontory locations of a great many of these roundhouse sites suggest that they were never of tower-like proportions although all of the excavated examples where wall structure has been examined indicate the presence of structural traits associated with broch architecture. Another Dun Bharabhat, for example, this time on Great Bernera off Lewis, seems to fit this description (Figure 7.6). This structure incorporates a massive wall containing intra-mural galleries and stairs facing the causeway that leads out to the islet. A scarcement ledge can be traced along the rear of this upstanding stretch of wall. The shape of the islet, however, and the steeply sloping rock on which the remainder of the wall is perched seems to preclude the construction of a broch tower and it appears that the sector of walling facing away from the causeway may have been less massive than the surviving frontal portion and the structure may thus have been somewhat irregular in shape. A number of sites previously classified as semibrochs, for example Dun Ardtreck and Dun Ringill in Skye, represent similar variants within the complex roundhouse class (although contra MacKie 1965 they were almost certainly wholly enclosed, roofed domestic buildings). Throughout the Hebrides elements of broch architecture appear to have been used simply because they were the architectural norm, or

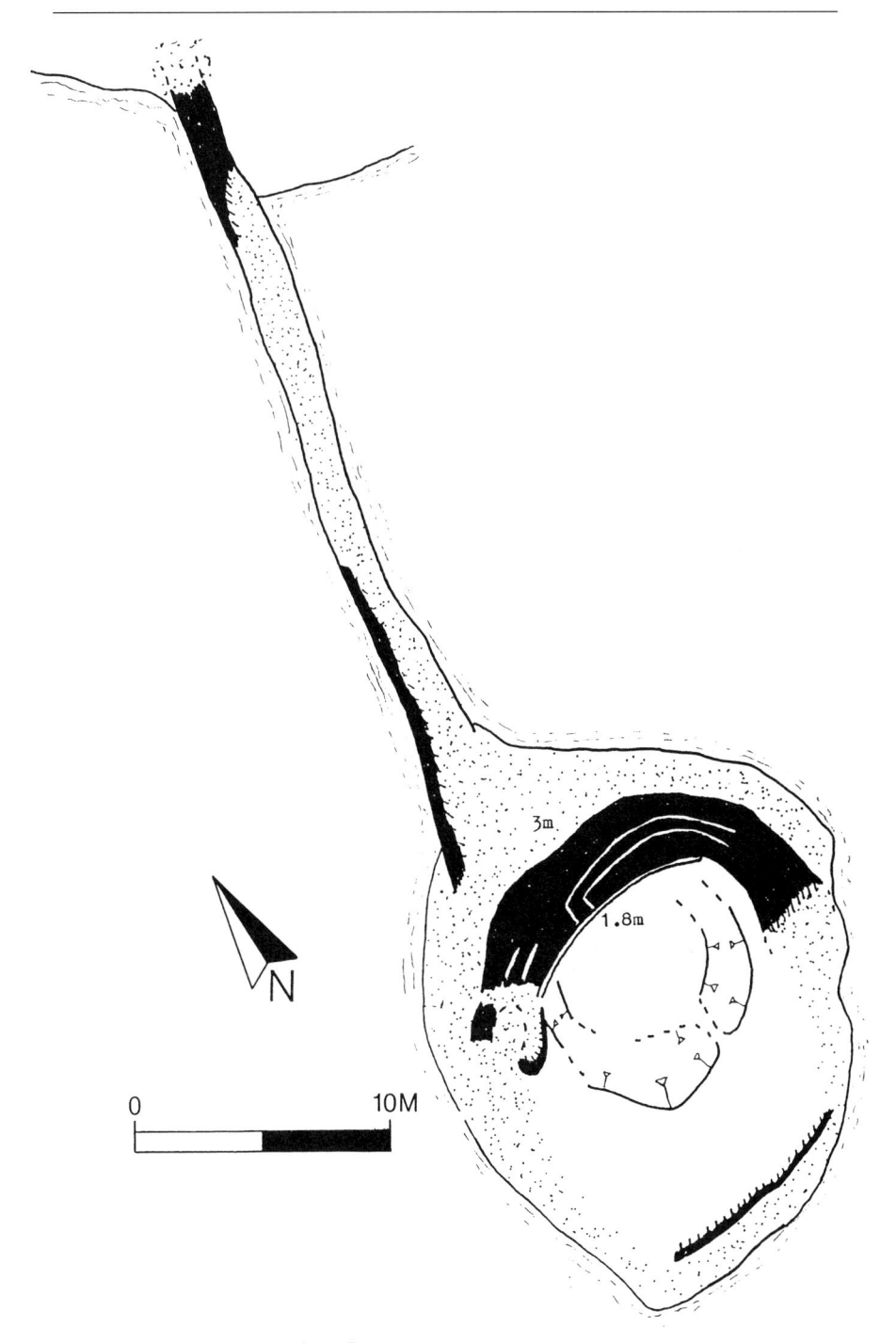

FIGURE 7.6. Dun Bharabhat, Great Bernera.

perhaps because their reference to broch towers was seen as transplanting some of the status of these buildings to the inhabitants.

Broch Towers

Loch na Berie

In the later centuries BC the Atlantic roundhouse tradition reached its apogee with the development of the broch towers. Although Dun Carloway is the best surviving Western Isles broch tower, there are a number of others which would, in their day, have been at least as impressive. The Loch na Berie broch tower in Bhaltos, on the west coast of Lewis, was partially excavated by the Callanish Archaeological Research Project from 1985–1989 (Harding and Armit 1990) at the same time as excavations were in progress at Dun Bharabhat some 500 m away, and subsequent excavations have been carried out more recently (Harding, pers. comm.). Although the excavated deposits relate mostly to the later, Pictish period structures inside it (see Chapter 9), the broch tower is of considerable importance in its own right. Before excavation, this structure was visible only as an unobtrusive mound in a sand-choked marsh (Figure 7.7). Local tradition held that the site was that of a broch but there was nothing visible to confirm this identification.

On excavation it transpired that this was indeed the site of a broch tower of quite exceptional preservation, the surrounding peat, and sand blown in from the coast, having swamped it almost completely. The Loch na Berie broch tower was built using the same architectural techniques as Dun Carloway and its proportions suggest that it would have stood at least as high. Once the upper parts had been excavated it became apparent that the present-day ground surface was in fact the first floor level in the broch tower, and that the first floor gallery was intact, with a set of steps leading up to the (now vanished) second floor (Figure 7.4). Two doorways opened from this first floor gallery into the central area, where a timber floor would once have rested on the projecting scarcement ledge. A further set of steps led downwards into the sludge which had filled the ground floor galleries. Through the gaps between the first floor gallery slabs could be seen the ground floor cells half-full of waterlogged debris. In the centre of the broch tower the debris of later occupation had gradually brought the floor level up to the modern ground surface.

The Loch na Berie broch tower clearly illustrates the futility of attempting detailed typological classification of Atlantic roundhouses from the surface evidence. Using the traditional models of classification the site would never have been accepted as a true broch prior to excavation. There is no reason to believe that other equally impressive structures do not remain to be recognised throughout the Hebrides.

FIGURE 7.7. Loch na Berie, causeway and surface remains.

Broch Villages?

In Orkney certain broch towers, notably Gurness and Midhowe, formed the focus for sizeable settlements clustered around their bases. This suggests that, in the Northern Isles at least, the development of the broch towers was accompanied by the emergence of several larger centres of population. These broch villages were laid out in a highly structured way with the broch tower acting as the physical and spatial centre of the settlement (Foster 1989). The social dominance of the tower's inhabitants was reinforced through the architecture of the village. In all aspects of their daily lives those living in the shadow of the tower would have tacitly acknowledged their subservience. The restrictions of access to certain areas and constraints on the freedom of individuals to move around the complex form striking parallels with the much earlier religious architecture of the Neolithic. Like the chambered tombs before them, these broch towers enabled the routine social relationships between members of the community to be constantly and silently reinforced in the normal business of daily life.

There is no sign, however, of this development in Skye or the Western Isles. Although some of the finest examples of broch architecture occur in the west, notably at Dun Carloway, Dun Troddan and Dun Telve (Figure 7.8), they remain isolated single-structure settlements. At Dun Colbost in Skye excavations in the enclosed area around the roundhouse have revealed traces of paving, drains and hearths, but no evidence of actual domestic buildings contemporary with the main structure (MacSween, pers. comm.). Excavations outwith the enclosed area produced no evidence of any activity. So although many Atlantic roundhouses had enclosures around them and possibly small external buildings, there is as yet no evidence for contemporary domestic structures. The architectural developments which enabled the construction of broch towers thus occurred in two very different contexts in Orkney and the Hebrides and we cannot, therefore, assume that their function and meaning would have been the same in both areas.

Castle or Farmhouse?

Traditionally the Atlantic roundhouses, and especially the broch towers, were seen as the defensive strongholds of a warrior aristocracy. Research in the past ten years, however, has shown that, while security was probably a consideration in the building of many broch towers, it was by no means the whole story and does not in itself provide an adequate explanation for the development of broch architecture.

Whilst their visual similarity to later castles and towerhouses immediately suggests a military function, the defensive capacities of broch towers were actually fairly limited. While promontory forts of broadly similar date took advantage of natural topography to secure quite substantial areas of ground in which stock and other possessions could be defended, broch towers would

FIGURE 7.8. Dun Telve.

have provided limited space. The single, narrow entrance might have been easy to defend but it could perhaps equally easily have been blocked up or set alight by determined attackers intent on smoking or starving out the defenders. The timber roofs would have been highly vulnerable to fire, particularly at sites like Loch na Berie where the building was overlooked from a nearby rocky hillside.

In fact the main defensive qualities of most of the Atlantic roundhouses in the Western Isles derive from their siting rather than from the structures themselves. The numerous islet-sited structures would have provided easily controlled access via their narrow causeways and many appear to have had sufficient space for stock to be held to the rear of the islet. Dun Loch an Duna at Bragar in Lewis displays several traits which recur on islet-sited roundhouses (Figure 7.9). Three separate cross-walls, possibly relating to different phases of the site's use, cut off the approach across the causeway and an enclosing wall encircles a large area of ground behind the roundhouse. At other sites, such as Dun Loch an Duin near Carloway in Lewis and Dun Thomaidh in North Uist, the causeway terminates abruptly some distance short of the islet, presumably indicating the former presence of a timber gangway that could be raised when necessary. On both of these sites the presence of the roundhouse seems almost incidental to the defensive capacities of the site. The control of access, the provision of space for stock

FIGURE 7.9. Dun Loch an Duna, Bragar.

and the separation of the vulnerable timber and thatch elements of the settlement from potential attackers were all achieved principally by careful choice of location, on islets, promontories or other topographically favoured spots.

The situation in Skye, however, appears to have been rather different. Anne MacSween's examination of the topography of the Skye roundhouses suggests that their builders often failed to maximise the defensive locations of the rocky knolls and promontories upon which most of the structures are located (1985, 13). Whilst this might, as MacSween suggests, indicate a reliance on the structures themselves for defence it is perhaps more likely to suggest that defence was a relatively minor consideration in the design and positioning of most Atlantic roundhouses.

Whatever their defensive capacities, Hebridean Atlantic roundhouses were essentially and routinely farmhouses. Excavations, principally in northern Scotland but also at sites like Dun Bharabhat, Cnip and Dun Vulan in South Uist have demonstrated that Atlantic roundhouses were permanently occupied domestic buildings often associated with enclosures and ancillary structures necessary to the farming economy of their inhabitants.

Broch Tower Reconstructions

Alan Braby's cut-away reconstruction drawing of Dun Carloway in occupation provides a starting point for a discussion of how a broch tower might have been used, based largely upon architecture and the combined evidence of numerous excavations albeit over a wide geographical area (Figure 7.10). Excavations at Dun Carloway itself, however, have been restricted to the intra-mural cells where the excavator found evidence of intermittent occupation spanning more than a millennium (Tabraham 1977).

It is certain that broch towers had multiple, superimposed timber floors. This is demonstrated very clearly at Loch na Berie where the intra-mural stairs lead to an entrance through the inner wall at the level of the scarcement ledge; a second entrance at the same level across the interior of the tower gave access to the first floor gallery and it could only have been reached by walking across the former timber floor. It appears then that at least some scarcement ledges acted as supports for a timber floor. It is less clear, however, whether the absence of a scarcement means that there was no such floor and it remains difficult to estimate the number of potential floor levels in structures like Dun Carloway. If we could make a simplistic equation between scarcements and floors then the ground floor at Carloway would have been relatively low and cramped whilst the first floor would have a vast space above it reaching up to the timber roof. This interpretation is perhaps more likely than the multiple floor scenario favoured in the reconstruction drawing.

Such a picture is consistent with research carried out recently by John Hope on the construction and use of broch towers. This research has concentrated principally on two exceptionally well-preserved broch towers situated only a few hundred yards apart in Glenelg on the mainland opposite Skye. Dun Troddan and Dun Telve (Figure 7.8) are amongst the tallest surviving examples in Scotland making their close proximity all the more surprising. Perhaps their remote setting in the narrow and economically rather unrewarding glen is the principal reason for their survival in this condition or perhaps they were always amongst the taller and most substantial of the broch towers. Principally on the basis of evidence from Dun Troddan, Hope has suggested that the ground floors of broch towers may have been less finely constructed and faced than the first floors. Together with their relative lack of height and recurrent presence of unlevelled rock outcrops protruding from their floors, this suggests that they may have been used to house stock or for storage, whilst the first floor formed the main domestic space. The height of the first floor, assuming there were no further upper floors would create an impressive domestic area on the inside, consistent

FIGURE 7.10. Dun Carloway, artist's reconstruction.

with the visually striking exterior of the tower. There would probably have been a central hearth from which smoke would have escaped into the space above and ultimately seeped out through the thatch. Voids in the inner wall let smoke and air out into the intra-mural cavity keeping it dry.

There is no reason to believe that Atlantic roundhouses had anything other than a simple conical timber roof common to timber and stone roundhouses alike. This would have provided the most stable and practical roofing form and could have been supported on an upper scarcement or the inner wall-head, protected from the wind by the lip of the outer wall.

Our knowledge of the internal furniture of the Hebridean roundhouses is hampered by a lack of excavated primary floors. It is worth noting, however, that if the first floor was commonly the main domestic space in the broch towers then excavation will be of little help. However many Atlantic roundhouses were not towers like Dun Carloway or Loch na Berie and some, like Dun Bharabhat, Cnip, had their domestic occupation focused on the ground floor. The internal area of Dun Bharabhat was very small (only some 5 m in diameter) and thus predictably there was little formal division of the interior which was dominated by a centrally placed hearth.

Domestic Activity

The paucity of excavated Atlantic roundhouse interiors in the Hebrides restricts our knowledge of the arrangement and organisation of domestic activities. As in the Neolithic and Beaker periods, pottery dominates the assemblage of finds; ceramics continue to be well-made and often richly decorated in a recurring range of incised and applied motifs. Neutron activation analysis of pottery from various Iron Age sites in the Hebrides appears to demonstrate that most of this material was made locally and seldom, if ever, traded or transported over significant distances (Topping 1986).

The profusion of decorated pottery from Hebridean Iron Age sites is in stark contrast to the situation in most of the rest of Scotland. Decorated pottery of similar styles does occur in the Northern Isles but it forms a much smaller proportion of the overall assemblages than in the west (Lane 1990). Further south, in lowland Scotland, the pottery record for the Iron Age is sparse in the extreme and vessels tend to be ruggedly functional and crudely made (Cool 1982).

Bone and antler would have remained important for a range of tools but these are rarely preserved in the acid soil conditions which pertain on most roundhouse sites. Fortunately the waterlogged deposits of the islet sites provides the opportunity for the recovery of other organic materials that do not normally survive on dryland sites. The deposits under the loch level around Dun Bharabhat for example have produced a small but tantalising assemblage of wooden artefacts including fragments of looms, opening up the potential for the analysis of an important and rarely seen aspect of Iron Age material culture (Harding, pers. comm.).

Despite the recovery of these important assemblages from recent excavations, it unfortunately remains the case that the great bulk of finds from Hebridean Atlantic roundhouses derive from early excavations where the standards of recording were very low. At Dun Fiadhairt in Skye, for example, the finds included a necklace of amber beads, a steatite armlet, quernstones, rubbing stones and worked flint as well as a substantial and varied assemblage of decorated pottery. Undoubtedly the most unusual find was a hollow terracotta object, apparently modelled to represent a bale of fleeces (Curle 1932, 289). This object has been interpreted as one of the very few items of Roman manufacture found in the Hebrides and Curle speculated that it may have originated as a votive offering to the gods, carried north by some Mediterranean trader. Its context within the site would have been of some importance both chronologically and for the interpretation of its function. Although it is reported to have been found at a low level of the interior, close to the natural rock, it is, sadly, impossible to ascertain whether it was intrusive to that level. Early excavations at Dun Beag, also on Skye, yielded a comparable assemblage of finds with the addition of a glass armlet and beads, numerous bronze objects including pins and rings, and iron objects such as a tanged knife and possible spearheads. Taken as a group however, the finds from both Dun Beag and Dun Fiadhairt typify the mixed and long-lived assemblages which can be expected to accumulate in structures that would have been foci for settlement centuries after their primary use had ended.

Prestige

Despite the architectural mastery displayed in their design and construction, Atlantic roundhouses were manifestly impractical and environmentally ill-adapted structures. Both earlier and later buildings in the Hebrides tended to share two key traits. First they were low, often achieving negative height by virtue of being dug into sand hills, middens or the ruins of old buildings. This characteristic is easily explicable in terms of the need for insulation and shelter from the perennial Hebridean winds. Secondly, they were constructed in such a way as to create a fairly minimal requirement for timber. Narrow sub-rectangular buildings or multi-cellular complexes could be roofed using small timbers; circular structures with substantial internal diameters require much more substantial lengths. Although broch towers represent a supreme achievement of drystone building it is important to remember the importance of timber in their design. Broch towers would have made serious demands on available timber supplies for their floors, internal fittings and roofs. Timber scaffolding would have been required for the construction of the upper parts of the larger towers, although the intra-mural galleries may have provided some limited access. All of this would have added further pressure to what must surely have been a scarce resource. The builders of Atlantic roundhouses seem deliberately to have consumed scarce timber for the same basic reasons of prestige and display that caused their ancestors to sacrifice fine metalwork in bogs and pools and, even earlier, to quarry, haul and erect great megaliths for constructions of no practical use.

The recent excavations at Dun Vulan in South Uist have revealed the presence of a substantial midden within the enclosure around the main structure. This midden appears to have been formed of domestic floor sweepings and contains a mix of debris similar to that which might be expected within the roundhouse floor. What is unusual about this find, however, is that the rich and fertile midden dump has been allowed to accumulate around the settlement rather than being spread as fertiliser across the surrounding fields. The excavator of Dun Vulan, Mike Parker-Pearson, has suggested that the midden may have been a potent symbol of fertility and may in itself have constituted a status symbol (pers. comm.). Thus the presence of substantial unused midden around the settlement may have been another means by which the inhabitants displayed their affluence and power.

Several aspects of the Atlantic roundhouse tradition, then, suggest that its development was based around the desire to demonstrate the power of the inhabitants, even if the scale and nature of that power varied radically. Atlantic roundhouses developed in complexity over time, with successive innovations enabling the construction of ever taller and more massive structures. Although we regard many of the brochs as towers, we should remember that none of them is taller than its diameter; surely a pre-requisite for the use of the term. The impression of great height is achieved by the tapering of the walls; these structures were clearly built to impress.

Hierarchy or Community?

If we accept that a large part of the reason for the construction of Atlantic roundhouses involved prestige and the display of power it still remains open to question which members of society were engaged in this process. Traditionally it had been thought that brochs were the homes of an elite group, analogous to the motte and bailey castles of the incoming Anglo-Normans in the medieval period on the mainland. This view was understandable in a context where only a select few structures were defined as 'true' brochs, the rest being sorry imitations or degenerate, late versions.

Study of the density and distributions of Atlantic roundhouses in certain parts of northern and western Scotland has led to a questioning of this traditional view. The number of Atlantic roundhouses on Barra, for example, is far larger than could be sustained by any likely Iron Age population level if their occupation was restricted to the upper echelons of society (Figure 7.11, Armit 1988, 1992) because these buildings are spread fairly evenly across the most environmentally favoured parts of the island; a fact which suggests that they were all broadly contemporary. In North Uist there were many more Atlantic roundhouses than there were tacksmen in the post-medieval period. This suggests that, if population levels were broadly similar, Atlantic roundhouse construction extended far lower down the social ladder than the level of minor aristocracy and was probably more likely to represent something approximating to the level of tenant farmer. Such comparisons are of course very crude, but they do demonstrate that, unless the Iron Age populations of the Western Isles were vastly in excess of eighteenth century levels, Atlantic roundhouses cannot have been confined to the ruling elite. It is much more likely that they formed the standard unit of settlement throughout much of the region and were inhabited by a variety of social

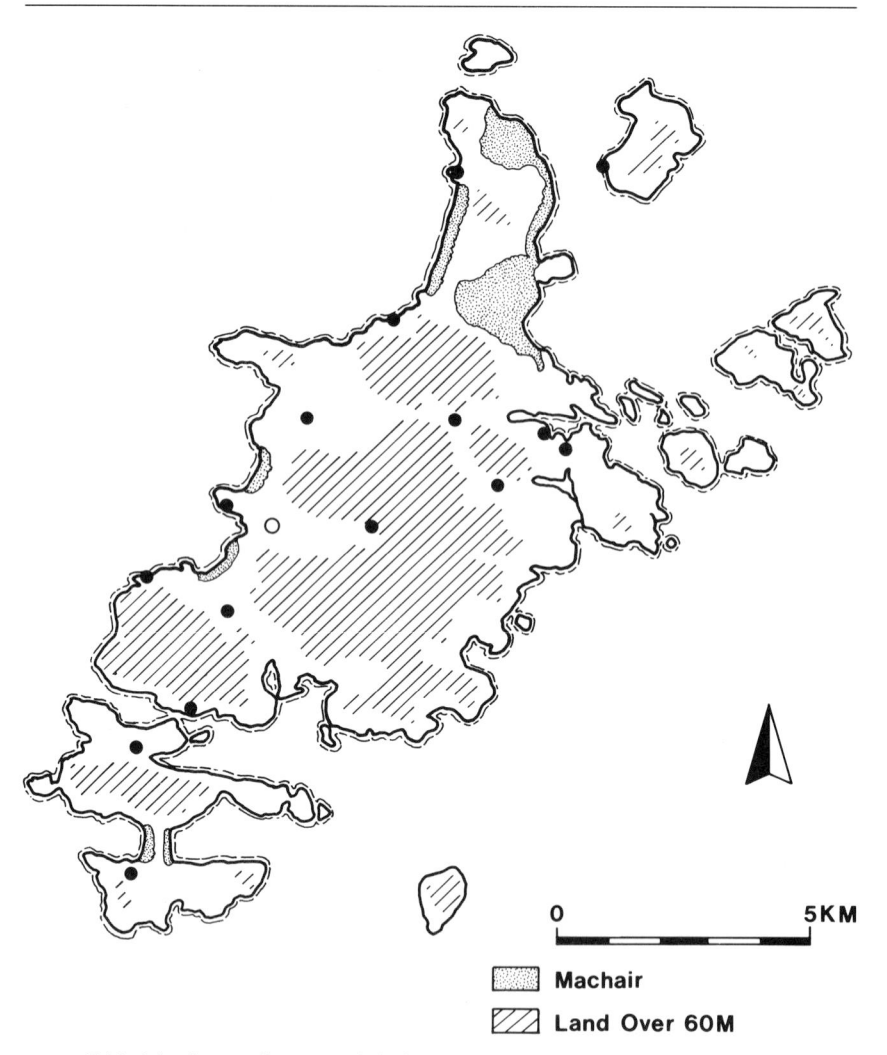

FIGURE 7.11. Atlantic roundhouses and the landscape, Barra.

levels from tribal chief down to modest farming families. This interpretation fits the evidence for the tremendous range in scale and quality of the structures themselves, perhaps most clearly demonstrated in the Bhaltos peninsula of Lewis where Dun Bharabhat and the Loch na Berie broch tower lie only 500 m apart and represent almost polar opposites in terms of size and quality of construction.

Atlantic roundhouses in the Hebrides seem, then, to have been built to express the local dominance over land and resources of the individual community. In Orkney, as we have seen, a pattern developed of increasing nucleation of settlement and centralisation of power which was expressed in the elaboration of the broch tower. Fewer but larger broch settlements emerged as Orcadian elites became more powerful. In the west, though, power over people does not seem to have been expressed through monumental domestic architecture. Undoubtedly there were significant differences in status among communities within the islands, but these must have found other modes of expression. The Hebridean Atlantic roundhouses were built by individual small communities. Even the tiny and currently uninhabited islands south of Barra supported populations that imprinted themselves upon the land by the construction of their own roundhouses. The roundhouse expressed the self-sufficiency of the community, its control of its small pocket of land and its permanence in the face of a hostile environment. Thus there never developed the spatial hierarchies that can be seen so clearly in the arrangement of subsidiary buildings around the central broch towers of the north.

Contemporary Structures?

The density of Atlantic roundhouses throughout the Hebrides strongly suggests that they represented a standard settlement form of the later centuries BC. MacSween, however, has identified two groups of structures in Skye – dun enclosures and promontory forts – that may relate to the later prehistoric period and have an uncertain chronological and functional relationship to the Atlantic roundhouses (1985). Promontory forts are also found widely in the Western Isles and numerous islet enclosures may parallel the dun enclosures of Skye. With the exception of a few cases, however, as at Barra Head Lighthouse, where these structures incorporate galleries or intra-mural cells, there is seldom any evidence to attribute even a broad date and there is little reason to assume that they represent any unitary class of monument, possibly incorporating medieval and Norse as well as perhaps pre-Iron Age sites amongst their number.

Recently an entirely new class of structure has been added to the roster of potential Atlantic roundhouse contemporaries, at least in Skye. Excavations by Roger Miket at the site of Tungadale revealed a substantial rectilinear building with an entrance in its short, east end (information from Roger Miket, Figure 7.12). This building was partially terraced into a hillside and formed of thick, stone-lined earthen walls. The spacious interior was dominated by a centrally placed hearth which had been replaced on several occasions. The most intriguing feature was the presence of a narrow souterrain, or underground passage, stone-lined and lintelled, leading off from the interior within the thickness of the wall. In the later stages of occupation the floor level inside the building had built up and the entrance to the souterrain had been cleared out and revetted with stone to allow the opening of a timber door. This lowered entrance is important because it means that the souterrain entrance could not have been hidden by placing timber furniture or

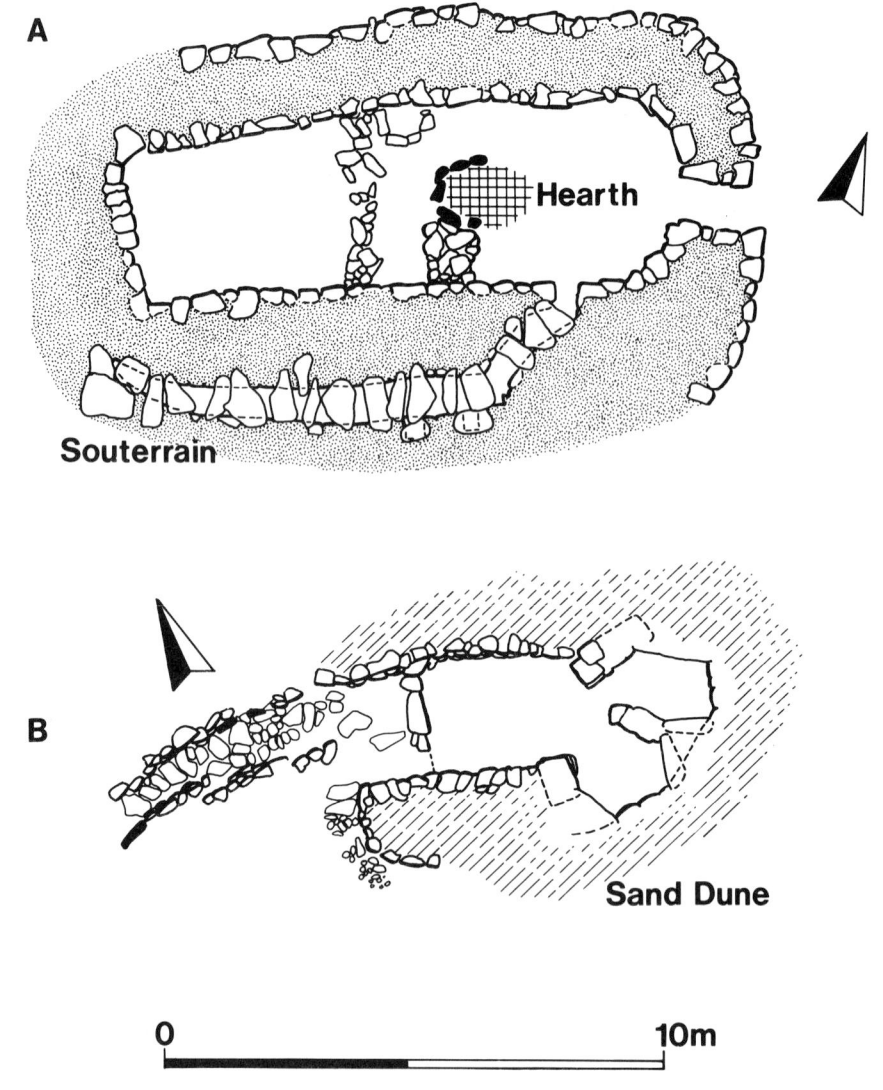

FIGURE 7.12. Rectilinear structures (a) an Iron Age building and souterrain at Tungadale, Skye; (b) the final phase structure at Cnip, Lewis.

other obstacles in front of it. This appears to rule out one traditional interpretation of such features: that they were for temporary refuge. Another more favoured explanation has been that souterrains were for the storage of foodstuffs. This, too, is unlikely in the case of Tungadale, as the souterrain was subject to water run-off from the hillside and required a drain in its floor to remove water. In this respect the Tungadale souterrain is unlike those larger semi-subterranean structures in eastern Scotland which date to a somewhat later period and were almost certainly used for the large-scale storage of grain.

Since the excavation, Miket has identified other structures associated with souterrains throughout Skye which may be of similar date and type. Radiocarbon dates suggest that the Tungadale building dates to around the third century BC, in the period when Atlantic roundhouses were almost certainly still being built. The relationship between these two markedly different architectural traditions must form an important subject for future research in Skye.

Hebridean Iron Age Economies

The Impact of Iron

The Atlantic roundhouse phenomenon has tended to attract the attention of archaeologists away from other aspects of the Hebridean Iron Age. This was, however, a time when important economic developments took place, not least of which was the arrival of iron itself. The adoption of iron, in preference to bronze, as the favoured material for tools and weapons happened at different times across northern and western Europe in the first half of the first millennium BC. The date of its first arrival in any area is notoriously difficult to assess because iron survives much less well on archaeological sites than either stone or bronze. In Orkney, for example, the first use of iron can be deduced by the disappearance of stone agricultural implements rather than by the appearance of actual iron implements.

The broch builders certainly used iron tools, although only rarely do these survive as anything more than depressing clusters of corrosion. Iron tools enabled more efficient agriculture and the raw materials were easier to obtain than those of bronze, although the latter material continued to be extensively worked for the production of decorative items. The change in metal-working technology, however, does not seem to have been as revolutionary as was once thought, when the introduction of iron was linked to the coming of new Celtic peoples with an accompanying package of cultural and social changes.

Environmental Stress

The period during which the Atlantic roundhouses originated appears to have been one of serious environmental stress throughout northern and western Scotland. The impact of climatic deterioration was felt, however, by prehistoric Scottish farmers several centuries before the appearance of monumental architecture. Recent work near Lairg in Sutherland, for example, has suggested that Later Bronze Age farmers were highly vulnerable even to relatively minor environmental changes (MacCullagh 1991), and that they retreated from the marginal uplands of Sutherland from the end of the second millennium BC and through the following millennium.

This work supports the conclusions drawn from earlier excavations in Sutherland at the hut circle complex of Kilphedir (Fairhurst and Taylor 1970).

It is notoriously difficult to make generalisations on the nature and impact of environmental deterioration from one area to another, even within Atlantic Scotland. Nonetheless there are indications from the settlement distributions in the Hebrides that a parallel process of settlement contraction may have occurred. The clearest evidence for this comes from North Uist where Atlantic roundhouse settlement is largely confined to the coastal belt, albeit off the machair, whilst apparently earlier, non-monumental settlement sites occur widely across the bleak interior of the island (Armit 1992). This pattern may reflect the combined effects of climatic change and human interference with the natural soils and vegetation cover conspiring to render much of the island useless for all but rough grazing and as a reservoir of peat. The coastal belt with its wider range of resources, terrestrial, marine and lacustrine, would thus have become the focus of island settlement as it has remained ever since. Such a process of settlement contraction would have serious social implications and, depending on its duration, may even have precipitated crises over the control of land and other resources. Such a background of land pressure and settlement dislocation may have promoted the concern with territoriality that led to the construction of the Atlantic roundhouses as symbols of the local dominance and legitimacy of established Hebridean farming communities.

Subsistence

Despite these indications of the broad-scale background to Iron Age Hebridean economies, it remains difficult to be specific about actual subsistence practices on Atlantic roundhouse settlements. The balance between arable and pastoral farming and the relative importance of fishing and fowling will have depended, as ever, on highly specific local conditions. The lack of substantial recent excavations on Hebridean Atlantic roundhouse sites together with the generally poor quality of bone preservation prevents any detailed discussion of the subsistence economy of these sites. The material recovered from older excavations is generally too poorly provenanced to address modern research questions. A reasonable bone assemblage was recovered from Dun Cuier in Barra, for example (Young 1955), including red deer, grey seal, pony and otter as well as the expected range of domesticated cattle, sheep and pig. Bird bones comprised principally shag and cormorant whilst several species of fish were represented including wrasse, black bream, cod, ling and saithe. Reinterpretation of this site, however, has demonstrated that its occupation stretched from at least the later part of first millennium BC when the roundhouse was built, until the immediately pre-Norse period when a secondary building housed the inhabitants within the ruins of the former structure. The bone assemblage, as with other finds from the site, cannot be attributed to any particular period of occupation and may mask a range of chronological changes. Similar problems pertain to the quernstones found at many sites and it seldom possible to make any specific statements concerning the subsistence economies of any of the Hebridean roundhouse sites in their primary periods of occupation.

Much new information may, however, come from the post-excavation work on the material from Dun Vulan in South Uist. Most of this assemblage derives from the enclosure around the complex roundhouse where excavations were concentrated. Preliminary indications suggest that a substantial and representative assemblage of both animal and plant remains may repay detailed analysis. Initial reports suggest that sheep dominate the faunal assemblage, with a substantial component of cattle and an unexpectedly high proportion of pig (Parker-Pearson 1992). As might be expected, numerous species of bird and fish are also represented. Hulled barley seems to have been the dominant crop with some wheat, oats and possibly rye. The occurrence of carbonised grain at this and other sites, and the ubiquity of saddle and later rotary querns from Iron Age sites demonstrates the existence of an arable component within the economies of the islands.

Beyond the Brochs

At some time around the turn of the millennium, the people of the Western Isles stopped building Atlantic roundhouses. We do not know when the last broch tower was built or how long occupation continued in the unaltered towers. What is clear is that in the last century BC, and certainly from the first century AD, a new form of settlement was becoming dominant in the islands. This new structural form, the wheelhouse, forms a sharp contrast to the broch towers, but it was still, in a different way, monumental and architecturally accomplished.

8 Wheelhouses

In the last centuries BC an entirely new and highly distinctive form of architecture appeared in the Hebrides. Wheelhouses are so-called because of their peculiar ground plan where the stone piers radiating from the central hub of the circular drystone building resemble the spokes of a wheel (Figure 8.1). These structures are found widely throughout the Western Isles but, oddly, none have been found in Skye or the Small Isles (Figure 8.2). This absence does not result from a lack of fieldwork since intensive survey carried out in Skye over the past few years has failed to produce any hints of wheelhouse architecture (Miket, pers. comm.). This highly specific distribution is reflected in the Northern Isles where wheelhouses identical in construction to the Western Isles examples have been identified in Shetland but not in Orkney despite the intensity of archaeological activity there over more than a century.

BUILDING A WHEELHOUSE

The dominance of the Atlantic roundhouses in the landscapes of northern and western Scotland has tended to over-shadow the wheelhouse architectural tradition. Nonetheless, as recent excavations have confirmed, wheelhouse architecture showed a sophistication and mastery of drystone building matching that of the more obviously monumental broch towers. The excavation in 1988 of a wheelhouse settlement at Cnip in the Bhaltos peninsula of Lewis, uncovered the remains of a wheelhouse with its roofing partially intact whilst an adjacent, apparently unfinished, wheelhouse provided information on the processes of construction. A series of reconstruction drawings by Alan Braby based on the excavated evidence from Cnip show the main stages of wheelhouse construction (Figure 8.3). These drawings compress

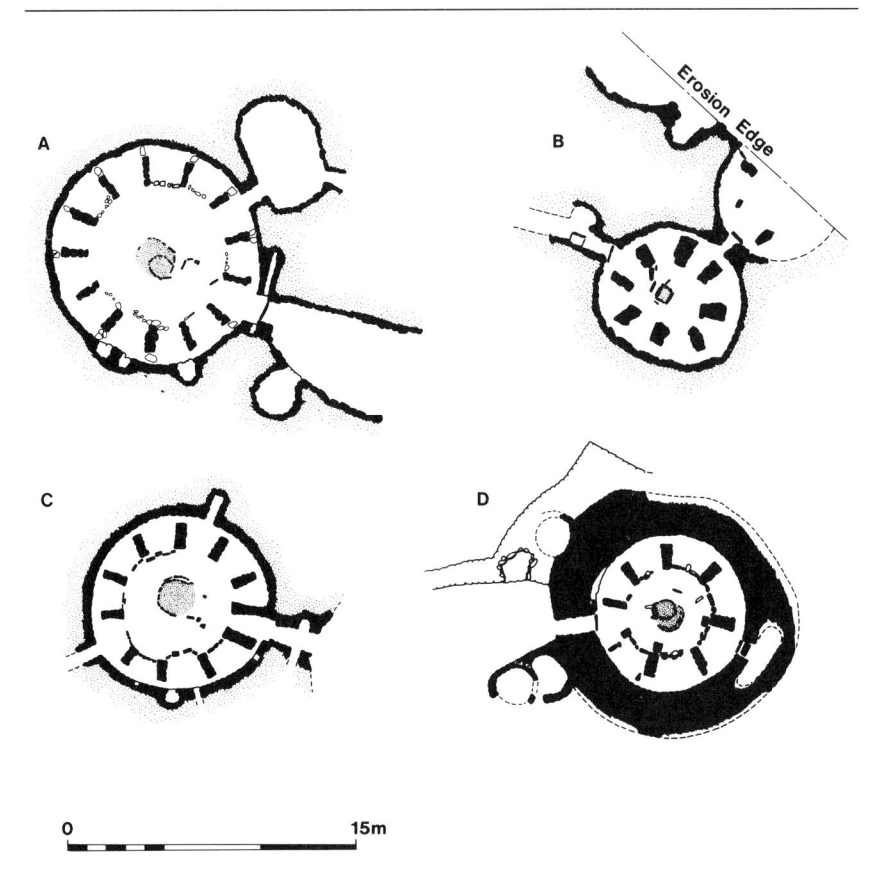

FIGURE 8.1. Wheelhouse plans from the Western Isles: (a) Sollas, North Uist; (b) Cnip, Lewis; (c) Kilpheder, South Uist; (d) Clettraval, North Uist.

together several activities that would probably have been sequential but they are indicative of the main building stages.

The first stage in the process was the excavation of a large circular pit in the natural sand dunes of Traigh Cnip, along with a linear trench which was to become the entrance passage and which would provide access during construction. This circular pit was cut to the exact size required for the wheelhouse wall which was backed directly into the natural sand. Once the pit was excavated it would have been essential to put the lower drystone wall courses in place quickly, since the pit was cut vertically up to shoulder height. Any delay would have led to the collapse of the trench sides so we must conclude that stone was stacked ready for use in the pit as its edges were cut back. The unfinished wheelhouse at Cnip contained stacks of building stone in its entrance passage that appeared to have been in place ready for construction.

The walls of the wheelhouse were a single stone thick, forming a simple skin of masonry to revet the sand. Once they were built to around shoulder

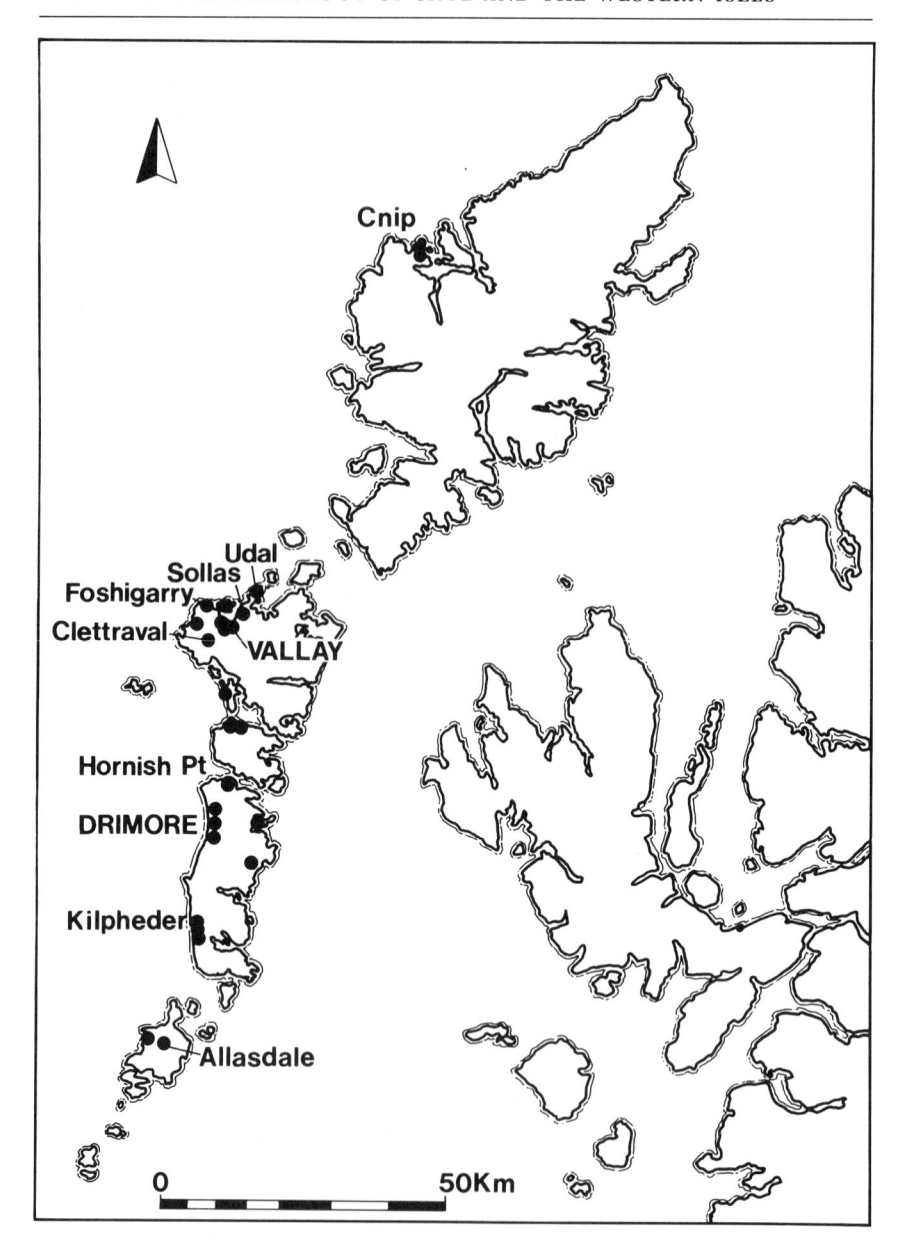

FIGURE 8.2. Distribution of wheelhouses in the Western Isles.

height and the edges of the pit were thus stabilised, the lower courses of the stone piers were put in place. At Cnip these were not bonded into the outer wall but separated by an intervening gap or aisle. At some other wheelhouses, for example Foshigarry A and Bac Mhic Connain in North Uist, the piers were bonded in and thus appear to have been built up with the outer wall. This may have been designed to give added stability since the 'aisled' wheelhouses like Cnip appear to have suffered some structural instability and the aisles were often later blocked up with stone to prevent complete collapse. Indeed at Foshigarry and at Jarlshof in Shetland there appears to have been a structural development whereby the later wheelhouses on each site had bonded piers.

As the wall was built up a series of votive offerings was placed behind it. At Cnip these included the head of a great auk, articulated cattle bones and a complete pottery vessel. At Sollas in North Uist numerous votive pits were excavated into the floor of the wheelhouse, some of them possibly at the stage of its construction (Campbell 1991). The contents of these votive pits and their possible meanings are discussed in more detail below but, together with the evidence from Cnip, there is a strong suggestion that at least some offerings were connected with the foundation of the new dwelling. The primary floors levels of the main wheelhouse at Cnip were not excavated so we cannot be sure whether similar pits were dug into the floors there.

Once the walls and piers were at the same height, large lintels were used to bond them together and provide the base for the corbelled stone roofs of the cells. The piers widened as they rose and each course of walling in the upper parts of the cells overlapped the one below to create a high domed roof over each cell. Thus each cell was individually corbelled, forming a solid ring of masonry around the still open central area. At Cnip, two of these cells survived with their corbelling almost intact, thus confirming the use of a technique suspected from earlier excavations. The entrance passage was probably lintelled although no direct evidence for this was preserved at Cnip. The upper courses of walling were packed against the sand dune with midden material, possibly brought from an older settlement nearby.

Once the ring of roofed cells was in place, the timber roof over the central area could be constructed. At Cnip this central area measured only some 4 m across and could thus have been roofed using fairly short timbers forming a conical frame resting at 45° on the cell roofs. The largest recorded central space of any wheelhouse is that at Sollas which measured some 7 m across and, even this, could easily have been roofed in the same way. A thatch, probably of heather, or perhaps of marram grass collected from the surrounding dunes, would have covered this timber structure, held in place by ropes weighted with stones. This central thatched roof would have drained over the individual roofs of the ring of cells which would each have been covered by a layer of turfs and possibly sealed with clay as was the case with the wallheads of more recent blackhouses in the Hebrides. Rainwater would thus have been channelled into the surrounding sand dune.

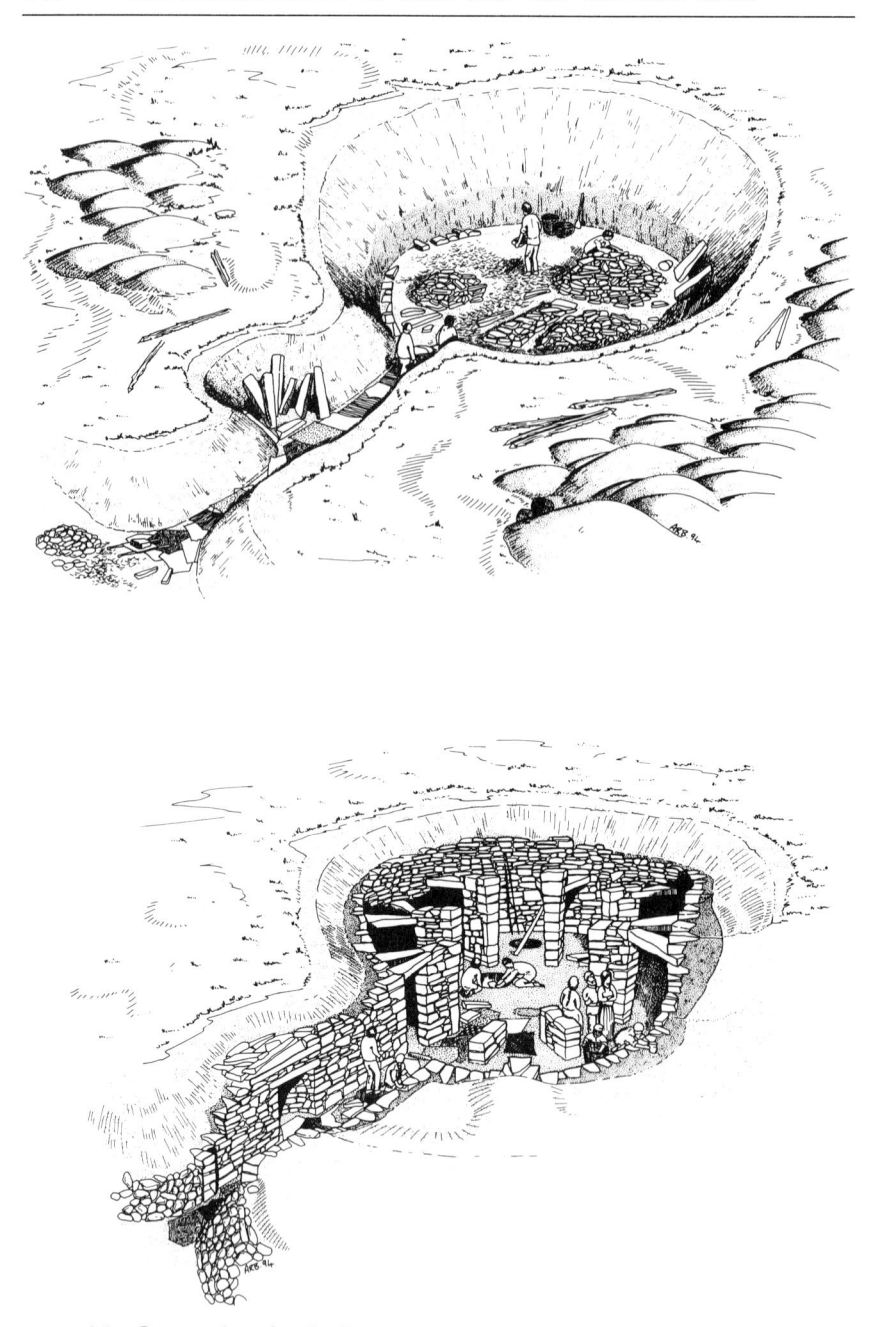

FIGURE 8.3a. Construction of a wheelhouse, 1.

WHEELHOUSES

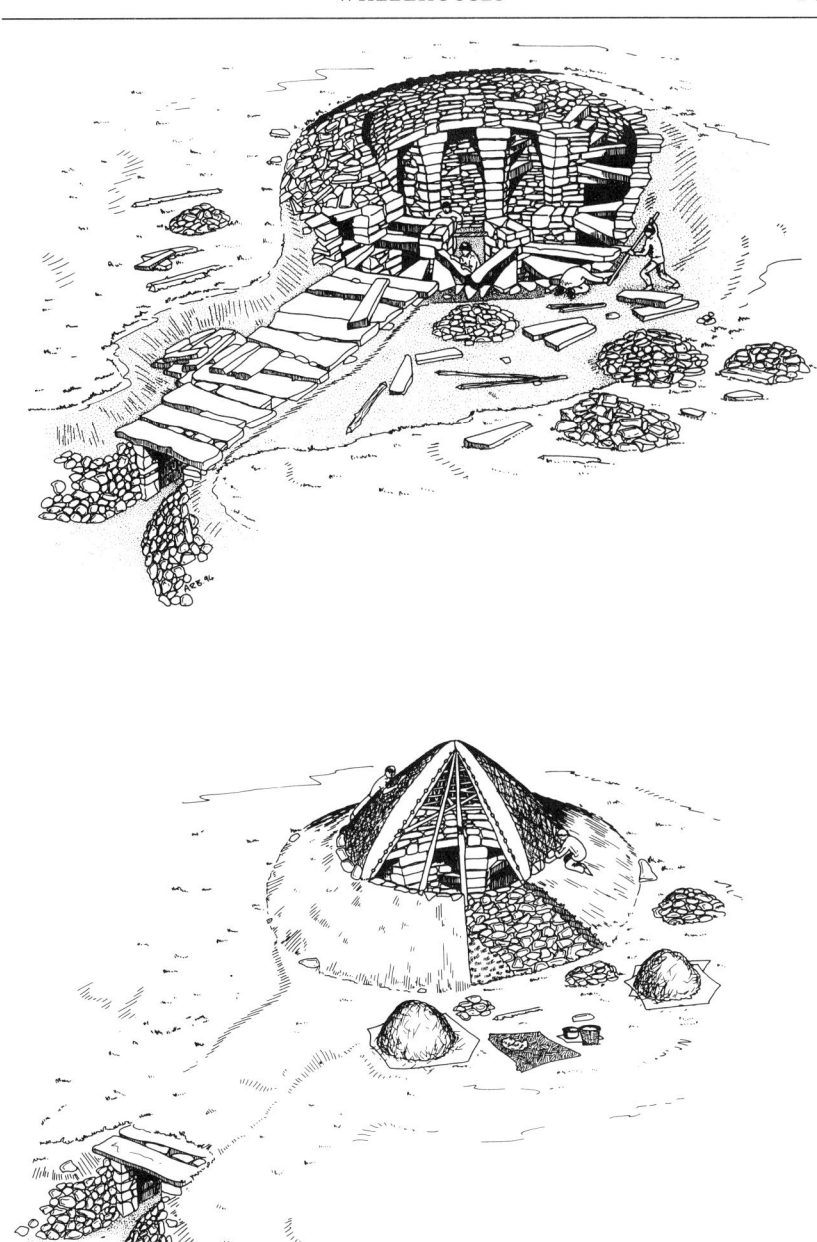

FIGURE 8.3b. Construction of a wheelhouse, 2.

FIGURE 8.4. Detail of stone pier and aisle in the Cnip wheelhouse.

The main wheelhouse at Cnip appears to have been typical of Hebridean wheelhouses in general although there were local variations. The occurrence of bonded piers has already been mentioned, and this may have been a structural development designed to stabilise the building. If, however, the aisles connecting the cells were used for access or communication, this development would have greatly affected the way in which space was used within the buildings, necessitating that all communication pass through the central space. At wheelhouses like Cnip, however, the aisles appear to have been largely blocked with domestic debris before they became unstable and thus it may be that the aisles were primarily a structural feature rather than a formal means of access between cells.

The majority of excavated Hebridean wheelhouses are found on the machair and are revetted into sand dunes or areas of midden. Others are set into the ruins of earlier Atlantic roundhouses, as appears to be the case with some of the Vallay sites in North Uist excavated by Erskine Beveridge, e.g. Garry Iochdrach and Cnoc a Comhdhalach (Armit 1992, Chap. 6). A few appear to have been built as *de novo* free-standing structures away from the coastal belt as at Allasdale in Barra (Young 1952). Clettraval in North Uist was partially free-standing and partially quarried into the remains of the Neolithic chambered tomb on the site (Scott 1948). In all cases the basic building techniques were apparently the same. The constructional method dictated a distinct and recurrent floor plan and restricted the possibility of variation in the size or arrangement of cells. Thus wheelhouse architecture can be readily identified from the uniformity of its ground plan in structures where the survival of the superstructure is limited.

In terms of their suitability for the Hebridean environment wheelhouses, had several advantages over Atlantic roundhouses. Their tendency to be dug into sand-hills or ruined buildings would have provided insulation and warmth. Their low roofs would have suffered much less from the ravages of the wind than those of the broch towers. The small central spaces over which the timber roof sat meant that small timbers would suffice for construction rather than the substantial lengths that must have been required to roof and floor the broch towers. Nonetheless, wheelhouses did not represent an abandonment of the tradition of monumental domestic architecture. Even the Cnip wheelhouse, which was one of the smallest of the excavated examples, was a monumental structure although this monumentality was expressed in an entirely different way to that of broch architecture. From the outside the wheelhouse would have been an unimposing bulge in the sand dune with only a low conical roof projecting above the surface. Yet inside the arches of the cells would have risen and widened impressively from the sand floor whilst the apex of the central roof would have been some 6 m above the central hearth. The nature of wheelhouse architecture dictates that there was no possibility of multiple floors so we must imagine that this substantial space would have been clear up to the roof. The wheelhouse, despite its advantages over Atlantic roundhouses in terms of design and economy of timber use, was by no means a modest utilitarian building.

WHEELHOUSE SETTLEMENT IN THE WESTERN ISLES

The most detailed excavation of the primary floor levels of a wheelhouse yet to be published was that at Sollas in North Uist, excavated in the 1950s by R. J. Atkinson and published recently by Euan Campbell (1991). The Sollas wheelhouse was one of a number of sites excavated in North and South Uist ahead of the, then imminent, construction of the Ministry of Defence's Hebridean rocket range and associated facilities. Although the Sollas wheelhouse had been previously excavated by Beveridge (published in his 1911 volume under its alternative name Machair Leathann) it was soon found that he had not penetrated the lowest layers of occupation material and a wealth of deposits remained to be excavated. At various times during the occupation of the site the wheelhouse had been re-floored with clean machair sand, sealing two accumulations of debris formed during occupation along with associated stone furniture. Although these accumulations are not likely to be absolutely primary to the use of the wheelhouse as a monumental building (see below) they do correspond to a period when the spatial configuration of the wheelhouse remained in use.

The interior of the Sollas wheelhouse was dominated by a large central hearth, replaced on at least one occasion, suggesting that the central area was the main communal focus of the house, where cooking was carried out (Campbell 1991). A stone-lined tank adjacent to the hearth may also have been associated with cooking or storage. There were clear differences between the surrounding bays in terms of the nature of the artefactual remains and deposits found within them. It has often been suggested that the bays served a range of functions including storage, sleeping accommodation and working areas and this sort of division might help explain the variety of archaeological remains in each. Cell 6 at Sollas, for example, was the only one to contain paving and also contained two shelves, or 'aumbries' built into the wall. The same cell (in relation to the entrance) at the South Uist wheelhouse of Kilpheder has a similar arrangement suggesting again a specialised function (ibid., 126). It appears that similar structuring principles governed the use of space in quite widely separate structures.

More detailed analysis of primary wheelhouse floors excavated under modern conditions may yet enable us to understand the specific functions of the wheelhouse bays and begin to approach these underlying structural principles. There may have been, for example, important divisions between back and front, right and left, etc. which were associated with different members of the community and with different activities, as has long been recognised in the ethnographic record (c.f. discussion in Parker-Pearson 1994).

Unlike the Atlantic roundhouses where space could be divided vertically between floors used for different functions, wheelhouse settlements had to be more horizontally organised if they were to maintain a similar range of differentiated spaces for various domestic activities. Most of the Hebridean wheelhouses, therefore, had one or more subsidiary cells leading off from the main structure. At Sollas this took the form of a fairly substantial oval cell with little evidence for its original function. At Cnip the unfinished wheelhouse 2 seems to have become a subsidiary structure leading off the main wheelhouse and possibly used for storage. In no case, however, is there solid evidence for the co-existence of two or more wheelhouses. At Foshigarry three wheelhouses lie closely clustered but appear to have been occupied sequentially, each new building utilising its predecessor as a yard or outbuilding (Armit 1992, Chap. 6). The wheelhouses appear to have carried on the Hebridean Atlantic roundhouse tradition of single-structure settlements, albeit with a similar range of outbuildings and working areas.

This 'solitary homestead' pattern is perhaps best exemplified by the two excavated inland wheelhouses at Allasdale in Barra and Clettraval in North

Uist (Young 1952; Scott 1948). In both cases the wheelhouses occur within small enclosures containing outbuildings as well as the expected subsidiary cells attached to the wheelhouses themselves. The Allasdale example also had a 9 m long souterrain, or semi-subterranean passage, leading off the wheelhouse. It may be of course that these settlements are multi-period accretions where subsequent settlement has usurped formerly isolated wheelhouse sites; the Hebridean tradition of building on or next to a handy stone source would of course apply here. Alternatively, it may be the case that these represented unitary wheelhouse farmsteads. The survival of such complexes would, after all, be more likely in the inland zone than on the intensively occupied machair. Only modern excavation of one of the inland examples is likely to resolve this question.

Sollas and Cnip; Dating the Wheelhouse Period

The dating of wheelhouses has undergone a significant change in recent years particularly with the realisation of the complexity and longevity of many wheelhouse sites and with the availability of radiocarbon dates from the excavations at Sollas and Cnip. Traditionally wheelhouses have tended to be dated on the basis of metalwork or artefacts with Roman associations found in early excavations. The mid-first millennium AD date commonly ascribed to wheelhouses had its roots in Stevenson's seminal paper of 1955 in which he discussed the typological affiliations of metalwork, particularly pins, from Hebridean sites. Much of this material, however, has been shown to have a highly uncertain relationship with the wheelhouses themselves and may derive from substantially later occupation on the sites (c.f. Armit 1992, 69). A sherd of Roman period Samian Ware from the wheelhouse at Bac Mhic Connain in North Uist, for example, has no recorded context and may relate to any part of a lengthy sequence of building and occupation. Similar problems occur with the glass beads and bone objects used to date these structures prior to the availability of radiocarbon dates.

A series of radiocarbon dates from Sollas wheelhouse have recently been used to argue for the construction of the site in the late first to early third centuries AD. Closer inspection of the contexts from which these dates derive, however, suggests that they may relate to the subsequent use of the wheelhouse rather than to its construction. Recent work on the nature of 'occupation' deposits within excavated buildings has cast some doubt on their common interpretation as the material casually discarded during the main period of occupation (Matthews, 1993). Instead it has been suggested that such accumulations commonly relate to the final phases of a building's use once its original domestic function has gone or once it is in decline. It is clear from excavations at Cnip that even the small cellular buildings that were inhabited after the wheelhouse had gone out of use were periodically scoured of floor deposits and restored to their clean sand floor (Armit 1988b). Given the investment of human and material resources in the construction of a deliberately monumental building it seems implausible that the structure would be allowed to fill up with domestic refuse. The idea of the wheelhouse inhabitants wading around in an unctuous ankle-deep soup of domestic waste does not sit easily with the care and organisation given to the construction of the home in the Hebridean Iron Age. Thus, at Sollas, it would be surprising if any of the excavated 'occupation' deposits relate to the primary use of the structure. Campbell identified a stratigraphic sequence in the ritual pits as a result of which he placed a number of large pits in the cells and the periphery of the central area in the earliest period of construction. The radiocarbon dates, however, were obtained exclusively from secondary pits dug later and commonly cutting into the upper fills of these larger pits. Since Campbell believed that all of the pits related to one basic period of ritual deposition this was not considered a problem. Given, however, that floor deposits would have been regularly scoured down to clean sand, these pits could have been excavated and ritual deposits placed within them at any time during the use of the building in its earliest, monumental form. Subsequently material was deposited within the structure, forming layers of occupation deposits and instead of being scoured down to sand these were covered over at least twice with clean sand from the machair. The same process was observed in the later phases at Cnip and seems a much more likely explanation for the occurrence of sand layers within the building than Campbell's suggestion, following Atkinson, that they represented accumulations of blown sand. Thus none of the Sollas dates seems likely to relate to the construction of the wheelhouse or to its earliest phase but rather to the period at which its original monumental function went into decline. This decline would then date to the period from the late first to early third centuries AD, most probably occurring in the second century with wheelhouse construction occurring perhaps decades or even centuries prior to this date.

The eighteen radiocarbon dates obtained from the excavations at Cnip provide a remarkably coherent series for the development of the settlement, although the dates for the construction and earliest occupation of the site remain somewhat ambiguous. A series of dates from Phase 2 of the occupation show that the wheelhouse had started to decay and lose its original form through a series of rebuildings in the mid–late first century AD. Occupation continued at least until the second century and possibly slightly later (these reoccupation phases are discussed in more detail in Chapter 9). These dates all derive from animal bone in the accumulating floor deposits, relatively late in the lifespan of the settlement. The range of dates for Phase 1, when the wheelhouse was occupied in its original form, is considerably wider, ranging from the mid-first millennium BC until the late first century AD. Articulated cattle bone placed as a votive deposit behind the wall of wheelhouse 2 ought to date the construction of the complex fairly accurately and this gave a date centred in the fifth century BC, suggesting that there is very little likelihood that the building was constructed later than the third century BC.

The Cnip dates provide an internally consistent series, particularly for the latter stages of the site's occupation. Nonetheless, the dates for construction and early occupation are considerably earlier than might have been expected, placing the building of the wheelhouse in the period when complex Atlantic roundhouses were being constructed. More dated sequences will be required, particularly from the construction and earliest occupation deposits of wheelhouses before we can establish securely the period at which this structural type emerged. The selection of material from contexts appropriate to provide these dates will be crucial, and should concentrate on clearly defined foundation deposits and material from primary pits, where these can be securely identified.

There are a few other indications of the chronology of wheelhouse construction and abandonment from artefacts found in earlier excavations in contexts that can be fairly securely interpreted. At Kilpheder and A' Cheardach Mhor both in South Uist, for example, rotary quern fragments had been built into the walls of the wheelhouses suggesting construction dates no earlier than the last two centuries BC. At Foshigarry in North Uist, by contrast, a saddle quern was recovered from wheelhouse C, the earliest wheelhouse on the site, suggesting that it may have had an earlier foundation (Beveridge 1930, c.f. Armit 1992, 69). A Romano–British brooch was found in an 'aumbrey' or shelf in the Kilpheder wheelhouse suggesting that the abandonment of this building did not occur before the mid or late second century AD (the date being based on a similar brooch from the Roman fort at Newstead, Collingwood 1953, 125).

Another series of radiocarbon dates comes from the excavation of a radially partitioned structure at Hornish Point in South Uist (Barber et al., 1989). This structure appears to have been a small circular domestic building with a series of radial partitions suggesting the same basic division of internal space as is seen in wheelhouses. Its irregular plan, however, demonstrated that it is most unlikely to have been a wheelhouse in the architectural sense, i.e. it would not have been a monumental building with a ring of indvidually corbelled bays. Clearly, though, it is a related type in terms of the division of domestic space. The dates from this building suggest that it was constructed in the fourth or fifth centuries BC (ibid.) but there are, potentially serious, distortions in this picture relating to the use of sea-shell as the sample material for dating. Full publication of these dates will have to be awaited before their significance can be properly judged and for this reason they have not been incorporated into the Appendix.

Dating the emergence of wheelhouse architecture thus remains somewhat problematic, although dates for the demise of the tradition are becoming fairly clear. At Cnip the main wheelhouse was losing its monumental stature by the latter part of the first century AD or perhaps a little earlier. At Sollas the same process seems to have occurred with the building most likely going out of use in the second century AD. Secondary structures appear to have been built over a wheelhouse at the Udal again in the first century AD (Crawford n.d., 9). A pattern is thus emerging for the decline of wheelhouse architecture, although not necessarily the abandonment of the sites, in the first two centuries AD and it is not clear whether any wheelhouses were being built as late as the first century AD.

Economy

Subsistence

The clearest picture of the subsistence economy of a wheelhouse site to emerge so far is that from Cnip although, as elsewhere, evidence for animal husbandry is far more easily attained than information on agricultural practices. As with most machair sites, animal bone was remarkably well preserved at Cnip and was present in sufficient quantities to enable some detailed discussion of the economy of the site's inhabitants, giving a much fuller picture than is currently possible for the earlier Atlantic roundhouse settlements.

The most striking feature of the Cnip bone assemblage was the extremely high proportion of red deer which equalled cattle and sheep in quantity (McCormick 1991). This contrasts with the situation in the Uists where red deer rarely feature in wheelhouse bone assemblages. The preliminary analysis of bone from the later reoccupation of the nearby Loch na Berie broch tower in the mid–late first millennium AD seems to indicate a similar dependence on deer (Harding, pers. comm.). The reason for this imbalance may lie in the proximity of Cnip to extensive areas of upland in the west of Lewis where red deer herds may have survived much longer than in the relatively crowded and intensively exploited Uists. There is some evidence, however, that the situation may not have been so simple and environmentally determined. At Dun Mor Vaul on Tiree, in the southern Hebrides, there was also a high proportion of red deer in the bone assemblage throughout most of the site's use despite the unsuitability of the island for the co-existence of human populations and wild deer herds. McCormick has suggested that the combined evidence from Cnip and Dun Mor Vaul indicates that certain communities in the Hebrides were treating red deer almost as a domesticated animal and using careful 'farm' management of herds to conserve and protect the resource (ibid.). Animals, when culled, tended to be semi-mature and at their fastest period of growth, again suggesting conscious management of deer herds. The collection of antler, as a vital raw material for toolmaking appears to have been conducted as a separate exercise from hunting or culling since most of the antlers used had been shed. It has also been suggested that deer, like domesticated animals, may well have been introduced into these islands by humans although this would, of course, have occurred long before the Iron Age and will be virtually impossible to demonstrate archaeologically (Serjeantson 1990, McCormick 1991). The Cnip deer were exceptionally small in stature, far smaller than the Mesolithic Hebridean deer from Oronsay, Iron Age deer from Howe in Orkney, or Early Historic assemblages from sites like Edinburgh Castle or even Iona.

Cattle and sheep were the principal conventional domesticates at Cnip, being present in more or less equal numbers, whilst pig represented a stable but minor component (McCormick 1991). The cattle were extremely small compared even to broadly contemporary herds on Orkney, for example at Howe. This could result from either isolated breeding or, perhaps, more likely, the limited good grazings in the vicinity of Cnip. The machair sands of the Bhaltos peninsula were limited in extent and probably used predominantly for tillage at this period. Thus McCormick suggests that cattle would have been predominantly restricted to low quality peatland grazings further inland.

The evidence of the age at death of cattle from Hebridean machair settlements such as Cnip, Baleshare and the Udal suggests that many animals were killed at a very young age with another peak representing old animals. McCormick has suggested that this pattern, rather than representing a dairy economy as has been traditionally suggested, represents the slaughter of excess male calves to meet short term requirements for meat. The characteristic age/slaughter patterns of a dairy economy, as demonstrated in Early Christian Ireland are very different and it does not appear that dairying played a significant role in Hebridean economies at this time (c.f. McCormick 1991a). Whilst sheep were roughly equal in numbers to cattle at Cnip, they appear to have played a far less significant part in the economy of the site's inhabitants than at other wheelhouses such as Sollas and other Iron Age machair settlements such as Hornish Point and Baleshare. Unlike the rather scrawny cattle, the Cnip sheep appear to have been of a common stature with other Iron Age populations in Scotland. A great many lambs appear to have been slaughtered in the second half of their first year, having been fattened over the summer and autumn.

A number of other species are represented casually in the bone assemblages of wheelhouse sites. Only one dog bone was found at Cnip but the gnaw-marks on other bones demonstrated their persistent presence throughout the lifetime of the settlement. A rare find of pony bones from secondary structures within the wheelhouse at A' Cheardach Mhor confirms that horses were also present in the islands at this time (Young and Richardson 1959). Seal and whale bone is commonly found in most of the machair wheelhouse sites and a number of pieces of burnt whalebone from Cnip suggest that it was used as a fuel (McCormick 1991).

The common occurrence of querns, both rotary and the earlier saddle varieties, on wheelhouse sites confirms that agriculture was practised though its archaeological traces remain fugitive. The siting of so many wheelhouses on the machair probably relates, in part at least, to a need to locate the settlement adjacent to the best available agricultural land. Unfortunately the light and highly mobile machair soils, cultivated long before and ever since the Iron Age, preserve next to nothing of the fields and land divisions that presumably surrounded the wheelhouse settlements. Indeed the best chance for the recovery of evidence for contemporary fields and land divisions lies in the more detailed exploration of the environs of an upland wheelhouse settlement like those at Clettraval and Allasdale, although these may, of course, have had a rather different range of functions.

Several wheelhouses have also produced evidence for the exploitation of fish and birds that would be expected of a Hebridean coastal community. At Cnip most of the bird bones came from sea-birds, commonly the shag and the, now-extinct, great auk. Other sea birds present were the common and black guillemot, puffin, gannet and diver. A few bones of grouse represented the only land-based bird. Migratory geese were also represented as a minor component of the assemblage. The assemblage from Sollas contained the same broad range of species, dominated again by sea birds.

The fish bone assemblage from Cnip was dominated by hake, a species obtainable only by trawl or long-line from boats as it does not inhabit shallow coastal waters. Other species represented were saithe, cod and ballan wrasse. At Sollas, cod and saithe seem to have been the principal species. A variety of shellfish species are present to some degree on all excavated wheelhouse sites.

Interestingly, this series of snapshots of local site economies in the Hebridean Iron Age is beginning to indicate that these did not behave according to a strictly environmentally determined model. The environs of Cnip were peculiarly unsuited to the raising of cattle, yet cattle were present in far higher proportion than on the sheep-heavy Uist wheelhouse sites. This might explain the apparently rather stunted nature of the Cnip cattle. At Dun Mor Vaul, too, the apparent reliance on red deer flies in the face of local environmental conditions. Whilst the husbandry of deer at Cnip, and probably also somewhat later at Loch na Berie, is more explicable it is still puzzling why deer rather than sheep should have been accorded so much attention. Deer, apparently uniquely, occur occasionally as a motif on Hebridean decorated pottery for example at the Kilpheder wheelhouses in South Uist and at Dun Borbaidh on Coll (Lethbridge 1952, 189), and on a fine wooden handle from Dun Bharabhat close to Cnip itself (Dixon, pers. comm.), and in medieval times their hunting and consumption was to acquire connotations of high status. This may be a local reflection of a much more widespread phenomenon since deer are also the only animals represented on late Iron Age painted pottery on the Continent (Ralston, pers. comm.). It is possible that the hunting and/or husbandry and consumption of red deer at monumental settlements like Cnip and Dun Mor Vaul may have been associated with a desire to demonstrate the status of the site's occupants. Similarly cattle, even if rather tawdry specimens, may have had a status value not accorded to sheep, as was the case in the Early Christian period in Ireland.

Domestic Crafts

Spindle whorls from a number of wheelhouse sites show that spinning was a routine domestic activity. Similarly bone and antler-working was commonly

FIGURE 8.5. Wheelhouse pottery: artist's reconstruction based on vessels from Cnip.

carried out within the wheelhouses as witnessed by the scatters of debris from this process at Cnip and elsewhere. Bronze and iron-working appear to have been fairly common on wheelhouse sites (c.f. Finlay 1985, 125) but whether these practices were carried out during the primary periods of occupation of the buildings is open to question. A possible specialist metal-working site has been identified and partially excavated within a few hundred metres of the Cnip wheelhouses (Armit and Dunwell 1992). There has been insufficient excavation to date this site precisely but it may be, in part, at least contemporary with the wheelhouse settlement.

Artefacts

Pottery

Like the Atlantic roundhouses, the various excavated wheelhouses of the Hebrides have consistently yielded large assemblages of highly decorated pottery (Figure 8.5). The Sollas wheelhouse, for example, produced around 3000 sherds from a range of cooking and storage vessels (Campbell 1991, 150). The Sollas pottery was formed of a range of gritty fabrics well-suited to cooking and was all hand made with some limited evidence for the use of a primitive wheel or simple turntable. The range of decoration was typical of wheelhouse assemblages: incised decoration in a variety of geometric motifs accompanied by the characteristic applied cordons; grooved and channelled decoration was also present to some extent. Campbell attempted to identify chronological changes in the sequence of pottery and indeed some of these do seem to hold good for the Sollas material. For example, everted rims seem to have been introduced to the site at around the same time as the wheelhouse was constructed since they were absent from an earlier residual structure nearby. Nonetheless, the possibility remains that the variation in the assemblages between the two structures is functional rather than chronological and better dating of everted rim pottery elsewhere will be required if a general developmental sequence is to be constructed. Campbell's suggestion that the use of everted rim pottery may be influenced by exposure to Roman forms is an intriguing one and should be possible to evaluate with the accumulation of more well-dated assemblages.

The recurrent forms and motifs that recur widely between different wheelhouse sites and different islands over a lengthy chronological span again, like the regularities of wheelhouse architecture and spatial organisation, emphasise the shared traditions and culture of the different communities inhabiting these structures. Topping has shown, using the technique of neutron activation analysis of pottery from fifteen Hebridean sites, that this material was locally made and locally distributed within individual islands (Topping 1986). Thus, the observable uniformity of styles relates not to any imposition of a common style from specialised centres of production, but rather to a shared background and understanding of what forms and motifs were appropriate. Enormous scope remains for the analysis of patterns of association between the different forms, motifs and contexts in which this material is found.

Bone and Antler

The alkaline conditions prevailing in the machair sands of the Uists have led to the recovery of substantial bone and antler assemblages from a number of wheelhouse sites, most notably perhaps from Beveridge's excavations at Foshigarry and Bac Mhic Connain (Beveridge 1930; 1931). These sites yielded a particularly impressive collection of heavy bone tools including hammerheads, spearheads and harpoons. Other characteristic finds in bone and antler materials include the so-called weaving combs (they may equally be hair combs) from sites like Foshigarry, Bac Mhic Connain and Cnip as well as a wide range of fairly functional items such as simple pins, awls, handles and borers. It remains a problem, however, that the bulk of the finds from wheelhouse excavations were recovered from early and, by modern standards, fairly basic excavations where the time-depth of the sites was not appreciated. Thus it is seldom possible to relate finds to particular structural types and thus to construct chronological sequences which might let us understand the development of Hebridean material culture.

Other Materials

Wheelhouses characteristically yield small numbers of finds in a variety of other materials. Occasional objects of bronze are found, often small pins, whilst corroded iron objects provide the sole illustration of a material that must have been very important for the manufacture of agricultural tools. Glass beads are also a recurrent, if not particularly common, find and like the bronze pins, probably represent casual losses. Stone tools such as grinding stones and hammerstones are often found incorporated into later walling, either casually, or perhaps deliberately in the light of the careful emplacement of votive material in wheelhouse walls and floors. The common appearance of quernstones in house walls may, for example, be associated with the symbolism of fertility and agricultural production.

Burial and Ritual

As for Scotland in general, there are notoriously few known funerary or overtly ritualistic sites dating to the Hebridean Iron Age but this probably reflects our inability to recognise them archaeologically. Sporadic discoveries have been made; at Northton, for example, two disarticulated male inhumations dug into the beaker period cist were found to be of Iron Age date. A recently excavated inhumation from Galson in Lewis was accompanied by a small vessel with incised decoration similar to material from wheelhouses such as Cnip and Sollas (Langhorne, pers. comm.). A further inhumation found during the construction of Stornoway airport was accompanied by three vessels (now disappeared), a weaving comb, and spindle whorl; apparently a classic Iron Age assemblage (ibid.). Clearly, then, there was some tradition of accompanied burial but it appears to have been relatively rare and the general paucity of such identifiable Iron Age graves suggests that the great majority were unaccompanied.

Despite the scarcity of dedicated funerary sites that can be placed in the Iron Age, the wheelhouses have produced a significant amount of material that is suggestive of a highly ritualised approach to the organisation of domestic life. Foremost among these sites is the Sollas wheelhouse where a mass of pits excavated into the sand floor of the building produced a wide range of ritual or votive deposits (Figure 8.6). In fact, of approximately 150 pits some sixty produced material of overtly ritualistic character (Campbell and Finlay 1991, 141).

The Sollas pits mostly relate to the early use of the wheelhouse before any occupation debris was allowed to accumulate on the sand floor, although a few appear to be later (Campbell 1991, 131, and supra). Nonetheless the pits seem to have been excavated over a protracted period as they are intercut on numerous occasions. In general though, it seems that there is a distinction to be made between a series of large primary pits containing few indications of animal burial and a large scatter of smaller pits excavated later which contain the bulk of the overtly ritualistic remains.

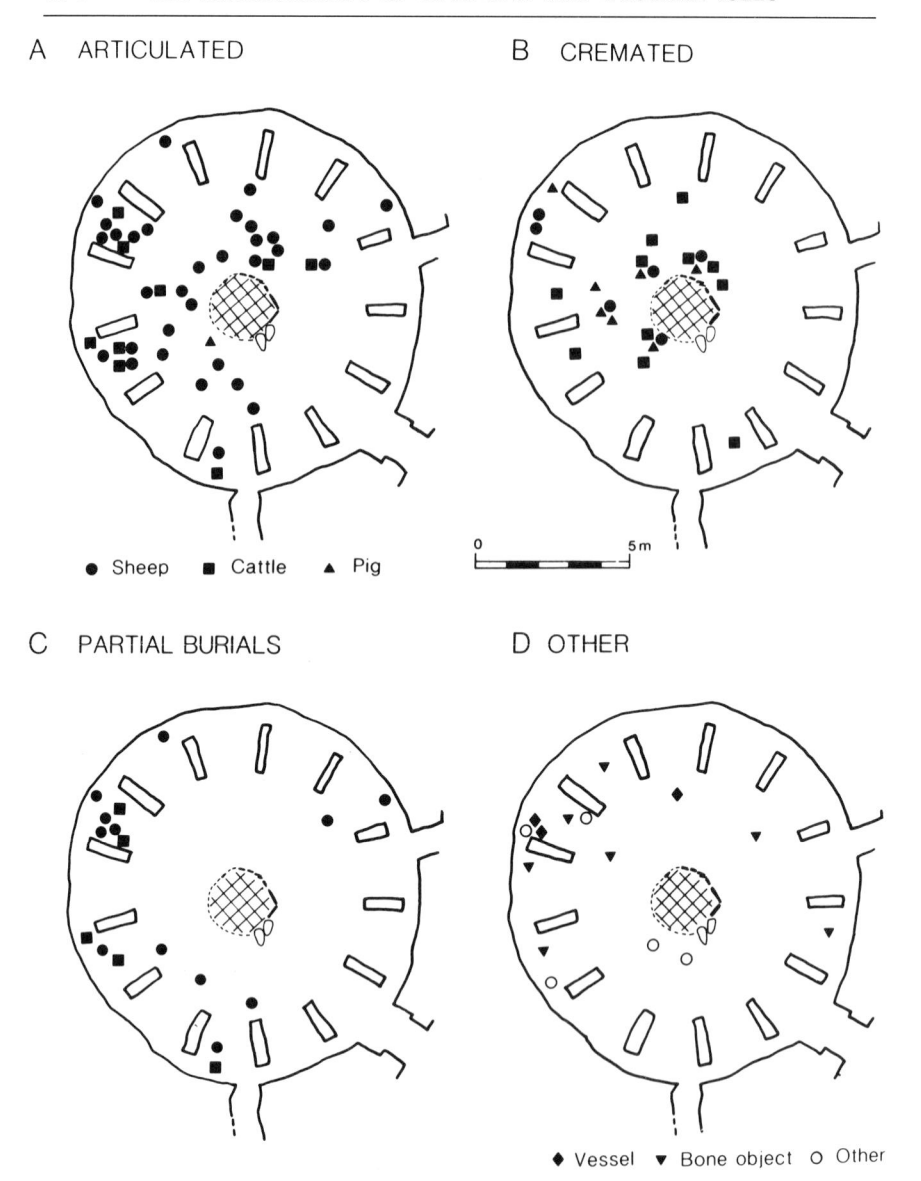

FIGURE 8.6. Ritual deposits in the wheelhouse at Sollas, North Uist.

The large primary pits appear to have been emplaced after the construction of the wheelhouse since they do not occur under piers or under the central hearth, suggesting that the structure was already inhabited (or at least habitable) when they were dug out. These pits vary from around 1–2 m in diameter and in five of the cells the pits virtually fill the floor area. Although the fills of these pits contained some bone and pottery there were no overtly ritualistic deposits and their function is, to some degree, interpreted on the basis of the nature of the later pits and the absence of any obvious functional explanation. Similar pits were found by Lethbridge at Kilpheder in South Uist where again they occupied the whole floors of some cells (Lethbridge 1952, 181). Lethbridge interpreted these as functional, working hollows but this does not seem a likely explanation, particularly in view of their depth, and they should probably be regarded as similar in nature to those at Sollas.

The smaller pits at Sollas tended to be less than 0.5 m in diameter and lacked the spatial order of the larger pits. This, along with the occurrence of some small pits in the later floors, suggests that these were dug periodically throughout the use of the wheelhouse rather than, as the excavation report suggests, prior to occupation commencing. A number of these pits contained the articulated remains of animals. Three, for example, contained entire sheep, dismembered to fit. In other cases the bones were jumbled, indicating the removal of the flesh before burial. Most of the animals represented by these articulated skeletal remains were sheep although there were some cattle and one pig. Other pits contained burnt bone and in these cattle predominated over sheep, pig and deer. Some of the later pits appeared to contain the residue of animal cremations and, in three cases, these were apparently contained in pottery vessels.

Other pits lacked animal remains but contained odd deposits of other kinds. In one tiny pit was a crucible used for bronze-working covered with carefully placed mica plates. Over another was placed an upper quernstone, its central perforation perhaps enabling the pouring of libations into the pit below or perhaps forming a conduit for communication with the ritual world (Campbell 1991, 147).

At Sollas there appears to have been a special status attached to the cell opposite the entrance; this was the location of the greatest number of ritual pits. Similarly at A' Cheardach Mhor, the cell opposite the entrance contained a peculiar deposit of sheep long bones thrust vertically into the cell floor. This focus on the area opposite the entrance seems to be a recurring feature of Hebridean domestic organisation across archaeological periods, recurring for example in later cellular buildings at Loch na Berie and secondary buildings at Cnip (see Chapter 9).

The closest parallel for the animal burials at Sollas comes from a building at Hornish Point in South Uist. This radially-partitioned structure, clearly related to the wheelhouse tradition of spatial organisation, has produced one of the most unusual deposits found in any site of the Scottish Iron Age. Into the floor of this building had been cut four pits holding the quartered remains of a child, probably a boy, aged around twelve years (Barber et al., 1989). He had been cut along the spine and dismembered, apparently some time after death and probably after a certain amount of decomposition. The pieces were then placed in the four pits accompanied by the skinned and filleted remains of a number of young cattle and sheep. Clearly feasting had accompanied the ritual deposition of the dead boy into a series of pits, possibly as an act of propitiation for the new building. There is nothing to suggest, however, that the boy had been deliberately killed (had this been so the corpse would probably have been fresh when dismembered) and the state of the corpse shows that, unlike the young animals, his flesh had not been consumed as part of the ceremony. Barber suggests that the boy may have died at sea and later been retrieved (ibid., 777). The ritual acts and the special treatment of the body may thus have been thought necessary to mitigate an otherwise ill omen. Alternatively, exposure of corpses may have been the normal method of disposal of the dead in the Hebridean Iron Age (accounting for the lack of conventional burials) and the boy may simply have been retrieved from the site of excarnation when the new building was erected.

Aside from ritual pits a number of wheelhouses held other deposits for which no functional explanation can be found. At A' Cheardach Bheag, for example, a kerb of red deer jawbones was found thrust down into the floor deposits, while a cache of thirty two ox teeth was also found in one of the cells (Fairhurst 1971). At Cnip, a series of votive deposits had been placed behind the walls of the unfinished wheelhouse 2 as it was erected. These included the head of a great auk, articulated cattle bone and a complete pottery vessel. There is no record of the careful removal of the walls of other wheelhouses which might show whether such deposits were common.

Other wheelhouses may well have held similar ritual deposits; the features at Kilpheder have been alluded to already. In the majority of wheelhouse excavations, however, there is reason to believe that the primary floor levels have not been fully excavated and so such pits may have been unrecognised. At A' Cheardach Bheag for example, the water table prevented excavation of the lowest deposits (Fairhurst 1971; 73). Similarly at Cnip, the primary floor deposits of wheelhouse 1 were not removed because they were not threatened with destruction. Beveridge appears seldom to have fully excavated the floor levels of buildings in his investigations. An Iron Age site at Eilean Olabhat in North Uist, whilst not of wheelhouse type, contained numerous small pits below its primary floor although the soil conditions prevented the survival of any bones which they may originally have contained (see Chapter 9).

There are a number of human bone fragments from wheelhouse sites that may have had a ritual purpose in their deposition. At Cnip part of a human skull seems to have been deliberately laid in the gradually infilling hollow of the unfinished wheelhouse 2. Another small skull fragment had been shaped and 'shaved' with a knife and subsequently dumped in a midden deposit.

Perhaps the oddest find was a skull fragment into which had been drilled an 'hourglass' perforation, although the fragment had broken during this process. The condition of the bone suggests that it was not fresh at the time of this attempted working and thus its origin as a human skull fragment may not have been significant (McCormick 1991). Knowing the special attention given to human remains in the Hebridean Iron Age, however, it seems improbable that the piece was not specially selected for working, even if it was casually found.

DISCUSSION

The presence of this highly distinctive architectural form in both the Western Isles and Shetland, together with its apparent absence in Orkney and elsewhere, is intriguing. It appears that whilst wheelhouses were being built elsewhere the larger broch villages were still flourishing in Orkney. At Jarlshof in Shetland a series of successive wheelhouses occupy a former complex Atlantic roundhouse site (Hamilton 1956), whilst an apparently isolated example was recently identified at Ward Hill (Smith, pers. comm.). These wheelhouses are extremely close in constructional methods and spatial layout to the Hebridean examples and must surely indicate close cultural contacts. Nonetheless, it is perhaps significant that the sites are very different in other ways, not least in the relative paucity of decorated pottery in Shetland. It may be that both Shetland and the Hebrides were increasingly closely involved in the orbit of larger political authorities perhaps centred in Orkney or Caithness where nucleated broch villages had emerged. Such conditions may have created some stability in the holding of land and rights to other resources which made the overt and provocative symbol of the broch tower unnecessary and anachronistic for communities without pretensions to political power.

Although their specific architectural form was unique to a fairly brief period in the later centuries BC and first century AD, wheelhouses belonged to a long tradition of radially partitioned domestic buildings. Similar spatial divisions occur for example in the Bronze Age structures at Jarlshof in Shetland (Hamilton 1956) as well as in northern broch towers such as Gurness and Midhowe. Interestingly, however, there is little evidence for this form of spatial arrangement in the west of Scotland prior to the wheelhouses. The wheelhouse-like structure at Hornish Point is currently the only well-documented example.

It appears that wheelhouses continued to serve the same basic functions as the Hebridean Atlantic roundhouses. Analyses of their distributions in well-studied areas such as Vallay Strand in North Uist show that they were neither more nor less common than their predecessors and commanded similarly sized parcels of land. They seem to have maintained the Hebridean tradition of the isolated single settlement with a cluster of outbuildings, built for the needs of an extended family group. Rather than using multiple floors for different domestic functions, the settlement was extended horizontally with subsidiary cells, cupboards and souterrains opening out from the main building.

There are some differences in terms of the location of wheelhouses relative to Atlantic roundhouses. Eilean Maleit in North Uist, for example, is the only known wheelhouse to occupy an islet site where it appears to occupy the ruins of a complex Atlantic roundhouse. Whilst other wheelhouses almost certainly lurk unrecognised in the ruined roundhouses of earlier islet sites, there is a clear shift of preferred settlement location onto the machair in this period. Wheelhouses were clearly not intended for defence. Indeed it is hard to imagine a less defensible structure. If there was serious defensive intent in the construction of Atlantic roundhouses then presumably this perceived requirement had receded by the period of wheelhouse construction.

The change from Atlantic roundhouse to wheelhouse building as the principal form of domestic architecture clearly signalled a major change in the perception of the domestic residence. There were environmental pressures involved perhaps; for example, the wastefulness of scarce timber and the unnecessary exposure to wind and cold in the roundhouses. But these pressures were not new and are not a sufficient explanation for the change. The inward-looking monumentality of the wheelhouses, compared with the outward-looking Atlantic roundhouses, suggests that contacts between communities and individuals may increasingly have been taking place inside these buildings. Competition and mutual suspicion over rights to resources may have been replaced by social competition aimed more at demonstrating the status of the wheelhouse inhabitants.

Besides their monumentality and apparent intent to impress, wheelhouses may hold clues to wider interpretations of the way in which Iron Age Hebrideans saw the world. The obvious ritual significance attached to the organisation and construction of the dwelling suggests that it represented the ideological as well as the physical centre of its inhabitants' world. Communal activity centred on the hearth formed the focal point of the building, whilst activities associated with the individual or smaller groups such as craftworking and sleeping were apparently carried out in the cells radially set around the hearth. Leading off from the cells were areas set aside for storage, presumably of agricultural produce and other foods. The whole was contained within an almost womb-like sunken building accessible through a single low and narrow passage from the outside world and surrounded by votive deposits mainly of domestic animals, possibly other organic offerings and occasionally human remains packed in walls and below floors. The whole nature of the architecture, the spatial organisation and the laying of votive deposits seems to stress the isolation and independence of the household and to insulate it from the outside world.

9 Picts and Scots

For the first millennium AD in Scotland contemporary, or near-contemporary, documentary sources of various forms complement the archaeological record, although the Hebrides themselves seldom appear directly. Most of the documentary evidence, with the exception of place-names, deals primarily with the activities of the political and social élite, initially the Roman military and subsequently the emergent kingdoms of the Scots, Picts, Angles and Britons (Figure 9.1). Such records provide, with varying degrees of vagueness, a broad outline of political developments and chart the stuttering emergence through the millennium of increasingly coherent and centralised kingdoms. Integrating documentary evidence, such as king lists and ecclesiastical records, with the raw archaeological material of structures and artefacts is notoriously problematic yet some overview of wider developments is essential in any attempt to make sense of the archaeological record.

Towards the end of the first century AD the southern parts of mainland Scotland had come within the reach of the expanding Roman Empire. Having overrun and largely consolidated England, the Roman army under the Flavian dynasty made initial incursions into southern Scotland at around about the time when, in the Hebrides, wheelhouses were ceasing to be maintained in their original monumental form. The Roman grasp on southern Scotland was to be a sporadic, and almost entirely military, one but nonetheless must have had a significant impact on native society and economy. The nature of that impact is a subject of considerable debate. For the northern parts of Scotland, however, including the Hebrides, the degree of Roman influence is even more difficult to assess. The political and military events that provide the framework for the study of the Roman period in the south need have little relevance to Atlantic Scotland and the paucity of Roman

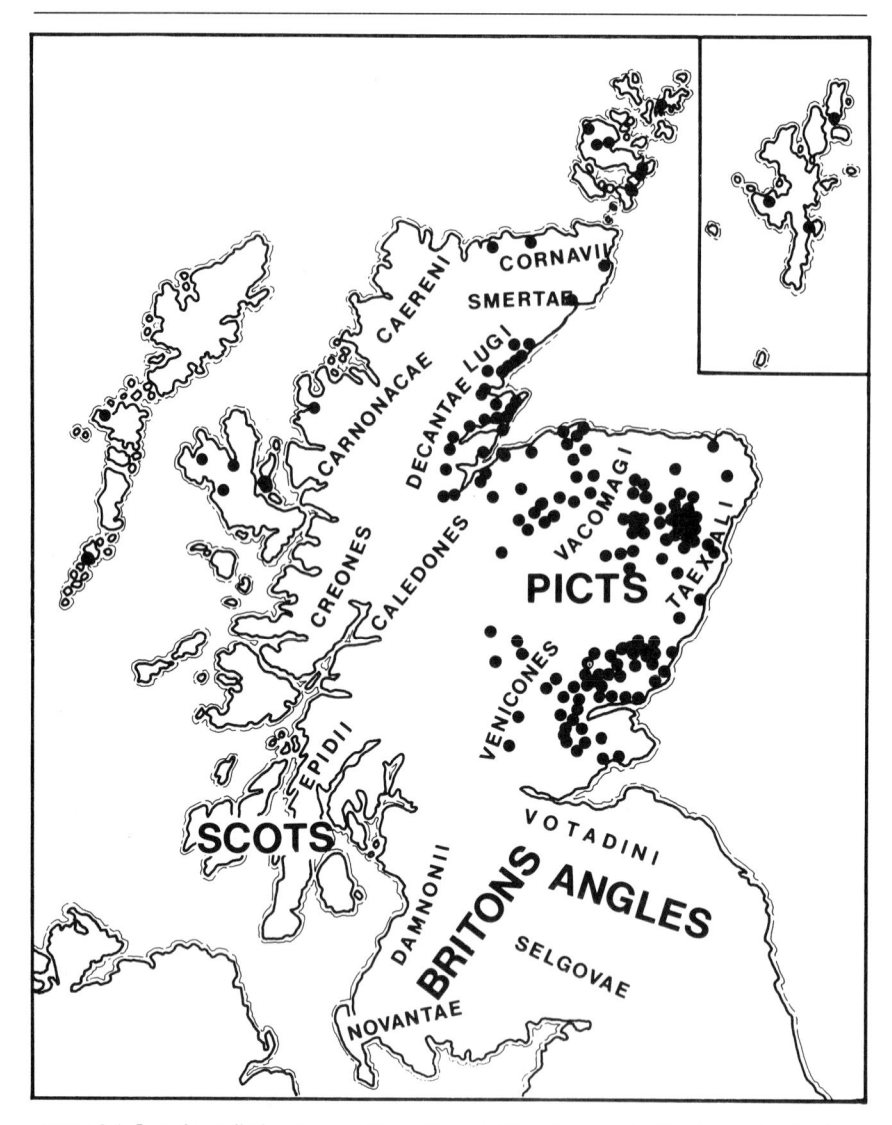

FIGURE 9.1. Iron Age tribal names and Early Historic Kingdoms of Scotland, and the distribution of Pictish symbol stones.

material in the region makes it difficult to establish even basic chronological connections.

Items of Roman influence or manufacture are scarce from the excavated sites of the Hebridean Iron Age. Sherds of Samian Ware pottery found in midden sites in Bhaltos in Lewis, Dun Ardtreck in Skye (Robertson 1970, 207), and a further sherd from the reoccupation of the nearby Loch na Berie broch tower, are rare examples of tangible connections with the Roman world (RCAHMS 1928, 29; Harding, pers. comm.), as is a Romano–British brooch from Kilpheder in South Uist (see below). The terracotta model of a bale of fleeces found at Dun Fiadhairt in Skye, and discussed in Chapter 7, may be another (Curle 1932, 289) as may some apparently Severan silver coins found in Benbecula in the last century (Robertson 1983, 417). Less direct connections have also been postulated, for example the possible influence of Roman forms on everted rim pottery (Campbell 1991), although this requires much closer dating of the appearance of these pottery forms.

Evidence for precocious contacts with the Roman world comes from the broch tower of Gurness in Orkney where sherds of a Roman amphora, used to hold wine or olives, and dated prior to AD 60, seem to indicate that the Orcadian elite had dealings with the Roman world at least twenty years before the first military incursions into southern Scotland. Fitzpatrick has used this evidence to breathe new life into the previously rather unfashionable idea, based on a fourth century account by Eutropius, that Orcadian rulers had submitted to Claudius at around the time of his invasion of southern Britain (Fitzpatrick 1989). If this is true it would suggest a greater degree of power and a greater range of diplomatic contacts than would generally be expected for the peoples of Atlantic Scotland at this time. During the AD 80s Agricola's forces circumnavigated Britain, subduing Orkney in the process but apparently retaining no military presence in Atlantic Scotland. The persistent mentions of Orkney may support suggestions that the centre of power in the Atlantic region was focused on these islands during the Iron Age (Armit 1990e).

Clearly, the people of the Hebrides would have been well aware of the Roman invasion further south and probably had first hand, albeit fleeting, experience of the Roman military. It is even possible that the Hebridean elite formed part of a wider political unit that had been in diplomatic contact with Rome over many decades. Nonetheless direct contact was, at best, brief and seems to have produced little recognisable influence on the material culture of the islands. Political influence is obviously much harder to gauge. Certainly the scant Roman references do seem to point to a gradual amalgamation of loosely affiliated Iron Age tribes in Scotland into larger confederacies through the early centuries AD. This process is repeated widely throughout the margins of the Roman Empire, for example among the Germanic tribes, and has been seen as a reaction to the proximity of Roman influence (c.f. Armit and Ralston 1995a). Interestingly, there is much less evidence for the circulation of Roman goods beyond the frontier in Scotland than there is among the area of the Germanic tribes, perhaps suggesting a lesser degree of influence from Rome.

Recognisable kingdoms had begun to emerge in Scotland by the middle centuries of the millennium. The most relevant of these kingdoms, for our purposes, were the Scots of Dalriada, based in Argyll, and the Picts, apparently occupying the rest of Scotland north of the Forth and Clyde. These kingdoms would, at least initially, have been rather unstable entities composed of numerous sub-groupings. The Pictish state for example seems to have been divided into northern and southern components between which controlling influence periodically shifted. We should be wary of equating these essentially political vehicles of the elite with ethnic or cultural divisions. The Pictish state clearly included peoples with a wide variety of Iron Age cultural antecedents, possibly encompassing several ethnicities and languages. Much effort seems to have been expended by the Scottic and Pictish authorities in stressing their own legitimacy and perhaps in drumming up a sense of ethnic affiliation through the use of material culture and, later, literacy and ecclesiastical endorsement.

Bannerman has placed the northern limits of Dalriada at Ardnamurchan and Coll and Tiree in the sixth century AD (1974), seeing Skye (and, perhaps by inference, the Western Isles) as probably Pictish at this time, whilst Ritchie has summarised the evidence for the Pictish character of the northern isles (1985). The complete absence of documentation relating to the status or affiliations of the Hebrides at this time forces us to rely on the archaeological information alone to identify areas of contact and possible political units. The latter in particular is a task for which it is notoriously unsuited. Aside from the few symbol stones from Skye and the Western Isles which are discussed below, there are few artefacts that could be classed as diagnostically Pictish. An ogam inscribed knife handle from Beveridge's excavations at Bac Mhic Connain (Beveridge 1931) and a possible painted pebble from Garry Iochdrach (Lane 1983, 375), both in North Uist, suggest Pictish cultural affiliations but are hardly enough in themselves to see the Western Isles as part of the Pictish world. On the basis of the clear Iron Age affiliations of the Hebridean zone with the northern isles and north mainland of Scotland, however, it seems most likely that if they had political affiliations in this period then these were with the northern part of the Pictish state. Clearly, however, their geographical marginality to the main axis of Pictish power and their close proximity to Dalriadic and ultimately Irish influences meant that their 'Pictishness' may have been rather ill-developed.

So for all the tantalising promise of the documentary record the first millennium AD in the Hebrides remains, in essence, a prehistoric period for which archaeology provides the vast majority of our evidence. The remainder of this chapter will consider this material from an archaeological perspective before returning to the question of its integration within the wider historical picture.

SETTLEMENT CONTINUITY ON THE MACHAIR

Most of the evidence for Hebridean settlement for the period from the first century AD until the eighth or ninth century Norse incursions comes from the machair of the Western Isles. The majority of these settlements occupied former wheelhouse sites, seldom with any evidence of a break in occupation and occasionally, as at Cnip, with evidence of direct continuity. Many of the early excavations, as at Foshigarry and Bac Mhic Connain,

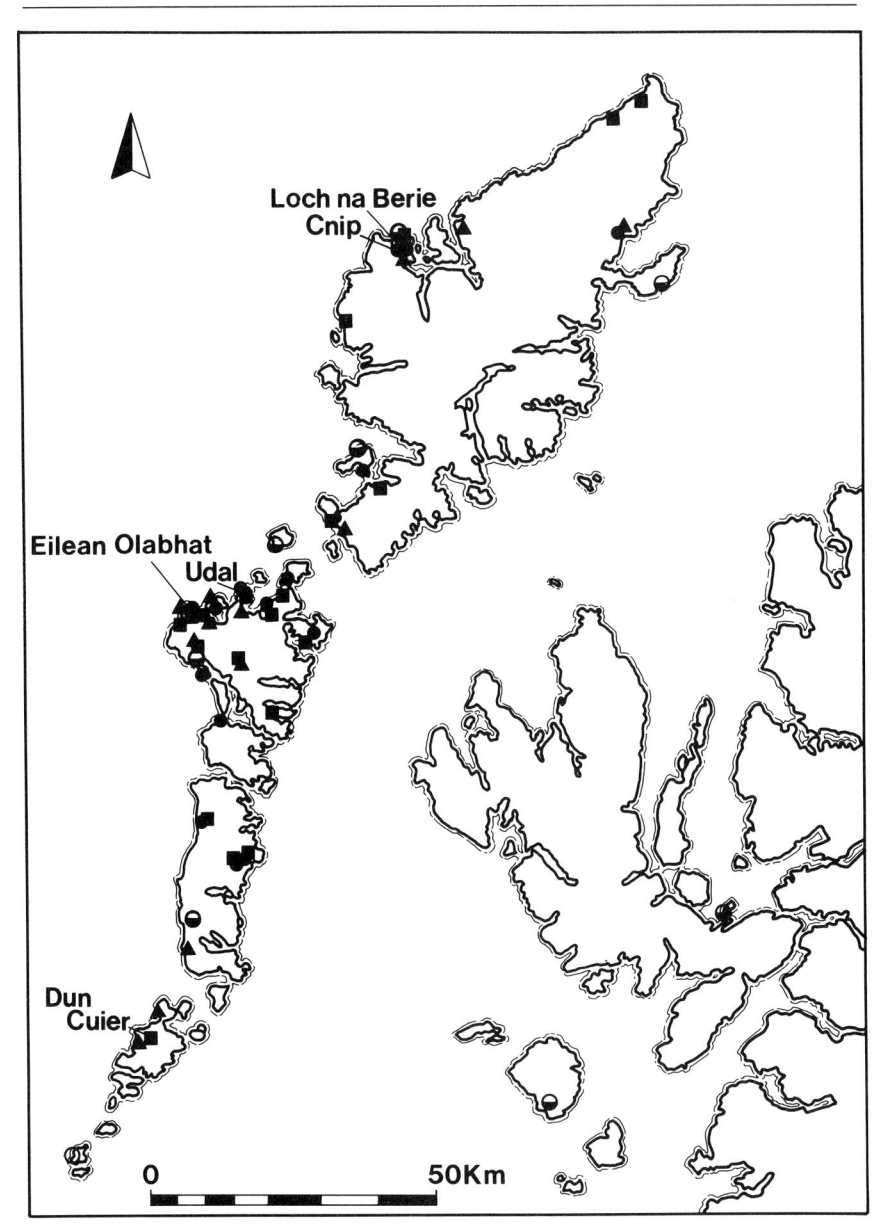

- **Linear Structures**
- **Plain Style Hebridean Pottery**
- **Cellular Structures**
- **Papar Place Names**

FIGURE 9.2. Distribution of pre-Norse sites in Skye and the Western Isles.

display considerable artefactual and occasional structural evidence for occupation through the first millennium AD, but it is only from more recent excavations at Cnip and the Udal that substantial evidence for the nature of that occupation is available.

Cnip, Lewis

By the late first or early second century AD the wheelhouse at Cnip in Lewis was falling into disrepair. Some of the aisles between the bays had been propped up with rubble to support strained lintels and occasional posts had been inserted to hold up the roofs of the bays. The structure had been less well-maintained for some time, with accumulations of rubbish being allowed to lie on the floor and form mounds against the backs of the bays. At some point the decision was taken to re-model the whole settlement and to abandon the spatial arrangements of the wheelhouse. There appears, however, to have been no break in occupation at any time between the construction of the wheelhouse and its eventual replacement by a series of small, interconnected cells.

The original wheelhouse remained the focus of the new cellular building but in a significantly re-shaped form (Figure 9.3). Several bays were blocked and apparently unused, with occupation focusing around the re-built central hearth. In the remains of the unfinished wheelhouse, leading off from the main wheelhouse, a small paved cell roofed with stone lintels, was built and survived intact. The paving and small size of this cell suggest that it may have been used for storage. Leading off the former wheelhouse entrance passage was a further cell with a substantial hearth close to its entrance. The dimensions of this cell are close to that of the re-used part of the former wheelhouse and it appears to have been a second, probably contemporary, domestic focus. The slabs forming the lowest course of walling in this cell were carefully graded in height with the largest standing opposite the entrance. A small niche or shelf was built into the wall on the right hand side of the entrance. The opposite wall was not sufficiently well-preserved to reveal whether or not this was one of a pair but recurrent features of this kind elsewhere suggest that it might have been (see below).

Apart from the remodelled wheelhouse, all of the cells shared a distinctive construction technique: revetted into sand, their lower courses were formed of vertical slabs topped by coursed walling. Aside from the one which was lintelled, the cells seem to have had timber roofs resting on the sand behind their wall-tops. As with the wheelhouses the bulk of the material found within these structures appears to date to the period of their decline. The lintelled cell had evidence for three successive hearths and had clearly been scoured out and cleaned regularly during its use. Substantial quantities of debris had accumulated on its floor only after it had ceased to be used as a domestic area.

The final phase of occupation at Cnip involved the construction of a

FIGURE 9.3. Cnip, Lewis, post-wheelhouse cellular building.

presently unique rectilinear building within the ruins of the wheelhouse and the decaying cells of the preceding period. Again there is nothing to suggest any intervening period of abandonment. No blown sand accumulated in the cells, for example, and the radiocarbon dates suggest that this last structure was built in the second century AD with occupation perhaps extending into the third century. Nonetheless this structure marked a radical break from the spatial layout of the previous phase and was, apparently, completely alien to the wheelhouse tradition. This final structure utilised parts of the earlier structures; it retained two original, still-roofed wheelhouse cells at its inner end and the earlier piers were incorporated within its coursed walls.

The rectilinear structure was a substantial building in its own right with internal dimensions of some 7 by 2.2 m. It was approached along the former wheelhouse entrance passage from the west over a newly laid path, with a small cobbled path providing alternative access from the south. The entrance led into a small area with a stone bench built into the wall along one side and separated from the inner chamber by a stone alignment that presumably supported a timber or wattle partition. Certainly no occupation debris had penetrated into this outer chamber so its function was clearly different from that of the inner area. The inner chamber was substantially larger (Figure 9.3) and, although lacking a formal hearth, contained significant quantities of peat ash and other occupation debris sealed at intervals by laid sand floors. At the inner end lay the two remnant wheelhouse cells. Their survival may have been fortuitous but it is also possible that they were deliberately maintained to provide an innermost area distinct from the main body of the building.

This building must have been roofed in timber since it was too wide for stone lintels. As with the cellular structure, the roof presumably rested on the sand above and behind the wallhead which survived intact at a height of around 2 m. After abandonment this roof appears to have been deliberately dismantled and the structure filled quickly with clean, blown sand. The site seems never to have been re-occupied, although subsequent settlement may simply have shifted outwith the areas available for excavation.

The Udal, North Uist

The great majority of known cellular structures in the Hebrides appear to relate to what remain, essentially, single isolated farmsteads. The exception to this appears to be the machair settlement at the Udal where several structures of cellular form were found, some of them contemporary (Crawford n.d., 12). The excavator has proposed a structural sequence whereby simple oval forms with satellite cells give way to a figure-of-eight form subsequently embellished with further subsidiary cells (ibid.). Such a proposal is intriguing although the absence of published archaeological plans and photographs of these structures prevents any serious comment at this stage.

Crawford has insisted that the appearance of these cellular buildings, associated as they are with Hebridean Plain Style pottery (see below), represents 'one of the rare total and precise watersheds in the archaeological record that are so complete as to compel an invasion interpretation' (Crawford and Switsur 1977, 129). The culprits have been termed 'Scotto-Picts' (ibid.). Alternatively, since the earlier material at the Udal lies some distance away and has no apparent physical or stratigraphic contact with the later material it may simply be that settlement drifted for a time outside the area of Crawford's excavations. Given the clear development of Hebridean Plain Style pottery from earlier, Iron Age styles and the demonstrable continuity of wheelhouse to cellular architecture at sites like Cnip, it is perhaps wiser to leave Crawford's invasion of 'Scotto-Picts' to one side for the moment. It is interesting to note that, even before the recovery of the more recent excavated assemblages, Lane had already cast doubt on the radical break between Iron Age styles and the later Plain Style pottery and suggested a continuity of population from the broch-builders through to the Early Historic period (1983, 374).

SETTLEMENT CONTINUITY IN ROUNDHOUSES

Aside from the continuing occupation of wheelhouse sites, the first millennium AD also saw the continued occupation of numerous Atlantic roundhouses in the Hebrides. Just as the excavation of prominent machair settlement sites has revealed the presence of individually slight cellular buildings of the first millennium AD so the excavation of Atlantic roundhouses has fortuitously enabled the discovery of a further series of contemporary structures. It is not clear from any of the excavated examples whether these cellular constructions represent direct continuity, as at Cnip, or whether the existence of ready-made stone sources and the shelter provided by the walls of the ruined buildings simply attracted later settlement. Perhaps also the symbolic associations of the roundhouses with power and prestige was a reason for the reoccupation of these sites. The lack of demonstrable continuity, however, may simply be a by-product of limited modern excavation. Indeed it is not possible either, to demonstrate discontinuity on any of the sites on the basis of the available evidence.

At Dun Bharabhat in Bhaltos the complex roundhouse was apparently re-modelled as a cellular structure in the last centuries BC after the premature collapse of the original super-structure (Harding and Armit 1990). Most such structures within former roundhouses, however, remain undated or, as at Loch na Berie, the excavated phases date to the later part of the first millennium AD.

Loch na Berie

The broch tower at Loch na Berie, sited on a small islet in a machair loch, has already been discussed in Chapter 7 as one of the finest of its type in the Hebrides. Excavations by Professor Dennis Harding continue to reveal the remains of successive structures, possibly from the disuse of the broch tower in its original form through to the seventh to early ninth centuries AD, i.e. immediately prior to the Norse incursions.

The earliest of the excavated post-broch tower structures are difficult to disentangle due to the continual re-building which has gone on within the confined space of the tower's interior. Nonetheless, they seem to have comprised a series of cellular buildings similar to those at Cnip (Harding 1993). Each of these seems to have been at least partially levelled to enable construction of its successor save for occasional wall fragments and stone furniture that were reused *in situ*. Some of the structures have survived sufficiently well to enable the recognition of house plans and internal features (Harding, pers. comm.). Interestingly, a sherd of Samian Ware was found stratified between two phases of paving within one of the cellular buildings indicating some contact with the

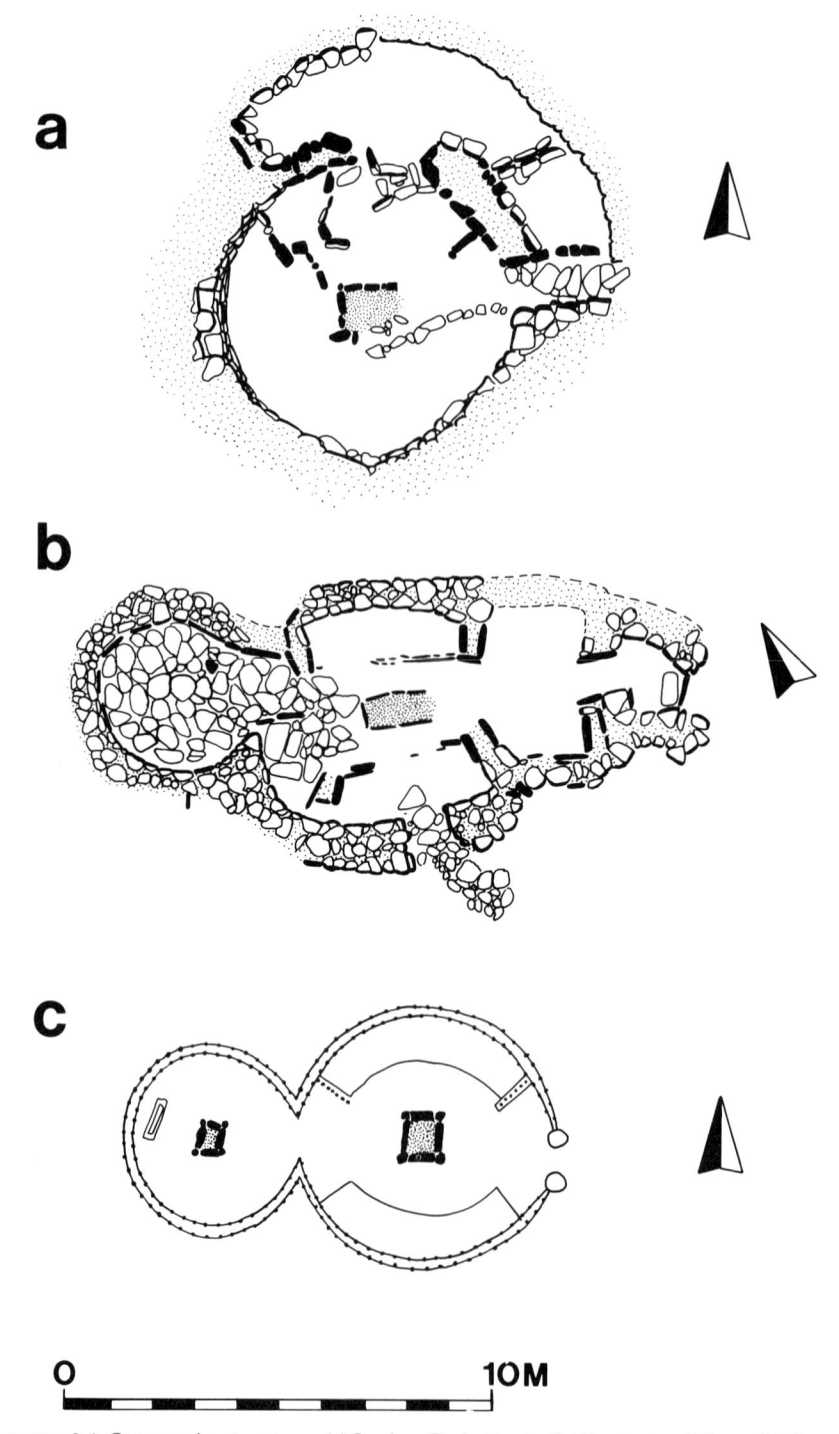

FIGURE 9.4. Comparative structures: (a) Loch na Berie, Lewis; (b) Buckquoy, Orkney; (c) Deer Park Farms, Ulster.

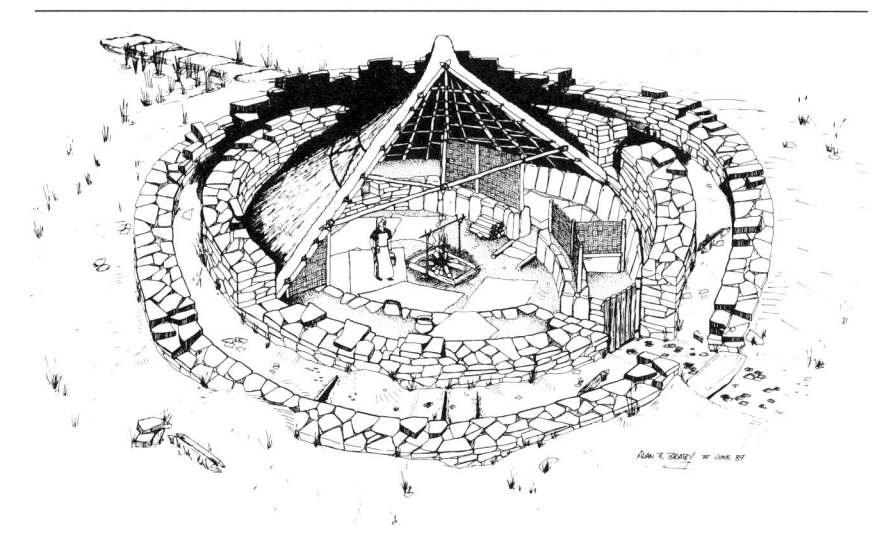

FIGURE 9.5. Loch na Berie, pre-Norse settlement, artist's impression.

Roman world and extending the likely date of the cellular structures back to the early centuries AD (Harding, pers. comm.).

The latest building within the tower was remarkably well-preserved and had been little disturbed since its abandonment. This latest structure was cellular in plan with a substantial circular cell leading in from the re-modelled broch tower entrance (Figure 9.4). The walls were formed of vertical slabs revetting back quantities of midden material packed against the inside of the broch tower walls. This created a level platform behind the walls that would have formed the base for the roof, itself sheltered from the wind by the residual stumps of the inner broch tower wall (Figure 9.5).

On entering the structure along a paved passageway the view would have been focused on the large central hearth and then, directly across it and opposite the entrance, two stone shelves or seats built into the wall. Indeed this part of the wall had been built in conventional coursing rather than vertical slabs, presumably to enable the construction of these features. Whether these were intended for display of objects or whether they did form actual seats they certainly appear to have occupied the most prestigious area of the building on which the entrance and hearth layout were focused. Paired niches, albeit less closely-spaced were identified in the secondary structure in Dun Cuier and at Cnip. This arrangement is also reminiscent of the concentration of ritual material in the bays opposite the entrances of several wheelhouses (see Chapter 8 and above).

Stone alignments around the periphery appear to have divided the main cell into separate functional areas. Although some of these features formed parts of the walls of underlying buildings their survival implies that they also played a functional role in the spatial divisions of the later structure. To the

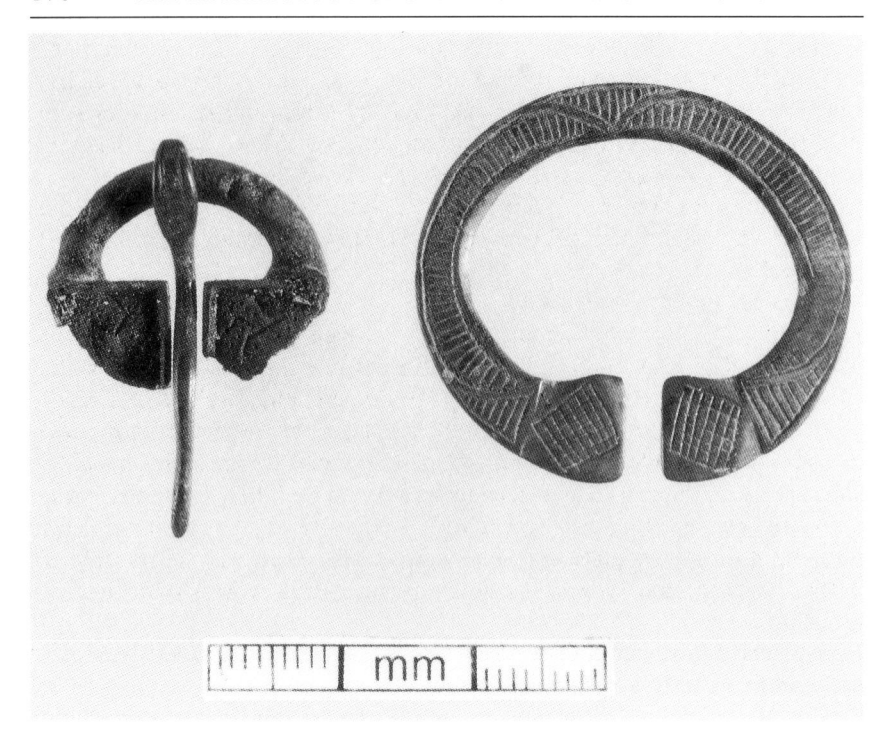

FIGURE 9.6. Brooches from the pre-Norse occupation at Loch na Berie, Lewis.

right of the hearth on entering the building was the entrance to the second, smaller cell which then curved back around the inner broch tower wall towards the entrance. There were fewer features and no hearth in this cell which may have been used for storage as has been suggested for similar cells leading off wheelhouses.

This final structure at Loch na Berie can be broadly dated by the occurrence in its floor deposits of a set of bronze tweezers decorated with a series of regular dots and an incised line echoing the outline. This find almost exactly parallels a set from Whitby Abbey dated to around 650–875 AD on the basis of associated coins (Peers and Radford 1943, 61). The absence of Norse, or Norse-influenced, material suggests that an abandonment date later than the early 9th century is unlikely for Loch na Berie. Two penannular brooches (Figure 9.6) from the immediately underlying structure suggest that it dated to the fifth or sixth centuries AD (Harding and Armit 1990, 103).

Dun Cuier, Barra

A close parallel for the cellular structures within the Loch na Berie broch tower comes from Dun Cuier in Barra. Like several of the Barra roundhouses Dun Cuier lies not in a loch but on the summit of a low hill commanding the surrounding area. This complex roundhouse was excavated before the full implications of multi-period construction within these sites were understood and its excavator therefore failed to distinguish between the original Iron Age roundhouse and the cellular structure inside (Young 1955). There may well have been other structures occupying the period between these two well-preserved buildings but, if so, these too were not recognised during excavation.

Reinterpretation of the site has shown that the original roundhouse was reoccupied by the construction of a large circular cell, possibly leading off to a smaller cell (Armit 1988). As at Loch na Berie, a thin skin of drystone walling revetted midden material packed against the inner wall of the roundhouse. This would have formed a platform to support the roof and provided insulation for the building. On entering the building through the re-modelled and paved roundhouse entrance, again as at Loch na Berie, the interior was dominated by a large central hearth and an entrance appears to have led off to the right into the smaller cell. Two wall niches or shelves to either side of the hearth have already been mentioned as recurrent traits for structures of this broad period.

As a result of the excavator's belief that the structure was essentially single-phase, it is impossible to assign the artefactual material from the site to any given structural phase. The material includes a wide range of pottery styles reinforcing the view that the structure was occupied from the first millennium BC until the immediately pre-Norse period. Decorated pottery confirms the presence of occupation from the earlier period whilst several decorative items (Figure 9.7), including a high-backed composite comb with Irish parallels (e.g. at Lagore) indicate a date in the second half of the first millennium AD (Young 1955, 316).

The cellular houses built within the ruined hulks of the Atlantic roundhouses and in the machair hills, were not monumental architectural constructions but were, nonetheless, substantial and carefully constructed buildings, well-adapted to their environmental conditions. They were well-insulated by their midden packing and relatively sheltered from the wind by the residual roundhouse walls. The smaller spans necessitated by their segmented construction meant that shorter timbers, such as could probably have been obtained from limited local resources and driftwood, would suffice for roofing. Spatial organisation within the dwelling remained important with a series of recurring stylistic and organisational traits being apparent, such as the focus on the area opposite the entrance. Clearly, as with the earlier wheelhouses, the external appearance of the settlement was not meant to impress or to demonstrate status. Unlike the wheelhouses, however, the interior architecture was no longer so manifestly a forum for display.

Parallels for the development of cellular architecture in the first millennium AD can be cited both in the northern isles and north mainland (the

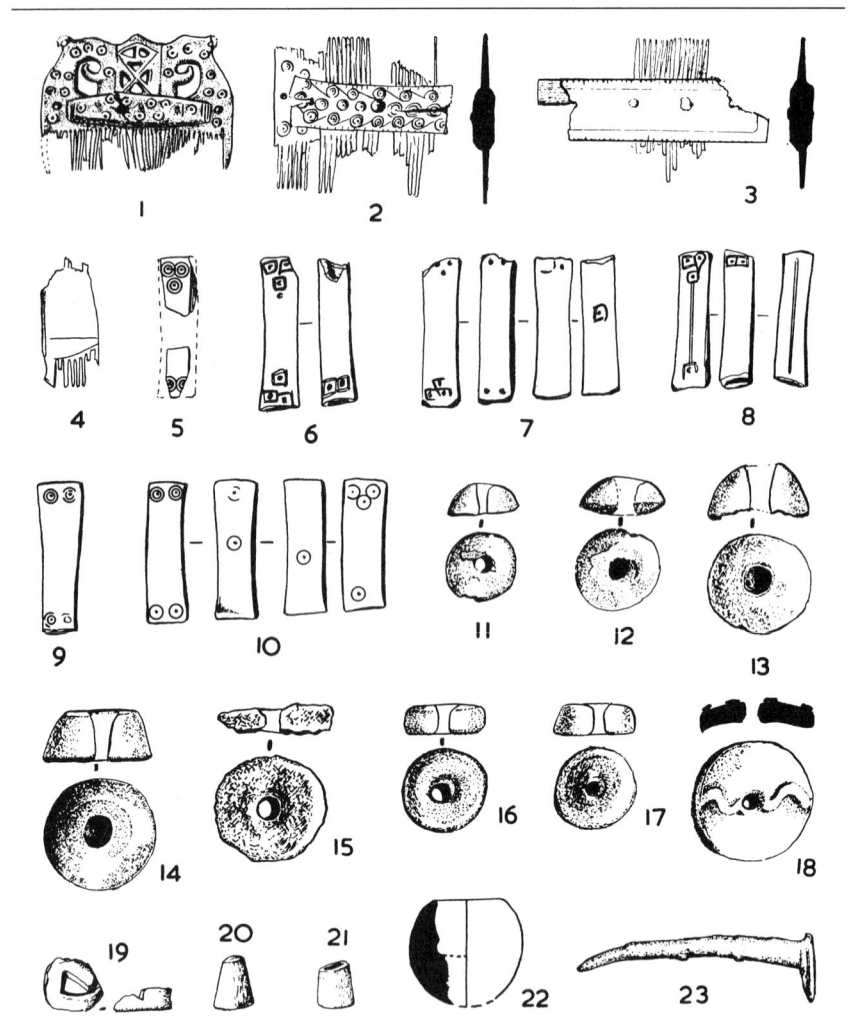

FIGURE 9.7. Finds from the excavations at Dun Cuier, Barra.

northern Pictish zone), and in Ireland; theoretically at least, a separate cultural area whose political affiliations in Scotland are traditionally thought to have been confined to Dalriada. The Pictish period houses at Buckquoy in Orkney best exemplify the similarities between the northern and western cellular structures (Figure 9.4) displaying distinct similarities to house plans from Loch na Berie and the Udal (Ritchie 1976). The figure-of-eight houses built of timber at Deer Park Farms in Ulster typify the related Irish structural tradition (Lynn 1987).

With so few sites excavated in modern times it remains difficult to identify the architectural development in any detail but it does appear to be the case that there was a distinct architectural tradition of cellular construction operating in the Hebrides with affinities to the wider Atlantic Scottish region and beyond.

EILEAN OLABHAT, NORTH UIST; SETTLEMENT AND WORKSHOP

The site of Eilean Olabhat in North Uist is presently unique in the Hebrides in having produced evidence for a small specialist metal-working workshop of the Early Historic period. The site was excavated in the late 1980s initially as an adjunct to the excavation of the Neolithic settlement of Eilean Domhnuill in the same loch (Armit 1990a; Armit and Dunwell 1993).

Eilean Olabhat is a small natural promontory, formerly an islet, projecting into Loch Olabhat from its south shore to the east of the Neolithic settlement of Eilean Domhnuill (see Chapter 4). The promontory is enclosed on three sides by a stone wall which excavation has shown to have been rebuilt on numerous occasions, presumably contemporary with at least some of the phases of internal occupation. Excavation, however, was concentrated on the summit of the promontory where a group of super-imposed stone and turf buildings had formed the focus of the various phases of occupation.

The Early Settlement

In its earliest stages, Eilean Olabhat appears to have been a settlement with one principal building sited on its low rocky summit. This early building was a small and simple oval construction measuring around 5 by 4 m internally with an entrance on its north-east or east side (Figure 9.8). This structure is particularly interesting for the profusion of pits excavated into its floor. These are reminiscent of the pits at the Sollas wheelhouse (see Chapter 8) although the soil conditions at Eilean Olabhat prevent the survival of bone, making it impossible to tell whether they held similar votive deposits. The structure itself is difficult to date with precision although the small pottery assemblage suggests that it was built in the last centuries BC (Campbell 1994). Structurally it bears no relation to the wheelhouse tradition and its simple form prevents ready comparison with later cellular settlements. Nonetheless, its construction methods, with a thin skin of walling revetting a slightly sunken floor, may have been rather similar to cellular structures on some of the former wheelhouse sites. Although the building had suffered heavily from disturbance by later constructions it retained a large and well-constructed horseshoe-shaped hearth and some residual traces of a compacted floor surface.

Subsequently this simple oval building was re-shaped to incorporate a substantial entrance passage (Figure 9.9). Again there is evidence for foundation ritual associated with the new building, for in one of two pits at the foot of the entrance piers a complete pot was found which fitted exactly

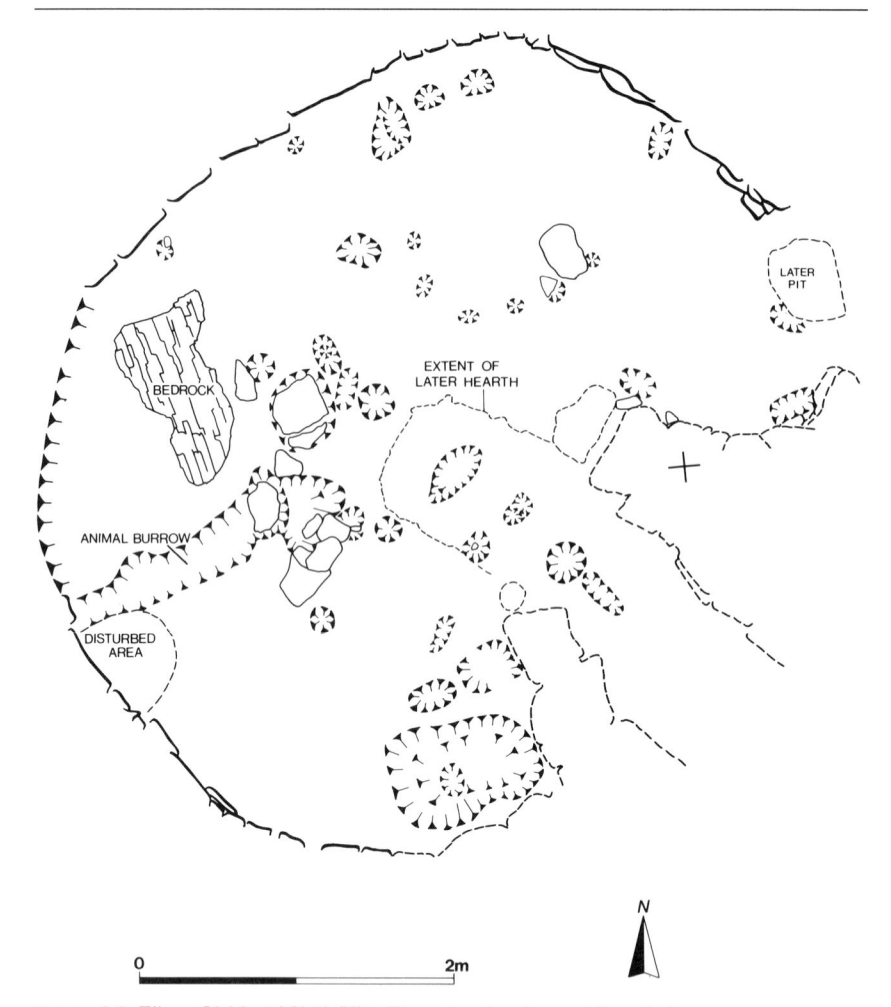

FIGURE 9.8. Eilean Olabhat, North Uist, Phase 1a, showing position of pits.

into the pit and had been deliberately shattered, apparently by driving a stake through it. The pit was then covered over by a patch of cobbling suggesting that it was not designed to hold a structural post. The centre of the building was occupied by a roughly triangular patch of paving with a socket stone apparently intended to support a central post. Such a post could not have been free-standing and was presumably intended to support the roof, suggesting a rather different roofing structure from the earlier building.

Unlike its predecessor this building had no surviving hearth and very little indication of any debris associated with occupation, although there were indications of displaced stone furniture around the paved area. It is tempting

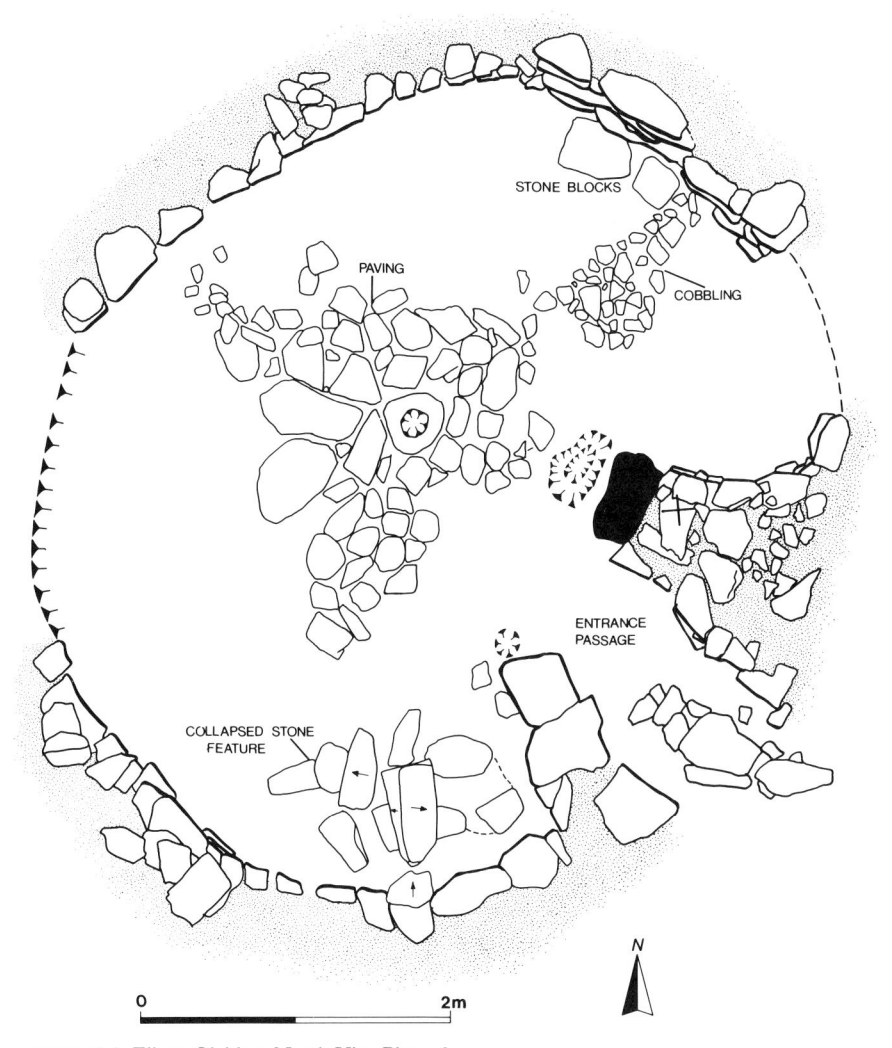

FIGURE 9.9. Eilean Olabhat, North Uist, Phase 2.

to suggest that it may have held some specialist, perhaps ritual, function although the absence of any other formal ritual structures and the wealth of ritual practice focussed on domestic buildings suggests that such an interpretation may be out of step with our current understanding of the Hebridean Iron Age. After a period of abandonment the structure was again re-modelled on a slightly different alignment and with the addition of a new internal pier. This building was, however, substantially damaged by later construction and little survived other than an indication of its wall position and localised patches of occupation debris.

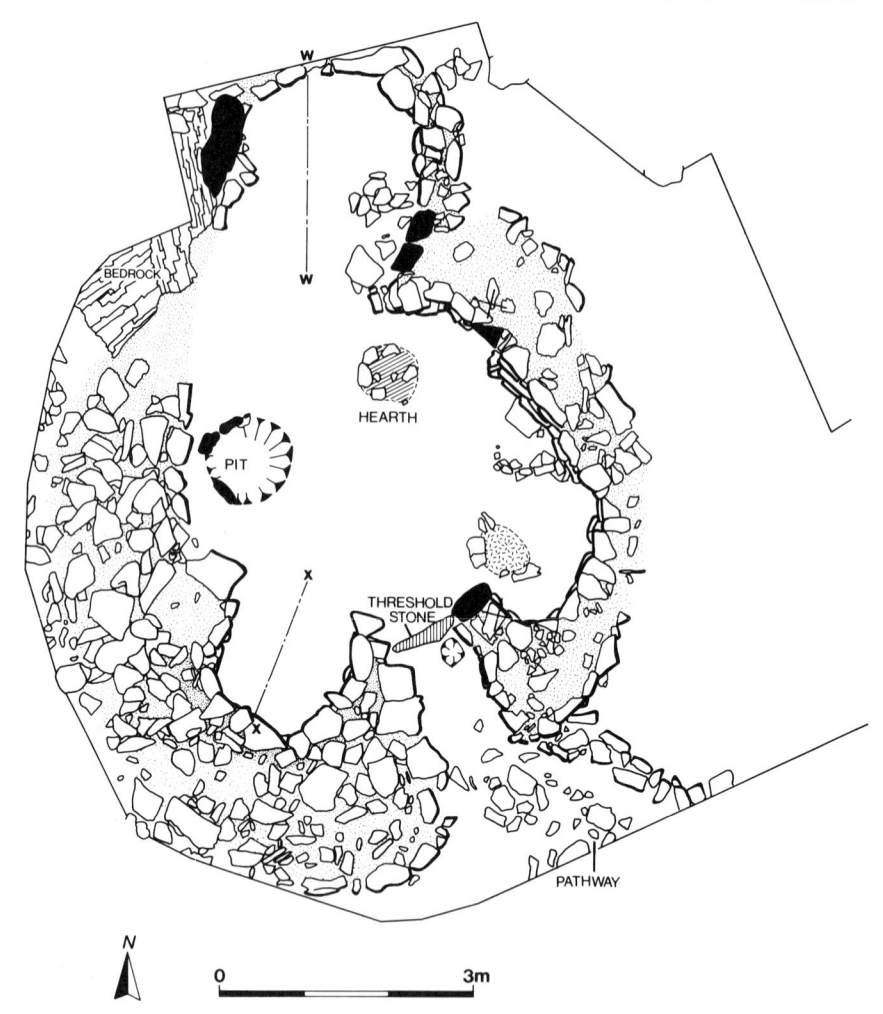

FIGURE 9.10. Eilean Olabhat, North Uist, Phase 3.

The workshop

The next phase of re-building on the site can be dated to around the sixth–seventh century AD, probably after the original settlement had long since become ruinous (Figure 9.10). This occupation consisted of a series of small cells, at least one of which was corbelled, set around the periphery of the earlier structures. The position of a gatepost at the entrance and the nature of the internal deposits suggests that the cells were all components of a single roofed building. The overall plan of this building is similar to that of broadly contemporary cellular buildings at Loch na Berie in Lewis and Buckquoy in Orkney (Figure 9.4).

This phase of activity produced substantial accumulations of debris, most of which were formed of hearth waste dumped in the cells as metal-working was carried out in the centre of the building. Interestingly the largest cell was almost free of hearth waste prompting the suggestion that it may have been utilised as living accommodation during the use of the workshop. Around 150 fragments of clay moulds, 185 crucible fragments (including several complete examples), pieces of tuyere and other metal-working by-products were recovered from this material, apparently representing a highly specialised toolkit (Spearman, pers. comm.) possibly for the working of precious metals as well as bronze (Figure 9.10). Despite the presence of this material there was no formal kiln and it appears that a simple hearth was sufficient for the scale of production required. A cobble-lined bowl hearth and a series of contemporary pits appear to relate to the metal-working activity.

The Products

Although, not surprisingly, none of the products of this metal-working activity remained on the site, the fragments of clay moulds indicate the range of items being made. These included small pins, ingots, penannular brooches and, most notably, a developed handpin of a characteristic Early Historic type. The arrangement of the 'fingers' of the handpin, in a straight line along the top, indicate that it is late in the typological sequence for this artefact type and probably dates to the sixth–seventh century AD (Campbell, pers. comm.). A mould for a roundel with triscele bosses parallels an example from Dunadd in Argyll, dating to the seventh century AD (Campbell, pers. comm.). These were clearly objects of considerable value and part of the mainstream of fine jewellery of the period.

Dating

A series of radiocarbon dates were obtained from hazel and birch charcoal, all deriving from small twigs and branches used to fuel the metal-working process (domestic fuel in other phases appears exclusively to have been peat). These dates revealed that the wood had been recovered from a variety of residual sources, possibly from nearby peat or even perhaps from the adjacent Neolithic site. The dates, therefore, gave a wide range which cannot be related to the metal-working material except insofar as this activity must be later than the latest date from the charcoal. This latest date centres on the period from around 550–650 AD and is thus consistent with the typological dates for the metalwork which would suggest a sixth–seventh century date.

Interpreting the Bronze-working Activity

The absolute quantities of metal-working debris at Eilean Olabhat are not particularly large, suggesting either that they represent simply the last episode in a sequence of use where the structure was generally cleared out, or that metal-working was a discrete final use of a ruined cellular building. The latter interpretation is perhaps the more attractive in that there is little to suggest that the cellular building was purpose-built for metal-working. The structure may thus have been a convenient sheltered spot for an itinerant bronzesmith to work for a short time, or for a specialist from a nearby settlement to work away from the rest of the community.

Whatever the status of the smith and the duration of the activity, Eilean Olabhat is an unusual site on which to find such concentrated activity for fine metal-working. The site appears at this time to have been a ruinous shell of a building on a disused promontory, the nearest known contemporary settlement being Foshigarry, a kilometre or so to the north along the coast. The production of fine jewellery at this period has often been interpreted as having been conducted under the close supervision and patronage of the élite (e.g. Alcock 1987, 85), the remainder of the population having limited access to the materials and products. Thus large assemblages of fine metal-working debris have been recovered from high status sites such as Birsay in Orkney (Curle 1982) and at Dunadd, a capital of the Scots of Dalriada. The Eilean Olabhat material would seem, by contrast, to imply localised production away from high status sites. Perhaps the petty aristocracy of the Western Isles, still inhabiting relatively small-scale scattered settlements relied upon itinerant specialists to provide them with status goods rather than supporting specialist craftspeople in larger, nucleated settlements.

ARTEFACTS

Pottery

Throughout the first millennium AD, prior to the Norse incursions, there appears to have been a steady decline in the quality of pottery manufacture, and in the range of forms and decoration. The rate of this change is hard to assess until more well-dated assemblages have been excavated but there do seem to be transitional forms between the profusely decorated and varied Iron Age assemblages and later plain vessels of the Hebridean Plain Style.

The pottery recovered from the cellular structures at Cnip appears to maintain the forms and motifs present during the occupation of the wheelhouse. Pottery traditions remained apparently unaffected for some time, despite the dramatic change in architectural and spatial arrangements, since the bulk of the material probably relates to the latter stages of the use of these cells. In the subsequent period at Cnip, however, when the rectilinear building was occupied, motifs became restricted to applied wavy cordons and the variety of forms declined sharply, presaging the markedly plainer assemblages of the mid–first millennium AD.

The first millennium AD Hebridean Plain Style pottery was defined by

Alan Lane initially on the basis of the substantial assemblage from the Udal in North Uist (Lane 1983, 1990). This pottery was, like earlier traditions, locally handmade and fired without a formal kiln, but unlike the earlier material it was entirely undecorated. The forms were predominately flat-based buckets and shouldered jars, many with flaring rims. This pottery was thought to predominate at the Udal for several centuries prior to the Norse incursions but the available radiocarbon dates have very wide standard deviations and provide little help in narrowing the date range of the style (Lane 1990, 117). What is apparent is that the style persists into the later eighth or ninth centuries, given its association with decorated metalwork of that period. The date of its initial appearance, however, is difficult to establish from the published Udal evidence.

Lane has identified Plain Style pottery similar to the Udal assemblage at numerous sites in the Western Isles (though none in Skye), but most of these sites were early excavations and provided ill-dated sequences where they provided any at all (Lane 1990, 120). Better evidence comes from the latest structure at Loch na Berie where the pottery was plain and often relatively coarse in a variety of simple forms similar to the Plain Styles at the Udal. By contrast, however, the immediately underlying structure contained a small element of pottery with decoration restricted to applied wavy cordons, associated with penannular brooches of probable fifth or sixth century date. Dun Cuier also produced an assemblage of Plain Style pottery, further reinforcing the evidence for its occupation through the first millennium AD.

The pottery assemblage from the metal-working site at Eilean Olabhat included numerous sherds decorated with the applied wavy cordons typical of Later Iron Age material in the Hebrides, and similar to that from the penultimate structure at Loch na Berie. Although the pottery analysis and report for this assemblage is still in progress it is clear that vessels with this type of decoration persisted through the sequence at least as late as the metal-working phase in the sixth or seventh centuries AD. The flaring rims of some of these vessels distinguish them from the latest pottery at Cnip where, although decoration had become restricted to applied cordons, everted rims were still present. The close association of cordoned, flaring-rimmed pottery with apparently sixth- or seventh-century metalwork at Eilean Olabhat seems to confirm that, in contrast to the Udal sequence, decorated pottery persisted here into the second half of the first millennium AD.

Given the apparently late date for cordon decorated pottery at Eilean Olabhat it seems that decorated pottery was produced at least until the sixth century and probably into the seventh in the Western Isles. This might suggest that the latest structures at Loch na Berie and the structures yielding Plain Style pottery at the Udal belong to a late pre-Norse horizon, perhaps in the eighth or early ninth centuries AD. Alternatively, it may be the case that decorated pottery continued to be used in specific functional contexts away from the mundane domestic domain, since the Eilean Olabhat vessels were apparently used when the site was a specialist smith's workshop.

Personal Items

Increasingly in the first millennium AD finely made decorative items such as jewellery and gaming equipment appear in the archaeological record. These include items manufactured in bone and glass as well as fine metalwork of the kind made at Eilean Olabhat. Overall there seems to have been an increasing emphasis on the manufacture of small items, made by specialists, destined for personal rather than communal ownership. This was by no means a trait restricted to the Hebrides or Atlantic Scotland but rather reflects the pattern across the whole of Britain and Ireland at this time.

One of the earliest dated examples of fine bronzework in the region is a Romano–British brooch found in a niche in the wall of the Kilpheder wheelhouse. This appears, on the basis of similar material from Newstead Roman fort in the Borders, to date to the latter part of the second century AD, and must have been deposited in the final stages of the use of the wheelhouse (Lethbridge 1952, 182–3). Decorative bronzework becomes more common in subsequent centuries, however, as witnessed by the occurrence of penannular brooches in the fifth or sixth century phases at Loch na Berie and a fine set of bronze tweezers from the final structure on that site. Decorative bonework from the Hebrides includes a fine series of combs from Dun Cuier, dating to the middle and later centuries of the first millennium, including a high-backed comb similar to Irish examples at Lagore dating to the sixth or seventh centuries AD (Young 1955). Bone dice from the long-lived sites at Foshigarry and Bac Mhic Connain on North Uist may date to a similar period.

Both the combs from Dun Cuier and the penannular brooches from Loch na Berie hint at Irish cultural connections, whilst the tweezers from the latter find their closest parallel in a similar set from Whitby in Northumbria. Clearly widespread cultural connections were in operation that did not split along ethnic or political lines.

RITUAL AND RELIGION

The pre-Christian Evidence

Pictish Symbol Stones

Mention has already been made of the few Pictish symbol stones from the Hebrides as one of the few overt signs of affiliation with the Pictish state (Figure 9.11). The overall distribution of these stones corresponds remarkably well with the presumed extent of Pictland (Figure 9.1). The Hebridean examples are all Class 1 stones i.e. decorated with a variety of recurrent symbols and lacking overt Christian motifs. Their lack of obvious association with archaeological sites makes their function difficult to interpret.

Class I symbol stones are generally thought to have emerged around the

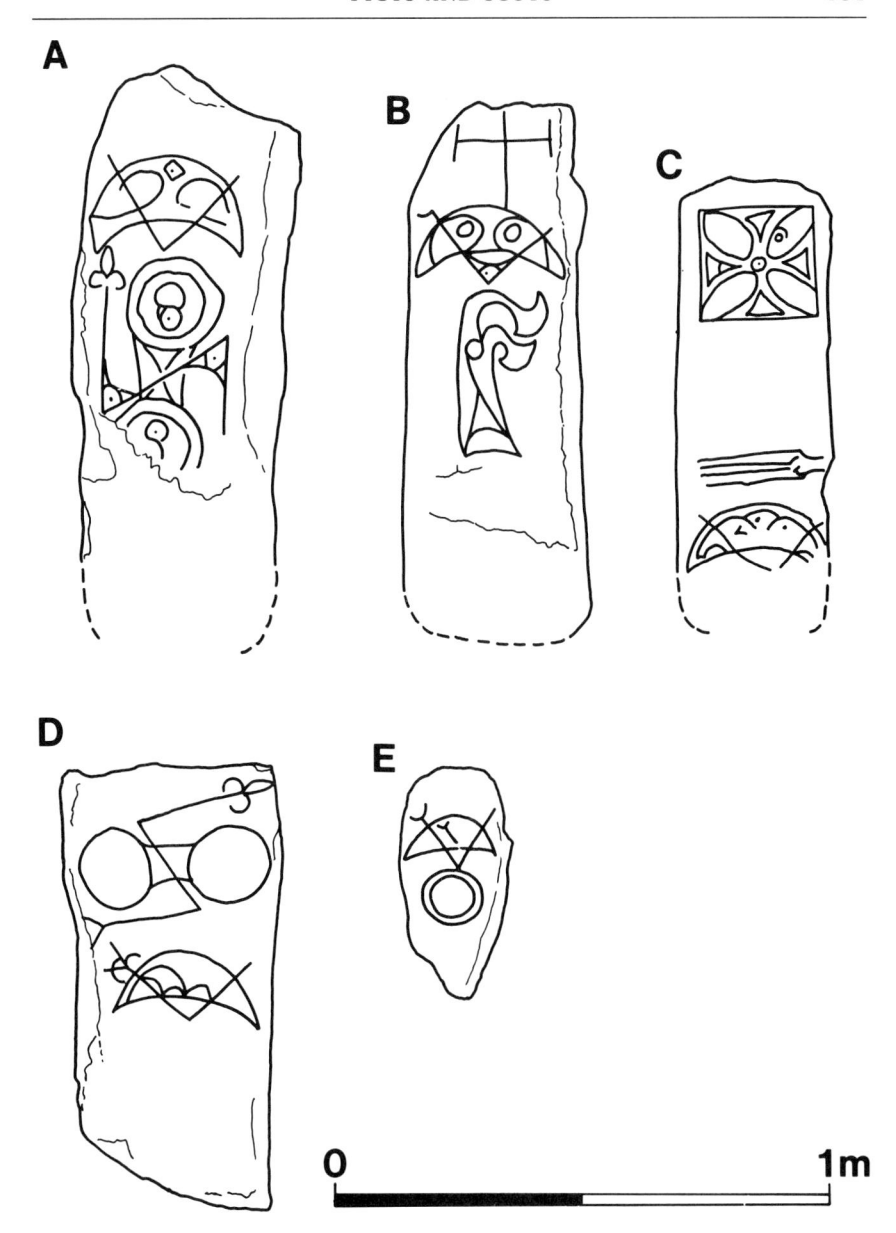

FIGURE 9.11. Pictish symbol stones on Skye and the Western Isles: (a) Clach Ard, Tote, Skye; (b) Bagh Ban, Pabbay; (c) Raasay House; (d) Fiskavaig Bay, Skye; (e) Dunvegan Castle, Skye.

sixth century AD and to have been superseded by the Christian Class 2 stones shortly thereafter. Interestingly, the Hebridean stones all share a symbol in common, the so-called crescent and V-rod (Figure 9.11), but otherwise carry an assortment of symbols found widely across Pictland. The lack of stones bearing Christian motifs in the Hebrides is unlikely to be of significance in itself given the small numbers involved and the position of the islands on the periphery of the overall distribution of the stones and of the Pictish kingdom itself. The purpose of these stones remains a matter of debate but presumably they transmitted messages of some form, possibly commemorative of certain people or events, and were used by local elites to display their status and record their achievements.

Burial

Few burials can be dated securely to the early part of the first millennium AD in northern Scotland and the Hebrides are, in general, no exception. At Galson, on the exposed north-west coast of Lewis, however, excavations have revealed a long cist cemetery dating to around the fourth century AD, associated with a site containing settlement remains of the first millennia BC and AD (Edwards 1923; Stevenson 1952;, Ponting 1989). In 1984 and 1985 erosion of the beach front brought to light a series of four cists of which two were excavated albeit not in ideal conditions. The cists were simple stone boxes sides formed of slabs and coursing, capped by thin slabs (ibid.). A layer of pebbles seems to have been deliberately placed over them. The graves were marked on the surface by rectangular stone kerbs. A small, elongated stone with a polished surface appears to have been the only clearly intentional offering placed with the dead whilst other finds, including fragments of pottery, may best be interpreted as casual inclusions.

The two excavated skeletons had both been buried with their heads to the west. One was a robust young woman, perhaps in her mid-twenties, who had apparently suffered illnesses in childhood; she had suffered back problems in life resulting from heavy work and pelvic damage resulting from childbirth trauma. The other was a muscular adult male, perhaps around 35–40 years old. He, too, would have suffered back pain resulting from heavy work. This evidence supports that adduced from five burials excavated on the site in the 1950s which, again, stressed the heavy workloads endured by each of the individuals examined (Wells 1952).

Christianity

In the second half of the first millennium AD the Celtic Christian church began to play an increasingly important political as well as religious role within the early kingdoms of Scotland, following the establishment shortly after AD 563 of the Columban community on Iona. Even the initially pagan Pictish state came increasingly under the influence of Celtic monasticism, deriving ultimately from Ireland, through the activities of missionary saints. The important church figures of the period were often high-ranking members of the secular elite, particularly amongst the Scots, and a symbiotic relationship was soon established between church and emergent state; the church providing divine legitimacy for the earthly rulers in return for patronage and the material requirements of the church establishment. The ordination in 574 of Aedan as king of the Scots by St Columba (who himself belonged to the Irish Ui Neill royal house) exemplifies the close link that existed even at this early stage. Such a bond between religion and political power was simply the continuation of much older traditions and did not relate specifically to Christianity. Nonetheless the 'international' character of the Christian church and the ideologies it promoted were consonant with the aspirations of the elite and the bond between church and state was to grow increasingly strong through the millennium despite the disruptions of the Norse who were also ultimately absorbed within the Christian world.

Direct evidence for Christian religious belief in the Hebrides during the pre-Norse period is slight. Given their proximity to the ecclesiastical centres of Dalriada and the Irish contacts represented by the artefactual record, it is unlikely that early Christian influence did not affect the Hebrides. Two passages in Adomnan's *Life of Columba* refer to the saint's visit to Skye and, although he does not appear to have visited the Western Isles, there is little reason to doubt that others did. One piece of evidence often cited for a pre-Norse Christian presence in the islands is the occurrence of the Norse island name, Pabbay, thought to refer to the island of a Christian 'papar' or priest, although we should not forget that there appears also to have been a pre-Christian preference for island retreats for holy men or religious communities (c.f. Burn 1969). Such islands were presumably areas of marginal economic importance granted by local or more distant lords. Pabbay names are fairly common in the Hebrides, as at Pabbay Mor just off the Bhaltos peninsula in Lewis, and may suggest a fairly well-established monastic presence prior to the Norse incursions (Figure 9.2). Other island names with the Norse suffix 'ay' (for island) following a saint's name may reflect pre-Norse associations of certain islands with particular saints. Taransay off Harris, for example, would appear to be associated with Pictish saint Taran or Ternan (RCAHMS 1928, xvi).

One of the most significant, identifiably early ecclesiastical sites in the Hebrides is Annait, situated in Waternish in Skye. The name means 'mother church' and was commonly used in Ireland and Scotland to denote the earliest monastic establishment within a given district. At Annait the monastic buildings appear to have been sited within a prehistoric fort; the domestic buildings were centred on a small chapel within an enclosure defined partly by a river and stream. The place name occurs elsewhere in the Hebrides: at Shader in Lewis, in the Shiant Isles and on Staffin Island off Skye. In these cases, however, there are no identifiable structural remains.

Physical remains of the early Christian period do appear to survive on the remote island of North Rona where a chapel and domestic buildings probably dating to this period have been identified (RCAHMS 1928, no. 9). The monastic settlement on this island, some fourteen miles north-north-east of the Butt of Lewis probably represented an offshoot from an established church in the northern part of Lewis, possibly at Europie where later remains and place name evidence suggest the presence of an important early religious centre. On North Rona an early chapel survives within a cemetery enclosure despite the presence of numerous medieval, domestic buildings on the site. Numerous incised cross-slabs of seventh–ninth century AD date point to the existence of an Early Christian monastic community that appears to have disappeared during or shortly after the Norse incursions. Further cross-slabs suggest reoccupation from the twelfth century onwards.

DISCUSSION

It appears then that in the middle centuries of the first millennium AD the successors of the Iron Age communities who had built the Atlantic roundhouses and wheelhouses, and who seem to have been part of a wider political scene with its centre in the north, were drawn into the northern part of the emerging Pictish state. Despite, or perhaps because of this, the people of the Hebrides continued to be exposed to a wide range of cultural influences, extending to Ireland and Northumbria as well as Pictland and any central Pictish authority would probably have been exerted only loosely.

Continuity from the Iron Age is manifested most clearly in the development of the cellular building tradition from the preceding wheelhouses and in the steady development of pottery forms. The continuation of occupation on existing settlement sites suggests that patterns of land-holding and economy continued more or less unaltered, although there is as yet precious little direct evidence relating to these important issues. So, although the political affiliations and loyalties of the Hebridean elite may nominally have come within the orbit of a larger and more distant authority, the local scene may have remained fairly stable.

There were, however, significant trends in the way in which power and prestige were displayed during the course of the millennium and these may hint at a rather greater local impact of the nascent Pictish state than is at first apparent. During the Iron Age, monumental architecture – first the Atlantic roundhouses and then the wheelhouses – was central to the lives of Hebridean communities. These buildings stressed the independence and authority of individual households at a local level. Elaborately decorated ceramics also seem to have been important and again these were probably objects of communal rather than individual ownership.

In the early part of the first millennium AD monumental architecture finally disappeared, whilst at the same time pottery became much less elaborately decorated and less varied. Instead there was an increasing emphasis on objects of personal ownership, generally portable and highly visible items such as jewellery. This implies that the perceived status of the individual was increasingly important, suggesting that certain individuals were now more mobile and engaged in more face-to-face contacts demanding that they carry the marks of their status with them rather than rely on the local and static monumentality of the home base. Patterns of land-holding may have been more formally fixed as the power of the state became more pervasive, reducing the need for ostentatious building. At the same time the more elaborate ranking and range of social relationships created by the state would have found expression in the attire and behaviour of individuals at all levels of society. Latterly the role of the Church became crucial in establishing the legitimacy of secular lords and providing a divine model for earthly authorities. The role of literacy in helping to establish the early church should not be overlooked, assuming that it must have had an almost magical significance for illiterate communities. Access to such arcane knowledge would have been a powerful symbol of power and prestige. The change in the nature of the archaeological record from the Iron Age to the mid–first millennium AD thus reflects both the changing concerns of Hebridean communities and the changing nature and scale of the world of which they were a part.

10 The Vikings

The Hebrides first attracted the attentions of Viking raiders some time close to AD 800. Documented attacks on the Christian centre of Iona in AD 795 would have taken the raiders through the Minch and it is most unlikely that Skye and the Western Isles escaped their attentions. Andersen has suggested that the initial raids ceased after a few decades, giving way to colonisation and that this latter process may itself have come to an end by around AD 870 when Norse sights had become set on Iceland and other Atlantic islands (1991, 133). Once colonised, however, the Hebrides remained part of the Norse world until their secession to Scotland in 1266.

The Viking raiders of the ninth century AD would have encountered in the Hebrides a society nominally part of the Pictish kingdom yet open to considerable Scottic and Irish influence. It was an area that had only recently begun to accept Christian monastic settlements but where at least the upper echelons of society would probably have been Christian. Politically it was apparently peripheral both to Pictland and the Dalriadic Scots and the local rulers could probably not have expected much assistance from either quarter in their opposition to the Viking raiders. A continuity of social and political development extending at least from the early Iron Age, and probably much earlier, was thus about to come to an end.

Although the Viking Age is a period for which contemporary or near-contemporary records exist there are very few written documents that mention the Hebrides and none that provide much help in defining the processes by which Norse power was established and maintained. The most prolific record for the period is perhaps that of Norse place-names (Figure 10.1). Several place-names or elements within them indicate Viking Age foundations for the settlements to which they refer. Place-name elements such as *stadir*, *setr/saetr*, *bolstadr* and *byr* all relate to various classes of

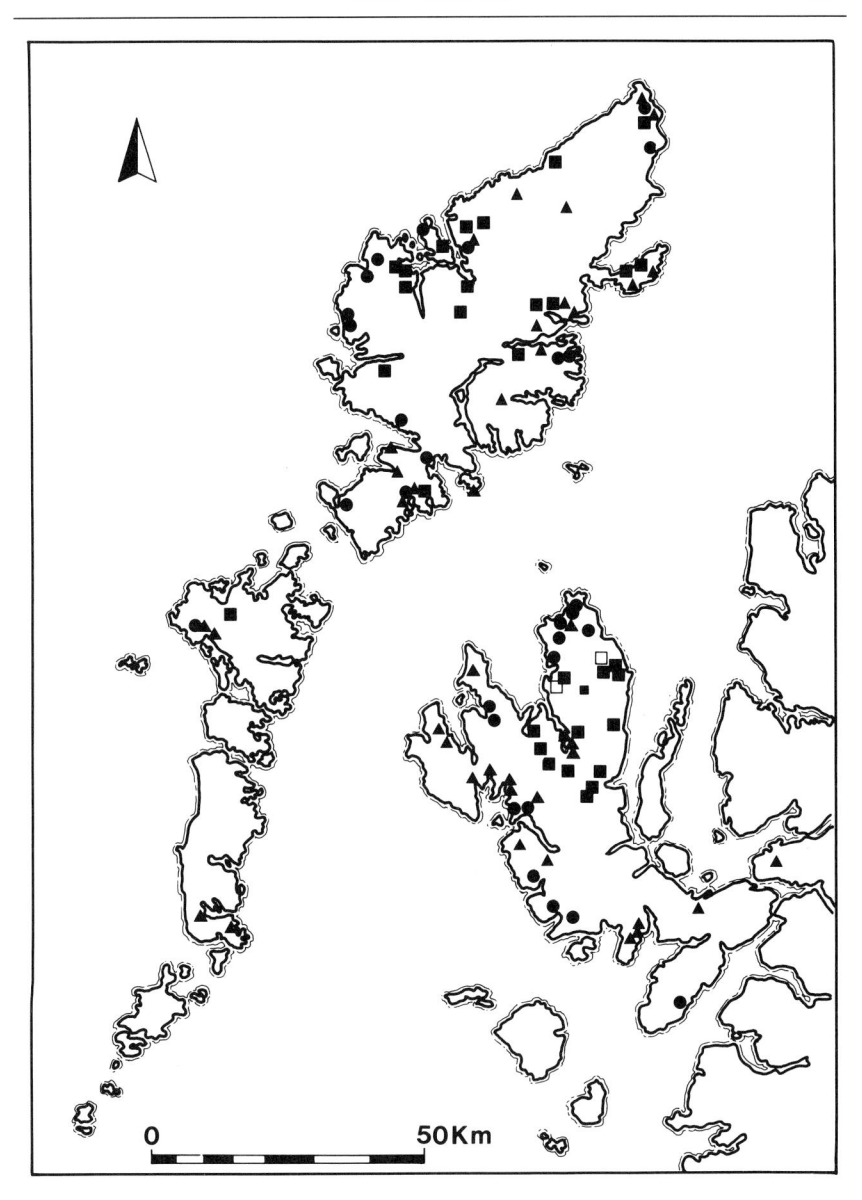

- ● **Stadir Place Names**
- ■ **Setr/Saetr Place Names**
- ▲ **Bólstadr Place Names**
- □ **Byr Place Names**

FIGURE 10.1. Some Norse place-names in Skye and the Western Isles.

settlement (c.f. B. Crawford 1987). Despite disputes over the detailed meaning and chronology of these place-names (usefully summarised by Andersen 1991) they nonetheless provide a broad-scale picture of the density and date of Viking settlement throughout the Hebrides.

The place-name evidence suggests that the northern parts of the Hebrides were densely settled, to an extent that implies the cultural if not physical obliteration of the indigenous population. This is particularly the case in Lewis where 99 of the 126 village names are of Norse origin while a further nine have Norse elements (Barber 1885, 70). In the southern part of the Hebrides actual immigration, as opposed to political control, may have been more sporadic and short-lived, the settlers being thus more easily assimilated into indigenous cultures. Such assumptions, however, may be simplistic since Norse place-names in these southern areas may themselves have been displaced later by the spread of Gaelic in the Later Middle Ages particularly in those areas south of Skye which in the pre-Norse period had been culturally Scottic rather than Pictish.

Viking Age Settlement

Despite the apparent density of Norse settlement in the Hebrides, archaeological sites of this period have proved exceptionally elusive. Even areas like Lewis that were linguistically swamped by the Norse retain few identifiable sites of the period. This situation has perhaps two main causes. First, Viking houses were rectilinear and would thus be better disguised by the mass of medieval and later settlement forms that litter the islands than their cellular and circular predecessors. Secondly, many of the farms and villages established by the early Norse settlers will have survived to the present day and evidence for their earliest phases will have been obscured by later building. Nevertheless these factors do not fully explain the elusiveness of Norse settlement in areas like Bhaltos in Lewis where there has been extensive survey and excavation and where Viking Age burials are plentiful (see below).

Drimore, South Uist

At present the only published excavation of a Hebridean Norse settlement relates to a single house excavated on the Drimore machair in South Uist (Maclaren 1974). This site was one of a number of principally Iron Age settlements excavated in advance of the construction of a rocket range in the 1950s. Maclaren interpreted the building as the nucleus of a small farmstead largely devoted to pastoral farming (1974, 14), although the difficulties of retrieving archaeological evidence for agriculture from machair sites has been remarked upon elsewhere. It was unfortunate that the very limited scope of the excavation, which lasted only two weeks, did not enable the excavator to explore the area around the excavated building.

THE VIKINGS 189

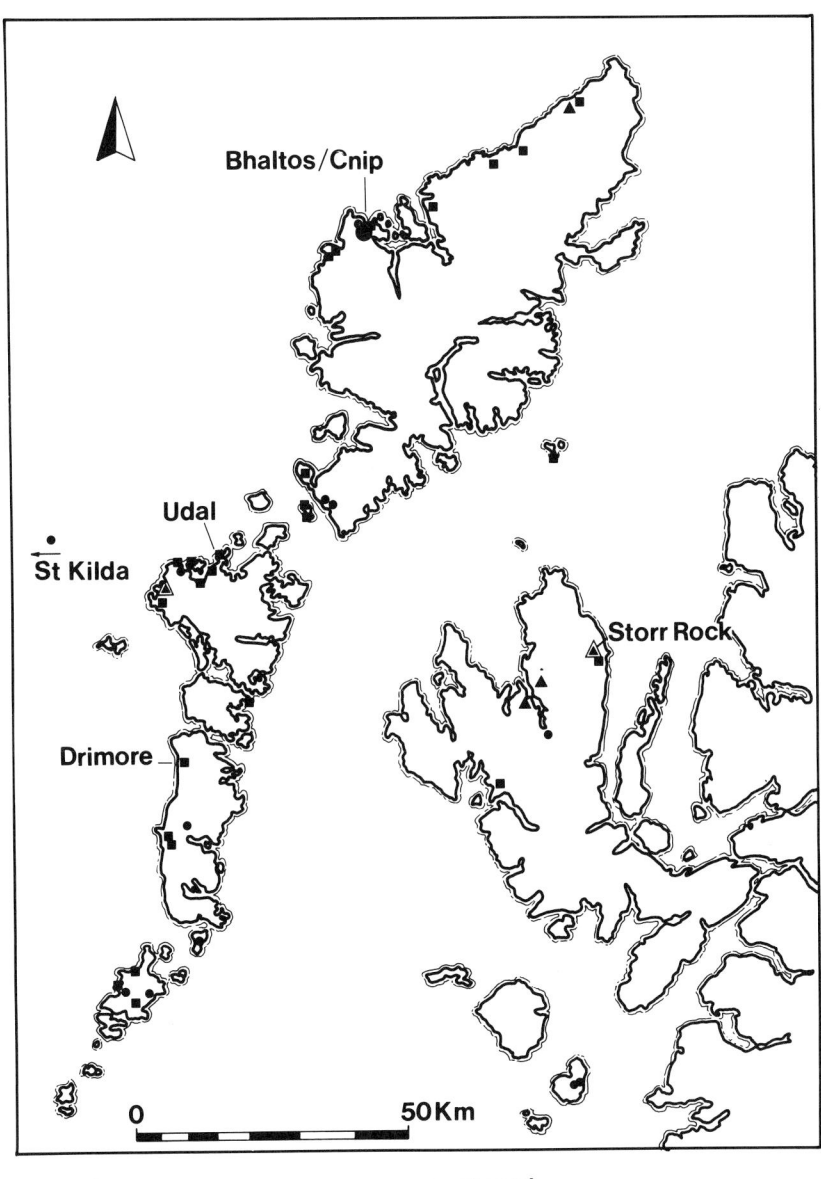

- Grave
- Cemetery
- Viking Pottery
- Hoard
- Coin Hoard

FIGURE 10.2. Norse sites in Skye and the Western Isles.

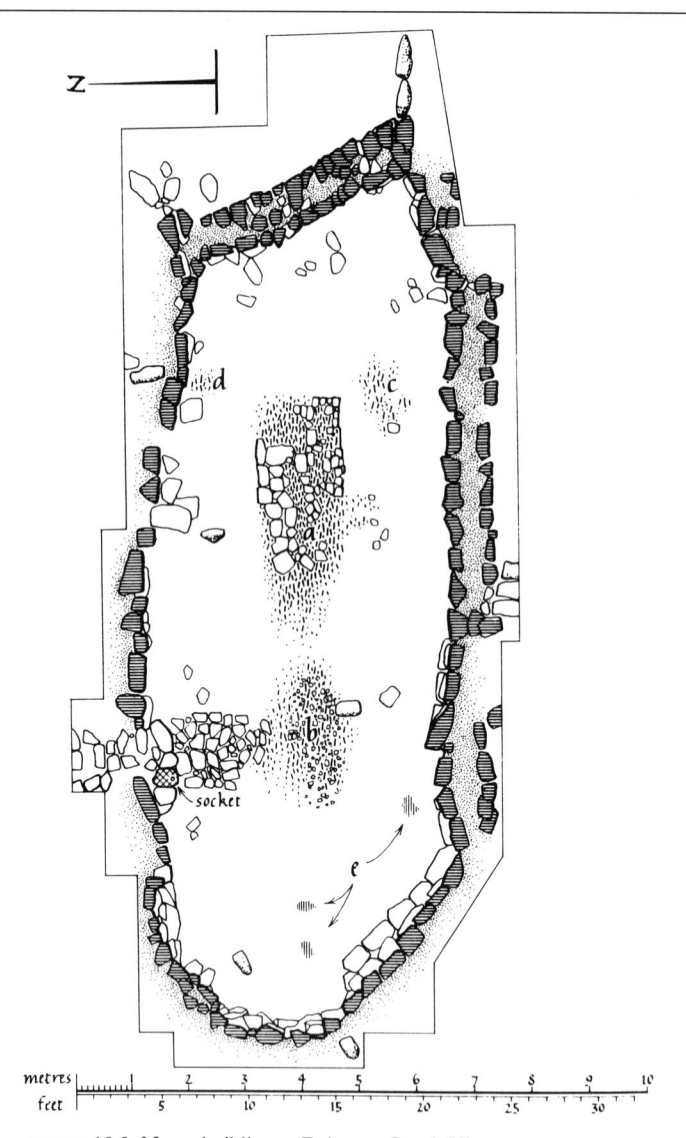

FIGURE 10.3. Norse building at Drimore, South Uist.

The Drimore house was of a completely different type to those of the preceding Early Historic period in the Hebrides (Figure 10.3). It was subrectangular with one end rounded and the other apparently re-built with a straight blocking wall. It was a substantial building measuring some 14 m long by 5 m wide internally, its long axis running east to west (Maclaren 1974). An entrance was set in the north side where a socket for the doorpost had been formed from a whale vertebra. Only the foundations of the walls survived intact and these were less than 1 m thick, formed of waterworn boulders ill-suited to supporting substantial walling. It appears that turf rather than stone may have formed the upper parts of the building.

The building was entered from a path leading in from the north. The paving carried on into the house up to the long rectangular hearth that dominated the interior. Unfortunately the severe waterlogging of the floor deposits made it impossible for the excavator to recover a detailed floor plan and there is little evidence one way or the other for internal divisions, postholes and other features. The almost complete lack of finds from the area to the west of the entrance, however, suggests that there may have been an internal partition at the entrance separating the eastern domestic end of the building from a western end used for storage or for housing livestock. The bone assemblage suggests that cattle and sheep were the predominant livestock with some pig, horse, dog and red deer also represented.

The Drimore house belongs to the 'hall-house' type known widely from the Norse world and has its closest parallels at Jarlshof in Shetland and a number of Orcadian sites such as Buckquoy and Birsay. Similar buildings have also been found in Iceland and Faeroe. House 1 at Jarlshof in Shetland dating to the earliest Viking period is the closest parallel in terms of groundplan although it is considerably larger (Hamilton 1956).

The site has been dated to the late ninth or early tenth centuries primarily on the basis of the building form and the finds assemblage. The latter includes a distinctive bone cleaver of a type also found in Norway in the later ninth century AD. Steatite spindle whorls and vessel fragments, and a single-sided composite bone comb reinforce the Viking Age date. Other finds tended to be undiagnostic. Despite some signs of re-building there is no stratigraphic evidence for a protracted use of the structure although, as with earlier buildings, it was probably regularly scoured out of occupation debris. Indeed Lane has cast some doubt on the interpretation of Drimore as a single-phase building, pointing out the occurrence of a fragment of medieval silver (1983, 298).

The Udal, North Uist

A more extensive Viking Age settlement has been identified at the Udal in North Uist where a series of buildings yielding Norse artefacts apparently overlaid earlier cellular structures (Crawford and Switsur 1977). The site has not yet been published and detailed information about the sequence and dating is not yet available. The excavator has claimed that the construction of a diminutive fort heralded the Norse arrival, implying a military take-over, but the only available radiocarbon date seems to suggest the structure was more likely to date to the tenth century than the early part of the ninth (see the Appendix) although some of the artefactual material, particularly a bronze strap-end, suggests a pre-AD 900 date for the Norse occupation (Graham-Campbell 1974, 18–20). Other buildings on the site appear to indicate a rather more mundane set of activities: these include a cornthreshing floor and metal-working areas as well as domestic buildings (Crawford and Switsur 1977, 131). The site continued in occupation throughout the Norse period, as an essentially domestic site, whilst finds such as a Norwegian silver coin of Harald Hardrada point to continued links with the wider Norse world (ibid.).

Barvas, Lewis

During the course of field survey of the Western Isles coastline in 1978 a number of sites were identified eroding from the Barvas machair on the north-west coast of Lewis. One of these transpired, on further, small-scale excavation, to be the remains of a Viking Age settlement (Cowie et al., forth). A dense midden mound yielding Viking Age pottery contained the remains of at least two domestic structures, both sub-rectangular in form with double-skinned drystone walls packed with turf. On the basis of pottery evidence Cowie has suggested that the site is a single-period Norse farming settlement dating from tenth–eleventh centuries AD.

One of the most important aspects of the Barvas excavation was the recovery of a wide range of animal and plant remains that enable a picture to be constructed of the economy of the Norse farm. Carbonised grains and seeds indicate that both barley and oats were staple crops. The latter is rare in prehistoric Scotland and more characteristic of medieval cropping regimes. Flax, too, was grown and a range of arable weeds present on the site may have been used for food on analogy with later, medieval practice.

The animal bone assemblage suggested that cattle and sheep were the dominant domesticates, whilst pig, red deer, horse and otter were present in small quantities (Harman, n.d.). Serjeantson's analysis of the ages at death of the cattle and sheep revealed interesting patterns that reflect the particular methods of animal husbandry practised by the site's inhabitants. The majority of calves were killed shortly after birth whilst sheep were kept for at least one summer and often two (Serjeantson, n.d.). In order for cattle to produce milk they must calve regularly, so the pattern of culling of very young calves suggests that milk production was important. Sheep would also have provided milk, and they were allowed to live until they had achieved a worthwhile meat weight whilst those surviving two summers would also have yielded a fleece. In the case of both cattle and sheep, only the minimum number of cows and ewes required to maintain the herds and flocks seem to have been kept alive. The indications of a dairy economy are supported by strikingly similar results from the analysis of animal bone from the Udal in North Uist (ibid.).

Fish remains, too, were common on the site, the predominant species being large cod, ling and saithe, suggestive of offshore fishing from boats. Flat-fish such as plaice, flounder and turbot are indicative of shallow water fishing as well, either from boats of from the shore.

Overall then, the economy of the Norse farm at Barvas was diverse; dairy production played a central part, with meat and fleeces also important. Fishing would have provided much of the basic subsistence of the site's inhabitants as would the cultivation of barley and oats. Other animal remains hint at less central aspects of the economy. Otter remains suggest the hunting of that animal for its pelt, occasional whalebones suggest the periodic exploitation of strandings, although in general marine mammals are surprisingly scarce on the site.

Viking Age Pottery

A distinctive Norse pottery style has been identified by Alan Lane, principally on the basis of the material from the Udal in North Uist (Lane 1983; 1990). This pottery comprises sagging and flat-based bowls and cups along with distinctive flat platters, all with minimal or no decoration. Around 40 per cent of the bases of Viking Age pottery from the Udal were distinctively grass-marked in contrast to pottery of other periods in the Hebrides (Lane 1983, 245) and suggesting links with broadly contemporary Irish grass-marked pottery. The excavator, however, has suggested that grass-marked pottery was also briefly present on the site in the fifth and sixth centuries AD (Crawford 1974) and similar sherds appear to relate to occupation several centuries earlier at Eilean Olabhat (Campbell, pers. comm.) so some caution must be exercised in the identification of this as a distinctively Norse trait. Grass-marked pottery also occurs, for example, in pre-Viking deposits at sites such as Pool in Orkney and Kebister in Shetland (Owen, pers. comm.). Decoration was restricted to occasional slashing or impressing of the rims, a trait which appears also to have persisted into the medieval period. Overall the range of form and fabric is quite different from the preceding Hebridean Plain Style pottery at the Udal.

The range of forms and fabrics of the Viking Age pottery does not appear to derive from any Hebridean precursor, suggesting that incoming Norse people may have had a major impact on the production of ceramics. Lane has suggested that the Hebridean Plain Style sherds recovered from Viking Age levels are likely simply to be residual material (1983, 242). This change in pottery type might relate, for example, to the introduction of new techniques of food preparation and serving, or to alternative modes of production. Pottery in this profusion is, however, extremely rare in the rest of the Viking Age world, especially the Viking colonies, although it is, of course, a persistent characteristic of the material culture of the Western Isles over thousands of years. The apparent radical break in the ceramic tradition in the islands, remembering that the evidence for this sequence is restricted to one site, cannot therefore be equated with a simple cultural replacement.

By examining older assemblages from earlier excavations, Lane has identified this tradition of Viking Age pottery throughout the Hebrides as far south as Tiree (1983, 129). Pottery comparable to the Udal material has been identified at a whole range of sites including former roundhouses such as Dun Cuier and Dun Chlif in Barra; Dun Carloway in Lewis and Eilean Maleit in North Uist; as well as machair middens at Barvas and Carinish in Lewis; and former wheelhouse sites such as Allasdale in Barra and Foshigarry in North Uist (Lane 1983, 303–20). Some sites which have produced surface collections of this type of pottery, such as at Mangersta and Bosta in Lewis, appear to be settlement mounds and would well repay more detailed study. Further sherds have been found close to the eroding Viking Age cemetery on Cnip Headland reinforcing the suggestion that the settlement inhabited by those buried on the site may not be far off.

SILVER AND GOLD

Characteristic of the Viking Age throughout those areas of Scotland subject to Scandinavian influence are hoards of silver or, more rarely, gold objects (Graham-Campbell 1976). Perhaps the most important of the Hebridean hoards is that found at Storr Rock, some eight miles from Portree in Skye towards the end of the last century (Figure 10.2). The 111 coins of Anglo-Saxon and Arabic origin that formed the bulk of the hoard suggest a date for its deposition of around AD 935, making Storr the earliest dated Scandinavian hoard in Scotland. As well as the coins, the hoard contained twenty three pieces of 'hack-silver' (fragments cut from a range of objects including penannular brooches and ingots). The derivation of these fragments suggested that a range of items of Scottish, Scandinavian and Irish origin had been used.

From around AD 950–1050 Scottish hoards of Scandinavian character are dominated by 'ring money': silver, penannular arm-rings which appear to have been of fairly standardised manufacture and have been interpreted as a form of currency (Graham-Campbell 1976). This interpretation is supported by studies of the weight of ring money which appear to show that the makers were aiming for, though not consistently achieving, a standard weight (Warner 1976). Complete ring money has been found in a hoard discovered under five feet of peat at Dibadail, near South Dell in Lewis where it had been buried along with two finger rings. A further, recently discovered, hoard from the grounds of Lews Castle in Stornoway, Lewis, contained thirty seven items, mostly hack-silver cut from ring money. The fragments had all been wrapped in linen, possibly sorted into different groups, and then deposited in a cattle horn. Two Norman coins date the Lews Castle hoard to around AD 990–1040.

The relative paucity of coins in the Scottish hoards compared to those of Ireland has led Graham-Campbell to suggest that the Norse settlers in Scotland were engaged in less overseas trade than their Irish counterparts (1976, 127). The apparent lack of proto-urban centres of Norse character in Scotland may support this interpretation, whilst the use of ring money may hint at a more insular and inward-looking economy.

Although scarce relative to silver, gold items of Scandinavian character are known from the Hebrides. A gold finger ring found at Dun Beag, an Atlantic roundhouse in Skye, and another from the same island with no detailed provenance may be casual losses unrelated to the phenomenon of hoard deposition. However a hoard of six and a half gold finger rings apparently from Oronsay, a small island off North Uist, does seem related to this wider phenomenon.

Much effort has gone in to the detailed cataloguing of the Viking Age silver hoards and the provenancing of the objects they contain. The most interesting question of all though, must surely be why so many items of such value were buried in the ground, never to be recovered, during the tenth and eleventh centuries. Traditionally they have been seen as a means of protecting private wealth in insecure times, or as the 'savings' of individuals. There would, however, seem to be many more practical ways of hiding such material for short periods than burying it in the ground, often in remote places where relocation would be extraordinarily difficult, and where any above-ground marking would be likely to attract unwanted attention. Despite the undoubtedly uncertain times in which these hoards were deposited, the recovery rate by the owners also seems peculiarly low. Given the assumption that only a fraction of the hoards still buried have been found by archaeologists, the rate of loss must have been enormous over these two centuries. It is perhaps more likely that much of the hoard deposition of the Viking Age was intended to placate or gain favour from the gods, as was the case in earlier periods, and that they were never intended to be recovered. The act of burial in the ground with its concomitant difficulties of relocation, the bizarrely low recovery rate by the original owners, and the frequent choice of remote places, all seem to make more sense in the context of ritual offerings than pragmatic storage.

Burials

Although Christian communities may have remained active in the Viking Age the incoming settlers were pagan, and this is reflected in the grave goods deposited with their dead. Christianity did not become the principal religion of the Norse settlers in Orkney until AD 995 when pressure was exerted from the Norwegian king Olaf Tryggvasson, and it is likely that, even then, its percolation to the bulk of the population was limited. A similar situation is likely to have pertained in the Hebrides. If Christian graves existed in this period they would, of course, be much harder to identify given their lack of grave goods.

Few Viking Age cemeteries have been identified in Scotland and the principal excavated site, that at Westness in Orkney, is unpublished. Only two such sites are known in the Western Isles and Skye (see below) although many of the isolated graves reported from the area may signal the presence of other cemeteries. To the south of our area, particularly in Islay, Colonsay

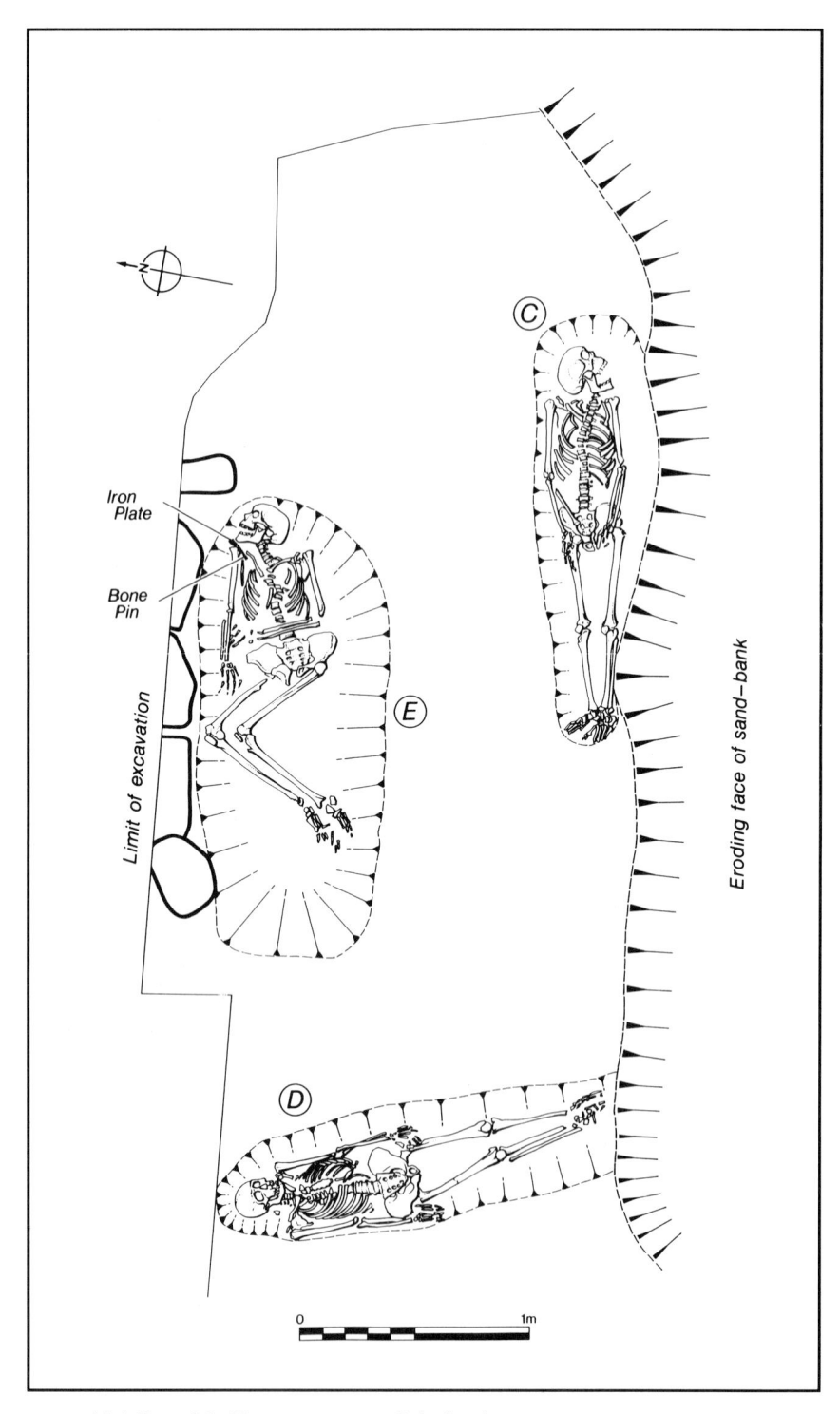

FIGURE 10.4. Part of the Norse cemetery at Cnip, Lewis.

and Arran, numerous Viking graves have been excavated, although mostly with primitive, antiquarian techniques. It is important to be aware that, in this period, the scatter of known graves and cemeteries in the Western Isles and Skye form part of a wider continuum from the Northern Isles through the west coast to the Isle of Man and Ireland.

The Viking Age Cemetery on Cnip Headland, Lewis

The largest known concentration of Viking Age burials in the Hebrides comes from an eroding cemetery in the machair on Cnip Headland on the Bhaltos peninsula of Lewis (Figures 10.4 and 10.5). The cemetery lies on the hillside overlooking Traigh na Berie, close to several later prehistoric settlements such as the Cnip wheelhouse and the Atlantic roundhouses of Loch na Berie and Loch Bharabhat (see Chapters 6 and 7). The Cnip Headland site has already been discussed in Chapter 5 with reference to a series of Bronze Age burials from the lower of two former ground surfaces exposed on the hillside. Perhaps coincidentally, or perhaps because the site was a traditional place of burial, the Viking Age cemetery directly overlies the Bronze Age burials on the upper ground surface. The nature of the erosion of the site has meant that there has been no single major excavation but rather a series of smaller investigations as burials became exposed in the years since 1979 when the first grave was discovered. So far seven burials have been recovered, five from a single cluster, one close by and one a short distance uphill.

The first burial to be excavated was also the only one to yield substantial quantities of grave goods (Figure 10.6). Unfortunately the excavation was not carried out by archaeologists, and evidence relating to the form of the grave has been lost. Nonetheless important information was obtained, mainly relating to the artefactual assemblage. The grave was that of a woman aged around 35–40 years, buried with a range of personal ornaments characteristic of Viking Age female burials throughout the Norse world in the tenth century AD (Welander et al., 1987). The grave goods were all personal items likely to have been used extensively in life rather than specially fashioned offerings or funerary gifts. They included two oval brooches in gilt bronze, highly ornamented with a series of zoomorphic designs. These brooches, one of which had been slightly damaged before being buried, would have been worn in life to secure the woman's clothing. The corpse also wore a necklace comprising forty four coloured glass beads and had an antler comb, a ringed pin and a bronze belt-buckle and strap-end. As well as these personal ornaments the woman had also been furnished with a small collection of more utilitarian items comprising an iron knife and whetstone, a sickle and a bone needle case containing the remnants of two iron needles. The sickle was a particularly light example and was perhaps used for cutting herbs rather than a heavier agricultural function (ibid., 163). Detailed analysis of the material from the grave confirmed the high quality of crafts-

FIGURE 10.5. Stone settings marking three adult Norse burials at Cnip, Lewis.

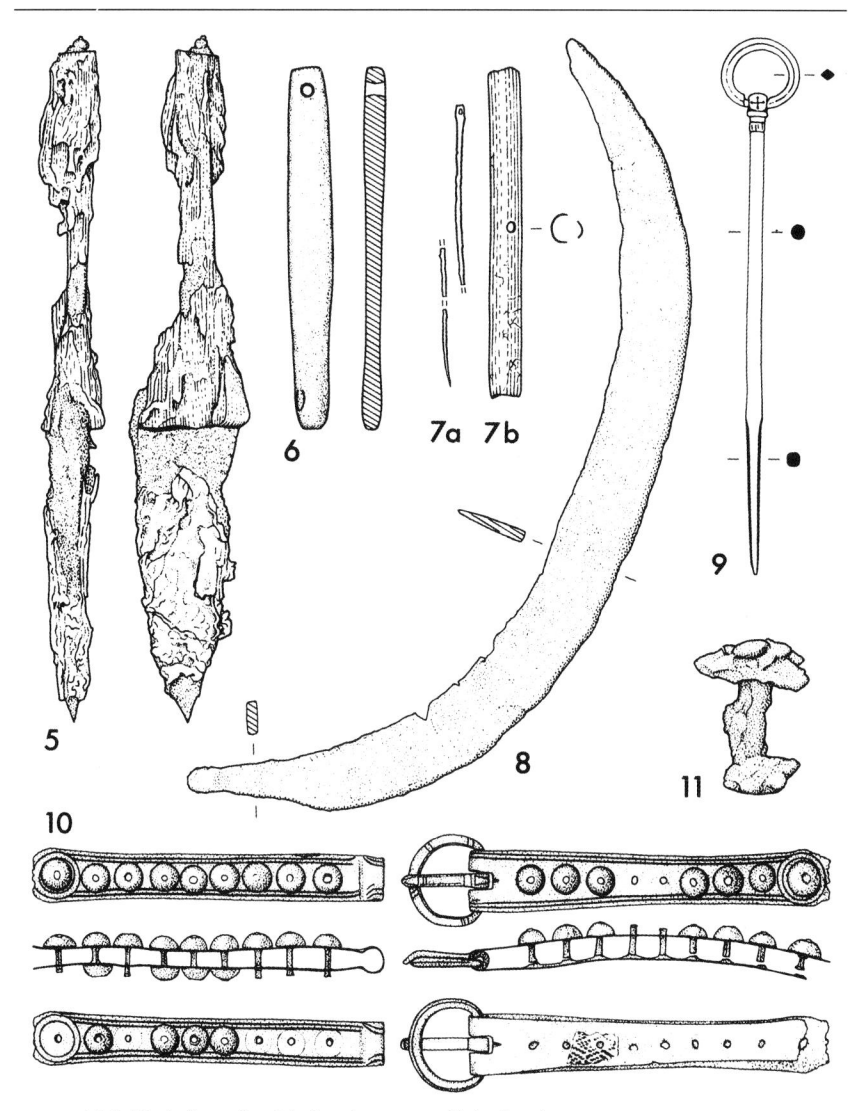

FIGURE 10.6. Finds from the rich female grave at Cnip, Lewis.

manship required to produce this small assemblage (ibid., 165). It has been suggested that the decorative metalwork and glass beads, for example, were almost certainly imported from specialist craft centres such as are known at Birka in Sweden or at Dublin (ibid.).

One further aspect of particular interest was the recovery of pieces of textile adhering to the oval brooches; remnants of the dead woman's burial clothing. Several fabrics were represented suggesting that the woman had been buried in the typical dress of a wealthy Viking Age Scandinavian woman; wearing a tunic under a pinafore-style skirt (Bender Jorgensen 1987). The fabrics are of a common Scandinavian type found widely in Denmark, Sweden and Norway as well as in Scotland, Ireland and the Isle of Man.

Further excavations on the site in 1992 and 1994 recovered a cluster of five burials close to the first grave (Dunwell et al., forth). These comprised three adults, one child of six–nine months and one new-born. A further child burial had been excavated some distance upslope in 1991. The three adults were all buried in simple shallow grave pits marked on the surface by low mounds kerbed by rectangular arrangements of stones. Two lay with their heads to the east and one to the north; two were in an extended position and one was slightly flexed. The three graves were all tightly packed together but did not inter-cut, suggesting that little time separated the funerals. The child burials apparently had no above-ground markers. One of the dead had its arms crossed suggesting that the body had been laid in the grave in a shroud. Another, the only female of the group, had a bone pin and perforated iron plate at her shoulder, presumably to secure the clothing in which she was buried.

Both the young child in the grave cluster and the other child buried upslope from this group had similar assemblages of grave goods. The former had been buried wearing a necklace of amber beads and clothing secured by a fine bone pin. The latter was also found with an amber bead and a pendant, both apparently worn around the neck. Given the paucity of grave goods associated with the majority of the adults it is possible that some special significance was attached to the untimely deaths of children. The number of burials so far recovered, however, is too small for any serious consideration of such variations in the treatment of the dead.

Two of the Cnip Headland graves, the rich female burial and the youngest of the children, contained single small iron rivets. These seem most unlikely to have been deliberate inclusions and perhaps came from wooden planks used to support the corpse during the funeral proceedings. Indeed the rivet from the rich female grave had the remains of wood embedded in its corroded surface (Welander et al., 1987, 163).

As a group, the skeletons from Cnip Headland provide some information about the conditions in which the Viking Age inhabitants of Lewis lived, although there are manifestly too few as yet for a proper statistical analysis. The adults had all reached maturity (certainly none was less than thirty years old at death) although the proportion of children is, of course, high relative to modern populations. Bruce has suggested that the small stature of the adults reflects poor conditions during childhood and there are signs from the skeletons of arduous working conditions later in life (Dunwell et al., forth). The teeth of all of the adults had suffered severe attrition caused by a coarse diet. Both adult males had suffered broken bones in life; one a fractured pelvis and one a broken arm, both of which had healed. At least one of the skeletons showed signs of spinal injury due to prolonged and arduous work. The female skeleton showed signs of minor injuries to her hand and shoulder. Despite this parade of assorted mishaps, however, none of the skeletons produced any evidence for their cause of death.

The radiocarbon dates for the Cnip Headland burials suggest that the cemetery was in use in the latter part of the ninth century AD. This implies a somewhat earlier date for the burial cluster than was suggested on artefactual grounds for the rich female burial. The recovery and dating of further burials will have to be awaited before it will be possible to judge whether this simply indicates that the cemetery was used over several generations.

The distribution of the graves so far discovered suggests that there are many more burials still present on Cnip Headland in what appears to have been a fairly extensive cemetery, albeit perhaps divided into small family clusters (Dunwell et al., forth.). The mix of men, women and children and their physical condition suggests that this was the burial ground of a settled farming community presumably living close by and probably farming the machair of the Traigh na Berie. The relationship of the rich female burial to the others is intriguing. Hers was the only richly furnished burial and the only one to show clear signs of wide-ranging contacts within the Norse world (although the more modest artefacts from the other graves do have Norse parallels in Scotland). The typological dates for the artefacts suggest a slightly later date than the radiocarbon dates from the grave cluster. Possibly she belonged to a different and wealthier family or came from a slightly later generation when the community was enjoying better fortunes. Perhaps ideas on what was appropriate to leave with the dead had changed. Alternatively, the poorly furnished burials may represent the graves of the descendants of the Pictish population whose burial traditions, following native precedents, were less ostentatious than those of the Norse settlers; in this case the variation within the cemetery may simply reflect the varying cultural affiliations present within the Hebrides in the ninth and tenth centuries. Only the recovery of a larger sample of burials will enable real patterns to be identified within the cemetery.

A Rich Burial at Bhaltos, Lewis

A further indication that there may be some substance to the idea that the native population formed part of the upper echelons of Viking Age cultural milieu comes from an apparently isolated rich Viking Age female grave from close to Bhaltos school, not far from Cnip Headland (MacLeod et al., 1916). The presence in this grave of two brooches and a belt buckle of Celtic design, including one penannular brooch, along with two Viking oval brooches, exemplifies the melding of cultural influences occurring in the Hebrides during the later part of the ninth century. Either this was a Scandinavian woman, a first or second generation settler, for whom Celtic fashions in personal ornaments were both available and apparently appropriate, or else she was a descendant of the indigenous peoples for whom Viking-style clothing and burial customs had become the norm.

A Viking Age Cemetery on Eigg

Three wealthy male burials excavated on Eigg, one of the Small Isles, in the nineteenth century, point to the existence of an important cemetery there. These burials each lay under substantial mounds and contained a range of artefacts including penannular brooches and a magnificent Norwegian sword hilt dating to the late eighth or ninth century AD (Greig 1940). The character of these graves suggests that they relate to a rather different community to the one using the Cnip Headland cemetery but, again, the lack of systematic excavation of a large sample of the cemetery prevents fruitful comparisons.

VIKING AND NATIVE

One of the key questions concerning the study of this period is the nature of the encounters between the indigenous population of the Hebrides and the incoming Norse. Was the Norse colonisation a brief, bloody and violent process or did cultural assimilation enable the peaceful co-existence of native and incomer? The place-name evidence suggests that Pictish culture and language were entirely usurped in at least the northern parts of the Hebrides whilst the scant documentary sources demonstrate the extent and duration of Norse political control. Although we should be wary of naive equations of material culture and language with identifiable ethnic groups there were clearly major social upheavals underway in the Hebrides of the ninth century AD. Initial attempts to reduce the Viking colonisation to a peaceful, neighbourly affair were predicated upon the idea that the Northern and Western Isles of Scotland were, if not 'empty islands', then at least under-used and sparsely populated (the arguments are usefully summarised by Crawford, 1981). This was evidently not the case and any attempt by a new social elite to impose themselves will inevitably have met with resistance of some kind.

The absence of material of Norse origin or displaying Norse influence in such settlements as Loch na Berie is striking, especially since the latest structure on this site appears to date very close to the Viking Age and was probably still occupied when Norse raids were beginning to plague at least parts of Scotland. It appears that in Bhaltos there may have been some major re-structuring of land-holding and settlement location coinciding with the period of Viking settlement (c.f. Armit 1994a). Nonetheless Viking Age pottery elsewhere demonstrates that many sites were not abandoned, whilst the settlement sequence at the Udal demonstrates the continuity of an apparently locally significant centre (Crawford and Switsur 1977). It appears likely that there was at least tolerance by the Norse settlers of the incipient Christian Church since the various islands incorporating the place-name element 'papar' presumably refer to Christian monks inhabiting these islands during the Viking Age occupation.

The evidence of the blending of cultural traditions apparent in the Bhaltos female burial is perhaps the best single indicator of the relationship between incomer and native. Although political authority and land rights would have changed at the top end of what was already a rather extended social hierarchy, the individual land rights and obligations of the native people may not have been so radically different. Changes in language do not necessarily reflect wholescale changes in population, particularly if the new language is associated with political power and prestige (c.f. Robb 1993); the domination of Norse language and place-names does not mean that the native people were obliterated or that earlier languages did not survive in daily parlance. Such a situation may help to explain the otherwise rather puzzling reassertion of Gaelic as the Norse grip relaxed in the later Middle Ages.

Andersen has suggested that the Viking settlement had its centre of gravity in the Western Isles but that there were considerable numbers of settlers even in the southern Hebrides (1991, 136). In areas like Lewis he suggests that the native Pictish population was reduced to a minority of the population. He further proposes that the subsequent gradual melding of language and culture took place amongst the existing members of this social milieu rather than being the result of later incursions of Gaelic speakers from further south (ibid.). On the whole this seems like a reasonable interpretation of the archaeological and historical evidence. We cannot be sure, however, from the evidence of either language or material culture that the incomers ever comprised more than the ruling elite within the islands, since the association of their language and customs with power and social status would rapidly have made them objects of emulation for aspiring Picts. Indeed this latter cultural context, where the majority of the population were native, is perhaps better suited than Andersen's model to explaining the decline of Norse influence.

In the light of the, admittedly scant, evidence for this period, accounts of genocidal Vikings engaged in wholesale 'ethnic cleansing' throughout the Hebrides seem a little extreme (Crawford 1981). Nonetheless life may have rapidly become rather unpleasant and insecure for the upper echelons of Hebridean society tied, as they appear to have been (however loosely), to a Pictish kingdom from which they were now effectively cut off and which was, in any case, shortly to disappear as a political entity.

THE LATER NORSE PERIOD

The Lewis Chessmen

A vivid illustration of the Later Norse period in the Western Isles comes from a find made in 1831. The greater part of four chess sets comprising elaborately carved naturalistic figures made of walrus ivory was found hidden in a stone cist in the sand dunes of Uig Bay on the west coast of Lewis. A number of draughtsmen and a belt buckle of the same material were found with them and, since some time elapsed between their discovery and acquisition by the British Museum and the National Museum of Antiquities in Edinburgh, other items may well have been lost.

The intricate carving of animal figures and foliage on the backs of the figures suggests comparisons with wood carvings on Norwegian churches of the mid-twelfth century and this has been used to provide the most likely date for their manufacture (Taylor 1978). Indeed a similar chess piece was found in early excavations at the church of St Olaf in Trondheim, dating to the same broad period. The combined evidence of the various parallels suggests that the pieces were probably made in Norway. They were clearly prestigious items and the reasons behind their burial remain obscure. Given that so many sets are represented it is probable that they belonged to a merchant rather than an individual, but this is hardly an adequate explanation for the peculiar circumstances of their deposition. This find, however, indicates the relative wealth and close contacts with the mainstream Norse world of at least some inhabitants of the Hebrides well into the medieval period, just as the graves at Cnip Headland and Bhaltos had confirmed for the earlier Viking Age.

A Late Norse Church?

Recently it has been suggested, on the basis of ground survey, that a group of buildings on a small promontory in South Uist represent the remains of a Late Norse church known as Cille Donnain (Fleming and Woolf 1992). The remains cap an apparently complex series of structures possibly dating to the later prehistoric period. If the identification is correct, this site would be potentially one of the most important for the period in the Western Isles. The plan of the structure identified as a church, however, appears very similar to pre-Norse cellular structures like those at Loch na Berie and at Buckquoy in Orkney and there are no other buildings of this distinct type on the promontory. Clearly excavation will be required to confirm the suspicion that the site represents a Norse ecclesiastical establishment.

Postscript

The Hebrides remained under Norse control for around 450 years after the initial Viking incursions. By the eleventh century they formed the northernmost part of the kingdom of Man and the Isles, their ruler owing allegiance to the King of Norway. The twelfth century, however, saw the establishment in the southern Hebrides and Argyll of Somerled's kingdom, the nascent Lordship of the Isles, and the consequent reassertion of Irish links, Gaelic culture and language. The Norwegian grip on Skye and the Western Isles continued, however, until the final secession of the Hebrides to the Kingdom of Scotland in 1266 by the Treaty of Perth, following the decisive defeat of King Hakon at the Battle of Largs three years earlier. Throughout the Norse period, however, as in the preceding centuries, these areas would not have been immune to influences from the south and ultimately from Ireland.

11 Lords of the Isles

The archaeology of the medieval and post-medieval periods in Skye and the Western Isles is, as for the rest of rural Scotland, badly under-developed. The bulk of archaeological endeavour has traditionally been directed towards prehistory with later periods remaining the preserve of the documentary historian. This has been the case despite the paucity of historical knowledge concerning the mass of the Scottish population for much of the medieval and later periods. Prior to the eighteenth century documentary records focused heavily on the activities of the ruling elite. Even for these privileged members of society, however, the available records delineate little more than a succession of bare events; battles, alliances, marriages and deaths. Little remains to tell us how even those people whom history does record saw and understood the world around them.

There has been a growing realisation in recent years, amongst both archaeologists and historians, that the two disciplines must work more closely together if a detailed picture of the history of the Scottish people is ever to emerge (c.f. Hingley 1993). Particularly in the highland areas of Scotland, archaeologists have begun to study the development of the landscape as a whole rather than simply the islands of preservation represented by individual archaeological sites. This trend has been particularly marked in field survey. In the Hebrides, for example, the work of the Royal Commission on the Archaeological and Historic Monuments of Scotland has recently included the survey of substantial areas of pre-Clearance landscape in Skye (RCAHMS 1993). Surveys by Roger Miket in Skye, Sheffield University in South Uist and Barra, and the Loch Olabhat Research Project in North Uist have adopted a landscape approach not restricted to specific archaeological periods.

Excavations too have begun to be directed at a wider range of periods than was traditionally the case. Crawford's excavations at the Udal in North Uist pioneered this approach, working backwards in time, on a single site, from the pre-Clearance period to the Neolithic (Crawford n.d.). Excavations at Eilean Olabhat and Druim nan Dearcag in North Uist, combined with field survey of the Loch Olabhat area have begun to sketch out the nature of settlement there in the medieval and later periods (Armit 1990a). Overall, however, excavation on sites of this period remains scarce and large scale research programmes focussed on medieval and later settlement have yet to be attempted.

Despite promising signs from recent work it is still too early to present an archaeological narrative of the period from the end of Norse control until the Clearances. This chapter therefore simply surveys the accumulating evidence against the backdrop of the available documentary sources and tries to give some idea of the potential of archaeology to illuminate the historical records. There is no scope here to deal with the embarrassment of riches that is the documentary record from the mid-eighteenth century onwards, or the large body of Gaelic oral tradition, nor indeed to describe in detail the political manoeuvrings and intrigues that characterise the relationship between the Hebrides and the Scottish Crown over the centuries following the removal of Norse suzerainty. Retaining an essentially archaeological perspective does, however, at least place the sites and landscapes of this period in the context of earlier developments in settlement, society and economy.

THE HISTORICAL BACKDROP

The historical picture for much of this period is dominated by the emergence, flowering and demise of the political entity that was the Lordship of the Isles and its irregular and fractious relationship with the Scottish Crown (c.f. MacLean 1981). The 'official' Lordship begins with John of Islay, invested in 1354 as *Dominus Insularum* or Lord of the Isles. His Gaelic title, however, *Ri Innse Gall* or Ruler of the Hebrides, had its origins with Somerled MacGillibride who, in the mid-twelfth century, carved out a power base from areas previously under Norse control; this domain had its political centre of gravity in Argyll and the southern Hebrides. Steer and Bannerman have suggested that Somerled represented an elite family (with a pedigree stretching back to Dalriada in the ninth century) whose power base may originally have been consolidated when the Dalriadan kings moved east to assume kingship over the united Pictish and Scottish kingdoms. Indeed they see, in the resurgence of Celtic culture that accompanied the emergence of the Lordship of the Isles, an echo of the Dalriadan kingdom itself (1977, 201).

Accepting the mid-twelfth century date for the appearance of the Lordship, its early incumbents were able to exploit a political ambiguity whereby they nominally owed allegiance both to the Scottish and Norwegian Crowns, whilst their own cultural links more naturally bound them to Ireland. During this period, and until the middle of the fourteenth century, overall power seems to have shifted between the various kinship groups or clans descended from Somerled, very much in the traditional Early Historic, Celtic pattern seen in Dalriada prior to the union of Picts and Scots. The position of Skye and the Western Isles within the wider political picture of the later centuries of Norse control are far from clear but they were clearly peripheral to the main territorial interests of the nascent Lordship.

With the end of Norse control over their island territories, the Lords of the Isles and their followers became increasingly drawn into mainland Scottish politics and thus more open to cultural influences flowing from lowland Scotland and England. The relationship between the Lordship and the Scottish Crown was always uneasy as the former sought to retain their autonomy and the latter to consolidate their rather toothless, nominal control over the West Highlands and Islands. The Lordship was officially recognised and subsumed to a degree within the Scottish feudal system, even if in practice this was largely a southern rationalisation of *de facto* Highland practice.

The difficult relationship between the Lordship and the Scottish Crown, however, was to bring about the eventual demise of the former. Deals were periodically struck between the Lords of the Isles and the English Crown in an attempt to maintain an appropriate distance from Scottish control. Such intrigues were to result in the final forfeiture of the Lordship, at least in its officially sanctioned form, in 1493. Several risings followed this forfeiture as the clans sought to maintain their distinct identity and political status. These were all to end in failure, however, and the death in 1545 of Donald Dubh, the last serious claimant to the Lordship, effectively snuffed out the institution for good.

The years that followed witnessed the wielding by the Scottish Crown of more direct authority over the islands and a further wave of cultural and social integration of the Hebridean elite into the mainstream of the Scottish aristocracy. The gradual removal of autonomous military muscle from the Hebridean clans and the exercise of direct power from lowland Scotland, completely changed the relationship between the elite of the islands and the wider population. Ties of kinship and power based on military capability were replaced by formalised economic ties and power based on commercial capability. Whilst the suppression of the clan system by the British government following the failure of the 1745 rising effectively symbolised the end of the relative autonomy enjoyed by the Hebridean elite, and ushered in the period of rampant commercialisation and Clearance, the processes that underlay these changes had been in sway for several centuries.

THE SEARCH FOR THE COMMON PEOPLE

The documentary records deal on the whole with a tiny minority of the population; the secular and ecclesiastical leaders and their families. Similarly, the best known monuments remain the castles and churches that housed these people and formed the power centres of their day. To support the military aristocracy of the Lordship of the Isles, however, required the labour and surplus economic production of the mass of the Hebridean population. The great majority of these people continued to live in modest settlements that remained largely unrecorded prior to the eighteenth century when estate records become more commonly available. The material conditions of their lives, the structures in which they lived and their basic economic practices remained substantially unchanged from prehistoric periods. Economies remained pitched more or less at subsistence level and settlements were formed of individually slight buildings. Indeed historical records for the eighteenth century suggest that perishable materials, predominantly turf, were the norm for domestic buildings in the Hebrides and that these were regularly taken down completely and used as manure on the fields (c.f. Dodghson 1993, 423). Recent excavations have begun to detect some of these buildings although so far these provide only snapshots, highly localised in time and space, and we cannot be sure how representative they are of more general settlement patterns. Indeed the fact that structures survive archaeologically and were not wholly dismantled may suggest that they are unrepresentative or relate to the final phase of occupation on the settlements to which they relate.

Eilean Olabhat, North Uist

The 1st millennium AD settlement and bronze-working site on the small promontory of Eilean Olabhat in North Uist has already been discussed in Chapter 9. The abandonment of this site in the sixth or seventh centuries AD did not, however, mark the end of the site's use (Armit and Dunwell 1993). Some time later a sub-rectangular drystone structure was built into the ruined cellular building and a small outbuilding was constructed close by, to the north-east (Figure 11.1). The new building was a fairly small structure (with internal dimensions of approximately 4.5 by 2.6 m) divided into two chambers. In the northernmost chamber lay the entrance and also a small hearth butted up against the internal partition. Subsequently this structure partially collapsed and further occupation seems to have been limited to occasional use of the ruin as a shelter or bothy.

The medieval or later reoccupation of Eilean Olabhat was associated with the use of a distinct ceramic assemblage that shows the continuing importance of pottery within the region even after the Norse period. This assemblage includes a series of flattened rim, globular vessels made in a hard black fabric apparently with rounded bases. They often display stabbed decoration confined to the top of the rim and/or the neck. Campbell has dated this type of pottery to the thirteenth–fifteenth centuries AD, during the floruit of the Lordship of the Isles (1994).

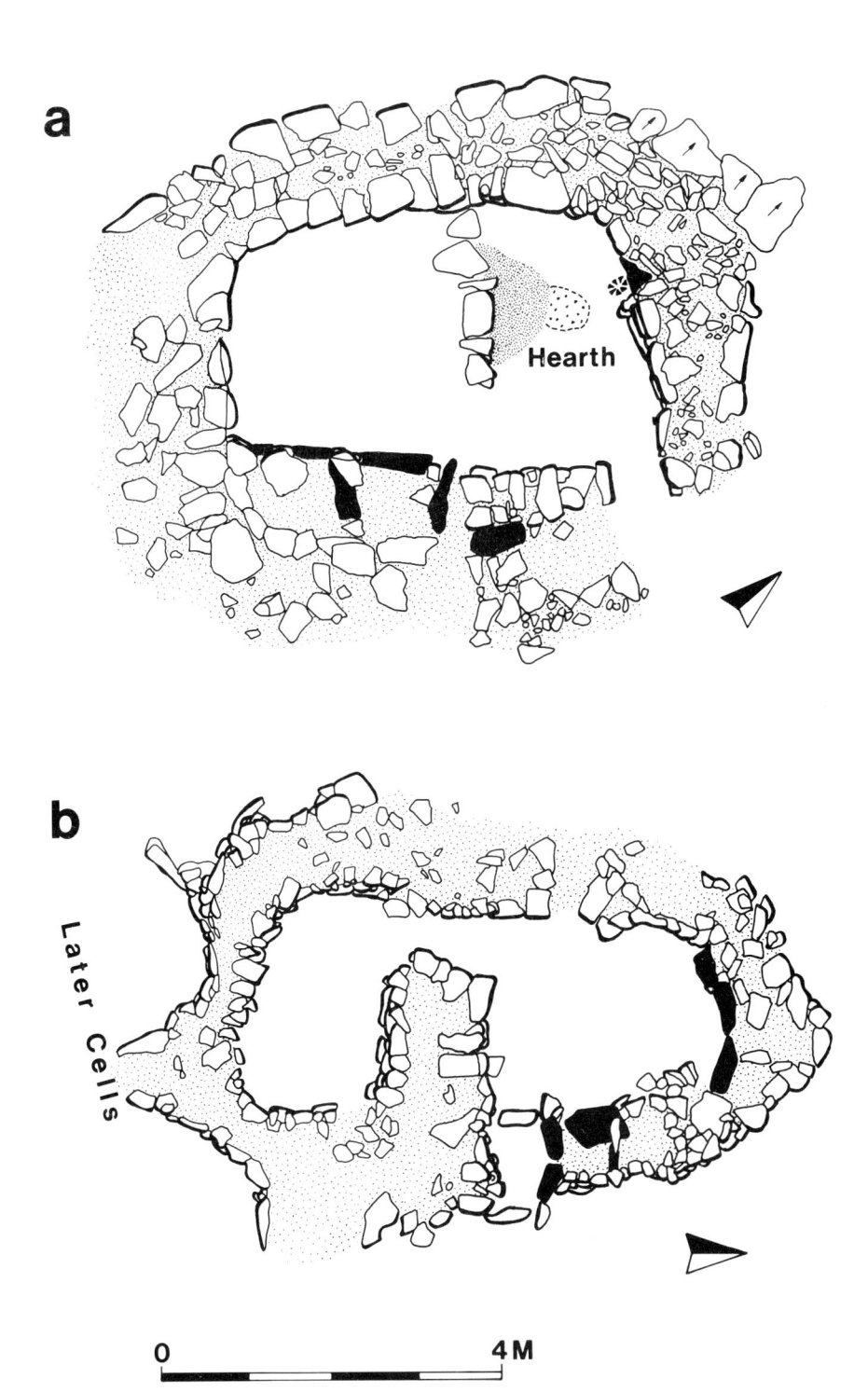

FIGURE 11.1. Medieval buildings in North Uist: (a) reoccupation of Eilean Olabhat, Loch Olabhat; (b) Druim nan Dearcag, Loch Olabhat.

Druim nan Dearcag, North Uist

The settlement of Druim nan Dearcag lies on the shore on the south side of Loch Olabhat, North Uist, close to the Neolithic settlement of Eilean Domhnuill and some 500 m from Eilean Olabhat. The site was excavated as part of the Loch Olabhat research programme, having been identified by field survey in 1986 (Armit 1990a, forth.). The main structures lie slightly set back from the loch, clustered around a rocky outcrop. The settlement comprises a cluster of five turf and stone-built structures, two rectilinear, two circular and a slab-built enclosure at the water's edge. Excavation concentrated on one of the rectilinear structures, which was revealed to have been a domestic building, and the two circular foundations that appear to have been simple stone-footed, turf-walled out-buildings.

Excavation of the rectilinear building revealed that it was, in its earliest phase, a boat-shaped structure with overall dimensions of $c.6 \times 4$ m, although the interior was a simple rectilinear shape (Figure 11.1). The inner walls were lined with upright slabs, whilst the outer wall was of simple stone coursing, forming the base of a turf superstructure. An informal hearth dominated the centre of the structure and a sloping outcrop of gneiss formed the eastern half of the floor. A series of ashy deposits overlying this floor represented the accretion of occupation debris.

After the collapse and decay of this structure the southern half was extended and rebuilt whilst the northern half was retained, in broadly, its original form. A partition wall divided the interior of the rebuilt structure into two small rooms and the entrance was shifted from the west wall to the east. This new entrance was paved and lined with orthostats, with threshold stones at both inner and outer ends. The gap between the two periods of occupation is difficult to establish from the excavated evidence. Subsequently, two small, ephemeral, semi-circular cells were built into the southern wall of the building. These are perhaps best interpreted as rough, temporary shelters, probably associated with the use of the adjacent drove road, some time after the abandonment of the settlement. A copper alloy belt buckle, probably dating to the eighteenth century, was found close to these structures and may relate to the period of their use.

The excavations and survey at Druim nan Dearcag combine to suggest that the site represents a small farming settlement comprising two houses and a series of storage structures and enclosures. It had at least two phases of occupation but it is not clear whether one or both houses were occupied at any one time. There is little evidence for the economy of the site due to the lack of survival of either bone or palaeo-environmental material. There is no evidence from surface traces of associated fields, rigs or clearance heaps which might suggest a predominantly pastoral function for the site, although such traces may lie under the extensive peat which encroaches on the land immediately to the south of the site.

The pottery from Druim nan Dearcag is of a distinctive type appearing to pre-date the craggan forms of the seventeenth century and later (Cowie, pers. comm.), but containing one glazed sherd of likely fifteenth or sixteenth century date (Caldwell, pers. comm.). The remainder of the assemblage is hand-made and superficially similar to much later prehistoric pottery from the islands. Decoration is restricted to occasional slashing of the rim in a fashion similar to the late material from Eilean Olabhat. Overall, a date in the fifteenth or sixteenth centuries is most likely for the assemblage, and thus for the initial phase of occupation of the excavated house. This would place the occupation late in the Lordship period and slightly later than the reoccupation of Eilean Olabhat.

The Olabhat Area

The layout of the settlement at Druim nan Dearcag has its closest recorded parallels at Clibhe in the Bhaltos peninsula of Lewis (Armit 1994a site 47). At this latter site, a similar rectilinear structure lies on a knoll overlooking Traigh Clibhe. This building is associated with a number of small annular structures which appear as raised turf platforms. There are other sites, however, within the immediate area of Druim nan Dearcag itself that also offer parallels from surface evidence. These sites appear to form components of a broadly contemporary settlement pattern of dispersed farmsteads and field systems which were subsequently truncated by the extensive rig and furrow cultivation system radiating out from the cleared township of Foshigarry to the north of Loch Olabhat. Trial excavations suggest that these structures were of a type similar to those at Druim nan Dearcag but dating evidence was not present in sufficient quantity to clarify their possible chronological relationships (Armit forthcoming).

It does seem likely, however, that Druim nan Dearcag, the final occupation at Eilean Olabhat, and the other structures excavated as part of the same project represent a tide-mark of survival of medieval and later settlement. This settlement system was subsequently largely obliterated by the growth of field systems focused on Foshigarry, which themselves went out of use as arable land in the early part of the nineteenth century. This settlement pattern appears to consist of regularly placed small, domestic sites occupying a strip of land set back some distance from the coast and focused on Loch Olabhat. To the south, any continuation of this settlement distribution is obscured by peat growth.

THE EVOLUTION OF THE BAILE

The emergence of the baile (plural *bailtean*) is one of the key issues facing medieval and later archaeology in the Hebrides, and one which archaeologists are well-placed to address. Bailtean were the distinctive nucleated settlements of tenant farmers that formed the backbone of Hebridean settlement in the eighteenth century when written records begin to shed light on the distribution of people in the Hebridean landscape (c.f. Crawford 1965).

The traditional view of the baile has been that it was a long-lived, traditional mode of settlement intimately associated with the organisation of open field and runrig cultivation. This interpretation has recently been challenged by Professor Robert Dodghson who has suggested, on the basis of field evidence throughout the West Highlands, that nucleated settlement and open field systems may only have begun to be adopted in the area from the thirteenth century onwards, and that the change may still have been taking effect in some areas as late as the eighteenth century (1993, 422). Dodghson has suggested that the eighteenth century Hebridean bailtean represented attempts to rationalise and reorder a previously diffuse settlement pattern associated with cultivation and husbandry based around the use of enclosures (ibid.). Maps of the bailtean of North and South Bragar in Lewis, for example demonstrate that, even in the first decade of the nineteenth century, vestiges of a former dispersed settlement system remained (ibid., 424-7). At Greaulin, Trotternish in Skye maps from the mid-eighteenth century seem to indicate a recently abandoned dispersed settlement pattern replaced by the nascent baile (ibid., 428).

The evidence from around Loch Olabhat has hinted that the field systems associated with the eighteenth century baile at Foshigarry may truncate elements of an earlier landscape of more dispersed settlement, thus complementing the largely map-based evidence from Bragar and Greaulin. If this is the case it would suggest that the development of the baile at Foshigarry may have occurred at a relatively late stage, after the abandonment of sites like Druim nan Dearcag, possibly as late as the seventeenth or even eighteenth centuries. Thus, rather than the Hebridean bailtean representing a long-lived settlement form derived ultimately from Norse period clustered settlement, it may be that the prehistoric pattern of dispersed settlement continued well into the present millennium. Such a pattern of replacement of dispersed settlement by nucleated settlement is a widespread phenomenon throughout much of Europe from the tenth century onwards and appears to have been closely associated with the spread of feudalism. In this context it may be that it was the demise of the Lordship of the Isles and subsequent flow of lowland ideas and economic practice into the islands that influenced the establishment of clustered joint farms from the later part of the sixteenth century onwards.

The Udal, North Uist

Settlement at the Udal in North Uist appears to have continued well into the present millennium, culminating in the appearance of the medieval baile (Crawford and Switsur 1977, 131). A series of 'long houses' appear to have been the principal units of settlement and these were associated with timber buildings, possibly byres or barns (ibid.). Decorated, hand-made pottery

FIGURE 11.2. Arnol blackhouse, Lewis.

continues into this period (ibid.), maintaining the, by now, rather ancient Hebridean tradition of ceramic elaboration despite its absence in most of the rest of Scotland. The eventual publication of this material, when compared with that from sites like Eilean Olabhat and Druim nan Dearcag, will help establish a more solid foundation for understanding the Hebridean pottery sequence in the second millennium AD. The dates of the various phases of settlement at the Udal in the present millennium, however, do not appear to be particularly well established, with the published accounts showing a rather touching faith in the equation of archaeological features with historical events. Nonetheless the termination of permanent settlement appears to be fairly well fixed from historical records at around the start of the eighteenth century (ibid., 133).

Blackhouses

It has always been tempting to attempt to trace the development of vernacular Hebridean housing as a continuous process leading to the familiar blackhouse, the typical Hebridean house form which persisted well into the present century. Blackhouses themselves varied greatly in design and construction, but essentially they were rectilinear buildings consisting of a series of activity areas, housing livestock as well as people. Latterly constructed of thick drystone walls with an earthen core (as at the late blackhouse in state care at Arnol in Lewis, Figure 11.2), early examples appear to have made use of turf for walls and possibly roofs. Their low roofs and rounded corners made them resistant to wind whilst the thick walls provided insulation, making them an eminently well-suited and thus conservative housing form in the islands. Whilst later examples were quite formally partitioned, with livestock screened off at one end from a living area and a separate sleeping area, earlier examples appear to have been in general smaller and less formally divided. Other changes through time included the replacement of central hearths and emplacement of chimneys at the gable end, the introduction of windows built within the walls rather than simple panes of glass covering windows in the roof, and the occasional use of mortared walls.

Exactly how early we can trace structures that can meaningfully be called blackhouses is a matter of some doubt. Traditionally it has been suggested that the basic design may date back to the Norse period, evolving ultimately from the Viking longhouse, but it is presently impossible to identify an intermediate sequence. The few excavated structures of the intervening period, as at Eilean Olabhat and Druim nan Dearcag, can hardly be related to either tradition, although how typical they were of medieval settlement generally remains to be established.

Some indication of the general state of Hebridean housing in the latter part of the eighteenth century comes from Samuel Johnson who characterised them as ranging from 'murky dens to commodious dwellings'. A range of building forms appear to have been present: some houses were of drystone with earth packing; others of turf, perhaps with wattle lining. Central fireplaces were still the norm as were floors of plain beaten earth. Archaeologically, one suspects, the picture will prove to have been complex with a variety of house forms of varying permanence and quality of construction, inhabited by the many gradations of society that were emerging in the incipient capitalist economies of the times. It is perhaps unlikely that there was any one form of 'proto-blackhouse' ancestral to the later forms that characterised the later nineteenth and early twentieth centuries, the ruins of which dominate the Hebridean landscape today (Figure 11.3).

Landscapes

The recent survey of the archaeological landscapes of the Waternish peninsula in Skye has demonstrated the potential for archaeology to address questions of settlement and economic development in the post-medieval and earlier periods (RCAHMS 1993). The conventional interpretation of the vast numbers of pre-crofting structures that litter the islands has been that they reflect the increase in the population of the islands in the eighteenth century, prior to the Clearances. Comparison of the numerous surveyed buildings and boundaries in the area, however, with estate maps from the late eighteenth century revealed that only a fraction of the visible sites were recorded in map form (ibid., 10). This implies that amongst the surveyed sites must be many that date significantly earlier than the period to which these maps relate. By contrast, however, in the rather more intensely settled Bhaltos peninsula in Lewis, many structures indicated as visible ruins on the first edition Ordnance Survey maps of the mid-nineteenth century have been so

FIGURE 11.3. Roof construction visible in a ruined dwelling close to Loch Olabhat, North Uist

FIGURE 11.4. Ridge and furrow cultivation, Callanish, Lewis.

thoroughly robbed that they are now barely visible as slight depressions in the ground (Armit 1994).

As well as individual settlement sites, extensive systems of rig and furrow cultivation (Figure 11.4) or 'lazy-beds' (a labour-intensive West Highland variant suited to poorer soils) cover much of the cultivable land of the Hebrides. Again, like the settlements, these field systems, and the numerous small enclosures and boundaries associated with them, encompass a considerable variety of forms and occupy a range of landscape niches. Like the pre-Clearance settlements, however, these agricultural landscapes still await detailed analysis that might enable us to understand their development over time and their relationships to the various forms of contemporary settlement.

The practice of transhumance, whereby cattle are removed from the cultivated lands to higher or more remote pastures during the summer months, characterised the medieval and later economies of many parts of upland

Scotland, including the Hebrides. Oral tradition and documentary records testify to this practice in the islands until relatively recent times. Patterns may have varied quite widely between different islands and even within islands, however, depending on the distribution of areas of rough grazing relative to the townships. The material relics of transhumance are principally shielings, small buildings, occurring in isolation or in small clusters, that were built and occupied by those tending the herds and flocks during the summer months. As well as providing accommodation, shielings were the focus for the processing of dairy products. Shieling sites are ubiquitous throughout the Hebrides although, until recently, they have not been subject to detailed survey and analysis. It is therefore difficult to trace their distributions with any certainty or to be sure what proportion of the many sites labelled as shielings actually served that purpose.

In the Waternish peninsula the RCAHMS identified a series of shieling types, including moderately substantial rectilinear structures with stone walls, turf-walled buildings often positioned on mounds built up through repeated use and reconstruction, and multi-celled structures with small cells placed around a central chamber (RCAHMS 1993, 10). The shielings investigated by Roger Miket at Torrin, also on Skye, have yielded radiocarbon dates indicating use in the twelfth–fifteenth centuries. They have also provided a further date, however, indicative of activity in the first millennium BC (Appendix, information from Roger Miket). Whether this represents a continuity of transhumance over millennia or rather the chance reoccupation of an earlier settlement can only be clarified by further excavation. The paucity of excavated or dated shielings, however, prevents any meaningful discussion at present of how widespread the practice of transhumance may have been or what its chronological limits were. Interestingly, however, the RCAHMS survey in Waternish noted few indications of transhumance on the 1790 estate maps other than the very occasional indication of a 'bothy' or 'cott' (RCAHMS 1993, 11), possibly indicating the decline of the practice in this part of Skye by the late eighteenth century. What is clear is that there is sufficient structural and distribution evidence to learn a great deal from the archaeology of transhumance within the islands, and the potential, within some of the longer-lived sites, to identify the chronological developments of the practice.

The Elite

From Fort to Castle

Late Duns

The RCAHMS survey of 1928 identified a series of monuments that appeared to indicate either the survival of the long-established Hebridean tradition of islet dwellings into the medieval period, or else the late re-establishment of that tradition (RCAHMS 1928, xi). The sites identified as 'late duns' are a heterogeneous group that may well span several centuries, as none has yet been excavated and securely dated. The best known are those in North Uist, for example Dun Ban in Loch Carabhat where a D-shaped enclosure contains the ruins of a lime-mortared, rectangular hall of medieval date (ibid., no. 215). There is no definite trace at Dun Ban of pre-medieval occupation though it would not be surprising if an earlier site had been adapted. At other sites in North Uist and elsewhere, however, Atlantic roundhouses on islets have clearly been reoccupied, often having secondary rectangular buildings constructed within their shells. At Dun an Sticer, for example, a well-preserved building probably of sixteenth century date nestles in the remains of the much earlier broch tower (Figure 11.5). Elsewhere local traditions or documentary records suggest the use of such sites well into the medieval and post-medieval periods. Dun Aonghas, also in North Uist, for example, has a strong association with Aonghas Fhionn (Angus the Fair) in the sixteenth century, and contains some traces of recti-linear buildings that may well date to that period (ibid., no. 213). Dun Carloway is associated with numerous oral traditions probably originating in the later medieval period. In Lewis the broch tower of Dun Loch an Duna, Bragar, was also apparently reoccupied in medieval times.

Without excavation it is impossible to determine whether there was an identifiable horizon of reoccupation of these islet sites, possibly centred around the sixteenth century in the last turbulent years of the Lordship of the Isles, or whether this was simply the latest period in which they were routinely occupied. It is possible that internecine strife created unstable conditions during the medieval period making islet settlements desirable. Or perhaps the late duns represent attempts by elites, drawing their authority from outside the locality, to display their legitimacy by re-occupying ruins associated with the ancestors and with traditionally held power, at the same time distancing themselves from the machair-dwelling, common people.

The chronology and distribution of the late duns of the Hebrides are poorly established and it remains difficult to relate them to any particular stratum of medieval society. Their relatively small numbers, however, compared, for example, to the Atlantic roundhouses of a much earlier period, suggest that they did represent elite settlements. It is a reasonable assumption, therefore, that they were the homes of a petty aristocracy drawing power from their ties of kinship with more powerful and distant chiefs, and controlling fairly limited areas.

This social stratum may perhaps be identified with that of the tacksmen who emerge in the written records by the seventeenth century as middlemen, still drawn from within the kinship-based clan system, who held land from the clan chiefs in return for its administration and the collection of rents.

Castles

The castles of Skye and the Hebrides, the fortified residences of the clan chiefs, represent centres of power of a rather higher order than the late duns.

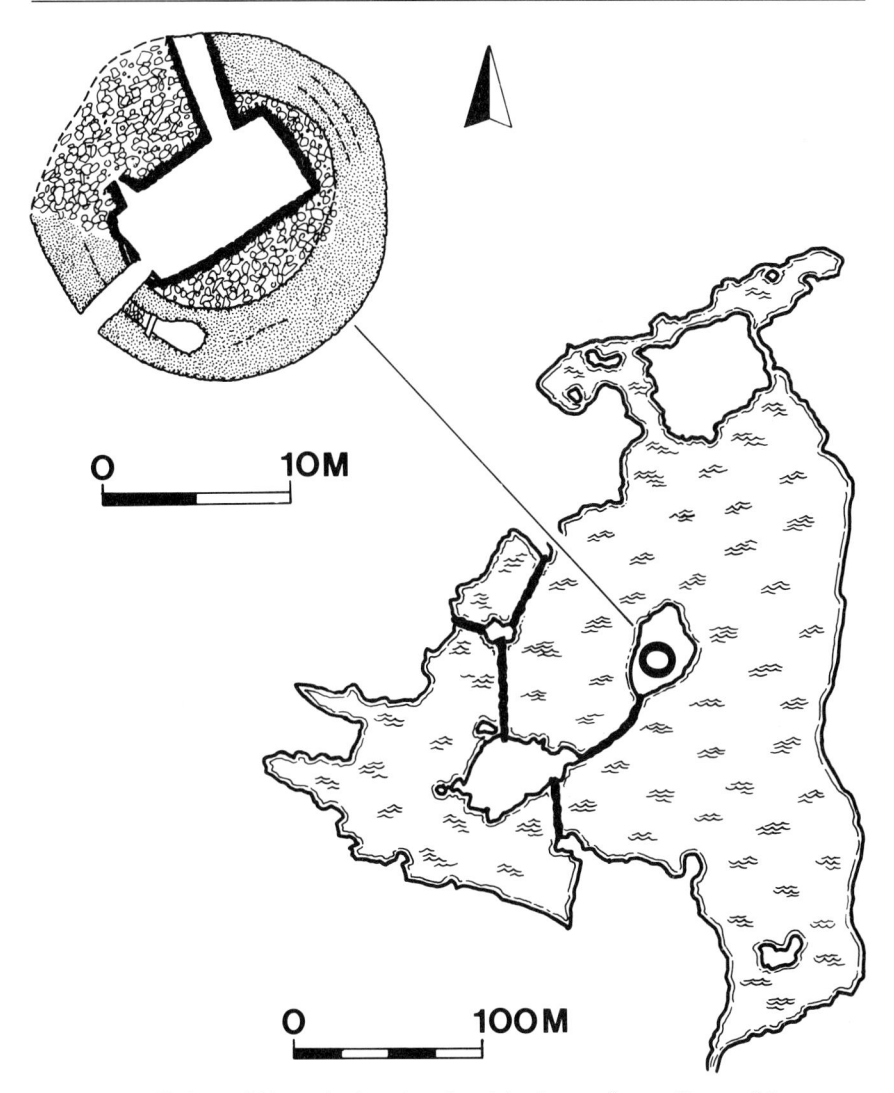

FIGURE 11.5. 'Tacksman's' house in the ruins of an Atlantic roundhouse: Dun an Sticer, North Uist.

These were 'symbols of the power and prestige of the clan' rather than the strategically placed military strongholds which appear throughout the lowlands in the medieval period (Miket and Roberts 1990, 5).

It is hard to draw the line between castles and late duns. For example, Dun Ringill in Skye, a complex Atlantic roundhouse, was substantially modified with the addition of lime-mortared walls to serve as the residence of the chief of Clan MacKinnon before being abandoned for Kyleakin in the late fourteenth or fifteenth centuries (ibid., 7). Although regarded as a castle by

FIGURE 11.6. Kisimul Castle, Barra.

Miket and Roberts it has a great deal in common with the late duns of the Western Isles.

There are few castles in the Western Isles, suggesting that the necessary resources to build and maintain them was invested in very few hands. Those that do exist represent considerably greater investments of labour and resources than any structures previously built in the islands. The construction of Kisimul Castle in Barra, for example, dating to the fifteenth century, at least in its presently visible form, was a major undertaking, particularly given the need to transport all the stone and other material to the island on which it was built (Figure 11.6). Quarrying of stone, timber preparation, mortaring and roofing would all have required a huge input of labour even apart from the construction of the walls still visible today. Interestingly, the choice of an island for the construction of this major symbol of authority in Barra appears to echo again the long tradition of islet occupation in the Hebrides.

Whilst the choice of location for Kisimul Castle may have been intended for a defensive purpose, this was clearly not the case with several other castles

FIGURE 11.7. Borve Castle, Benbecula.

built in the Western Isles. The towerhouse with attached ranges at Borve Castle for example, seems sited for convenience rather than defence, although its location in the low-lying, sandy, plain of Benbecula does let it command the views for some distance around a geographically pivotal point in the islands (Figure 11.7).

Despite the problems of chronology, the medieval period does appear to witness the emergence of a greater range of elite dwellings and a firm separation of those from the more transient homes of the common people of the islands. This implies that the emergence of powerful and wide-ranging authorities embodied in the Lordship of the Isles, and the kinship-based power structures associated with it, produced a society far more hierarchically organised and unequal in access to wealth than the societies that preceded it in the Norse and Pictish periods and earlier.

Divine Authority and the Tombs of the Elite

One of the most impressive memorials to the Lordship of the Isles is the collection of late medieval monumental sculpture found throughout the West Highlands and Islands (Figure 11.8; Steer and Bannerman 1977). This body of sculpture takes the form principally of grave slabs, tombs and effigies, and free-standing crosses, profusely decorated with complex patterns of foliage and interlace and incorporating a range of decorative motifs and the use of relief carving. A blend of influences, dominated by Romanesque but with elements from Pictish, Anglo–Saxon, Norse and Gothic, combined to create

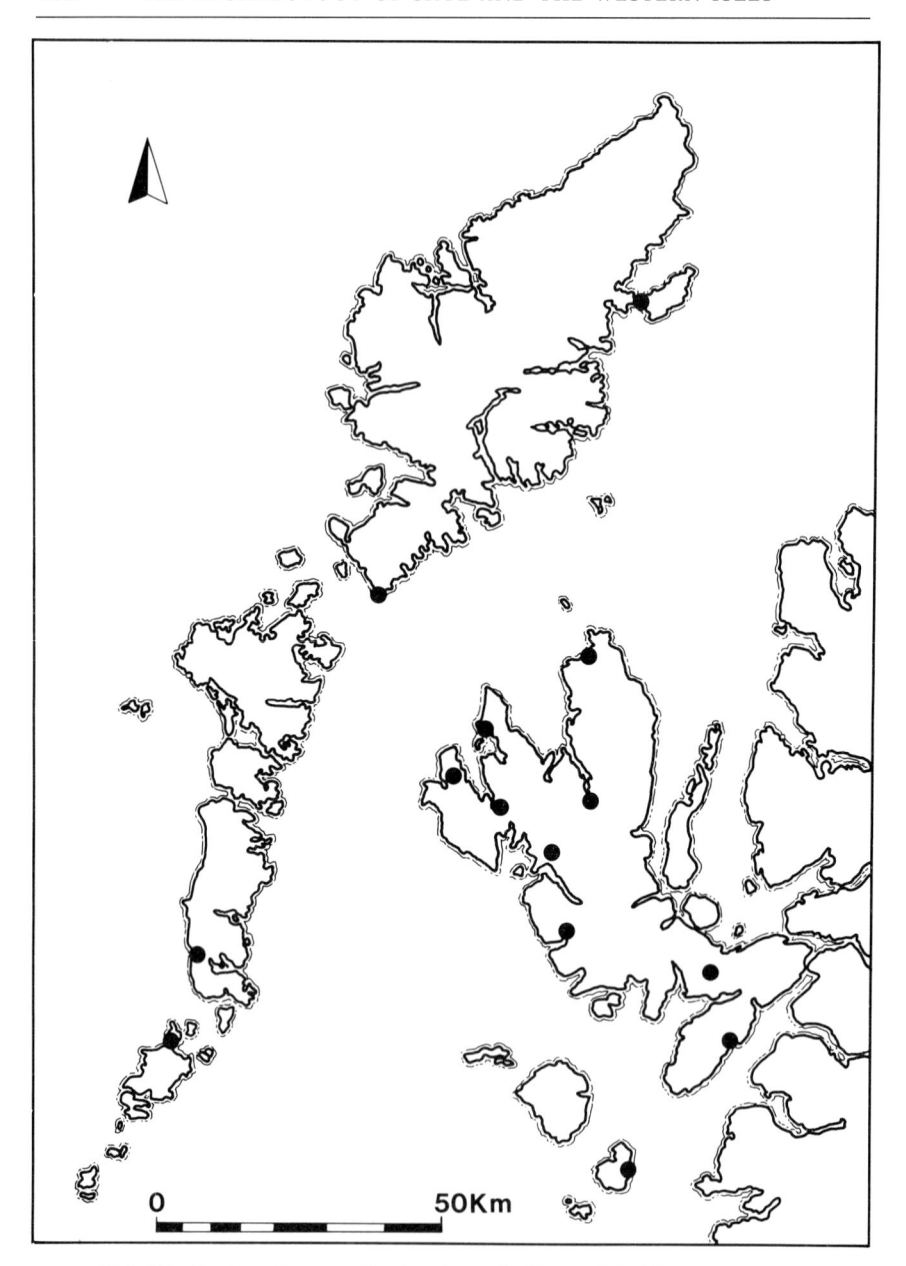

FIGURE 11.8. Distribution of later medieval sculpture in Skye and the Western Isles.

a unique and vibrant West Highland tradition (ibid., 5). Like the art on the earlier Pictish symbol stones, this decorative style was presumably applied to artefacts of wood, leather and other perishable materials, and was probably not confined to items with overtly Christian affinities. Nonetheless, aside from a handful of survivals, the corpus is confined now to carved stone monuments.

The concentration of carved monuments, as might be expected, reflects the political centre of gravity of the medieval Lordship in Argyll, the southern Hebrides and the spiritual centre of Iona. An important series of monuments is, however, present in Skye and the Western Isles, many of which seem to represent a late flourishing of the tradition in the first half of the sixteenth century after the official forfeiture of the Lordship of the Isles (Figure 11. 8). Steer and Bannerman have suggested that this phenomenon represents a shift in power towards the MacLeods of Dunvegan at a time when the traditional centres had been stifled by external political pressure (1977, 77).

The purpose of these monuments appears to have been to display the status and power of the individual to whom each was dedicated and of the clan hierarchies that they represented. The motifs used on the tombs and grave slabs provide some insight into the ideologies of the clan chiefs in the later medieval period. The effigies and associated material culture indicate a highly male-dominated society with a strong emphasis on martial symbolism. The most common symbol is the sword, and, in the sixteenth century, the double-handed claymore. The dead were generally portrayed as armoured warriors, whilst scenes on the tombs portray warships, castles and hunting scenes.

The tomb of Alasdair Crotach (Alexander MacLeod) chief of the MacLeods of Harris and Dunvegan is a prime example both of the art style itself and the motives underlying its use. This tomb is one of three lying within the small church of St Clement's at Rodel in the south of Harris (Figure 11.9). An effigy of the dead man, in full armour and with sword, lies on a recessed tomb under arching panels covered in Christian and martial symbolism (Figure 11.10). That such an impressive construction as Alasdair Crotach's tomb at Rodel should be built after the demise of the official Lordship and at a very late stage in the development of the art style as a whole is perhaps no accident. These tombs and grave slabs symbolised the martial power and autonomy of the highland clan chiefs. At the same time, however, the Hebridean elite sought to legitimise the clan hierarchy through the context of art, in its association with churches, rites of burial and martial and religious symbolism, by linking it to divine authority and the power of the Church.

Indeed, patronage of the Church appears to have been an important means by which the Hebridean elite legitimised their own secular authority from early in the Lordship period, as elite groups had done for centuries. Teampull na Trionaid (the Church of the Holy Trinity) at Carinish in North

FIGURE 11.9. Rodel Church, Harris.

Uist was, according to tradition, a place of learning in the thirteenth and fourteenth centuries established by the patronage of clan hierarchies under the Lordship. St Clement's itself, established around 1500, represents an even more potent link between the secular and ecclesiastical elite.

Clan leaders like Alasdair Crotach clearly wanted to demonstrate that the Lordship of the Isles was a rightful institution, drawing its authority and legitimacy from divine sanction rather than simply the feudal gift of the Scottish Crown. By the time his tomb was built though, the autonomy of the highland chiefs was substantially eroded and the Rodel tomb appears as a rather desperate display of bravado from an elite whose absolute local power was almost gone.

By the middle of the sixteenth century a combination of the final demise of the Lordship of the Isles and the effects of the Reformation on religious art had conspired to extinguish the tradition of monumental sculpture almost completely. Portrayals of clan chiefs as mighty and godly warriors had, in any case, become increasingly anachronistic as Scottish power over the islands was consolidated and the Hebridean elites gradually absorbed cultural and social influences from the lowlands.

Towards the Modern Era

The demise of the Lordship of the Isles saw the Hebrides marginalised

FIGURE 11.10. Alasdair Crotach's tomb, Rodel Church, Harris.

culturally and politically as fringe territories of Scotland. This is perhaps most aptly symbolised by the attempted 'colonisation' of Lewis at the end of the sixteenth century by the Fife Adventurers, a band of lowland gentry instructed by James VI to settle at Stornoway and exploit the, rather optimistically, viewed agricultural and fishing potential of the island. Although unsuccessful, this enterprise may have been responsible for the formal establishment of the modern town of Stornoway (Fojut, Pringle and Walker, n.d.).

The relatively stable conditions of the seventeenth and eighteenth centuries appear to have witnessed considerable growth in population and the appearance in the written records of the bailtean (c.f. Crawford 1965). The minor aristocracy had by then abandoned all semblance of defensive settlement for more comfortable and convenient accommodation. Indeed by the time written records become available, the settlement patterns had already adopted their recognisable pre-Clearance form. These settlement patterns, however, were not to last. The widespread currents of the Agricultural Improvements that swept Scotland in the eighteenth and early nineteenth centuries were reflected in the Hebrides by the desire of landowners to maximise income from their holdings by the wholesale switch to sheep-farming, involving the complete reorganisation of existing patterns of tenure and often the forcible clearance of the population.

Macinnes has characterised the change in attitudes of the clan hierarchies in the post-medieval period as a switch from 'resource management under clanship to demand management under commercial landlordism' (1994, 1). The change in economic emphasis, where efforts were directed at meeting external markets at the expense of the indigenous subsistence economy, reflected the adherence of the Hebridean elites to the values and attitudes of the Lowlands and England. This was particularly the case from the seventeenth century onwards when the children of the clan hierarchies were routinely sent south for their education. Maintenance of people on the land ceased to be a priority when clan leaders counted their status in terms of commercial rather than military power.

The Archaeology of Hebridean History

The potential for the detailed study of the medieval and later periods in the Hebrides is vast. There is a tremendous range of known settlement sites, from the ordinary farmsteads of the peasantry through the periodically defended and moderately elaborate homes of the petty aristocracy, to the relative splendour of the elite residences. The scale of preservation of relict landscapes allows for the analysis of broad-scale as well as site-specific economic activity. There is a wealth of symbolic material from the traditions of stone-carving and religious and funerary architecture. Add to this a political understanding of the period provided by the written documents and the additional layer of information available through oral tradition and it is clear that inter-disciplinary study could reveal an enormous amount about the development of Hebridean society in what was, perhaps, its Golden Age.

12 Tracing Change

One of the main contributions archaeology makes to the study of human society is the insight it gives into long-term change. The preceding chapters have set out the archaeology of Skye and the Western Isles in broadly chronological terms, dealing in detail with particular archaeological periods. It is almost inevitable in a book of this kind that these periods will appear as a series of discontinuous vignettes. The organisation of the subject, where most archaeologists tend to specialise in a particular period, encourages the construction of such chronological ghettos. Often the crucial questions of how and why changes occurred between these comfortably segregated periods are unjustly neglected. Similarly, continuities in human culture and society across such arbitrary boundaries can often go unappreciated. This final chapter presents the opportunity to summarise some of the main recognisable changes and continuities in Hebridean archaeology that can be discerned, with varying degrees of uncertainty, from the archaeological record.

SETTLEMENT CHANGE

In the nine thousand years or so since the first detectable human settlement of the Hebrides the environment of the islands has changed beyond recognition and has, inevitably, forced island populations to adapt their economic practices and settlement patterns. With a few notable exceptions, like the catastrophic machair movements of recent centuries, these changes would have been too slow to be perceived by the islands' inhabitants. Thus there was no continuous, conscious struggle between people and nature, but rather the choice of economic options and areas for settlement was gradually but inexorably narrowed as peat spread, the climate worsened and the sea encroached. People played their own significant part in these changes:

clearance of woodland, intensive and prolonged cultivation and over-grazing all contributed to accelerating and intensifying environmental degradation.

There are indications from the distribution of domestic sites of various periods in the Western Isles, and in particular from North Uist, that there has been a progressive concentration of human settlement on the machair. Maps from the eighteenth century onwards show a virtually exclusive concentration in these areas (c.f. Crawford 1965). Clearly, by the post-medieval period, the interior of the island (and indeed most of the rocky east coast), was regarded as unfit for human settlement, its uses restricted largely to the provision of fuel and rough pasture.

The first archaeological traces of human habitations in North Uist, however, suggest a very different picture. The identification of Neolithic settlements at Eilean an Tighe and Eilean Domhnuill suggests that the occupation of the numerous causewayed, but otherwise largely featureless, islets strewn across the lochs of the interior and east of the island may date to the earlier prehistoric period. Palaeo-environmental study shows that these areas would have been early victims of peat encroachment and, by the Iron Age, the Atlantic roundhouse settlements focus heavily on the coastal areas, although with a greater coverage than the bailtean of more recent centuries. With the advent of the wheelhouses, at the cusp of the first millennia BC and AD, the dominance of the machair as a settlement focus became even more marked. Thus, over these millennia, human settlement, initially widespread and occupying most available environmental niches, seems to have become narrower in focus as environmental conditions deteriorated.

Future excavation and survey in North Uist, particularly of the putatively early sites, will will be required to test this very general model of settlement shift. Even if the model holds good for North Uist, however, its more general applicability remains to be evaluated. Smaller islands, such as Barra, with its significantly different topography and different proportions of various environmental niches, may have witnessed rather different processes. Skye, lacking the relatively clear-cut division of machair lands and peatlands would have been different again. Nonetheless, it is likely that each island experienced the effects of environmental degradation and settlement contraction over the millennia.

The response of human communities to environmental adversity was seldom one of straightforward retreat. In the Iron Age people appear to have flouted environmental conditions by the construction of overtly ill-adapted monumental buildings making copious use of scarce timber. In the present millennium the reclamation of substantial areas of peatland for agricultural use shows that the spread of peat did not necessarily remove areas from productive use for all time. Technological advances would also have had some impact in counteracting environmental deterioration, particularly through the introduction first of bronze and then iron for the manufacture of tools.

The impact of environmental change would also have depended greatly on its timescale. Degradation of inland areas may have happened so slowly that populations gradually and painlessly adjusted. Other events, such as the drowning of the Vallay Strand machair, probably in the first millennium AD, may by contrast have happened relatively suddenly and given rise to serious social dislocation. Such 'sudden' events were, however, usually more local in their extent and impact.

SOCIAL CHANGE

The evidence for social organisation in the Hebrides is highly variable throughout the period covered by this book, and at no point could it be described as abundant. Nonetheless, it is important to examine the evidence as it stands and to attempt to identify changes within Hebridean society, if only to establish a focus for future research.

The social organisation of the earliest settlers in the Hebrides appears to have been relatively loose if not exactly egalitarian. Of Mesolithic society we know next to nothing, although there are hints from outside our area that communities of this period may have been concerned with personal status and adornment and with the marking of ethnic identity. In the Early Neolithic the picture is similar although the evidence of the numerous chambered tombs suggests that small, localised groups or households held a considerable degree of autonomy, although probably recognising wider tribal or ethnic affiliations. The perceived need physically to stamp the authority of the community onto the landscape through the building of elaborate tombs was probably related to the adoption of farming and the greater investment by people in particular patches of ground. The link between the community and the land seems to have been symbolised by the presence of the community of ancestors contained within the tombs. Although tomb architecture hints at a degree of status differentiation within these groups there is little to suggest much difference in status between them. In this respect there is little evidence of major changes in social organisation between the Mesolithic and Early Neolithic periods despite the gradual adoption of new economic practices, technologies and artefacts.

This picture changes somewhat in the Later Neolithic and Bronze Age with the appearance of monuments apparently dedicated to individuals rather than the faceless mass of ancestors, suggesting that power may have begun to be gathered into fewer hands. Indeed the monuments of the ancestors fade from view, being replaced as communal monuments by stone circles and standing stones suggestive of celestial gods. Both the monuments themselves and the artefacts associated with them (particularly beaker pottery) demonstrate widespread cultural links throughout and beyond Scotland and it appears that the Hebrides shared in a general trend towards the emergence of elite groups drawing on 'divine' legitimacy and external contacts for their earthly power. The resources, in terms of people and time, required for the construction of the Callanish complex is in excess of any chambered tomb and implies that labour from a number of communities could be mustered and marshalled, or that such projects were tackled over an extended period of time. Perhaps certain lineages had emerged from the earlier tomb-building communities as locally recognised leaders. The concentration of megalithic monuments at Callanish suggests that this area (rather than North Uist, where the greatest concentration of earlier chambered tombs is found) had become a focus for ritual activity associated with these elites. Nonetheless, there are few signs of significant social change throughout most of the Hebrides as the earlier pattern of small, single-household settlements persisted. This pattern contrasts with the apparent trend in Orkney for the emergence of nucleated villages suggestive of greater social cohesion. It does not appear, from the available evidence of both monuments and settlements, that elite groups in the Hebrides achieved the level of power enjoyed by their northern contemporaries.

Throughout Britain the elite groups represented by the major ritual centres, of which Callanish was the Hebridean reflection, seem to have lost their power to mobilise large numbers of people and resources by the latter part of the Bronze Age. Elite groups are again visible in the archaeological record in the earlier part of the first millennium BC but the traces are highly fugitive. Elaborate metalwork began to be deposited in hoards which were never intended to be recovered, suggesting that the conspicuous disposal of wealth was now being employed to display status and power. As before, access to elaborate and exotic artefacts appears to have been one manifestation of power but the appearance of weaponry and the disappearance of large communal monuments suggests that an ideology associated with force and physical power may have usurped the previous reliance on the supernatural for legitimacy. This change may signal the emergence of wholly new elites after a period when social organisation had once again dissipated to the level of the individual locality and household.

Perhaps the most remarkable reassertion of the autonomy and authority of the household came in the mid-first millennium BC with the appearance, throughout the Hebrides, of large numbers of Atlantic roundhouses, including the broch towers. These monumental domestic buildings appear to have been the standard settlement form for several centuries and were presumably inhabited by groups of a variety of social levels. Certainly their numbers and distribution, including some on small and fairly unproductive islands, suggest that these groups could not realistically be called elites. Indeed the wealthy Late Bronze Age owners of metalwork such as the hoard deposited at Adabrock cannot be traced through the second half of the first millennium BC. Like the chambered tombs, the Atlantic roundhouses stamped the authority of the household onto the land although instead of making reference to the ancestors, these structures hint at a legitimacy established through physical power. This change in emphasis may be in part the result of increased competition for land and resources in the much less favourable environmental conditions of the Iron Age.

Through the first millennium AD until the Norse incursions at around

AD 800 the development of Hebridean society must be framed in terms of its relationship with the emerging state of Pictland, and particularly the northern Pictish kingdom, or sub-kingdom. Although the Picts do not emerge in historical documents until the third century AD there is little doubt that the centralisation of power amongst their constituent peoples was underway earlier. In Orkney this appears to be manifested in the appearance of nucleated villages around certain broch towers, a development not reflected in the west. This difference in social and settlement development is a striking parallel with that observed in the Later Neolithic when Orcadian society also appears to have shown a capacity to become more tightly organised and hierarchical.

Orcadian broch towers, such as Gurness and Midhowe, appear to have been transformed from symbols of local autonomy and control over land and resources to symbols of dominance over people. It is possible that the end of Atlantic roundhouse construction in the west, at the expense of wheelhouses, may relate in part to the islands having come under the sway of political authorities centred in the north. The limited evidence for the first millennium AD does indeed suggest that Skye and the Western Isles were affiliated (if they were affiliated at all) to Pictland until the disruptions brought about by the Viking raids. If so, this would appear to be the first period in which ultimate power in the Hebrides was wielded by external authorities.

The replacement of the monumental wheelhouses with more utilitarian cellular structures during the first millennium AD was part of a wider process in which the status of the individual rather than the household seems to have become the main focus for the display of power. Personal ornaments and, presumably, clothing would have established the ranks of individuals in a rather more mobile and hierarchical society than had existed in earlier centuries. The spread of Christianity and its intimate links with secular powers would have helped to consolidate the rather remote power of the emerging Pictish kingdom from the middle of the millennium.

The nature of the social changes wrought by the Norse incursions and subsequent settlement is difficult to gauge. Certainly the native, presumably Pictish, elite were deposed, the Norse language became dominant and the islands came under the distant authority of Norway. What is not clear is how pervasive these changes were in terms of the mass of the population and the organisation of settlement and economic activity. The lack of surviving pre-Norse place names compared with the boundless supply of Norse farm names suggests that many settlements may have been established *de novo* at this time and there is evidence, too, from Bhaltos that there may have been a conscious avoidance of earlier settlements in some areas (Armit 1994a).

The Viking Age appears to be the first period after the initial Mesolithic colonisation of the islands when there is evidence for substantial population movement into the islands. Previously migrationist explanations have been advanced for other periods: these have included Neolithic colonists bringing agriculture; the 'Beaker Folk'; the Atlantic roundhouse builders; and the

'Scotto-Picts'. As we have seen in previous chapters, only for the Neolithic is there a serious case to be made on present evidence but even here the continuities with the western Scottish Mesolithic are sufficiently strong as to undermine any straightforward diffusionist explanation.

Even in the Viking Age, however, the scale of immigration is unclear, as is the question of how far down the social hierarchy significant change occurred. Recent work on the complexity of language change has shown that the adoption of the Norse tongue need not have signalled a wholesale replacement of population (Robb 1993). Nonetheless population movement on a smaller scale would have been a significant factor in cultural change throughout all archaeological periods. Movement brought about through marriage, trade, pilgrimage, etc. could all have spurred the interchange of ideas. On a slightly larger scale, warfare and the dominance of small but powerful elite groups over farming populations would undoubtedly have occurred throughout the prehistoric as well as historic periods and would have had some impact on culture change. It is likely therefore that there would always have been some inflow and outflow of people from the Hebrides, particularly at the upper end of the social scale and amongst those whose primary activities were other than subsistence agriculture. The proportion of the population able to achieve such mobility may be expected to have increased in broad terms as society became more hierarchical, as apparently happened for example in the Later Neolithic and again from the Later Iron Age onwards.

In the medieval period, with the establishment of the Lordship of the Isles, the hierarchical nature of Hebridean society seems to have reached a new peak. The vast gulf in wealth and power between the clan chiefs and their subjects manifested both in their dwellings and material culture far surpasses anything found in prehistory, or even in the period of Norse dominance. By comparison with the power manifested in the construction and maintenance of the castles of the Lordship period, the efforts of earlier island elites appear rather feeble.

Continuity

Despite the great changes that transformed Hebridean societies over the millennia covered by this book there are several remarkable signs of continuity. One of these is the great time-depth of settlement evidenced in certain locations. Perhaps the best known is the Udal in North Uist which has yielded settlement evidence from one small locality dating from the Later Neolithic to the post-medieval period (Crawford n.d.). The gaps in this sequence which have been highlighted elsewhere in this volume may attest periodic abandonment but, given the dynamic nature of the machair environment, may simply relate to periods when activity had shifted to areas now eroded by the sea or otherwise inaccessible to the excavator.

There is no reason to regard the Udal as a unique instance of preservation;

indeed the time-depth of the settlement was entirely unsuspected prior to excavation. Numerous other sites that have been subject to partial investigation hint at similar depths of occupation. The former township of Foshigarry, for example, just a few miles west of the Udal, has yielded evidence of occupation throughout the Iron Age and is capped by a baile cleared in the 1820s, with every likelihood of continuous occupation between the two known periods. This is but one of numerous machair midden sites containing enormous depths of settlement deposits. Indeed, few sites in the Hebrides seem to be 'single-period' settlements. Much of this continuity may relate to the paucity of suitable niches for settlement in the Iron Age and later, by which time peat growth was well-established, or to the availability of building stone on sites of former settlement. It may, however, also indicate an over-riding conservatism representing a broad continuity of population and economic organisation over much of prehistory. A modern reflection of the processes that caused these sites to be formed can be seen throughout the Hebrides today where ruined blackhouse lies next to its abandoned, 'improved' successor and modern bungalow.

The recognition of this tendency for settlements to remain fairly static in location enhances the significance of identifiable settlement shifts. A recent study of the Bhaltos peninsula in Lewis has identified apparent discontinuities that may represent times when the established economic organisation was altered (Armit 1994). One such dislocation appears to coincide with the arrival of the Vikings, since the numerous pre-Norse sites contain no apparent evidence for subsequent occupation. This may reflect a reorganisation of land-holding and settlement structure associated with the arrival of the first Viking settlers. A further settlement dislocation seems to occur in the medieval period with the abandonment of the machair plain and a retreat of settlement onto the lower hill-slopes. Rather than being the result of a major social change, however, this may relate instead to the climatic worsening associated with the Little Ice Age in the middle of present millennium, when the rise of the winter water table may have made the machair unsuitable for permanent structures.

There are numerous other indicators of cultural continuity in the islands that cross archaeological periods and defy easy interpretation. The long-lived tradition of islet settlements that we can trace from the Neolithic (Eilean Domhnuill and Eilean an Tighe) to the medieval period (Dun Ban and Kisimul Castle) is one particularly impressive instance. Islet settlements occur throughout Scotland and Ireland but seldom in such concentrations and never (so far as has been shown) with such longevity. The tradition of local pottery manufacture is even more long-lived, stretching as it does from the Early Neolithic to the nineteenth century. Decorated ceramics were produced consistently over the intervening millennia even in periods when the rest of Scotland was virtually aceramic. Although developments in pottery form and decoration were clearly open to outside influence distinctive Hebridean characteristics were almost always present to some degree.

FIGURE 12.1. Our Lady of the Isles; a mid-twentieth century monument on South Uist.

Prospect

Hebridean archaeology is arguably healthier today than at any time since its inception. Several major research projects have been underway since the mid-1980s and many of these are now making their way towards publication. Central amongst these are projects aimed at the reconstruction of the Hebridean environment as it evolved during the period of human settlement. The long decades in which Atlantic Scottish archaeology virtually ignored the west in favour of the Northern Isles appear to have finally been banished. Sufficient interest now exists amongst professional archaeologists to enable the setting up of a 'Hebridean Forum' to promote the exchange and dissemination of new ideas on the subject.

The islands have been recognised as of central significance within Scottish archaeology. In certain periods, particularly the Iron Age, they are at the centre of debate within a wider British context, as a session at the 1995 meeting of the British Iron Age studies group in Durham has recently demonstrated (Armit, forth. a; Sharples and Parker-Pearson forth.). As I write this final chapter, the Western Isles Council have pronounced 1995 as their 'Year of Archaeology' and are promoting a series of events to promote the archaeological heritage of the islands. A new visitor centre has just opened at Callanish and the new Museum nan Eilean has recently opened in Stornoway, providing a much-needed and, hopefully permanent, introduction to the archaeology of the islands for visitors and islanders alike.

In terms of active research, level of debate and public dissemination of results, the present situation is a major step forward from that which existed even ten years ago. Nonetheless, significant problems remain. The Western Isles remain one of only three Scottish regions with no local authority archaeologist in post to protect and promote the islands' heritage. Given the quality of the islands' archaeology and the enormous threats posed by coastal erosion in particular, this is an appalling situation which one has to hope will be remedied before too long.

I hope that this book has shown that the archaeology of Skye and the Western Isles is exceptionally rich and worthy both of preservation and study. In particular, the continuity of settlement within both individual sites like the Udal and small, self-contained areas like the Bhaltos peninsula presents rare opportunities for the study of human history on a timescale of millennia rather than decades or centuries.

Year by year the wind and weather tear at the most fragile remains in the islands. The processes that formed the Hebridean machair and preserved its archaeology also ultimately destroy it. The peat-covered inland regions remain all but unexplored by archaeologists. Nonetheless, the recognition and quantification of these problems is an essential first step to their solution. If the present momentum in research can be maintained, then it is to be hoped that the provisional and rather tentative outline of Hebridean archaeology presented here can be rendered obsolete before too long.

Appendix

Radiocarbon Dates from Skye and the Western Isles

The following is a list of archaeological radiocarbon dates from Skye and the Western Isles. Dates published prior to 1986 were obtained from a list compiled by Dr Ian Ralston (1986). Post-1986 dates sponsored by Historic Scotland were supplied by Patrick Ashmore of Historic Scotland. Dates from Skye were provided by Roger Miket, Museums Officer for the Skye and Lochalsh District Council. Additional dates were supplied prior to publication by Andrew Dunwell of the Centre for Field Archaeology, University of Edinburgh (Cnip Headland Viking Age and Bronze Age burials).

The dates have been calibrated using the computer package CALND which uses the high-precision dendrochronological data of Stuiver and Pearson (1986) and calibration procedure of Robinson (1984). Dates prior to 8000 bp were calibrated by Patrick Ashmore of Historic Scotland. Radiocarbon dates should be used, as ever, with the greatest caution: biases exist at all stages in the process of selection, recovery, processing and interpretation. Nonetheless they provide a useful indication of the calendar dates of many sites discussed in this volume.

Dates obtained as part of AOC's Western Isles Project have been omitted pending their publication and the resolution of problems associated with the use of marine shell samples. The series of dates from Eilean Olabhat, North Uist, has been excluded because of strong evidence that they derive from old wood used in the metal-working process (Armit and Dunwell 1993). The dating evidence for this site is summarised in Chapter 9. One date from the extensive sequence at Cnip has been excluded (GU2750) because it was clearly contaminated (c.f. Armit n.d.). Also excluded are dates relating to non-archaeological, palaeoenvironmental data, including those from Kinloch and Carinish not directly related to anthropogenic deposits, and dates obtained by the British Geological Survey from offshore boreholes.

APPENDIX

Key

Name	Name of site, context and sample material
Code	Laboratory reference number
Date	Uncalibrated date with standard deviation (bp)
68%H	68% confidence upper (oldest) limit
68%L	68% confidence lower (youngest) limit
95%H	95% confidence upper (oldest) limit
95%L	95% confidence lower (youngest) limit
Centroid	Weighted average (centroid) after calibration

Name	Code	Date	68%H	68%L	95%H	95%L	Centroid
MESOLITHIC							
Kinloch, Rhum fill of pit, carbonised hazel-nut shell	GU1873	8590 ± 95	7694 BC	7504 BC	7903 BC	7439 BC	**7549 BC**
Kinloch, Rhum fill of pit, carbonised hazel-nut shell	GU2040	8560 ± 70	7582 BC	7503 BC	7837 BC	7445 BC	**7543 BC**
Kinloch, Rhum fill of pit, carbonised hazel-nut shell	GU1874	8515 ± 190	7832 BC	7327 BC	7964 BC	7044 BC	**7534 BC**
Kinloch, Rhum fill of pit, carbonised hazel-nut shell	GU2146	8080 ± 50	7044 BC	7004 BC	7246 BC	6771 BC	**7035 BC**
Kinloch, Rhum fill of pit, carbonised hazel-nut shell	GU2039	7925 ± 65	7021 BC	6693 BC	7063 BC	6618 BC	**6811 BC**
Kinloch, Rhum fill of hollow, carbonised hazel-nut shell	GU2147	7880 ± 70	6828 BC	6629 BC	7046 BC	6572 BC	**6732 BC**
Kinloch, Rhum fill of pit, carbonised hazel-nut shell	GU2145	7850 ± 50	6717 BC	6621 BC	6825 BC	6577 BC	**6677 BC**

Name	Code	Date	68%H	68%L	95%H	95%L	Centroid
MESOLITHIC (continued)							
An Corran, Skye bevelled bone tool	OxA4994	7590 ± 90	6488 BC	6397 BC	6590 BC	6208 BC	**6429 BC**
Kinloch, Rhum	GU2149	7570 ± 50	6462 BC	6414 BC	6485 BC	6276 BC	**6423 BC**
Kinloch, Rhum buried soil, charcoal and hazel-nut shell	GU2211	7140 ± 130	6110 BC	5873 BC	6202 BC	5742 BC	**5998 BC**
EARLIER NEOLITHIC							
Carinish hearth spread, charcoal	GU2669	5520 ± 90	4477 BC	4337 BC	4546 BC	4208 BC	**4376 BC**
Carinish hearth spread, charcoal	GU2458	4490 ± 50	3339 BC	3076 BC	3368 BC	3021 BC	**3185 BC**
Shulishader axe haft	OxA3537	4470 ± 95	3358 BC	2994 BC	3389 BC	2914 BC	**3149 BC**
Carinish hearth spread, charcoal	GU2671	4430 ± 100	3307 BC	2932 BC	3380 BC	2892 BC	**3089 BC**
Northton Neolithic I, bone	BM 705	4411 ± 79	3218 BC	2933 BC	3359 BC	2910 BC	**3055 BC**
Carinish occupation deposit, charcoal	GU2670	4370 ± 50	3049 BC	2926 BC	3173 BC	2912 BC	**2986 BC**
Carinish	GU2672	4280 ± 130	3043 BC	2737 BC	3319 BC	2565 BC	**2897 BC**

APPENDIX

Name	Code	Date	68%H	68%L	95%H	95%L	Centroid
LATER NEOLITHIC/BRONZE AGE							
Kinloch, Rhum 'midden', charcoal	GU2148	4080 ± 60	2817 BC	2559 BC	2882 BC	2480 BC	**2651 BC**
Paible beaker midden, shell	GU1088	4060 ± 135	2855 BC	2475 BC	2929 BC	2245 BC	**2620 BC**
Rosinish beaker period ploughsoil, shell	GU1065	3920 ± 55	2490 BC	2388 BC	2581 BC	2261 BC	**2443 BC**
Rosinish primary midden containing beakers	GU1064	3850 ± 75	2479 BC	2228 BC	2540 BC	2077 BC	**2337 BC**
Kildonan I pit associated with huts, charred seeds	OxA3353	3710 ± 80	2255 BC	2010 BC	2398 BC	1901 BC	**2120 BC**
Northton beaker I, bone	BM 706	3604 ± 70	2088 BC	1891 BC	2167 BC	1772 BC	**1974 BC**
Kildonan I pit associated with huts, charred seeds	OxA3354	3560 ± 80	2031 BC	1811 BC	2140 BC	1705 BC	**1914 BC**
Udal	Q1134	3560 ± 100	2061 BC	1769 BC	2197 BC	1676 BC	**1915 BC**
Northton Beaker II, bone	BM 707	3481 ± 54	1896 BC	1744 BC	1992 BC	1678 BC	**1804 BC**
Udal deposits containing AOC beaker, shell	Q1133	3470 ± 120	1981 BC	1673 BC	2122 BC	1515 BC	**1799 BC**

Name	Code	Date	68%H	68%L	95%H	95%L	Centroid
LATER NEOLITHIC/BRONZE AGE (continued)							
Udal inhumation under kerb cairn	Q1478	3425 ± 80	1847 BC	1668 BC	1949 BC	1543 BC	**1739 BC**
Cnip inurned cremation, human bone	GU1174	3410 ± 55	1776 BC	1672 BC	1875 BC	1614 BC	**1718 BC**
Cnip cist, human bone	GU3488	3360 ± 50	1727 BC	1577 BC	1869 BC	1494 BC	**1665 BC**
Sheshader beneath field wall, peat	GU1665	2900 ± 100	1285 BC	976 BC	1411 BC	845 BC	**1111 BC**
Sheshader organic object, cattle hair	OxA3536	2860 ± 85	1201 BC	948 BC	1319 BC	839 BC	**1053 BC**
EARLIER IRON AGE							
Cnip	GU2756	2600 ± 150	916 BC	531 BC	1086 BC	399 BC	**755 BC**
Dun Bharabhat under foundation of roundhouse, wood	GU2436	2550 ± 50	807 BC	671 BC	827 BC	483 BC	**733 BC**
Alt a'Ghasgain hut circle	B66137	2370 ± 190	794 BC	242 BC	906 BC	10 BC	**469 BC**
Cnip votive deposit, animal bone	GU2754	2370 ± 130	685 BC	360 BC	815 BC	151 BC	**463 BC**

EARLIER IRON AGE (continued)

Name	Code	Date	68%H	68%L	95%H	95%L	Centroid
Stornoway wooden bowl	OxA3012	2370 ± 90	595 BC	395 BC	789 BC	241 BC	**451 BC**
Cnip wheelhouse phase 1, animal bone	GU2758	2280 ± 140	456 BC	197 BC	792 BC	22 BC	**356 BC**
Tungadale secondary floor, post-pad, charcoal	GU3808	2310 ± 70	424 BC	354 BC	535 BC	222 BC	**384 BC**
Torrin, Skye Period 1, pits, charcoal	GU3492	2219 ± 60	399 BC	218 BC	410 BC	134 BC	**297 BC**
Tungadale primary hearth, charcoal	GU3810	2150 ± 100	380 BC	87 BC	413 BC	40 BC	**208 BC**
Dun Bharabhat secondary occupation, charcoal; secondary hearth, charcoal	GU2435	2100 ± 50	245 BC	74 BC	367 BC	AD 35	**145 BC**
Dun Bharabhat secondary occupation, charcoal	GU2434	2010 ± 50	101 BC	AD 33	168 BC	AD 65	**31 BC**
Sollas Period B2 pit, animal bone	GU2591	2010 ± 60	104 BC	AD 40	184 BC	AD 87	**31 BC**
Dun Ardtreck roundhouse foundation, charcoal	GX1120	2005 ± 105	160 BC	AD 68	347 BC	AD 217	**29 BC**
Dun Flodigarry immediately post construction, charcoal	GU1662	1995 ± 65	100 BC	AD 53	180 BC	AD 122	**14 BC**

Name	Code	Date	68%H	68%L	95%H	95%L	Centroid
EARLIER IRON AGE (continued)							
Cnip wheelhouse phase 1, animal bone	GU2755	1990 ± 50	93 BC	AD 47	123 BC	AD 85	**8 BC**
Cnip wheelhouse phase 1, animal bone	GU2757	1960 ± 90	94 BC	AD 189	189 BC	AD 227	**AD 25**
Cnip Phase 3, animal bone	GU2742	1940 ± 70	55 BC	AD 118	108 BC	AD 215	**AD 49**
Cnip Phase 3, animal bone	GU2743	1930 ± 50	AD 11	AD 113	96 BC	AD 188	**AD 59**
Loch a'Ghlinne wooden bowl	UT1698	1930 ± 50	AD 11	AD 113	96 BC	AD 188	**AD 59**
Cnip phase 2, animal bone	GU2746	1930 ± 90	75 BC	AD 147	159 BC	AD 268	**AD 60**
Cnip wheelhouse phase 1, animal bone	GU2749	1920 ± 60	AD 11	AD 123	97 BC	AD 214	**AD 71**
Cnip phase 2, animal bone	GU2752	1900 ± 50	AD 30	AD 127	21 BC	AD 216	**AD 93**
Cnip phase 2, animal bone	GU2748	1890 ± 50	AD 43	AD 151	2 BC	AD 222	**AD 104**
Alt na Cille floor surface, charcoal	GU3829	1890 ± 90	AD 11	AD 214	105 BC	AD 317	**AD 106**

APPENDIX

EARLIER IRON AGE (continued)

Name	Code	Date	68%H	68%L	95%H	95%L	Centroid
Cnip phase 2, animal bone	GU2747	1890 ± 50	AD 43	AD 151	2 BC	AD 222	**AD 104**
Sollas Period B1 pit, animal bone	GU2590	1890 ± 100	3 BC	AD 220	110 BC	AD 354	**AD 107**
Sollas Period B1 pit, charcoal	GU2562	1880 ± 50	AD 52	AD 178	AD 12	AD 228	**AD 115**
Sollas Period B1 pit, animal bone	GU2565	1880 ± 50	AD 52	AD 178	AD 12	AD 228	**AD 115**
Sollas	GU2564	1870 ± 50	AD 56	AD 194	AD 15	AD 235	**AD 127**
Cnip phase 3, animal bone	GU2745	1870 ± 70	AD 44	AD 214	51 BC	AD 300	**AD 129**
Cnip phase 2, animal bone	GU2751	1850 ± 50	AD 66	AD 214	AD 28	AD 284	**AD 151**
Talisker wooden bowl	OxA3542	1830 ± 80	AD 62	AD 264	AD 4	AD 377	**AD 177**
Cnip phase 3, animal bone	GU2741	1810 ± 190	19 BC	AD 412	263 BC	AD 622	**AD 200**
Cnip phase 3, animal bone	GU2744	1770 ± 80	AD 125	AD 355	AD 54	AD 419	**AD 250**

EARLIER IRON AGE (continued)

Name	Code	Date	68%H	68%L	95%H	95%L	Centroid
Kyleakin wooden bucket	UB3186	1730 ± 35	AD 238	AD 351	AD 212	AD 391	**AD 298**
Galson human skeleton	GU2115	1710 ± 70	AD 226	AD 402	AD 126	AD 513	**AD 323**
Sollas Period B1 pit, animal bone	GU2566	1670 ± 80	AD 254	AD 428	AD 172	AD 542	**AD 371**
Kildonan III buildings and barley cultivation, charred seeds	OxA3356	1670 ± 75	AD 258	AD 426	AD 184	AD 536	**AD 371**
Rosinish upper midden, iron age, shell	GU1066	1655 ± 55	AD 304	AD 424	AD 239	AD 526	**AD 390**
Udal north mound, layer XIV (post-wheelhouse), whalebone	Q1131	1610 ± 120	AD 276	AD 557	AD 129	AD 646	**AD 435**
Cnip late midden, animal bone	GU2753	1570 ± 140	AD 314	AD 624	AD 132	AD 684	**AD 475**
Udal north mound, layer XIII, whalebone	Q1137	1500 ± 80	AD 439	AD 631	AD 391	AD 656	**AD 555**
Udal north mound, layer XII, bone	Q1132	1355 ± 115	AD 581	AD 762	AD 440	AD 912	**AD 673**
Udal north mound, layer XI, wood	Q1139	1275 ± 115	AD 638	AD 872	AD 549	AD 984	**AD 745**

APPENDIX

Name	Code	Date	68%H	68%L	95%H	95%L	Centroid
NORSE							
Cnip grave b., human bone	GU3486	1200 ± 50	AD 753	AD 881	AD 674	AD 957	**AD 814**
Cnip grave c., human bone	GU3487	1180 ± 50	AD 765	AD 910	AD 694	AD 975	**AD 839**
Cnip grave a., human bone	GU3485	1150 ± 50	AD 780	AD 955	AD 753	AD 986	**AD 879**
Cnip child burial	GU3489	1150 ± 50	AD 780	AD 955	AD 753	AD 986	**AD 879**
Newtonferry midden, shell	GU2162	1150 ± 70	AD 772	AD 973	AD 684	AD 997	**AD 877**
Kildonan III buildings and barley cultivation, charred seeds	OxA3355	1115 ± 70	AD 790	AD 984	AD 752	AD 1022	**AD 919**
Stornoway wooden bowl	OxA3011	1100 ± 80	AD 866	AD 990	AD 750	AD 1131	**AD 933**
Udal north mound, layer X, Norse 'fort', whalebone	Q1136	1090 ± 40	AD 894	AD 984	AD 830	AD 1000	**AD 956**
Udal north mound, layer IXc, charcoal	Q1135	1040 ± 150	AD 789	AD 1148	AD 658	AD 1262	**AD 990**
Torrin, Skye Period 2, hearth and mound, charcoal	GU3491	930 ± 50	AD 1015	AD 1156	AD 983	AD 1206	**AD 1105**

Name	Code	Date	68%H	68%L	95%H	95%L	Centroid
NORSE (continued)							
Udal north mound, charcoal	Q1138	850 ± 40	AD 1143	AD 1220	AD 1069	AD 1256	**AD 1193**
MEDIEVAL AND LATER							
Tungadale secondary floor in late cell, charcoal	GU3807	750 ± 50	AD 1229	AD 1274	AD 1192	AD 1290	**AD 1264**
Dun Carloway final hearth, shell	GX3428	650 ± 150	AD 1230	AD 1412	AD 1073	AD 1489	**AD 1321**
Torrin 2, Skye Period 1, hearth	GU3490	520 ± 70	AD 1339	AD 1427	AD 1285	AD 1467	**AD 1404**

Bibliography

Abbreviations

Brit. Arch. Reports	British Archaeological Reports
Curr. Archaeol.	Current Archaeology
Glas. Arch. Jour.	Glasgow Archaeological Journal
Proc. Preh. Soc.	Proceedings of the Prehistoric Society
Proc. Roy. Soc. Edin.	Proceedings of the Royal Society of Edinburgh
Proc. Soc. Antiq. Scot.	Proceedings of the Society of Antiquaries of Scotland
Scott. Arch. Forum	Scottish Archaeological Forum
Scott. Arch. Rev.	Scottish Archaeological Review
Scott. Geog. Mag.	Scottish Geographical Magazine
Scott. Jour. Geol.	Scottish Journal of Geology
Trans. Bot. Soc. Edin.	Transactions of the Botanical Society of Edinburgh
Trans. Inst. Br. Geog.	Transactions of the Institute of British Geographers
World Archaeol.	World Archaeology

Alcock, L. (1987), 'Pictish studies: present and future', in A. Small (ed.), *The Picts: A New Look at Old Problems* (Dundee), pp. 80–92.

Andersen, S. (1991), 'Norse settlement in the Hebrides: what happened to the natives and what happened to the Norse immigrants?', in I. Wood and N. Lund (eds), *People and Places in Northern Europe 500–1600: Essays in Honour of Peter Hayes Sawyer*, pp. 131–47.

Angus, S. (1993a), 'Statistics relating to the Western Isles', *Hebridean Naturalist*, 11, pp. 36–40.

Angus, S. (1993b), 'Cetacean standings in Lewis and Harris in 1990', *Hebridean Naturalist*, 11, pp. 13–14.

Angus, S. and Elliot, M. M. (1992), 'Erosion in Scottish machair with particular reference to the Outer Hebrides', in *Proceedings of the 3rd European Dune Congress*, Galway.

Armit, I. (1985), 'The later prehistoric defensive structures of Lewis and Harris', unpublished MA dissertation, University of Edinburgh.

Armit, I. (1987), 'Excavation of a Neolithic island settlement at Loch Olabhat, North Uist 1987', Department of Archaeology, Edinburgh University, Project Paper No. 8.
Armit, I. (1988), 'Broch landscapes in the Western Isles', *Scott. Arch. Rev.*, 5, 78–86.
Armit, I. (1988a), 'Excavations at Loch Olabhat, North Uist, 1988', Department of Archaeology, Edinburgh University, Project Paper No. 10.
Armit, I. (1988b), 'Excavations At Cnip, West Lewis 1988', Department of Archaeology, Edinburgh University, Project Paper No. 9.
Armit, I. (ed.) (1990), *Beyond the Brochs*, Edinburgh: Edinburgh University Press.
Armit, I. (1990a), 'The Loch Olabhat Project 1989', Department of Archaeology, Edinburgh University, Project Paper No. 12.
Armit, I. (1990b), 'Monumentality and elaboration: a case study in the Western Isles', *Scott. Arch. Rev.*, 7, pp. 84–95.
Armit, I. (1990c), 'Brochs and beyond in the Western Isles', in I. Armit (ed.), *Beyond the Brochs*, Edinburgh: Edinburgh University Press, pp. 41–70.
Armit, I. (1990d), 'Broch-building in Atlantic Scotland; the context of innovation', *World Archaeol.*, 21, pp. 435–45.
Armit, I. (1990e), 'Epilogue', in I. Armit (ed.), *Beyond the Brochs*, Edinburgh, pp. 194–210.
Armit, I. (1992), 'The Hebridean Neolithic', in N. M. Sharples and A. Sheridan, (eds), *Vessels for the Ancestors*, Edinburgh: Edinburgh University Press, pp. 307–21.
Armit, I. (1992a), *'The Later Prehistory of the Western Isles of Scotland'*, Brit. Arch. Reports, 221, Oxford.
Armit, I. (1994), 'Archaeological field survey of the Bhaltos (Valtos) peninsula, Lewis', *Proc. Soc. Antiq. Scot.*, 124.
Armit, I. (1996), 'Human responses to marginality', in G. Coles and C. Mills (eds), *On the Edge: Human Settlement in Marginal Areas*, Oxford.
Armit, I. (n.d.), 'The radiocarbon dates from Cnip wheelhouse, Lewis; an interim report', typescript.
Armit, I. (forthcoming), 'Excavation of a post-medieval settlement at Druim nan Dearcag, Loch Olabhat, North Uist'.
Armit, I. (forthcoming a), 'Cultural landscapes and identities: a case study in the Scottish Iron Age', in C. Haselgrove and A. Gwilt (eds), *Time, Space and Culture in Iron Age Britain*, 1996.
Armit, I. and Dunwell, A. (1992), 'Excavations at Cnip, sites 2 and 3, Lewis, 1989', *Proc. Soc. Antiq. Scot.*, 122, pp. 137–48.
Armit, I. and Dunwell, A. (1993), 'Eilean Olabhat, North Uist: interim summary', unpublished report.
Armit, I. and Finlayson, W. L. (1992), 'Hunter-gatherers transformed: the transition to agriculture in northern and western Europe', *Antiquity*, 66 (1992), pp. 664–76.
Armit, I. and Finlayson, W. L. (1995), 'Social strategies and economic change: pottery in context', in W. Barnett and J. Hoopes (eds), *The Emergence of Pottery*, Washington: Smithsonian Institution Press.
Armit, I. and Ralston, I. B. M. (1996), 'The Iron Age', in K. Edwards and I. B. M. Ralston (eds), *Environment and Archaeology in Scotland*, London: Wiley.
Ashmore, P. J. (1983), 'Callanish: making a stone stand again', in M. Magnusson (ed.), *Echoes in Stone*, Edinburgh: HMSO, pp. 41–4.
Ashmore, P. J. (1984), 'Callanish', in D. J. Breeze (ed.), *Studies in Scottish Antiquity*, Edinburgh, pp. 1–31.
Ashmore, P. J. (n.d.), *Callanish: Standing Stones and Chambered Cairn*, Edinburgh: Historic Scotland guide leaflet.

Ashmore, P. J. (forthcoming), *Temples and Tombs*, London: Batsford.
Atkinson, R. J. C. (1953), 'A prehistoric vessel from North Uist', *Proc. Soc. Antiq. Scot.*, 87, pp. 198–200.
Bannerman, J. (1974), *Studies in the History of Dalriada*, Edinburgh: Scottish Academic Press.
Barber, J. W. (1982), 'Arran', *Curr. Archaeol.*, 83, pp. 358–62.
Barber, J. W. (1985), *Innsegall*, Edinburgh: John Donald.
Barber, J. W. (forthcoming), *Western Isles Excavations*, Edinburgh.
Barber, J. W. and Crone, B. A. (1993), 'Crannogs; a diminishing resource? A survey of the crannogs of southwest Scotland and excavations at Buiston Crannog', *Antiquity*, 67, pp. 520–33.
Barber, J., Halstead, P., James, H. and Lee, F. (1989), 'An unusual Iron Age burial at Hornish Point South Uist', *Antiquity*, 63, pp. 773–8.
Barclay, G. (1993), *Balfarg: the Prehistoric Ceremonial Complex*, Glenrothes: Fife Regional Council.
Barnett, W. (1995), 'Putting the pot before the horse: early pottery and the Neolithic transition in the western Mediterranean', in W. Earnett and J. Hoopes (eds), *The Emergence of Pottery*, Washington: Smithsonian Institution Press.
Bennett, K. D., Fossitt, J. A., Sharp, M. J. and Switsur, V. R. (1990), 'Holocene vegetational and environmental history at Loch Lang, South Uist, Western Isles, Scotland', *New Phytologist*, 114, pp. 281–98.
Beveridge, E. (1905), *Coll and Tiree*, Edinburgh.
Beveridge, E. (1911), *North Uist*, Edinburgh.
Beveridge, E. (1930), 'Excavation of an earth house at Foshigarry and a fort, Dun Thomaidh, in North Uist, *Proc. Soc. Antiq. Scot.*, 65, pp. 299–357.
Beveridge, E. (1931), 'Earth houses at Garry Iochdrach and Bac Mhic Connain in North Uist', *Proc. Soc. Antiq. Scot.*, 66, pp. 32–67.
Birks, H. J. B. (1973), *Past and Present Vegetation of the Isle of Skye, a Palaeoecological Study*, London.
Birks, H. J. B. and Madsen, B. J. (1979), 'Flandrian vegetational history of Little Loch Roag, Isle of Lewis, Scotland, *Journal of Ecology*, 67, pp. 825–42.
Birks, H. J. B. and Williams, W. (1983), 'Late Quaternary vegetational history of the Inner Hebrides', *Proc. Roy. Soc. Edin.*, 83, pp. 269–92.
Boardman, S. (1993), 'The charred plant remains, in Crone'.
Bohncke, S. J. P. (1988), 'Vegetation and habitation history of the Callanish area, Isle of Lewis, Scotland', in H. H. Birks, H. J. B. Birks, P. E. Kaland and D. Moe (eds), *The Cultural Landscape – Past, Present, Future*, Cambridge: Cambridge University Press, pp. 445–61.
Boyd, W. E. (1988), 'Cereals in Scottish antiquity', *Circaea*, 5, pp. 101–10.
Burgess, C. (1980), *The Age of Stonehenge*, London: Dent.
Burl, A. (1993), *From Carnac to Callanish: the Prehistoric Stone Rows and Avenues of Britain, Ireland and Brittany*, Yale.
Burn, A. R. (1969), 'Holy men on islands in pre-Christian Britain', *Glasg. Arch. Jour.*, 1, pp. 2–6.
Blundell, F. O. (1913), 'Further notes on the artificial islands in the Highland area', *Proc. Soc. Antiq. Scot.*, 47, pp. 267–302.
Bradley, R. (1993), *Altering the Earth*, Edinburgh: Society of Antiquaries of Scotland.
Callander, J. G. (1921), 'Report on the excavation of Dun Beag, a broch near Struan, Skye', *Proc. Soc. Antiq. Scot.*, 55, pp. 110–30.
Campbell, E. (1991), 'Excavation of a wheelhouse and other iron age structures at Sollas, North Uist', by R. J. C. Atkinson in 1957, *Proc. Soc. Antiq. Scot.*, 121, pp. 117–73.

Campbell, E. (1994), 'Eilean Olabhat, North Uist: the pottery', typescript.

Campbell, E. and Finlay, J. (1991), 'The ritual deposits of Period B1, in Excavation of a wheelhouse and other iron age structures at Sollas, North Uist', by R. J. C. Atkinson in 1957, *Proc. Soc. Antiq. Scot.*, 121, pp. 141–7.

Case, H. (1993), 'Beakers: deconstruction and after', *Proc. Preh. Soc.*, 59, pp. 241–68.

Clarke, D. V. (1971), 'Small finds in the Atlantic Province: problems of approach', *Scott. Arch. Forum*, 3, pp. 22–54.

Close-Brooks, J. (forthcoming), 'Excavation of a cairn at Kneep, Uig, Lewis', *Proc. Soc. Antiq. Scot.*

Close-Brooks, J. and Ritchie, J. N. G. (1978), 'Beaker pottery from Skye', *Proc. Soc. Antiq. Scot.*, 109, pp. 99–103.

Clutton-Brock, T. H. and Ball, M. E. (1987), *Rhum: the Natural History of an Island*, Edinburgh.

Coles, J. M. (1960), 'Scottish Late Bronze Age metalwork: typology, distributions and chronology', *Proc. Soc. Antiq. Scot.*, 93, pp. 16–134.

Coles, J. M. (1964), 'Scottish Middle Bronze Age metalwork', *Proc. Soc. Antiq. Scot.*, 97, pp. 82–156.

Coles, J. M. (1969), 'Scottish Early Bronze Age metalwork', *Proc. Soc. Antiq. Scot.*, 101, pp. 1–110.

Collingwood, R. G. (1953), *Roman Britain*, London.

Colquhon, I. and Burgess, C. B. (1988), *The Swords of Britain*, Prahistoriche Bronzefunde IV.5, Munich.

Cormack, W. F. (1973), 'Traigh na Beiridh', *Discovery and Excavation in Scotland*, 48.

Cowie, T. (1986), 'Barvas', *Discovery and Excavation in Scotland*, pp. 52–3.

Cowie, T. (1987), 'Barvas', *Discovery and Excavation in Scotland*, 62.

Cowie, T. (1994), 'A Bronze Age Gold Torc from the Minch', *Hebridean Naturalist*, 12, pp. 19–21.

Cowie, T. et al., (forthcoming), 'Excavations at Barvas, Lewis'.

Crawford, B. E. (1987), *Scandinavian Scotland*, Leicester: Leicester University Press.

Crawford, I. A. (1965), 'Contributions to a history of domestic settlement in North Uist', *Scottish Studies*, 102, pp. 34–63.

Crawford, I. A. (1974), 'Scot (?), Norseman and Gael', *Scott. Arch. Forum*, 6, pp. 1–16.

Crawford, I. A. (1977), 'A corbelled Bronze Age burial chamber and beaker evidence from the Rosinish machair, Benbecula', *Proc. Soc. Antiq. Scot.*, 108, pp. 94–107.

Crawford, I. A. (1981), 'War or peace – Viking colonisation in the Northern and Western Isles of Scotland reviewed', in H. Bekker-Nielson, P. Foote and O. Olsen (eds), *Proceedings of the eighth Viking Congress, Arhus, 24–31 August 1977*, Odense, pp. 259–69.

Crawford, I. A. (n.d.), *The West Highlands and Islands; a View of 50 Centuries*, Cambridge: Great Auk Press.

Crawford, I. A. and Switsur, V. R. (1977), 'Sand-scaping and C14: the Udal, North Uist', *Antiquity*, 51, pp. 124–36.

Crone, A. (1989), 'Excavation and survey at Bharpa Carinish, North Uist', in *Archaeological Operations and Conservation Annual Report 1989*, Edinburgh.

Crone, A. (1993), 'Excavation and survey of sub-peat features of Neolithic, Bronze and Iron Age date at Bharpa Carinish, North Uist, Scotland', *Proc. Prehist. Soc.*, 59, pp. 361–82.

Curle, C. L. (1982), *Pictish and Norse Finds from the Brough of Birsay 1934–74*, Society of Antiquaries of Scotland monograph series No. 1, Edinburgh.

Curle, J. (1932), 'Objects of Roman and provincial Roman origin', *Proc. Soc. Antiq. Scot.*, 66, pp. 277–400.

Curtis, M. and Curtis, R. (1994), *Callanish: the Stones, the Moon and the Sacred landscape*, Callanish.

Dodgshon, R. A. (1993), 'West Highland and Hebridean settlement prior to crofting and the Clearances: a case study in stability or change', *Proc. Soc. Antiq. Scot.*, 123, pp. 419–38.

Dunwell, A. J., Neighbour, T. and Cowie, T. G. (forthcoming), 'A cist burial adjacent to the Bronze Age cairn on Cnip headland, Isle of Lewis', *Proc. Soc. Antiq. Scot.*, 124.

Dunwell, A. J., Neighbour, T., Cowie, T. G. and Bruce, M. F. (forthcoming), 'A Viking Age cemetery at Cnip (Kneep), Isle of Lewis', *Proc. Soc. Antiq. Scot.*, 124.

Edwards, A. J. H. (1923), 'Report on the excavation of an earth house at Galson, Borve, Lewis', *Proc. Soc. Antiq. Scot.*, 58, pp. 185–203.

Edwards, K. J., Whittington, G., Coles, G. M. and Lomax, T. (1994), 'Environmental change in the Callanish area of Lewis, Scotland', report submitted to Scottish Natural Heritage and Comhairle nan Eilean, typescript.

Ennew, J. (1980), *The Western Isles Today*, Cambridge: Cambridge University Press.

Evans, J. G. (1971a), 'Notes on the environment of early farming communities in Britain', in D. D. A. Simpson (ed.), *Economy and Settlement in Neolithic and Early Bronze Age Britain and Europe*, Leicester: Leicester University Press, pp. 11–26.

Evans, J. G. (1971b), 'Habitat change on the calcareous soils of Britain: the impact of neolithic man', in D. D. A. Simpson (ed.), *Economy and Settlement in Neolithic and Early Bronze Age Britain and Europe*, Leicester: Leicester University Press, pp. 27–74.

Evans, J. G. (1975), *The Environment of Early Man in the British Isles*, London: Paul Elek.

Fairhurst, H. (1971), 'The wheelhouse site at A'Cheardhach Bheag on Drimore Machair, South Uist, *Glasg. Arch. Jour.*, 2, pp. 72–106.

Fairhurst, H. and Taylor, D. B. (1970), 'A hut circle settlement at Kilphedir, Sutherland', *Proc. Soc. Antiq. Scot.*, 103, pp. 65–99.

Finlay, J. (1985), *Faunal Evidence for Prehistoric Economy and Settlement in the Outer Hebrides*, unpublished Ph.D. thesis, University of Edinburgh.

Finlayson, W. L. (1994), 'Complexity in the Mesolithic of the western Scottish seaboard', in *Man, Sea and the Mesolithic Conference Proceedings*.

Fitzpatrick, A. P. (1989), 'The Submission of the Orkney Islands to Claudius: New Evidence?', *Scott. Arch. Rev.*, 6, pp. 24–33.

Fleming, A. and Woolf, A. (1992), 'Cille Donnain: a late Norse church in South Uist', *Proc. Soc. Antiq. Scot.*, 122, pp. 329–50.

Fojut, N., Pringle, D. and Walker, B. (n.d.), *The Ancient Monuments of the Western Isles*, Edinburgh: HMSO.

Foster, S. M. (1995), *Picts, Gaels and Scots*, London: Batsford.

Fowler, P. J. (1971), 'Early prehistoric agriculture in western Europe: some archaeological evidence', in D. D. A. Simpson (ed.), *Economy and Settlement in Neolithic and Early Bronze Age Britain and Europe*, Leicester: Leicester University Press, pp. 153–82.

Gibson, A. M. (1984), 'Problems of beaker ceramic assemblages: the north British material', in R. Miket and C. Burgess (eds), *Between and Beyond the Walls: Essays on the Prehistory and History of North Britain in Honour of George Jobey*, Edinburgh: John Donald, pp. 74–96.

Glentworth, R. (1979), 'Observations on the soils of the Outer Hebrides', *Proc. Roy. Soc. Edin. 1979*, pp. 123–37.

Gowen, M. (1988), *Three Irish Gas Pipelines: new archaeological evidence in Munster*, Dublin: Wordwell.

Graham-Campbell, J. A. (1974), 'A preliminary note on certain small finds of Viking Age date from the Udal excavations, North Uist', *Scot. Arch. Forum*, 6, pp. 17–22.

Graham-Campbell, J. A. (1976), 'The Viking Age silver and gold hoards of Scandinavian character from Scotland', *Proc. Soc. Antiq. Scot.*, 107, pp. 104–35.

Hallen, Y. (1992), 'Animal bone from Eilean Domhnuill, Loch Olabhat', typescript.

Hamilton, J. R. C. (1956), *Excavations at Jarlshof*, Edinburgh: HMSO.

Hamilton, J. R. C. (1968), *Excavations at Clickhimin*, Edinburgh: HMSO.

Harding, D. W. (1984), 'The function and classification of brochs and duns', in R. Miket et al., (eds), *Between and Beyond the Walls*, Edinburgh: John Donald.

Harding, D. W. (1993), 'Loch na Berie', *Discovery and Excavation in Scotland*, pp. 110–11.

Harding, D. W. and Armit, I. (1990), 'Survey and excavation in west Lewis', in I. Armit (ed.), *Beyond the Brochs*, Edinburgh: Edinburgh University Press, pp. 71–107.

Harman, M. (forthcoming), 'Barvas: the animal bone, with particular reference to mammals', in T. Cowie et al., (forthcoming).

Hawkins, G. S. (1965), 'Callanish, a Scottish Stonehenge', *Science*, 147, pp. 127–30.

Hedges, J. W. (1984), *Tomb of the Eagles*, London: John Murray.

Hedges, J. W. (1985), 'The broch period', in A. C. Renfrew (ed.), *The Prehistory of Orkney*, Edinburgh: Edinburgh University Press.

Hedges, J. W. (1987), *Bu, Gurness and the Brochs of Orkney*, Vol. 1–3, Brit. Arch. Reports, Oxford, pp. 163–5.

Hedges, R. E. M., Housley, R. A., Bronk-Ramsey, C. and van Klinken, G. J. (1993), 'Radiocarbon dates from the Oxford AMS system: Archaeometry datelist 16', *Archaeometry*, 35, Part 1, pp. 147–67.

Henshall, A. S. (1963) and (1972), *The Chambered Tombs of Scotland*, Vols. 1 and 2, Edinburgh: Edinburgh University Press.

Hingley, R. J. (ed.) (1993), *Medieval and Later Rural Settlement in Scotland: Management and Preservation*, Historic Scotland, Ancient Monuments Division, Occasional Paper No. 1, Edinburgh.

Hirons, K. (1990), 'The post-glacial environment', in C. R. Wickham-Jones, *Rhum, Mesolithic and Later Sites at Kinloch, Excavations 1884–6*, Society of Antiquaries of Scotland, Monograph Series No. 7, Edinburgh, pp. 137–42.

Hodder, I. (1984), 'Burials, houses, women and men in the European Neolithic', in D. Miller and C. Tilley (eds), *Ideology, Power and Prehistory*, Cambridge: Cambridge University Press, pp. 51–68.

Hodder, I. (1990), *The Domestication of Europe*, Oxford: Blackwell.

Hunter, J. R. (1994), 'Archaeological fieldwork on the islands of Canna and Sanday, Inner Hebrides, Summer 1994', typescript.

Jensen, J. (1982), *The Prehistory of Denmark*, London: Methuen.

Johnson, S. (1774), *Journey to the Western Islands*, London: Oxford University Press.

Kent, M., Brayshay, B., Gilbertson, D., Wathern, P. and Weaver, R. (1994), 'A biogeographical study of plant communities on South Uist, Outer Hebrides, Scotland', *Scottish Geographical Magazine*, 110 (2), pp. 85–99.

Lane, A. (1983), 'Dark Age and Viking Age pottery from the Hebrides with special reference to the Udal, North Uist', unpublished Ph.D. thesis, University of Glasgow.

Lane, A. (1987), 'English migrants in the Hebrides: 'Atlantic Second B' revisited', *Proc. Soc. Antiq. Scot.*, 117, pp. 47–66.

Lane, A. (1990), 'Hebridean pottery: problems of definition, chronology, presence and absence', in I. Armit (ed.), *Beyond the Brochs*, Edinburgh: Edinburgh University Press, pp. 108–30.
Lethbridge, T. C. (1952), 'Excavations at Kilpheder, South Uist, and the problem of brochs and wheelhouses', *Proc. Prehist. Soc.*, XVIII, pp. 176–93.
Lynn, C. (1987), 'Deer Park Farms', *Archaeology Ireland*, Vol. 1, Part 1, pp. 11–15.
Macaulay Institute for Soil Research (1982), *Soil Survey of Scotland – Outer Hebrides*, Aberdeen.
MacCullagh, R. (1991), 'Lairg', *Curr. Archaeol.*, 31, pp. 455–9.
Maclaren, A. (1974), 'A Norse house on Drimore machair, South Uist', *Glasg. Arch. Jour.*, 3, pp. 9–18.
Macleod, D. J. et al., (1916), 'An account of a find of ornaments of the Viking time from Valtos, Uig in the Island of Lewis', *Proc. Soc. Antiq. Scot.*, 50, pp. 181–9.
MacKenzie, W. C. (1905), 'Notes on the Pigmies Isle at the Butt of Lewis, with the results of the recent exploration of the Pigmies Chapel there', *Proc. Soc. Antiq. Scot.*, 39, pp. 248–58.
MacKie, E. (1965), 'The origin and development of the broch and wheelhouse building cultures of the Scottish Iron Age', *Proc. Preh. Soc.*, 31, pp. 93–146.
Macinnes, A. I. (1994), 'Landownership, land use and elite enterprise in Scottish Gaeldom: from clanship to clearance in Argyllshire, 1688–1858', in T. M. Devine (ed.), *Scottish Elites*, Edinburgh: John Donald, pp. 1–42.
Macleod, F. T. (1915), 'Notes on Dun an Iardhard, a broch near Dunvegan excavated by Countess Vincent Baillet de Latour, Uiginish Lodge, Skye', *Proc. Soc. Antiq. Scot.*, 49, pp. 57–70.
MacLean, L. (ed.) (1981), *The Middle Ages in the Highlands*, Inverness: Inverness Field Club.
MacSween, A. (1985), 'The brochs, duns and enclosures of Skye', *Northern Archaeology*, Vols. 4 and 5.
Martin, M. (1716), *A Description of the Western Isles of Scotland*, London: Mercat Press.
Martlew, R. (1985), 'The excavation of Dun Flodigarry, Staffin, Isle of Skye', *Glas. Arch. Jour.*, 12, pp. 30–48.
Matthews, K. (1993), 'A futile occupation? Archaeological meanings and occupation deposits', in J. W. Barber (ed.), *Interpreting stratigraphy*, Edinburgh: AOC Scotland Ltd, pp. 55–61.
McCormick, F. (1991), 'The mammal bones from Cnip wheelhouse, Lewis', typescript.
McCormick, F. (1991a), 'Evidence for dairying at Dun Ailinne?', *Emania*, 8, pp. 57–9.
Megaw, J. V. S. and Simpson, D. D. A. (1961), 'A short cist burial on North Uist and some notes on the prehistory of the Outer isles in the second millennium BC', *Proc. Soc. Antiq. Scot.*, 94, pp. 62–78.
Mellars, P. A. (1987), *Excavations on Oronsay, Prehistoric Human Ecology on a Small Island*, Edinburgh: Edinburgh University Press.
Miket, R. and Roberts, D. L. (1990), *The Medieval Castles of Skye and Lochalsh*, Skye: Maclean Press.
Miles, A. E. W. (1989), *An Early Christian Chapel and Burial Ground on the Isle of Ensay, Outer Hebrides, Scotland, with a Study of the Skeletal Remains*, Brit. Arch. Reports, 212, Oxford.
Morrison, I. (1985), *Landscape with Lake Dwellings*, Edinburgh: Edinburgh University Press.
Newell, P. J. (1988), 'A buried wall in peatland by Sheshader, Isle of Lewis', *Proc. Soc. Antiq. Scot.*, 118, pp. 79–93.

Noddle, B. (1980), 'Animal bone', in J. N. G. Ritchie and A. M. Lane, Dun Cul Bhuirg, Iona, Argyll, *Proc. Soc. Antiq. Scot.*, 110, pp. 225–7.

O'Nuaillain, S. (1972), 'A neolithic house at Ballyglass, Co. Mayo', *J. Roy. Soc. Antiq. Ireland*, 102, pp. 49–57.

Ovrevik, S. (1985), 'The second millennium and after', in A. C. Renfrew (ed.), *The Prehistory of Orkney*, Edinburgh: Edinburgh University Press, pp. 131–49.

Parker-Pearson, M. and Sharples, N. (1992), *Dun Vulan, South Uist, Western Isles: an Interim Report on the 1992 Excavations*, Sheffield: Sheffield University Press.

Parker-Pearson, M. and Richards, C. (1994), 'Architecture and order: spatial representation and archaeology', in M. Parker-Pearson and C. Richards (eds), *Architecture and Order: Approaches to Social Space*, London: Routledge, pp. 38–72.

Pearson, G. W. and Stuiver, M. (1986), 'High-Precision Calibration of the Radiocarbon Time-Scale 500–2500 BC', *Radiocarbon*, 28 no. 2b, pp. 839–62.

Peers, C. and Radford, C. A. R. (1943), 'The Saxon monastery at Whitby', *Archaeologia*, 89, pp. 27–88.

Pollard, A. (1990), 'Down through the ages: a review of the Oban Cave deposits', *Scott. Arch. Review*, 7, pp. 58–74.

Ponting, M. R. (1989), 'Two iron age cists from Galson, Isle of Lewis', *Proc. Soc. Ant. Scot.*, 119, pp. 91–100.

Ponting, G. and Ponting, M. R. (1984), 'Dalmore', *Curr. Archaeol.*, 91, pp. 230–5.

Ralston, I. B. M. (1986), 'Radiocarbon dates (Scotland) Version 2', typescript.

Ralston, I. B. M. and Armit, I. (1996), 'The Early Historic Period: an archaeological perspective', in K. Edwards and I. B. M. Ralston (eds), *Environment and archaeology in Scotland*, London: Wiley.

Ranwell, D. S. (1974), *Sand Dune Machair: report of a seminar at coastal ecology research station Norwich*, National Environment Research Council, Institute of Terrestrial Ecology.

Ranwell, D. S. (1980), *Sand Dune Machair 3: report on meeting in the Outer Hebrides, 14–16th July 1978*, National Environment Research Council, Institute of Terrestrial Ecology.

Renfrew, A. C. (1979), *Investigations in Orkney*, London: Society of Antiquaries.

Renfrew, A. C. (ed.), (1985), *The Prehistory of Orkney*, Edinburgh: Edinburgh University Press.

Ritchie, A. (1976), 'Excavation of Pictish and Viking Age farms at Buckquoy, Orkney', *Proc. Soc. Antiq. Scot.*, 108, pp. 174–227.

Ritchie, A. (1983), 'Excavation of a neolithic farmstead at Knap of Howar, Papa Westray, Orkney', *Proc. Soc. Antiq. Scot.*, 113, pp. 40–121.

Ritchie, A. O. (1985), 'Orkney in the Pictish kingdom', in Renfrew (ed.), *The Prehistory of Orkney*, Edinburgh: Edinburgh University Press, pp. 183–204.

Ritchie, J. N. G. (ed.), (1996), *The Prehistory of Argyll*, Edinburgh: Edinburgh University Press.

Ritchie, J. N. G. and Crawford, J. (1978), 'Excavations at Sorisdale and Killunaig, Coll', *Proc. Soc. Antiq. Scot.*, 109, pp. 75–99.

Ritchie, J. N. G. and Ritchie, A. (1981), *Scotland: Archaeology and Early History*, Edinburgh: Edinburgh University Press.

Ritchie, J. N. G., Thornber, I., Lynch, F. and Marshall, D. (1975), 'Small cairns in Argyll: some recent work', *Proc. Soc. Antiq. Scot.*, 106, pp. 15–38.

Ritchie, J. N. G. and Welfare, H. G. (1983), 'Excavations at Ardnave, Islay', *Proc. Soc. Antiq. Scot.*, 113, pp. 302–67.

Ritchie, W. (1966), 'Sea level and coastal changes in the Uists', *Trans. Inst. Br. Geog.*, 39, pp. 79–86.

Ritchie, W. (1967), 'The machair of South Uist', *Scott. Geog. Mag.*, 83, pp. 161–73.

Ritchie, W. (1976), 'The meaning and definition of machair', *Trans. Bot. Soc. Edin.*, 42, pp. 431–40.
Ritchie, W. (1979), 'Machair development and Chronology in the Uists and adjacent islands', *Proc. Roy. Soc. Edin.*, pp. 107–22.
Ritchie, W. (1985), 'Inter-tidal and sub-tidal organic deposits and sea-level change in the Uists, Outer Hebrides', *Scott. Jour. Geol.*, 21 (2), pp. 161–76.
Robb, J. (1993), 'A social prehistory of European languages', *Antiquity*, 67, pp. 747–60.
Robertson, A. S. (1970), 'Roman finds from non-Roman sites in Scotland', *Britannia*, 1, pp. 198–226.
Robertson, A. S. (1983), 'Roman coins found in Scotland 1971–82', *Proc. Soc. Antiq. Scot.*, 113, p. 417.
Robinson, S. W. (1986), *A computational procedure for the utilisation of high-precision radiocarbon calibration curves*, open file report, United States Dept. of the Interior Geological Survey.
Rowley-Conwy, P. (1983), 'Sedentary hunters: the Ertebolle example', in G. Bailey (ed.), *Hunter-gatherer economy*, Cambridge: Cambridge University Press, pp. 111–26.
Rowley-Conwy, P. (1985), 'The origin of agriculture in Denmark: a review of some theories', *Journal of Danish Archaeology*, 4, pp. 188–95.
Roy, J. R. (1980), 'Comments on the astronomical alignments at Callanish, Lewis', *Journal of the Royal Astronomical Society of Canada*, 74.1, pp. 1–11.
RCAHMS (1928), *The Outer Hebrides, Skye and the Small Isles*, Edinburgh.
RCAHMS (1993), *Waternish, Skye and Lochalsh District, Highland Region: an archaeological survey*, Edinburgh.
Saville, A. and Hallen, Y. (1994), 'The "Obanian Iron Age": human remains from the Oban cave sites, Argyll, Scotland', *Antiquity*, 68, pp. 715–23.
Scott, W. L. (1932), 'Rudh an Dunain chambered cairn, Skye', *Proc. Soc. Antiq. Scot.*, 66, pp. 183–213.
Scott, W. L. (1934a), 'External features of Rudh an Dunain chambered cairn', *Proc. Soc. Antiq. Scot.*, 68, pp. 194–9.
Scott, W. L. (1934b), 'Excavations of Rudh an Dunain cave, Skye', *Proc. Soc. Antiq. Scot.*, 68, pp. 200–23.
Scott, W. L. (1947), 'The problem of the brochs', *Proc. Prehist. Soc.*, XIII, pp. 1–37.
Scott, W. L. (1947a), 'The chambered tomb of Unival, North Uist', *Proc. Soc. Antiq. Scot.*, 82, pp. 1–48.
Scott, L. (1948), 'Gallo–British colonies; the aisled roundhouse culture in the north', *Proc. Prehist. Soc.*, XIV, pp. 46–125.
Scott, L. (1950), 'Eilean an Tighe; a pottery workshop of the 2nd millennium BC', *Proc. Soc. Antiq. Scot.*, 85, pp. 1–37.
SEARCH (1992), *The Western Isles Project, 5th Interim Report*, Sheffield: Sheffield University Press.
SEARCH (1993), *The Western Isles Project, 6th Interim Report*, Sheffield: Sheffield University Press.
Serjeantson, D. (1990), 'The introduction of mammals to the Outer Hebrides and the role of boats in stock management', *Anthropozoologica*, 13, pp. 7–18.
Serjeantson, D. (forthcoming), 'The Cattle and Sheep from Viking Barvas, with Observations on Animal Husbandry', in T. Cowie et al., (forthcoming).
Sharples, N. (1984), 'Dalmore', *Curr. Archaeol.*, 91, p. 235.
Sharples, N. and Parker-Pearson, M. (forthcoming), 'Cultural landscapes of Atlantic Scotland: reviewing the problem of the brochs', in C. Haselgrove and A. Gwilt (eds), (1996), *Time, space and culture in Iron Age Britain*.

Shepherd, I. A. G. (1976), 'Preliminary results from the beaker settlement at Rosinish, Benbecula', in C. Burgess and R. Miket (eds), *Settlement and Economy in the Third and Second millennia BC*, Brit. Arch. Reports, 33, Oxford, pp. 209–16.

Shepherd, I. A. G. and Tuckwell, A. N. (1977), 'Traces of beaker-period cultivation at Rosinish, Benbecula', *Proc. Soc. Antiq. Scot.*, 108, pp. 108–13.

Sheridan, A. (1992), 'Scottish stone axeheads; some new work and recent discoveries', in N. M. Sharples and A. Sheridan (eds), *Vessels for the Ancestors*, Edinburgh: Edinburgh University Press, pp. 194–212.

Simpson, D. D. A. (1971), 'Beaker houses and settlement in Britain', in D. D. A. Simpson (ed.), *Economy and settlement in Neolithic and Early Bronze Age Britain and Europe*, Leicester: Leicester University Press, pp. 131–52.

Simpson, D. D. A. (1976), 'The later neolithic and beaker settlement at Northton, Isle of Harris', in C. Burgess and R. Miket (eds), *Settlement and Economy in the Third and Second Millennia BC*, Brit. Arch. Reports, 33, Oxford, pp. 209–20.

Steer, K. A. and Bannerman, J. W. M. (1977), *Late Medieval Monumental Sculpture in the West Highlands*, Edinburgh: Edinburgh University Press.

Stevenson (1952), 'Long cist burials, particularly those at Galson (Lewis) and Gairloch (Wester Ross), with a symbol stone at Gairloch', *Proc. Soc. Antiq. Scot.*, 86, pp. 106–14.

Stevenson, R. B. K. (1955), 'Pins and the chronology of brochs', *Proc. Prehist. Soc.*, 21, pp. 282–94.

Stevenson, J. B. (1984), 'The excavations of a hut circle at Cul a Bhaile, Jura', *Proc. Soc. Antiq. Scot.*, 114, pp. 127–60.

Stuiver, M. and Pearson, G. W. (1986), 'High-Precision Calibration of the Radiocarbon Time-Scale AD 1950–500 BC', *Radiocarbon*, 28 no. 26, pp. 805–39.

Taylor, M. (1978), *The Lewis Chessmen*, London: British Museum.

Thom, A. (1967), *Megalithic Sites in Britain*, Oxford: Clarendon.

Thomas, F. W. L. (1870), 'On the primitive dwellings and hypogea of the Outer Hebrides', *Proc. Soc. Antiq. Scot.*, 7, pp. 153–95.

Thomas, F. W. L. (1890), 'On the duns of the Outer Hebrides', *Archaeologia Scotica*, 5, 365–415.

Topping, P. G. (1986), 'Neutron activation analysis of later prehistoric pottery from the Western Isles of Scotland', *Proc. Prehist. Soc.*, 52, pp. 105–29.

Tuan, Y. (1979), *Landscapes of Fear*, Oxford.

Walker, M. J. C. (1984), 'A pollen diagram from St Kilda, Outer Hebrides, Scotland', *New Phytologist*, 97, pp. 99–113.

Warner, R. (1976), 'Scottish silver arm-rings: an analysis of weights, *Proc. Soc. Antiq. Scot.*, 107, pp. 136–43.

Welander, R. D. E., Batey, C. and Cowie, T. G. (1987), 'A Viking burial from Kneep, Uig, Isle of Lewis', *Proc. Soc. Antiq. Scot.*, 117, pp. 149–74.

Wells, L. H. (1952), 'A note on the human remains from the Gairloch and Galson cist burials', *Proc. Soc. Antiq. Scot.*, 86, pp. 112–15.

Wickham-Jones, C. R. (1986), 'The procurement and use of stone for flaked tools in prehistoric Scotland', *Proc. Soc. Antiq. Scot.*, 116, pp. 1–10.

Wickham-Jones, C. R. (1990), *Rhum, Mesolithic and Later sites at Kinloch, excavations 1994–6*, Society of Antiquaries of Scotland Monograph Series No. 7, Edinburgh.

Wickham-Jones, C. R. and Collins, G. H. (1978), 'The sources of flint and chert in northern Britain', *Proc. Soc. Antiq. Scot.*, 109, pp. 7–21.

Wildgoose, M., Burney, C. and Miket, R. (1993), *Coile a Ghasgain, by Ord, Sleat, interim report*, Skye.

Wilkins, D. A. (1984), 'The Flandrian woods of Lewis (Scotland)', *Journal of Ecology*, 72, pp. 251–8.

Woodman, P. C. (1985), *Excavations at Mount Sandel 1973–77*, Belfast.
Young, A. (1952), 'An aisled farmhouse at the Allasdale, Isle of Barra', *Proc. Soc. Antiq. Scot.*, 87, pp. 80–106.
Young, A. (1955), 'Excavations at Dun Cuier, Isle of Barra, Outer Hebrides', *Proc. Soc. Antiq. Scot.*, 89, pp. 290–328.
Young, A. (1961), 'Brochs and duns', *Proc. Soc. Antiq. Scot.*, 95, pp. 171–99.
Young, A. and Richardson, K. M. (1959), 'A Cheardhach Mhor, Drimore, South Uist', *Proc. Soc. Antiq. Scot.*, 93, pp. 135–73.

Index

A' Cheardach Mhor, South Uist 31, 147, 155
Adabrock hoard, Lewis 101–2, 108, 230
Adomnan 27, 183
Aedan 183
Allasdale, Barra 143–5, 150, 194
Alt Chrysal, North Uist 56, 93–4, 105
Altnacloiche, Skye 104
An Corran, Skye 14, 34–6
Angles 159
Annait, Skye 183
Ardnamurchan 162
Ardnave, Islay 94
Argyll 4–5, 14, 177, 204, 206
Arnol, Lewis 213–14
Arran 59, 83, 103, 197
Ashmore, Patrick 82
astro-archaeology 84
Atkinson, R. J. C. 143, 146
Atlantic Europe 6–7
'Atlantic Province' 4
Atlantic roundhouses 11, 15, 109–36, 142–4, 184, 197, 228, 230–1
  broch towers 4, 8, 15, 114–15, 120–31, 157, 231
  complex roundhouses 105, 115–20, 158, 171
  construction 109–12
  continuity from Bronze Age 115–16
  function 122–31
  re-use 167–173, 218
  simple roundhouses 115–16

Bac Mhic Connain, North Uist 139, 145, 152, 162, 180
baile settlements 16, 211–12, 225, 228

Baleshare, North Uist 28, 99, 149
Balfarg, Fife 80
Ballyglass, Ireland 50
Barber, John 12, 14, 28, 156
Barnett, William 39–40
Barpa Langass, North Uist 70–5, 95
Barra 3, 11, 104, 143, 170, 193, 205, 220
  Atlantic roundhouses 13, 113, 129–31, 134
  Barra Head 115, 131
  Bronze Age burials 96
  Bronze Age settlement 93
  Neolithic settlement 56
  rainfall 19
  settlement change 228
Barvas, Lewis 91, 99, 105, 192–4
Battle of Largs 204
'Beaker Folk' 89, 105, 231 (*See also* pottery; beaker)
beaker burials 94–5, 105
Bedburg, Germany 39
Benbecula 3, 12, 92, 161, 221
Beveridge, Erskine 8–11, 43–5, 48, 50, 71, 95, 143, 152, 162
'Beyond the Brochs' 11
Bhaltos, Lewis 96, 136, 160, 167, 183
  absence of Viking settlement 188
  Atlantic roundhouses 117, 120
  continuity of settlement 231, 233–5
  excavation programme 13–14
  medieval settlement 211
  post-medieval settlement 214
  Viking graves 197, 201–4
Bharpa Carinish, North Uist 15, 43, 54–7, 64–5, 70
Birka, Sweden 199

INDEX

Birsay, Orkney 178, 191
blackbird 25
blackhouses 213–14, 233
Blackshouse Burn, Strathclyde 80
bloodstone 38, 94
Blundell, Rev. Odo 8, 11
Bonsall, Clive 41
Borve Castle, Benbecula 221
Bosta, Lewis 194
Bradford University 14
Bragar, Lewis 212
Britons 159
Brittany 75
Broadford, Skye 30
brochs 7, 11–12, 52 (*See also Atlantic roundhouses*)
Bronze Age 25, 52, 55, 64, 229 (*See also Early Bronze Age, Middle Bronze Age, Later Bronze Age*)
   burials 7, 86–9, 94–9, 107, 197
   bronze manufacture 86–7, 151, 155
   economies 90–4, 106–7
   introduction 86, 228
   re-use of tombs 75
   settlements 88–95
   society 15, 107–8
Buckquoy, Orkney 176, 191, 204
Bu, Orkney 114, 116
Burl, Aubrey 82
Butt of Lewis 3, 31, 52, 184

Caithness 5, 53, 83, 116, 157
Callander, J. Graham 8
Callanish, Lewis 24, 81, 103, 216, 235
   Archaeological Research Centre 13, 120
   chambered tomb 79, 83
   excavations 82–3
   function 82–4
   stones 7–8, 15, 81–4, 95, 108, 229
Campbell, Ewan 143, 146, 152, 208
Canna 1, 14, 21
Carn Liath, Skye 69
carved stone balls 62–3
castles 218–21, 223
cattle
   Bronze Age 106
   introduction of 31
   Iron Age 134–5, 148–50, 156
   Medieval 216
   Neolithic 64
   Norse 191–2
cellular structures 164–76
'Celtic' Europe 108
Central Excavation Unit 12
Centre for Field Archaeology 98
chambered cairns (*See chambered tombs*)
chambered tombs 4, 11–12, 15, 67–85, 107, 109, 122, 143
   chronology 69
   Clyde cairns 70, 75

re-use 75–6, 94–5
siting 65, 77–8
symbolism 53–6, 67, 229–30
typology 69–70
Christianity 180–6, 202, 231
chronology 17
Cille Donnain, South Uist 204
Clan MacKinnon 219
Clearances 206–7, 214, 216, 226
Clettraval, North Uist
   chambered tomb 11, 69–70, 72, 76, 83, 94–5, 143
   wheelhouse 137, 143–5, 150
Clibhe 211
Close-Brooks, Joanna 96
Cnip, Lewis
   Bronze Age burials 96–9, 105–7, 117
   Viking cemetery 98, 193, 196–202, 204
   wheelhouse complex, Lewis 31, 132, 136–157, 162, 164–7, 169, 178–9, 197
Cnoc a Comhdhalach, North Uist 143
Coile a Ghasgain, Skye 103–5
Coles, John 108
Coll 10, 150, 162
Colonsay 195
Columba 27, 182–3
continuity of settlement 16
Cowie, Trevor 12, 192
crannogs 8, 19, 52–4, 88, 105, 118, 217, 228
Crawford, Iain 166, 202, 206
Crone, Anne 54
Crosskirk, Caithness 116
Crotach, Alastair 223–5
Cuillin Hills 1, 3, 19, 22, 72, 93
Cul a Bhaile, Jura 103
cup-marked stones 79–80
cursus monuments 82
Curtis, Margaret 80, 84
Curtis, Ron 80, 84
Cyprus 31

Dalmore, Lewis 87, 92, 105–7
Dalriada 4, 161–2, 172, 178, 183, 186, 206–7
Deer Park Farms, Ireland 172
de Latour, Countess 8
Dell, Lewis 103
Denmark 200
Dibadail, Lewis 194
diffusionist archaeology 5, 11–12, 41, 88, 114, 129
Dodghson, Professor Robert 212
dogs 31, 149, 191
Donald Dubh 207
Drimore, South Uist 188–91
Druim nan Dearcag, North Uist 206, 210–14
Dublin 199
Dunadd, Argyll 177–8
Dun an Sticer, North Uist 219

Dun Aonghas, North Uist 218
Dun Ardtreck, Skye 12, 118, 160
Dun Ban, North Uist 218, 233
Dun Beag, Struan, Skye 6, 9, 128, 195
Dun Bharabhat, Bhaltos, Lewis 24, 103, 105, 117–20, 124, 127, 130, 150, 167
Dun Bharabhat, Gt Bernera, Lewis 118–19
Dun Borbaidh, Coll 150
Dun Carloway, Lewis 15, 109–12, 120, 122, 125–7, 193, 218
Dun Chlif, Barra 193
Dun Colbost, Skye 122
Dun Cromore, Lewis 105
Dun Cuier, Barra 134, 169–73, 179–80, 193
Dun Fiadhairt, Skye 127–8, 161
Dun Loch an Duin, Carloway, Lewis 123
Dun Loch an Duin, Shader, Lewis 105
Dun Loch an Duna, Bragar, Lewis 123–4, 218
Dun Mor Vaul, Tiree 148, 150
Dunragit 80
Dun Ringill, Skye 118, 219
duns 11–12, 44, 52, 131
Dun Telve 122–3, 125
Dun Thomaidh, North Uist 123
Dun Torcuill, North Uist 9
Dun Troddan 122, 125
Dunvegan, Skye 223
Dun Vulan, South Uist 124, 128–9, 135

Early Bronze Age 4, 15, 72, 88, 117
  metalwork 101
  settlements 88–95
Early Historic period 52, 148, 167, 173, 177, 190, 207
  bronze-working 173–80
  burials 182
  ritual deposits 173–5
Edinburgh
  Castle 148
  University 13
Eigg 1, 21, 202
Eilean an Tighe, North Uist 50–2, 56–7, 61, 65, 76, 118, 228, 233
Eilean Domhnuill, North Uist 14–15, 43–53, 55–65, 76, 94, 118, 173, 210, 228, 233
Eilean Maleit, North Uist 158, 193
Eilean Olabhat, North Uist 14, 45, 173–80, 193
  Medieval period 206, 208–11, 213–14
  metal-working 176–8
  ritual deposits 156
England 6, 33, 159, 207, 226
Ensay, Sound of Harris 79
Ertebolle 39–41
Evans, John 25
Eye peninsula, Lewis 61

Faeroe Islands 191

farming
  introduction of 15, 38–41
farm mounds 231
Fife Adventurers 225
Finlaggan, Islay 52
Foshigarry, North Uist 139, 147, 152, 162, 178, 180
  continuity of settlement 233
  Viking pottery 194
foxes 31
France 6, 39

Galson, Lewis 153, 182
Garrafad, Skye 95
Garry Iochdrach, North Uist 143, 162
Gerisclett, North Uist 95
goats 31
Grant, Capt. 11
great auk 31, 139, 150, 156
Great Langdale 61
Greaulin, Skye 212
Gurness, Orkney 122, 157, 161, 231

handpins 177
Harding, Prof. D. W. 13, 167
Harris 12, 32, 43, 55–6, 80, 90–1, 113, 183, 223
  Harris Hills 4, 19, 25, 65
  machair 28
  topography 22
Hedges, John 78–9
henges 80, 86
Henshall, Audrey 12, 69–70, 83, 95
hoards 100–3, 128, 194–5, 230
Hornish Point, South Uist 147, 149, 155–7
Howe, Orkney 117, 148–9
Hunter, John 14
hut circles 14, 103–5, 134

Ice Ages 22–3, 28, 30, 33
Iceland 186, 191
Inner Hebrides 8, 10, 27
Inner Isles (*See Inner Hebrides*)
Institute of Terrestrial Ecology 28
Iochdar, South Uist 101
Iona 148, 182, 186, 223
Ireland 6, 61, 149, 171–2, 180, 193–4, 186, 200, 204, 206, 233
  crannogs 52
  Early Church 183–4
  Later Neolithic 80
  megaliths 82
  Neolithic settlement 48, 50
  Viking graves 197
Iron Age 8, 11–15, 24–5, 28, 31, 44–5, 52, 54–5, 59, 105, 108, 113, 184, 186–8, 233–5
  economies 133–5, 148–53
  environment 133–4
  introduction of iron 133, 228

iron manufacture 151
re-use of tombs 75–6
ritual 139, 153–7
society 122–31, 157–8
warfare 122–5
Isbister, Orkney 78–9, 85
Islay 94, 105–6, 195
Isle of Man 6, 197, 200, 204
islet settlements (*See crannogs*)

Jarlshof, Shetland 115, 139, 157, 191
John of Islay 206
Johnson, Dr Samuel 6, 214
Jura 103

Kebister, Shetland 193
Kensaleyre, Skye 95
kerb cairns 96–8, 108
Killin 61
Kilpatrick, Arran 103
Kilpheder, South Uist 137, 143, 147, 150, 155–6, 161, 180
Kilphedir, Sutherland 134
Kinloch, Rhum 13–14, 27, 34–8, 41, 55
Kisimul Castle, Barra 220, 233
Knap of Howar, Orkney 50–1, 64–5
Kneep (*See Cnip*)
Kyleakin, Skye 219

Lagore, Ireland 171
Lairg, Sutherland 133–4
Lane, Alan 166, 179, 191, 193
late duns 217–20
late medieval sculpture 12, 221–6
Later Bronze Age 13, 88, 99–105, 107–8, 115
  absence of evidence 13, 15, 99
  metalwork 99–103, 230
  settlement 103–5
Later Neolithic 4, 25, 80, 86, 107, 229–32
'lazy beds' 216
Lewis 15, 192, 212, 218 (*See also Bhaltos, Butt of Lewis, Cnip and Stornoway*)
  archaeological research 13
  Bronze Age 87, 91–2, 101–5
  environmental history 24–5, 31–2
  geology 22
  Iron Age 109–11, 113, 123
  Neolithic 61, 64, 80, 81
  rainfall 19
  topography 28
Lewis Chessmen 203
Lews Castle, Lewis 194
'Life of Columba' 27
Linearbandkeramik culture (LBK) 41
literacy 185
Little Ice Age 233
Little Loch Roag 24, 108
Liveras, Skye 95

Loch Awe 52
Loch Bharabhat, Lewis 197
Loch Carabhat, North Uist 218
Loch Hellisdale, South Uist 24
Loch Lang, South Uist 24, 36
Lochmaddy 3
Loch na Berie, Lewis 197, 202, 204
  broch tower 112, 120–1, 125, 130
  cellular structures 155, 160, 167–71, 176, 179–80
  faunal assemblage 148, 150
Loch Obisary, North Uist 4
Loch Olabhat, North Uist 14, 43, 50, 66, 173, 210–12, 215
Loch Olabhat Research Project 14, 205
Loch Roag, Lewis 81
Loch Tay 52
Lords of the Isles 52, 204–10, 212, 218, 221–4, 232

MacArthur Cave 40
machair 5, 14, 28, 55, 75, 162, 188, 192–3, 218
  Bronze Age 88–92
  continuity of settlement 227–9, 233–5
  development 22–3, 28
  distribution 3, 29
  wheelhouse settlement 142–3, 145, 148–9, 158
Machrie Moor, Arran 83
MacKay Cave 40
MacKie, Euan 12
Macleods 223
MacSween, Anne 131
Maes Howe, Orkney 107
Mangersta, Lewis 194
marginality 5–6, 13
Martin Martin 7, 31, 82
Mathieson, Sir James 8, 81
McCormack, Finbar 148–9
Medieval period 13, 16, 206, 233
  economy 207, 210–11
  settlement 207–11
megalithic tombs (*See chambered tombs*)
Mesolithic period 13, 24, 27, 30, 33–41, 77, 232
  cemeteries 40
  economies 34–6, 40–1
  social organisation 38–40, 229
  structures 36–7, 57
  technologies 38
  transition to farming 38–41, 229
Middle Bronze Age 101
Midhowe, Orkney 122, 157, 231
Miket, Roger 14, 103–4, 131, 133, 205, 217, 220
Minch 101, 186
monumentality 15, 67, 107–8, 112–13, 143, 146, 184–5, 230–1
Mount Sandel, Ireland 37

Muck 1
Mull 21, 41
Museum nan Eilean 235

Neolithic period 15–16, 22, 25, 27–8, 31, 36, 67–85, 88, 105, 206
　definitions 41
　economies 62–6
　end of 86, 107
　'package' 41
　population 78–9
　ritual 15 (*See also chambered tombs*)
　settlements 42–57, 90, 93–4, 228
　society 15, 77–9, 84–5, 229
　warfare 52, 85
Ness, Lewis 101
Newstead 147, 180
Norse (*See Vikings*)
Northern Isles 6, 12, 15, 115, 122, 127, 136, 171, 235 (*See also Orkney and Shetland*)
North Rona 184
North Tolsta crannog, Lewis 52, 105
Northton, Harris 12, 25
　Beaker period 86–7, 90–4, 105–7
　Bronze Age burials 98–9
　Iron Age burials 153
　Neolithic 43, 55–7, 64
North Uist 3, 209, 218–19, 232 (*See also Eilean Domhnuill, Loch Olabhat and Vallay*)
　archaeological research 8–12, 16
　Bronze Age 90, 99
　Iron Age 113, 123, 129, 134, 139, 156–8
　location of tombs 77–8
　Neolithic 54, 69–70, 72, 75, 83
　topography 22
　Vikings 162, 191, 193–5
Northumbria 180, 184
Norway 191–2, 195, 200, 202, 204, 206, 231

Obanian culture 36, 40
Orkney 3, 5, 107–8, 136, 148, 176, 178, 204
　archaeological research 7, 10, 12
　Atlantic roundhouses 114–17, 122, 130–3
　chambered tombs 70, 77, 80, 83, 95
　contact with Rome 161
　henges 80
　Neolithic population 78–9
　Neolithic settlement 50, 57, 62, 94
　social change 230–1
　Viking sites 191, 193, 195
Oronsay 34, 148, 195
otters 31
Outer Hebrides *See Western Isles*

Pabbay Mor 183
Palaeolithic period 33
Parker Pearson, Mike 129
peat expansion 23–7, 77, 228
Perthshire 103

Picts 4, 16, 159–62, 180–8, 202–3, 206–7, 221, 231–2
Pictish symbol stones 162, 180–2, 223
pig 64, 134–5, 155, 191–2
Pool, Orkney 193
Portree, Skye 1, 27, 194
Post-Medieval period 16
pottery 39–41, 233
　adoption of 39
　Beaker 75, 83, 86–95, 105–6, 108, 127, 229–30
　Bronze Age 96
　cinerary urns 89, 95–9, 106
　Ertebolle 39
　Food Vessels 106
　Grooved Ware 75, 80, 83
　Hebridean Ware 55–9, 76, 106
　Iron Age 127, 151–2, 157, 166, 171
　Medieval 207, 210–13
　Mesolithic 40
　Neolithic 41, 50, 55–9, 72–6, 93, 105, 127
　'phalluses' 59–60
　Plain Bowls 57
　Plain Style 166, 178–9, 193
　red deer motif 150
　Samian Ware 145, 160, 167–9
　Unstan Ware 55–9, 76, 106
　Viking 192–4
promontory forts 155, 122, 131
pumice 61, 72–5, 95
Pygmies Isle, Lewis 52

Quanterness, Orkney 78
querns 64, 135, 147, 149, 153, 155

Raasay 1, 22
rabbits 30–1
Rathlin Island, County Antrim 61
rats 31
RCAHMS 4, 10, 14, 205
red deer 33
　as pottery motif 150
　introduction of 31
　Iron Age 134, 148, 155–6
　Neolithic 64–5
　Norse 191–2
　ritual use 38–9
reindeer 33
Renfew, Colin 77
Rhum 1, 13–14, 21–2, 27, 30, 34–8, 55, 61, 94
Ring of Brodgar, Orkney 83
Rinyo, Orkney 94, 108, 115
Rodel, Harris 223–3
roe deer 31
Roman artefacts 127–8, 145–7, 152, 160–1, 167–9, 180
Roman invasion 113–14, 159–61
Rosinish, Benbecula 12, 92–3, 96–9, 105–7
Rousay, Orkney 77

Rudh an Dunain, Skye
  cave 93–4, 107
  chambered tomb 11, 72–6, 83, 93, 95

St Clement's Church, Rodel 223–5
St Kilda 3, 11, 31
St Olaf 204
Sardinia 31
Scandinavia 6, 39–40, 93, 194, 199–201
Scots 16, 159, 161–2, 178, 183, 207
Scott, Sir Lindsay 11–12, 50, 56, 72, 74–5, 93–4
sea-craft 34
seals 32, 134, 149
SEARCH Project (*See Sheffield University*)
sedentism 39–41
Shader, Lewis 183
sheep 226
  Bronze Age 106
  introduction of 31
  Iron Age 134–5, 148–50, 155–6
  Medieval 216
  Neolithic 64
  Norse 191–2
Sheffield University 13–14, 56, 205
shell middens 34
Shepherd, Ian 12
Sheshader 'Thing' 102–3, 107
Shetland 3, 22, 136, 139, 157, 191, 193
Shiant Islands 101, 183
shielings 14, 217
Shulisader, Lewis 61
Simpson, Prof. Derek 12
Sithean an Altair, North Uist 96
Skara Brae, Orkney 94, 108, 115
Skye
  climate change 18–21
  colonisation 33
  fauna 30–2
  geology 21–3
  history of research 6–14
  monument types 4
  origin of name 1
  peat growth 23–7
  population 1
  rainfall 19–20
  sea-level change 27–30
  topography 1–2, 21–3
  woodland 23–7
Small Isles 4, 22, 136, 202
Sollas, North Uist 137, 139, 143–55, 173
Somerled 204, 206–7
Sorisdale, Coll 94
souterrains 14, 131–3
South Dell, Lewis 194
South Uist 101, 113, 125, 135, 143, 147, 155, 188, 204–5, 234
  archaeological research 13
  environmental history 24, 31
  topography 29

Staffin Island 183
Star Carr, North Yorkshire 38–9
Stenness, Orkney 83
Stevenson, RBK 145
stone axes 41, 61, 86
stone circles 15, 67–8, 80–6, 109
Stonehaven 57
Stornoway 3, 22, 61, 194, 225
Storr Rock, Skye 194
Sutherland 5, 103, 133–4
Sweden 199–200

tacksmen 218–19
Talisker, Skye 101
Tankardstown, Ireland 50
Taran 183
Taransay 183
Taversoe Tuick, Orkney 95
Teampull na Trionaid, North Uist 223–4
Thom, Alexander 84
Thomas, Capt. F. W. L. 8
timber 25, 65, 128, 143, 171
Tòb nan Leobag, Lewis 24, 36
Tormore, Arran 103
Torrin, Skye 217
tower houses 122
Tiree 10, 148, 162, 193
Traigh Bhaltos, Lewis 96
Traigh Clibhe, Lewis 211
Traigh na Berie, Lewis 5, 96, 197, 201
transhumance 216–17
Treaty of Perth 204
Trondheim, Norway 204
Tulloch of Assery, Caithness 53
Tungadale, Skye 131–3

the Udal, North Uist 12
  Bronze Age 90–2, 105
  continuity of settlement 16, 232–5
  Early Historic 164, 166–7, 172, 179
  Iron Age 147, 149
  Medieval 206, 212–13
  Neolithic 55–6
  Viking 191–3, 202
Uig Bay, Lewis 203
Uig, Skye 30
Ullinish Lodge, Skye 69
Ulva, Mull 41
Unival, North Uist 11, 69, 72, 74–5, 78, 80, 83, 95

Vallay, North Uist 8, 10, 14, 96, 143
Vallay Strand, North Uist 8, 11, 30, 157, 229
Vikings
  economy 192–5
  finds on earlier sites 170
  gold and silver 194–5
  graves 98, 195–203
  incursions 13, 16, 178–9, 183–4, 186–8, 202, 221, 230–1

place names 16, 186–8, 202–3, 231
settlement 186–93, 214

Ward Hill, Shetland 157
Waternish, Skye 1, 14, 183, 214, 217
Wessex 80, 82, 113
Western Isles
  climate change 18–21
  colonisation 33
  difficulties of survey 11
  early names 3
  fauna 30–2
  geology 21–3
  history of research 6–14
  monument types 4
  peat growth 23–7
  population 3
  rainfall 19–20
  sea-level change 18, 27–30, 34
  topography 2, 21–3
  woodland 23–7
Westness, Orkney 195
whales 32, 64–5, 149, 193
wheelhouses 8, 11–12, 15, 31, 136–59, 162, 164–5, 171, 173, 184, 231
  chronology 145–8
  construction 136–43
  distribution 13–18
  ritual deposits 139, 153–7
Whitby Abbey 170, 180
Wickham-Jones, Caroline 13
wild boar 27, 33
wildcat 25
wolves 31
woodland history 19, 23–7, 40, 65–6, 228

Young, Alison 12–13